The Comic
Art of War

The Comic Art of War

*A Critical Study of
Military Cartoons, 1805–2014,
with a Guide to Artists*

Christina M. Knopf

McFarland & Company, Inc., Publishers
Jefferson, North Carolina

LIBRARY OF CONGRESS CATALOGUING-IN-PUBLICATION DATA

Knopf, Christina M., 1980–
The comic art of war : a critical study of military cartoons,
1805–2014, with a guide to artists / Christina M. Knopf.
p.   cm.
Includes bibliographical references and index.

ISBN 978-0-7864-9835-2 (softcover : acid free paper) ∞
ISBN 978-1-4766-2081-7 (ebook)

1. War—Caricatures and cartoons.   2. Soldiers—Caricatures and
cartoons.   3. Military life—Caricatures and cartoons.   I. Title.

U20.K58 2015   355.0022'2—dc23   2015024596

BRITISH LIBRARY CATALOGUING DATA ARE AVAILABLE

On the cover: *COMPANY DIS-MISSED!* by Abian A. "Wally" Wallgren
which appeared in the final World War I issue of *Stars and Stripes* (vol.
2 no. 19: p. 7) on June 18, 1919. It features the artist dismissing
his models, or characters, from duty at the end of the war.

Printed in the United States of America

*McFarland & Company, Inc., Publishers
Box 611, Jefferson, North Carolina 28640
www.mcfarlandpub.com*

Acknowledgments

It is said that writing is a solitary activity. This is true, but it fails to take into account the researching, planning, and revising stages, which are not solitary and indeed depend on the kindness and brilliance of others. Therefore, this book would not have been possible without the support of numerous people.

My gratitude to all the professionals in their respective fields whose expertise and kindness was invaluable: Kent Bolke, curator of the 10th Mountain Division and Fort Drum Museum, whose parallel exhibits of Bill Mauldin's Pine Camp cartoons and Steve Opet's Camp Victory cartoons sparked the idea for this research; Walter Biggins, for seeing my conference paper title in the National Communication Association 2012 program and suggesting that it would make a good topic for a book; Jeffrey Boshart, at Eastern Illinois University, for helping a stranger find "Molly Marine," and Nancy Wilt and Sara Phoenix of the Women of the Corps Collection, for introducing me to her; the staff of the Special Collections department at the E.S. Bird Library of Syracuse University, who granted me access to the Vic Herman papers; the librarians of the Veterans History Project at the Library of Congress, especially Megan Harris, for fulfilling my last-minute request to see the physical copies of Robert Bindig's work; and the audiences and fellow panelists at the Eastern Sociological Society 2014, who showed tremendous interest in chapter 6 and offered their own thoughts and experiences to make the work better, and at the Rhetoric Society of America 2014, who asked probing questions of chapters 4 and 5.

My eternal thanks to loved ones whose support is central to my success in all things: my mother, Sandra Knopf, who proofread the manuscript not once but twice with attentiveness and good humor and was my personal cheering section and any-time-of-day sounding board for every new comic discovered and every new idea conceived; my father, Donald Knopf, who long ago shared with me the secret of camouflage-by-clipboard, thus enhancing my appreciation for military humor; and Pixie, for the much-needed hugs while working—even if it did mean a lot of one-handed typing.

I would be remiss if I did not also thank the comic artists, amateur and professional, who served their countries. I learned much through your work, and this book is an effort to bring your insights, your experiences, and your humor to others. I have tried to represent your work fairly and accurately, and if I have not always succeeded, no disrespect was intended. Special thanks to Doctrine Man and Steve Opet for allowing me to include their artwork in these pages.

Table of Contents

Preface
Recon

The human race has one really effective weapon, and that is laughter.—Mark Twain

"Recon" is the shortened term for military reconnaissance, which is the gathering of information about unknown or outside areas for analysis and use. In essence, it is gathering information about what to expect, just as this preface will let you know what to expect of this book. There is an aphorism that claims generals are always fighting the last war; as such, it seems only fitting that this book on military comics begins with its backstory—a kind of tale of my own reconnaissance on warriors' graphic narratives. It all started, though I did not know it then, on a winter's day in late 2010. I was perusing the military history stacks at a local used bookstore when I discovered Barsis's *They're All Yours, Uncle Sam!*, a 1943 story of "babes in arms who become women at arms."[1] I was at once enchanted and bemused by the gentle, gendered humor about WAACs and WAVES and wondered if there were other books of its kind. My search discovered two Winnie the WACs: the first created by Cpl. Vic Herman during World War II[2] and the second created by Owen Fitzgerald in the 1950s as part of the *Here's Howie* comics published by DC.[3] I soon discovered other military and paramilitary heroines of the Second World War: Wonder Woman, of course, and War Nurse, Pat Parker and her Girl Commandos, Flyin' Jenny,[4] and then Molly Marine by real-life lady leatherneck Barbara Bristol[5] and an autobiographical "ripple" by WAVE Dorothea Byerly.[6] Before long, I happened upon other comics by and for military personnel. In November 2011, I visited the 10th Mountain Division and Fort Drum Museum, on the Fort Drum base just sixty-five miles south of my university, SUNY Potsdam. On one wall, there was a small display of World War II–era cartoons by Bill Mauldin, who had trained there (when it was Pine Camp) with the 45th Division. On the opposite wall

1

was a monitor scrolling through cartoons by 10th Mountain reservist Steve Opet drawn while he was deployed to Iraq in 2008. The following summer, I perused a small assortment of boot camp comic books while visiting the Sampson Museum at the old Sampson Naval and Air Force Base in upstate New York. And in November of 2013, while in Washington, D.C., for the National Communication Association conference, I was delighted by an exhibit at the Smithsonian's National Museum of American History highlighting the role of the entertainment industry in World War II, with particular attention to animated cartoons and comic books with messages supporting the civilian and military war efforts.

When I took on the mission of writing a book about military comics, I had no idea that during the next two years I would discover hundreds of military cartoonists spanning centuries and continents—the standards for which are Britain's Bruce Bairnsfather of the Great War and America's Bill Mauldin of the Second World War. Bairnsfather is sometimes credited as "the Man Who Won the War"[7] because of his morale-boosting, if brutally honest, cartoons. His work was developed into a 1926 film, *The Better 'Ole*, starring Syd Chaplin. Mauldin was considered the Bairnsfather of World War II.[8] Decades later, Steve Opet was called the Bill Mauldin of Iraq,[9] and W.C. Pope was dubbed "the Bill Mauldin of the Air Force,"[10] while Chris Grant's Iraq cartoons prompted *Stars and Stripes* to proclaim: "Bill Mauldin, meet the 'Bohica Blues.' Like the famed creator of World War II's Willie and Joe comic strip, Staff Sgt. Chris Grant is putting pen and ink on paper to humorously capture the feelings, desires and daily routine of soldiers deployed to Iraq."[11] Mauldin's work not only has been repeatedly emulated, but also was given numerous acknowledgments in popular culture by fan and fellow cartoonist Charles Schulz.

Despite the centrality of Mauldin's influence in military cartooning, the styles of art vary widely from the heavy and dark drawings of Bairnsfather and Mauldin, who both relied mostly on single-frame cartoons with captions placed below the usually black-and-white image, though Mauldin's work was slightly less exaggerated, or "cartoonish," than Bairnsfather's. Opet's cartoons were also single-frame images, but with combined speech/thought bubbles and captions. They appeared in either black and white or color, and the bold strokes and bright tints call to mind boardwalk caricatures. Pope's cartoons, also color or black and white in single-frame, use either speech/thought bubbles or captions to give voice to simplistic drawings that emphasize characters. Grant's single-frame, black-and-white cartoons rely on speech/thought bubbles and are sketchy in appearance, bringing small details to otherwise simple drawings. Other cartoonists have relied on stick figures, replicated and/or created by computers, digital graphics, and other mixed media to generate comic art that ranges from the gritty realism of Mauldin's work, to assorted animals in military uniforms, to androgynous geometric shapes—all conveying the experience of military service and warfare.

As I neared the completion of the book's first draft in April 2014 I read an article by Stephen Walt in *Foreign Policy* that asked when laughing at the military had become taboo. Walt's article begins:

> War is not a funny topic, but military life used to be a bountiful source of comic inspiration. The grim reality of the battlefield prompts plenty of black humor and the rigid orthodoxies of modern military organizations have been ripe fodder for satire in the past. Given that the United States has been at war for two out of every three years since the end of the Cold War, you'd think there would be lots of dark comedy and irreverent commentary on military topics, and not just when some randy commander gets caught with his pants down.
>
> Yet Americans no longer see the military as a worthy target for political satire.[12]

Walt goes on to argue that at the height of the Cold War until the 1970s, military humor was abundant in books such as *Mister Roberts*, films such as *Kelly's Heroes*, television shows such as *Gomer Pyle, USMC*, and comic strips such as *Beetle Bailey*. But after the Vietnam War, a serious approach took hold through a series of anti-war works, and since the early 1980s mass-market treatment of the military has been mostly respectful. There have, of course, been some exceptions, such as *Private Benjamin, Stripes, Hot Shots, Major Dad*, and, more recently, *Enlisted*—but their humor does not work to undermine the military in any way. He suspects the reason that Americans do not joke about the military anymore is that most Americans do not serve in uniform anymore and so do not feel comfortable laughing at those who do. Additionally, the "support the troops" fervor of the post–Vietnam era, magnified by the post–9/11 "war on terror," creates a climate inhospitable to mocking the military[13]: "Unfortunately, losing our ability to laugh at the military comes with a price. No human institution is perfect, and none should be given a free pass by the rest of society. Humor and ridicule are potent weapons when trying to keep powerful institutions under control."[14]

Walt is partially right. Military humor is important for keeping the institution in check and in perspective, and for serving a host of other social and political functions, which will be explored in this book. And a general population without military experience *does* contribute to a lack of mainstream military humor. After all, satire only works if an audience can recognize the conventions that are being lampooned.[15] Additionally, the general population has simply grown weary of war narratives.[16] But military humor has not disappeared quite so completely. There is the satiric online military news source *The Duffel Blog*—like *The Onion* for the Armed Services—and gag comic strips such as *Doctrine Man, Power Point Ranger, Terminal Lance*, and *Delta Bravo Sierra*, to name just a few. In fact, insider military humor, such as that expressed through comics and cartoons, is a persistent and consistent aspect of military culture, as this book will demonstrate at length.

Simply put, the work here focuses on the content of comics and cartoons—the stories told about the military and about war as seen through the inside jokes that are shared through the medium—and what we, as scholars, civilians, or fans, can learn about military experiences through that content. Beyond demonstrating how the military experience is constructed through cartoons and comics, it is hoped that this study will also contribute to an understanding of how comics work and how they serve cultural and identity functions, through its focus on comics developed within the tightly defined and rigidly constructed group of a military organization. Additionally, the work here will showcase the graphic works of artists and writers who may be little known to the broader public, introducing new audiences to this particular type of cartooning. A number of the artists included here may be known through their work for Disney, Marvel, Harvey Comics, the *New Yorker*, or Madison Avenue, but may yet be unknown for these particular creations. Other artists are likely to be entirely new to the reader. The book interweaves the work and contributions of a great many people and multiple academic disciplines: the military artists themselves; other servicepersons; journalists; and researchers in communication and rhetoric, sociology and political science, history and geography, psychology and medicine, and literature, art, and folklore. Hopefully none will feel misrepresented in the final picture I present, and for any errors of fact or misunderstandings of intention, I alone take full responsibility.

Introduction

Vocabularies of the Visual-Verbal

> I have a profound need to share, to communicate, and comics are
> a wonderful form of communication that will be hugely important
> to our evolutionary development as a 21st-century species.
>
> —Ales Kot

This book can be conceptually divided into two parts. The first part, consisting of the preface, introduction, and chapter 1, offers an orientation to the subject matter. The second part explores the work of military cartoonists. To begin with, a brief overview of comics studies and of comics types is needed in order to situate a more specific discussion of military-created comics. This introduction will present a truncated history of the study and lexicon of comics, with special attention to those types of works represented by the military artists studied here. It will also provide an explanation of how the research for this project was conducted. Chapter 1 will then discuss military culture and cohesion with attention to the place of humor in the military environment, introduce humor types and trends in war and the military, and review how comics function in the military setting.

"Comics' content and their social context are inextricably linked."[1] Comprising a "bewildering assortment of artistic styles, stories, characters, and seeming purposes,"[2] comics tell us about history—ours and theirs.[3] But the very definition of comics is said to be "the most befuddling and widely debated point" in comics studies.[4] One of the most used, and argued, definitions of comics calls them "juxtaposed pictorial and other images in deliberate sequence."[5] In fact, comics have even been reduced to a simple "sequence of binary symbols."[6] Cartoons, on the other hand, have been defined as "any whimsical, facetious graphic expression which parodies any aspect of human behavior."[7] These definitions, however, omit one of the most significant components of comics and cartoons: They tell *stories* with their unique blending of visual and verbal. Even single-panel comics and gag comics tell stories, because the point or the punchline is found in the implied storyline, of which only a single moment or brief time is seen. Relying on distortion and symbolic abstraction to tell these stories,[8] comics are a language, "an original ensemble of productive mechanisms of meaning"[9]; they use universally accepted markings that represent physical, temporal, spatial, and emotional effects.[10] Moreover, because so much of the story occurs between or outside the panels—in the "gutters"—comics actively engage the imagination of the readers, who must infer the information not on the page while processing the dynamics of the visual, linguistic, and spatial content of the panels. This individual self-creation with the multimodal rhetoric of comics subsequently supports a kind of pluralistic democratic individualism.[11]

The broader, if somewhat vague, moniker of "graphic narratives"[12] is accepted for this project as a general term for the combination of images, including words and other symbols, in an apparent or implied sequence, acting as either a pictorial story or exposition.[13] This term refers to the multiple approaches to graphic narratives including comic strips, comic books, manga, and graphic novels, as well as gag and editorial cartoons—recognizing the medium of comics along cultural lines as a verbal/textual language, rather than according to structural elements.[14] Fans and critics typically find it useful to make further delineations among these forms, because though the assorted types of graphic narratives share several key similarities, they are often seen as more different than alike.

Comic strips are drawings that usually include dialogue, featuring the lives of particular characters for the audience's entertainment.[15] Rodolphe Töpffer, a Swiss teacher, author, and artist who lived 1799–1846, is considered the creator of the comic strip. Töpffer used picture stories to satirize issues such as war, absolutism, bureaucracy, religion, and science.[16] In the American context, comic strips were nourished by the cultural milieu and political changes of the 19th into the 20th centuries and became a staple of newspapers during the publication war between William Randolph Hearst and Joseph Pulitzer, an era marked by the character of the Yellow Kid.[17] Their development has been classified generationally: the Innocent Age includes somewhat naïve strips from the turn of the 20th century to the 1920s; the Modern Age covers approximately 1920 to 1960 with strips that were both nostalgic and prescient in their reflections of society's shift from a rural to an urban, mass production-consumption society; and the third generation of comics was dubbed the Age of Confusion and began with the turbulence of the 1960s and comics that became more socially aware and involved.[18]

The technical hallmarks of the comic strip are speech balloons, also known as *fumetti*, and narrative breakdown.[19] Comic strips, nonetheless, need neither be comical nor appear in strip format.[20] They do, however, rely on an international set of cartoon symbols, referred to as *comicana*, used to develop characters and express actions and emotions. Cartoonist Mort Walker originally developed the language of comicana as satire, but the international research he represented in his work has now become the accepted language of both artists and critics. Facial expressions, or total *teteology*, rely on the interactions of eyes, mouth and tongue; body language depends on *morfs* (shapes), types, and stereotypes. Once the character has been developed, actions and reactions are portrayed through *indicia*—representations of emotions and motions. Environments are created through straight lines called *vites*, *dites*, and *cross-hatching*, and curved lines called *lucaflect*. Borders, shading, onomatopoeia, and other kinds of *symbolia*, plus standard gags known as *bulbonics*, also make up the system of comicana.[21]

Comic strips may be classified according to genre. The two primary genres are gag or anecdotal strips, which end with a punch-line, and continuity or serial strips, which may have a punch-line but always carry the story forward to the next installment. Continuity strips are typically characterized as humorous, soap opera, or adventure.[22] Gag strips may be multi- or single paneled. In the early part of the 20th century, gag strips dominated the funny papers, but by the 1920s, adventure strips reigned—until the creation of *Beetle Bailey*, and then *Peanuts*, in 1950.[23] Falling somewhere between these two common types is the emerging genre of the diary strip, made possible by the publication options, and ease, of the Internet. Written and released daily, diary strips bring the mundane incidents of the day-to-day life of the artists to the public through a genre that blends the blog and the four-panel gag strip. As a narrative, the diary "microcomic" strip uses a generic blending of diary, memoir, and lyric poetry; its stories are anecdotal, though still sequential, lacking the closure and interpretive significance of an autobiographical retrospective—but still created with a public audience in mind.[24]

Within the anecdotal genre are found editorial cartoons, which are typically "topical outbursts of image and text," frequently found in newspapers, that communicate attitudes or summary snapshots of situations.[25] They may be classified as political, seeking to bring order in and through government actions with biting partisan comment on current events, or as social commentary, designed to make life bearable; the latter are also referred to as "supportive comic strips" since they help audiences to cope with their world.[26] With their reliance on stereotypes and common symbols, editorial cartoons offer a rich resource for the study of culture and history.[27] They can frequently operate as an "inside joke," uniting a mass audience with shared, culturally situated allusions, and also offer audience members a way to vent their frustrations with leaders or situations, while making them laugh, by either reflecting the impressions of the public or making an issue salient to the public.[28] Editorial cartoons are a uniquely visual form of communication for orienting social issues, both offering and triggering deep reflection.[29] By drawing on various cognitive mechanisms, conceptual integration, and cognitive and cultural models, editorial cartoons can use humor as a form of criticism or commentary, and they can present a new vision, or frame, of a personality or event, often captured in a single image.[30] Comics have long offered a safe venue for dissent; the uses of parody, word-image dissonance, and Aesopian strategies of textual resistance have struck responsive chords in readers and allowed comics to critically mock society when others in the public forum could not.[31]

The earliest comic books, appearing in 1934, were reprinted collections of comic strips, or "funnies."[32] Quickly, though, as comic books developed in their own right, the two forms became very different. Comic books and comic strips are separated by matters of production, distribution, art form, and marketing. Comic strips are most often supplementary features to other media, reaching and appealing to a broad audience and using brevity to accommodate a confined space, whereas comic books have more creative freedom to be tailored to specific audiences who must deliberately purchase them. Therefore, there has never been a social stigma attached to either the children or adults who read comic strips—some sixty to seventy million each day—whereas comic books, and their readers, have often faced criticism as low-brow and prurient.[33] Comic books and their lengthier, more literary, progeny, graphic novels, emerged as a distinct medium in the mid-to-late 1930s and by the mid–1940s were America's most popular form of entertainment. By the end of the same decade comic books were under attack for promoting juvenile delinquency with their dark stories of crime and horror and, as a result, faced over a decade of socially imposed and self-enforced censorship.[34] Just as "comic strips" may be neither comical nor in strip form, "comic books" is also a misnomer; they are usually not humorous and are frequently more a pamphlet, or "floppy," than a book.[35]

The trajectory of comic book development is commonly classified according to eras: the Golden Age, the initial comic book boom of the 1930s–1940s, with varied tales of Westerns, crime, romance, horror, comedies, and adventure—all doing their part for morale at home and abroad during the war; the Silver Age of the 1950–60s, during which the industry struggled with stigma and censorship and the old, stale superhero stories took a grittier and more scientific or nuclear-age turn, while day-in-the-life teenage stories proliferated; and the Bronze Age, during the social turmoil of the 1960–70s through the 1990s, when a gap between cultural phenomena and comics content appeared and grew[36]—a gap that was filled by the advent of "comix," underground countercultural comic books with adult content ranging from political to profane.[37] Because these categories leave no room for a renaissance, some critics have reversed the colors, so that we are now in the Golden Age, or have used other descriptors such as "Industrial," to capture the period of ingenuity and creativity from the 1930s to the 1970s, and "Heroic," to describe the noble efforts of comic artists and fans to garner respect and permanence for the medium since the 1980s.[38] In recognition of the reciprocal importance of political turbulence to comics, the eras of World War II, the swinging Sixties, the Reagan/Thatcher years, and the Bush/Blair "war on terror" period have also been identified as critical comic book eras.[39] Whatever the classifications, the industrial and political eras are tightly intertwined with the content and reception of comic books. The most common genres of comic books during these decades have been these: crime, detective, educational, funny animal, horror, jungle, kid, kung fu, memoir, movie, promotional, romance, science fiction, superhero, sword-and-sorcery, teen humor, war, and hybrids of the same.[40] There is also the often overlooked genre of special-purpose comics, also referred to as industrial comics, giveaways, premiums, promics, or promos; this genre encompasses comics created for the practical objective of promoting an idea, purpose, or product—from winning a war to buying a Chevy.[41]

Graphic novels are comic books that are usually of novel length, though they may also be collections of shorter works unified by a common theme. The name first appeared in the 1960s and was popularized in 1978 with the publication of Will Eisner's *A Contract with God and Other Tenement Stories*. The graphic novel genre took hold in popular culture in the mid-to-late 1980s with the publication of three key texts that led to a boom in sales and attention from literary and arts scholars: Alan Moore and Dave Gibbons' *Watchmen* and Frank Miller's *The Dark Knight Returns* explored the dark side of superhero lore, and Art Spiegelman's *Maus* depicted the horrors of the Holocaust with furry animals.[42] For some fans, the distinction between a graphic novel and a comic book is one of ideology or marketing and suggests a "higher" form of graphic narrative or sequential art than the common superhero fare, and even suggests class distinctions among readers.[43] A variant of the graphic novel is the graphic memoir; autobiographical comics first began appearing within the comix movement in the early 1970s and their popularity has surged since the early 1990s, leading to greater elite acceptance of the sequential arts. The work of graphic autobiographers uniquely and intimately engages embodied aspects of identity and representations of temporal experiences, aiming to trigger particular emotional or cognitive responses from an audience, while challenging traditional assumptions of autobiographical authenticity.[44] The genre of comics journalism is also often found in graphic novel form. Closely aligned with alternative comics—those that fall outside the commercial mainstream—comics journalism is serious nonfiction that blends visual storytelling with reporting of current events. It first began appearing as a distinct genre in the mid–1990s. The narrative structure of comics journalism is not unlike that of standard news reporting and draws on the same devices, such as conducting interviews, incorporating both personal and source observations, and selecting and using quotes; the visual component of the comics helps to focus readers' attention on the particular parts of this content, often in a style reminiscent of a print photograph or broadcast screen.[45]

Comic books and graphic novels also house the genre of *manga*. Manga are transnationally circulated Japanese comics; they saw a boom in the 1950s and had their own Golden Age around the 1960–70s. Manga has its own generic divisions, including story manga, with an ongoing plot typically published in book form; essay manga, which offer short, semi-autobiographical stories drawn with a simple style and usually found in women's or general interest magazines; *shōjo manga*, girls' comics often featuring characters with particularly large, star-filled eyes; BL, or Boys' Love, manga, male homoerotic comics created primarily by and for women; and *senki-mono*, or records of war, which particularly focused on aerial, frontline, combat during World War II.[46]

Society, Superheroes and Strips

Like other elements of popular culture, comics can both reflect and challenge social norms; a powerful element of socialization, they send messages about preferred beliefs and behaviors.[47]

> When you look at a comic book, you're not seeing either the world or a direct representation of the world; what you're seeing is an interpretation or transformation of the world, with aspects that are exaggerated, adapted, or invented. It's not just unreal, it's deliberately constructed by a specific person or people. But because comics are a narrative and visual form, when you're reading them, you *do* believe that they're real on some level.... So the meaning of the comic's story within the world we see on the page is different from its meaning within the reader's world.[48]

Comics offer a symbolic environment that mirrors, yet manipulates, society.[49] People relate to comics by identifying with the characters and their struggles, recognizing in them shared hopes and fears; this is reinforced through the comics-culture of not only consuming the content, but also communicating about it with others and sharing the experience, thereby producing popular cultural memory.[50] Despite appearing unsophisticated in content, some comics use erudite narratives related to philosophy, mythology, or literature.[51] Such sophisticated content coupled with the ability to engender strong identification and community make comics useful teaching aids in literacy, writing, business, science, sociology, and history.[52]

The art form has a long and winding history: the graphic novel is the descendent of the comic book, which was born from the comic strip. The comic strip developed from humorous drawings in magazines and serial novels, following the appearance of picture stories in Europe that succeeded illuminated texts and medieval icons. Some have even argued that cave paintings, Egyptian hieroglyphs, and medieval tapestries, as visual storytelling devices, were the earliest forms of what would become the graphic narrative mediums.[53] Perhaps it is this longevity that makes comics such a valuable source of historical evidence. Since cartoons are cultural artifacts, historians have long used them—and the conditions of their creation and reception—as indicators of what happened in politics, religion, and social culture.[54] Though comic books were originally intended as escapist fare and shied away from real-world matters, the advent of World War II had a strong influence on the artists and writers and current events began to seep into the four-color pages; now, comics often raise controversial issues of the day, challenging audiences to choose between escaping from the real world or creatively wrestling with it. It has been argued, for example, that superhero comics are their most poignant during political and social unrest, especially during times of war. Hitting their peak during World War II, superhero comics, an American innovation, depict idealized, and often nationalistic, citizenship and contribute to the public discourse around U.S. foreign policy.[55] Of course, superheroes are not the only comics characters to go to, or take on, war.

"War offers cartoonists a set of subjects—lethal conflict, hyperbolic destruction, SNAFUs, reckless energy, human cruelty, and the self-destructive stupidity of our adversaries—that are laughably appropriate to the medium of cartooning."[56] During war, editorial cartoons sustain nations through recording and reinforcing the underlying beliefs about or in the cause.[57] American cartooning first began to bloom during the War of 1812 and really took root during the country's Civil War, during which battlefield artists played an important journalistic role.[58] During the Cold War era, many comics engaged in narrative battles with the communist menace,[59] and a range of characters, such as Reddy Kilowatt, Atomic Mouse, Atomic Rabbit, Atom the Cat, Doctor Solar, and the monstrous antihero Incredible Hulk dealt with themes of nuclear power.[60] At the same time, a proliferation of kid strips helped to spread American ideology through metaphoric conquest narratives,[61] while *MAD Magazine*'s "SPY vs. SPY" cartoon worked to undermine these same political rhetorics.[62] The official "9/11 Commission Report" was turned into a graphic novel to encourage alternate readings and audience political engagement, as did other graphic novels dealing with the subject.[63] Many comics have also dealt with wars retroactively and historically, including *Frontline Combat, Two Fisted Tales, Classics Illustrated, War Between the States*, and *The 'Nam*.[64] Even the Sunday funnies have gone to war: a beagle has re-fought the "Red Baron" from his doghouse-turned-

Sopwith-Camel, and a lazy army private has avoided the hardships of life at Camp Swampy. In a more serious vein, Garry Trudeau's *Doonesbury* has taken audiences through the darker, and more political, side of war with strips that, like *The 'Nam*, attempt to present an accurate and realistic portrayal of the war and soldiers' experiences.[65]

In the spirit of accuracy, realism, and soldiers' perspective, another source of war and military comics exists: those created by warriors themselves. Cartoons such as infantryman Bill Mauldin's Willie and Joe characters, beleaguered rank-and-file soldiers of World War II, spoke to and for the average soldiers of the war, expressing their shared emotions of exhaustion, grief, and hope, and they let the people at home better understand what the soldiers were experiencing.[66] Mauldin's work and other graphic narratives and the warrior-artists who create(d) them will be discussed in more detail in the next chapters. (Note that "warrior" is used herein to demarcate military servicepersons as a gender-neutral representation of all branches of service, in line with terminology used by the many Western militaries.) Some, like Mauldin's, are traditional comic strips, appearing in print periodicals. Some of those strips have been collected into published volumes, like the original *Famous Funnies* comic book. Others are more like comic books, or perhaps "graphic novellas," particularly of the special-purpose genre. Some of the strips are anecdotal, while others are more editorial. And whether a strip or a book, they tend to resemble diary comics or graphic memoirs and, throughout their history, have often served as comics journalism.

Research on Military and War Comics

There have been a number of studies of war or military comics and their cinematic counterpart, animated cartoons, over the years—most focusing on editorial cartoons,[67] historical comics,[68] or themes of warfare.[69] Comics of the Cold War have been an especially popular topic of inquiry.[70] There has also been some attention to pro- or anti-war messages in particular comics or genres,[71] such as discussion of nationalistic and militaristic themes in superhero comics.[72] Other studies have examined propaganda in cartooning,[73] often with particular attention to depictions of enemies.[74] Few have considered the comics drawn by[75] or for[76] warriors, and those few have often been limited in scope, looking at only a single conflict, specific title, or particular artists. This is not surprising, as relatively little has been written about the informal activities of the military, particularly in wartime.[77] Plus, in America, at least, war comics generally have been a marginal genre, enjoying prime popularity in the 1950s.[78]

In his defense of soldier cartoons as historical evidence, historian Jay Casey identified a categorical pattern of content based on military service that follows warriors' activities and the daily course of conflict as well as significant historical events, with common themes of military bureaucracy and hierarchy, food, technology, and gender and race relations. He wrote, "It is instructive to evaluate some of the ways individual cartoonists in uniform selected material that falls into predictable categories."[79] This book seeks to do just that, but with a broader scope than earlier studies, by considering more than two centuries' worth of comics by hundreds of artists from more than thirteen countries. The main focus of the book is comics drawn by warriors, though those drawn for warriors are also included, as it is not always possible to be sure whether or not artists, particularly those employed by the government, were officially members of the military.

These graphic narratives are valuable firsthand accounts of war:

> The visual record of wartime comics deserves to see the light again, not only for what the images tell us about a certain part of the past but because much of it is still funny, if poignantly so. The work of soldier cartoonists presents a valuable area for research in that veiled social commentary, as opposed to more obvious forms of editorial content, often informed their work. The intent was to deliver an escape from the realities they witnessed as a necessary part of gathering material for their cartoons. While humour remained the point, cartoonists familiar with the experiences of soldiers at the front often provided editorial comment in their attempts to recreate realistic scenarios.[80]

The comics discussed, analyzed, and highlighted in the following chapters offer the broadest representation available to the author. Accessing the work of many artists was unfortunately not practical: Many have only limited circulation in particular editions of *Stars and Stripes*, *Yank Magazine*, or base and division publications, with restricted archives. The work of others is long out of print, with scattered issues sitting only in private collections or far off libraries, if they were not long-since recycled in paper drives for the war effort. Some works exist only in personal correspondence and private diaries. Those acquired were found in dozens of primary and secondary sources. They are predominantly American, because of restricted translation and acquisition abilities, but every effort has been made to incorporate comics of other nationalities, including those of Australia, Canada, China, England (including British India), Germany, Japan, Korea, New Zealand, Scotland, Vietnam, Wales, and Yugoslavia. Relevant cartoon artwork from other countries, including Burma, France, and Russia, is also referenced, though the works of military cartoonists from those countries could not be identified. Conflicts represented include the Napoleonic Wars, the American Civil War, the Spanish-American War, the Boer War, the Great War, World War II, the Korean War, the Cold War, the Vietnam War, Operation Desert Storm, Operation Enduring Freedom, and Operation Iraqi Freedom. A complete comicography of the collected graphic narratives included in the analysis—more than 200 sets, each ranging in size from one to 700 stories—is provided in the appendix.

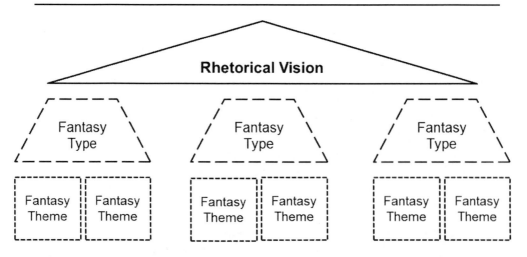

Fig. 0.1: Relationship of fantasy themes, fantasy types, and rhetorical vision.

Comics Criticism

Graphic narratives have been evaluated on literary, artistic, and cinematic grounds[81] but are best analyzed in terms that recognize the distinctiveness of the medium: "Great comics will be those that tell affecting and powerful stories—but they will tell those stories by exploiting to the fullest the unique potential of the art"—the sequential blending of word and image. Four graphic threads are considered useful for comic strip analysis: narrative breakdown, layout, panel composition, and style.[82] Additionally, the six elements of the taxonomy of graphic discourse are particularly useful in understanding editorial cartoons; these elements are: (1) naming the *topoi*; (2) identifying any literary or cultural allusions; (3) observing the traits of the featured characters; (4) noting idiosyncratic situational factors; (5) examining the forms of graphic disposition—contrast, commentary, and/or contradiction; and (6) critiquing the rhetorical style, including the use of line and form, the relative size of objects, exaggeration of features, placement, and relation of text to imagery.[83] This approach, however, has faced criticism for inadequately considering and explaining the peculiarities of the genre; a Burkean approach drawing on the strategy of perspective by incongruity has been used to better capture the negative attitude of political cartoons, and Burke's master tropes have been used to uncover their persuasive abilities. Meanwhile, Burke's dramatistic pentad has been used to look at longer comic storylines.[84] Content analysis has also frequently been used to critique comics, particularly comic strips,[85] to look for patterns of meaning, whereas mythic criticism has helped scholars to uncover culturally symbolic meanings.[86] Various other textual approaches have also been used to unpack the messages of comics, including rhetorical, feminist, queer, cultural, historical, political, economic, and sociological approaches.[87]

Fantasy Theme Analysis (FTA) is the tool of Symbolic Convergence Theory (SCT) and has also been repeatedly used by scholars to critique editorial cartoons and other comics.[88] SCT "provides a universal explanation of human communication."[89] Symbolic convergence promotes the achievement of empathic communication. Dealing with the human tendency to give meaning to symbols, it refers to the way in which two or more individual symbol-worlds align or join.[90]

SCT originated in work with small groups, asserting that members in small groups engage in communication that fosters shared group identity through the development of a common viewpoint unique to that particular group. This perspective was eventually expanded to include the ways in which larger groups can also enhance cohesion through communication.[91] Given the importance of group convergence in the military,[92] FTA is well-suited for inquiry into warrior-created graphic narratives. Though SCT most often looks at small group dynamics[93] it has also proven useful in understanding larger organizational dynamics,[94] as well as both mediated and non-mediated public, socio-political dynamics.[95] While FTA is not specific to the study of graphic narratives, it has much to offer their study because it allows for both simultaneous and distinct consideration of images and words. FTA evaluates rhetorical discourse with a focus on the message, rather than the speaker or audience, and "provides a clear technical vocabulary for the general analysis of imaginative language."[96] It is based on the assumption that people build a shared sense of reality through communication that can best be analyzed through the rhetorical concept of fantasy, which conveys meaning, emotion, and motive.

The communication that makes symbolic convergence possible is a dramatizing message—creative and imaginative interpretations of the "there-and-then" that can bring clarity to situations.[97] When these messages, whether they are shared through interpersonal or public exchanges, catch on they can "chain out," or spread through lively agreement and retelling.[98] SCT suggests several levels in the process of symbolic convergence: from lowest to highest, these are fantasy themes, fantasy types, and rhetorical vision.[99] The most basic unit is the fantasy theme, which is the content of a successful dramatizing message.[100] Fantasy themes that are intrinsic to a society's rhetoric, rooted in longstanding values or ideals, are modal societal fantasies.[101] One aspect of this theory that makes it particularly useful for the study of graphic narratives is the observation that "once the dynamic process of sharing a group fantasy creates symbolic convergence for a group of people, they will exhibit the 'inside joke syndrome,'" wherein a communicator needs only allude to a shared fantasy by means of a related symbol to spark a response.[102] This is particularly apt for such an insular group as the military. A cluster of related fantasy themes creates a fantasy type—an abstraction that incorporates several concrete fantasy themes that exist when shared meaning is accepted without question. At the highest level, both of abstraction and in the symbolic convergence process, is a rhetorical vision. A rhetorical vision is the unification of the various fantasy themes and shared scripts that gives group members a broader view of things, particularly a culture's social reality. Rhetorical visions may usually be indexed by some slogan or label, though they have multi-staged life cycles and exist along multiple continua. The body of people who share this common symbolic reality, who participate in the social vision, is a rhetorical community.[103]

The method of FTA works with individual messages, a series of messages, or a corpus of messages. The fantasy theme, fantasy type, and modal societal fantasy are the basic concepts and units of analysis when using FTA. The method's structural elements involve the key pieces of a rhetorical vision: *dramatis personae* (the characters), plotlines (the story or actions of the vision), scenes (the time and place), sanctioning agents (source of legitimacy), and master analogue (righteous, social or pragmatic orientations). FTA's critical evaluation essentials involve a rhetorical community (mentioned earlier), a reality link to here-and-now phenomena (elements of credibility that make the rhetorical vision more believable), and a dramatistic rhetorical strategy (the part of the vision that is emphasized in a message—character, plot, scene, or agent).[104] Critical probes for FTA ask of a story line what the characters are like, what the options for group action are, how both success and morality or correctness can be measured, and why things happen as they do.[105] Coding fantasy themes involves discovering "cryptic allusions to symbolic ground"—evidence of, or references to, a group's inside joke—which are often visible through repeated mentions or appearances, with attention to the vision components of characters, scene, and plotline. From this information, the critic can discern minor and major fantasies, or types, and then construct a rhetorical vision.[106] This may even be represented visually,[107] as in Figure 0.1. Discovering this symbolic ground builds an understanding not only of how the communication of graphic narratives works in the group, but also of that group's outlook, worldview, or "rhetorical vision," of themselves, of society, and of their place in society.

The challenge of this approach with warrior graphic narratives is in a group outsider being able to catch the inside jokes, and in a present-day researcher being able to recognize cultural references of other eras. But, as Jay Casey noted, "Cartoon images often provide a trail leading back to larger issues relating to specific historical events and broader cultural attitudes."[108] Additionally, this research draws not only from the comics but also from available cartoonist biographies and from resources regarding military culture, folklore and slang, war rhetoric, enemy archetypes, military geography, gender relations in the military, and more, to help understand and explain the rhetorical vision of the warrior. Searching for the meaning behind the drawings, and between the lines, can help outsiders to better understand not only the graphic narratives but also the warriors' experiences they express.[109]

Preview

The second part of this book—encompassing chapters 2 through 9—highlights the recurring themes in warriors' graphic narratives, exploring the types of content and the substance of the stories within different thematic areas. Chapters 2 through 8 each open with a brief review of the history and research on the particular theme in the military, and, where appropriate, its treatment in graphic narratives. These chapters then follow with a discussion of the ways in which these themes are developed in the graphic narratives, providing many examples from the artworks. (Please note that all graphic narratives given as examples are indicated in the endnotes and are found in the appendix.)

Chapters 2 and 3 discuss comics about the military lifestyle—arguably the most prevalent theme throughout the graphic narratives. The military organization has three distinct features: the communal character of life, strongly influenced by the degree of normative orientation of military employees to the institutional goals and values of the military; the formal hierarchy that exists to enact and enforce the official regulations of the military; and discipline and control, closely connected to the chain of command inherent in the hierarchy. Warriors' graphic narratives frequently reference one or all of these features that demarcate daily life in the military. Chapter 2 primarily looks at daily routines, touching on such issues as training, uniforms, food, health care, communal living, and branch rivalries. The frequency and nature of these topics in the graphic narratives emphasize the importance of community within the military establishment. Chapter 3 extends this discussion by focusing specifically on hierarchy in the military establishment, examining graphic narratives about courtesy, officers, bureaucracy, and politics—causes of frustration for military personnel. From the camp goldbrick to the brass hat, personalities are the defining characteristic of these graphic narratives.

Chapters 4 and 5 look to themes central to military operations: those of international interactions. In war, there are enemies and allies. Governments use the idea of a common enemy to maintain control, to reinforce dominant values, to mobilize action and allies, and to renew commitment to a common cause or ideology. Enemies are established by the state apparatus as legitimate targets of force, sanctioning killing as honorable, though in combat scenarios the enemy is more likely to be practically categorized by the seriousness of the perceived threat that they pose. Chapter 4 examines graphic narratives about both so-called allies and so-called enemies, touching on depictions of difference and similarity in what may be understood as the cultural factors of military geography. Chapter 5 looks more toward the physical factors of military geography. Military geographies are about the material and discursive control of land, involving economics, information, social order, space, environments, and landscapes. The physical factors of military geography include spatial relationships, topography, geology, vegetation, bodies of water, climate and weather, daylight and darkness, and gravity and magnetism—characteristics important to the probable effects on a military mission. Whereas Chapter 4 is concerned with Other people, chapter 5 examines graphic narratives about Other places, with emphasis on the climate, especially rain and cold, and terrain, such as rocks, sand, and mud, encountered in training, deployment, and combat. Warriors tend to express resentment towards anything, whether a person or a place, that interferes with their chances of survival.

Chapter 6 continues to look at graphic narratives about Others, this time focusing on gender and sexuality. During World War I, countries, such as England, that suffered heavy casualties began recruiting women for combat service roles such as cooks, or for temporary clerical work in Army Pay Department offices. In the early years of U.S. involvement in World War II, five female corps of the American military branches were established. Over the years, the role of women in the military has changed, with variations in each force and each country. While many Western democracies have increasingly adopted inclusionary policies that meet personnel demands and reflect diversity and gender equality, the same militaries' cultures and doctrines challenge women's inclusion by emphasizing a distinctly masculine warrior spirit, which has also created challenges for the service of gays in the military. Comics about sex and gender tend to reinforce these ideas by expressing the military in terms of virile masculinity.

Chapters 7 and 8 look at graphic narratives that represent what might be called the outcomes of military service. Chapter 7 examines representations of combat and the effects of combat: physical and emotional or mental wounds, and death. Combat experience has been linked to a range of positive and negative outcomes. Warriors report that they are better able to cope with adversity and have improved self-discipline, greater independence, and a broader perspective and appreciation for life's value. But they also report feelings of anxiety, misery, and loss. Such influences and life changes contribute to the phenomenon known as the civil-military gap. There is a tendency for current understandings of military service and civilian experience to be polarized, resulting in a sense of military alienation from civilian leadership and society, a growing gap between the military institution and civilian society at large, increasing politicization of the military and military resistance to civilian oversight. Chapter 8 explores such tensions between the civilian lifestyle and mindset and the military lifestyle and mindset, and the apparitions of those effects both upon entering and leaving military service.

The book's conclusion draws together all of these themes—culture, hierarchy, enemies and allies, climate and terrain, gender and sexuality, combat and casualties, and civil-military relations—into a broader discussion of the military worldview, or rhetorical vision, in which fraternity and experience are both central and universal. The conclusion begins by exploring the graphic narratives' characters, plotlines, scenes, sources of legitimacy, and moral orientations, before looking at the historical and international continuity of the themes rendered possible by the military's primary mission of violence.

1

GI Joking

Military Humor and Graphic Narratives

If you have to explain a joke, it ain't!—CWO Qill Eisner

In 1969 the British variety show *Monty Python's Flying Circus* ran a sketch sometimes known as "Joke Warfare." Set during World War II, it features the creation of a joke so funny its own writer dies from laughing. After the joke spreads and the death toll mounts, the British Army has the joke translated into German, eventually using it in open warfare. When the Germans try counter-joke tactics, the English are un-amused. Ultimately, the countries agree to a Joke Warfare ban at the Geneva Convention.[1] Research suggests that humor *can* play a part in paths to peace or war.[2] "Joke Warfare," however, has not yet been attempted, though during World War I, an artist with *Stars and Stripes*, Abian A. Wallgren, used multiple pen-names to make the Germans believe the paper had a large staff of cartoonists, and in World War II the cartoon character "Sad Sack," in the cartoon of the same name by Sgt. George Baker, was accused in *Yank Magazine* of being a Nazi spy,[3] and the military does make other regular and practical uses of humor. Homer Litzenberg, a brigadier general in the U.S. Marine Corps, stated, "As any military man will tell you, humor is a necessity on the battlefield."[4] Military leaders successfully use humor to improve morale, group cohesiveness, and teamwork, to relieve stress, to promote creativity and communication, to enhance leadership, and to accomplish organizational objectives while strengthening the organizational culture.[5] Humor reduces the tedium and pain of training, provides a way for the lowliest ranks to mock superiors, and unites the group against common rivals.[6] "Griping," in particular, is believed to be both a common form of amusement and a way to make life more tolerable.[7]

"Since the principal ingredients of humor are anachronism and inexplicability, you can't define, dissect, explain, or outline it without destroying it."[8]

Nonetheless, philosophers, psychologists, and scientists have offered their interpretations of humor, which is most commonly understood as something that may be found amusing or laughable, in varying degrees. In the military setting, humor develops a distinct essence because of special conditioning and unique fields of operation. Generally, aspects of the military environment that both encourage and influence humor include political leadership and control, particularly regarding the complicated and often inadequate allocation of resources; security and secrecy, which can, if taken too far, hinder efficiency; authoritarianism and the hierarchical structure, especially the disciplinary rigidity; communication of orders, as related to military hierarchy, with attention to detail that can go to absurd extremes; ceremonial pomp and circumstance and spit and polish, as related to the bisociation of the human and the mechanical; the juxtaposition of dignity and fun, as childish pranks are not uncommon among officers or enlisted; and the perpetual search for inventions to best the enemy, which may result in rejecting effective technology or adopting ineffective technology.[9]

Different branches, and branch rivalries, are instrumental in military humor, as each branch operates in different environments with different needs. For example, air force pilots face high risk and need high *personal* initiative and self-discipline, whereas sailors in the navy face the strict *formal* discipline and tradition. Additionally, "the relationship among Allies always involves conflicts of cultures, values, and interests which sometimes lead to a humorous situation in the bisociation of two operative fields."[10] In fact, there are some distinct variations of humor among nationalities, though underlying themes in the military tend to be the same. For example, Britain's long history of military action has resulted in a utilitarian sense of humor that is confident of victory but prepared for defeat, which allows the British military to trivialize crises and not take itself too seriously. The French military is a contrast to the British in that it is flamboyant in victory and self-pitying in defeat, shaped by the more individualistic French culture in general.[11]

War Jokes

Combat, too, brings its own variety of humor, brought on by the elements of surprise, uncertainty, and absurdity—and aided by the tendency for practical joking to ease tensions. The allure of combat for many warriors involves the depth of feeling they have for their comrades in arms and the desire to rise to a challenge, however difficult it may be. The perspective of combat as a challenge allows for a light-hearted attitude to combat situations, which helps to frame life-and-death scenarios into manageable terms of games or athletics.[12] Combat comedy is also a way to directly engage suffering, rather than hiding from it,[13] and the wars of history have triggered particular strains of humor both within the armed forces and in the broader societies they serve.

The French Revolutionary Wars saw the first official war cartoonist in James Gillray. Gillray was present during the Flanders Campaign in 1793, drawing on-the-spot portraits of allied commanders. His later caricatures of Napoleon Bonaparte helped to make the "Little Corporal" a stock figure of cartoon humor during the Napoleonic Wars. Napoleon was the most mocked figure of his time, though commanders and monarchs of the allied forces were also popular targets of satire, and he had a shrewd awareness of the power of caricature—an art form that was flourishing through satirical magazines and a rapidly expanding market for prints.[14] The impact of these cartoons and caricatures grew through the wars of the British Empire thanks to specialty publications that appeared between 1830 and 1876, including the French *La Caricature* and *Le Charivari*, the English *Punch, Fun, Judy, Moonshine*, and *Vanity Fair*, the German *Fliegende Blätter, Kladderadatsche*, and *Simplicissimus*, and the American *Puck* and *Judge*. The wars of the Empire offered plenty of humorous content, from the new combat technologies to the showy uniforms of the Brits and Scots and the ornate uniforms of the Ashanti, Chinese, Indians, Sudanese, and Zulus. Jokes were often long-winded, but familiar sexist, racist, and classist themes were common, and politicians, commanders, and monarchs were frequently targeted.[15]

During the American Civil War,

Fig. 1.1: An example of Civil War humor: mockery of president of the Confederate States Jefferson Davis.

many met the grisly events with bold and honest comedy. Bored soldiers in camp and anxious relatives back home filled their letters with nervous laughter. Prisoners of war joked about their desperate search for blankets, and nurses snuck "comic papers" under the pillows of wounded soldiers. Cabinet members noted that Abraham Lincoln read those same papers aloud in meetings.... By the second half of the conflict, even polite newspapers printed "Off-Hand" amputation puns and reported pranks played on battlefield gravediggers.[16]

The proliferation of humor during the grim years of 1861 to 1865 was inextricably tied up in the advancements of the print medium. Political cartoons, novelty song sheets, comic Valentines, pictorial envelopes, books, and more were printed by the thousands and sold for pennies. Visual humor was a priority in the print war, but most studies of Civil War humor have focused on popular persona-comedians.[17] Studies of visual humor in the era tend to focus on the work of Thomas Nast and other political cartoonists of the day.[18]

The jokes themselves relied on ironic satire and linguistic puns, though content varied widely, with the purpose of managing the horrors of war and the people's growing despair. There were marked differences in the humor of the Union and the Confederacy, with the latter being much quicker to find the wit in war and to adopt colder, more cynical, "hard war humor."[19] Some of the major themes that emerged from Civil War comedy included the presidents; the fears and hardships of soldiering, such as discomfort and boredom, but particularly death and, more so, disfigurement; and race relations. Confederate humor also emphasized insulting Union, or Yankee, stereotypes—making it easier to kill the enemy without hesitation. Combat and camp humor alternatively comforted and disturbed loved ones at home by either offering reassurance that the soldiers remained in good spirits or raising concerns about their levels of depravity.[20]

The War of 1898, more commonly known as the Spanish-American War, brought on the rapid creation and transmission of both hawkish and cautionary editorial cartoons, spurred by advances in media technology and fierce newspaper competition. Villainy and violence were the dominant themes, with liberal artistic interpretations of the truth playing on and piquing emotions.[21] Such politicized humor gave way to more soldier-centric humor during World War I thanks to the diverse mix of Americans, with limited world and military experiences, that were thrust together to fight. Cartoons in particular emphasized common themes of new and awkward situations, the perspective of the lowly private, and a dislike for officers and military police. American soldier, or "doughboy," humor went through four phases, in line with the progression of service: Stateside Training Camp humor, which emphasized the recruits' lack of military understanding; Overseas Service humor, which highlighted new places, foreign culture and language, and French women; Army of Occupation humor, which was frequently about the desire to go home; and Veteran humor, which was darker and more politically critical, touching on issues of joblessness, maladjustment, and "shell shock" (now recognized as Post-Traumatic Stress Disorder, or PTSD):

> Doughboy humor helped to make the inevitable difficulties in adapting to military life more bearable by revealing these experiences as universal, and by viewing them as something that could be discussed and laughed at. The overall tone of doughboy humor was good-spirited, and, despite the hardships suffered, most doughboys held a positive view about their military service.[22]

One of the best-known doughboy comics was *Wally's Cartoons of the A.E.F.* by Pvt. Abian Wallgren, printed in and reprinted from *Stars and Stripes*, which often featured light-hearted interpretations of military procedure. But Wallgren was only one of dozens of cartoonists in the Great War, and comic art was not limited to the United States.

England's Captain Bruce Bairnsfather was the most famous cartoonist of World War I. His ironic strips demonstrated humor through every possible difficulty and challenge. Bairnsfather was sometimes known as "the Man Who Won the War" for the morale boost through laughter that his soldier characters, Old Bill, Bert and Alf, gave to those at the frontlines and on the home front.[23] Australian soldiers were represented in *Humorisities* by Corporal Cecil L. Hartt, AIF, and in *Digger Days* by Frank Dunne. The duration of British Empire's involvement in the war meant that the works of Bairnsfather, Hartt, and Dunne tended toward realistic images "that traded in war's brutality and insanity," whereas the American artists such as Wallgren focused more on the vagaries of soldiering and were colored with slapstick comedy.[24] Germany, too, had its cartoons; Lieutenant General Theodor von Wundt of the 26th Division at the Somme commissioned artist Albert Heim for eighty cartoon paintings of German soldiers on the Western Front. Like the doughboy comics, many poke fun at the officer class, while others emphasize supply issues, all while ignoring the filth of trench warfare.[25] In France, the *Canard Enchaîné* weekly used satire and visual humor to question the war, irony being a key mechanism for making the lengthy war tolerable in Europe.[26]

Evidence of Western Allied humor from the Second World War is as ubiquitous as the cartoon "Kilroy Was Here" graffiti left by American soldiers throughout the world,[27] thanks to the extensive mobilization of men, women, and children through cultural and, more significantly, popular appeals. Humor in pop culture was a way to motivate and comfort those on the home front. For those in combat, humor was a means to record the experience:

> The GI's world often encompassed no more than his immediate occupations and surroundings, what he could actually see or sometimes only hear or feel. Con-

sequently, much of his humor was strictly local humor, based on down-to-earth perceptions of realities close at hand. Therein lies that humor's faithfulness, its documentary warrant, its historicity, if you will.[28]

With 9 percent of Americans serving in the armed forces,[29] the military humor easily filtered into broader civilian society. For example, members of the military use an informal, or folk, vocabulary that distinguishes them as an organization and helps to add humor to dull or dangerous situations while, ostensibly, improving communication. In conscript forces, such as those of World War II, some of these humor-tinted terms, such as "snafu" (situation normal: all fucked up), entered civilian vocabularies.[30]

Spoofs of the enemy were a favorite theme of World War II humor, particularly in comics, for all sides in the conflict.[31] Walt Disney's *Der Fuerher's Face* and the Spike Jones novelty song it bore, starring Donald Duck, is an epitomic example from the United States of spoofing the Nazis. In China, "cartoon warfare" against the Japanese invasion portrayed the enemy as demons, ghosts, and dogs.[32] In Germany, funny-animal-style animated cartoons presented childlike versions of anti–Semitism.[33] Tragic humor was also used effectively in propaganda, particularly by the Allies, in order to foster a sense of despair and bitterness in the enemy, and the postwar years saw a surge of war-related absurd and dark humor in literature.[34] Frontline humor, reportedly crude, racist, and subversive, also buoyed the spirits of the Soviet's Red Army, though little is known about it because the secret police banned the recording of soldiers' jokes, which were intimate, insider expressions of the moment.[35]

Cartoons were an especially popular form of entertainment during the Korean conflict, thanks in part to military morale officers who recognized and supported the value of comics in publications. Many of the comics took a silly, though informational, slant on life in a foreign country, the expectations of military service, interservice rivalries, depictions of the enemy (a common theme of both American and Chinese comics), extreme weather conditions, authority, alcohol, media, weapons, and vehicles. They made light of potentially deadly situations and gave soldiers something to laugh at when life was not that funny.[36] Humor in Vietnam was often satirical, particularly in the proliferation of underground newspapers that took aim at politics and government censorship.[37] Much of it focused on themes similar to those of previous wars, such as disgust for superiors, discomforts of combat, or disdain for the enemy,[38] though with an added bitterness about the situation.[39] "There were innumerable jokes about politicians, bureaucracy and the Brass," marked by disillusionment and cynicism.[40] Much of the humor was presented musically, fitting for what the *New York Times* named the "first rock and roll war,"[41] though it was also found in troop graffiti,[42] and one cartooning army captain found that soldiers enjoyed cartoons about war and created the blithe series *Grants Grunts* on the absurd-ities and miseries of Vietnam. Vernon Grant, who is credited with introducing the manga style to English cartooning, served in the army from 1958 to 1968, after which he became a regular cartoonist for the *Pacific Stars and Stripes*. He also published two books that took a humorous look at soldiering, *Stand-By One* and *Point-Man Palmer*, distributed to troops in the 1970s.[43]

In the United States, government-issued comic books became a key tool in recruitment and propaganda during the postwar and inter-war years. *Time of Decision* and other recruiting comics were distributed on college campuses, emphasizing ideas and ideals of heterosexual masculinity to glorify military service. Comics designed to undermine support for Cuban leader Fidel Castro were circulated in South and Central America.[44] In American society at large, satire was a prominent component of Cold War humor, used to undermine the hypocrisy and hyperbole of these kind of anti–Communist and pro-government messages.[45]

A game analogy of combat was pronounced in Operation Desert Storm (ODS) of 1991, as the conflict in the Persian Gulf was quickly dubbed "the Nin-tendo War." This narrative promoted humorous understandings of the war and its media coverage.[46] The game metaphor was again key in 1999 during Oper-ation Allied Force in Kosovo.[47] In the immediate aftermath of the September 11, 2001, terrorist attacks, the United States was not in a joking mood. The *New Yorker* magazine was published without any cartoons for only the second time in its history—the first was following the bombing of Hiroshima.[48] Eventually, though, humor returned, bitterly at first. A plethora of formulaic, enemy-directed, politically incorrect jokes emerged from the ashes of September 11, and enemy archetypes were numerous in political cartoons as Operation Endur-ing Freedom (OEF) got underway.[49]

Then came a new genre of digital disaster jokes, rife with ironic self-awareness, which spread on the Internet through e-mail, newsgroups, and Web sites, as a way for people to separate themselves from the mournful public and media discourses.[50] Eventually, late-night talk shows used humor to help educate the American public about Operation Iraqi Freedom (OIF), balancing the audience's need for information for a need for escape and levity.[51] There is, however, no research yet on humor within the military during these conflicts—except for recognition that humor is a frequent coping mechanism of troops in situations of high uncertainty and anxiety.[52] Following the 2003 invasion of Iraq, the U.S. military distributed *Baghdad Kids* comics to promote hygiene, safety, and pro–American news of OIF. It also continued its long-standing prac-tice of comics for the soldiers, with comics-format manuals—now using manga style, a graphic novel about being a navy corpsman in Iraq, and army web-comics.[53]

Fig. 1.2: An example of light humor from the Second World War—Kilroy "graffiti" on the World War II Memorial in Washington, D.C. Photograph by C.M. Knopf.

Military Humor

Though comics are not necessarily comical, the majority of comics drawn by and/or for warriors have a humorous bent, with different audiences, different artists, different circumstances, and different goals influencing the kind of humor used. Some war humor is labeled "irrelevant." It is "that humor, aimed at an audience consisting primarily of non-service people, which has very little to do with actual life in the services, and even less to do with the war."[54] American pop culture is filled with irrelevant war humor—television shows such as *Enlisted*, *Hogan's Heroes*, *Gomer Pyle USMC*, and *McHale's Navy*; movies such as *Father Goose*, *Stripes*, and *Hot Shots*; books such as journalist Marion Hargrove's *See Here, Private Hargrove* and Mac Hyman's *No Time for Sergeants*; and comic strips such as Mort Walker's *Beetle Bailey*. Private Beetle Bailey, who has been lazing about newspaper funny pages for more than sixty years, may be one of the most recognized military cartoon characters created by a military veteran.

Artist Mort Walker was drafted into military service in 1942 and discharged as a first lieutenant in 1946, four years before he penned his first *Beetle Bailey* cartoons. Accepted by King Features for syndication, *Beetle Bailey* was the last feature personally approved by William Randolph Hearst. Beetle was a college student until 1951. With audiences cooling, and the Korean War heating up, Walker put Beetle in the army, and he landed at Camp Swampy under the command of General Halftrack. "The potential readership for a strip about army life was enormous. Every able-bodied American male had been in military service or was in military service—or would be in military service. Military experience was the great common bond. And ... Walker drew upon his own experience."[55]

Walker partially attributed the strip's success to the humorlessness of the old U.S. Army from the 1940s and '50s, the army in which he himself had served. Indeed, the military newspaper *Stars and Stripes*, which carried numerous warrior cartoons for soldiers throughout the war years, twice banned the *Beetle Bailey* strip: once, in the early 1950s, for its disrespectful portrayal of officers, and again in 1970 when Walker introduced an African American officer, Lt. Jack Flap. The censorship resulted in hundreds of new civilian subscriptions. By the 1990s, military sex scandals in the real world influenced gender relations at Camp Swampy; women had long been unhappy with the ogling of women portrayed in the strips, so the general went to sensitivity training to ensure that *Beetle Bailey* was not seen as condoning sexual misconduct in the army. Ultimately, however, *Beetle Bailey* is about amusement, not politics, and not the military. It is driven by the characters, who are drawn in a simplistic and elastic style, more than by its setting. Walker explains, "I want the broadest possible readership. I'm in the business of entertaining people."[56]

"Light, jokey, inside humor or gags" is a broad category that often overlaps or intersects with the other kinds of war humor.[57] This category includes military jargon such as "FUBAR" (fucked up beyond all recognition), and "BOHICA" (bend over, here it comes again), images such as Kilroy, and other amusing references or allusions with which any warrior or veteran can easily identify. Light humor is a common theme among warrior comics, which are rich with inside jokes. One of the clearest examples of light humor comics is found in the various boot camp souvenir books published in the 1940s and 1950s. Many are written by Ted Ritter and Bob Gadbois, featuring the different branches of U.S. armed services, and humorously illustrate the hardships and concerns that all new recruits and draftees faced, such as early mornings, screaming drill sergeants, physical training, and unpleasant duty assignments. Such books both made the training experience universal within military service, and therefore made it a shared burden of a particular group, and helped to demonstrate to new personnel how to act.[58] They reinforced community with pages for autographs and sections that could be filled out with particulars from the owner's own boot camp experience, such as space for date of enlistment, the basic training outfit, the name of the commanding officer or platoon officer, and duty assignment. Additionally, a number of light humor comics during World War II helped to illuminate the new experiences for women in military service.

One of the best known of these servicewomen's comics was *Winnie the WAC* by Corporal Vic Herman. Herman was an advertising illustrator who was commissioned to create a morale-boosting cartoon for his army base newspaper during the war; Winnie's appearance was modeled after real-life WAC (Women's Army Corps) Althea Semanchik, but her experiences were based on every Wac. Winnie was a hero to the Women's Army Corps, to civilian children, and even to the male army who voted her Ordnance Joe—an honor that had always gone to a living man. Winnie's trials and tribulations began around 1943 and were syndicated in 1,200 of the army's camp newspapers; she was introduced to the American public through features in *Life* and *Look* magazines and through a bound collection, with a forward by actress Carole Landis, in 1945 that sold 85,000 copies and was later reprinted in 2002 as a morale booster for those serving in Afghanistan. *Winnie the WAC* was described by Landis, who played Winnie in a film adaptation that never made it to theaters, as the "baby" of the WACs because she teased them kindly, not cruelly. Winnie and her creator went on recruiting and morale-boosting tours, received hundreds of fan letters, and served as inspiration for both males and females to serve their country. Herman was called a hero to all Wacs for his ability to tell their story.[59]

More recently, a woman's perspective has been captured in a light humor comic named *Jenny, the Military Spouse*, written by military spouse Julie L. Negron. The only comic strip about life as a military spouse, it follows the (mis)adventures of a young air force wife named Jenny Spouse, determined to meet the challenges of the military lifestyle. Relying on the actual experiences of the cartoonist and other contributors for its content, "Jenny's experiences reflect the humor, ingenuity, and sheer determination necessary to be successful as the spouse of an active duty military member."[60] A features editor for *Stars and Stripes* describes the strip as perfectly blending visual style and humor to depict and shed light on the aspects of life that are common for those who live in military communities—from frequent deployments to lines at the commissary, and many military spouses express the sentiment that it is a relief to know they are not alone in what they go through physically and emotionally.[61]

"Serio-comic social commentary" has been considered the most important kind of war humor, as it is sobered by the experience of combat. It is "the kind of humor, really, that only someone who was part of the action of the war could truly understand."[62] This humor is not laugh-out-loud funny, but is more of a shared smile through misery or a wry chuckle at truth. It is reflective and raw. Bill Maudin's "Willie and Joe," or *Up Front*, comic epitomizes the serio-comic tradition in warrior comics. "Bill Mauldin, the Pulitzer-prize winning artist from the *Mediterranean Stars and Stripes* staff, had a knack for spotting the inequities in Army life—and then quickly turning inequity into ink."[63] Willie and Joe were privates, referred to as "dogfaces," drawn to look, as General George Patton described, like "goddamn bums." They served in Europe, primarily Italy, and were often shown enduring the hardships of climate and terrain and the degradation of officers.[64] The bedraggled and resigned characters were able to represent battle fatigue when other mediums could not get the topic past censors. Mauldin also deftly handled other subjects too taboo for strictly textual journalism and commentary, such as sex, alcohol, obscenity (conveyed visually rather than verbally), and even defecation.[65]

Though "Willie and Joe" were read by civilians at home, eager to get a glimpse of war's reality, the necessity of combat experience for true understanding of the comic's humor is easily seen in an analysis of World War II comic strips done by psychologist Carmen Moran. With an eye toward potential nationalistic differences in humor, Moran compared the American Mauldin's work to Australian Alex Guerney's strip *Bluey and Curley*. Guerney was a war correspondent who visited troops overseas, whereas Mauldin was an infantryman on the front. Moran noted that Guerney's work was more traditionally laughable, whereas Mauldin's work was a grim record of war meant only to enable soldiers to fight ruthlessly and still smile at themselves.[66] Though Moran considered these humor differences as potentially indicative of nationalistic culture norms or personality differences of the cartoonists, it is also likely that the disparities involve the experience of combat—both in the creation and interpretation of the comics.

Gags and social commentary easily overlap; laughable jokes are not necessarily devoid of insight, criticism, or commentary. Indeed, many of the modern warrior comics use prurient and scatological "barracks humor" to point out inequities and other concerns. This is certainly the case with one of the most recent, and increasingly popular, additions to warrior comics: *The Further Adventures of Doctrine Man!!* Written anonymously, and drawn crudely with stick figures and digital images in single- to four-frame strips, by a career army officer, the strip uses snarky humor to address key social, political, and military issues, helping the author and his following to vent their frustrations and navigate the complexities and absurdities of military life both at home and abroad. Published and released online through Facebook since March 2010, many strips mock the military's attempts to domesticate combat zones; others feature revenge fantasies; many, as suggested by the title, point out the irony in military doctrine, and some of the humor is inside humor, resonating only with actual military experiences. The work has been compared to Joseph Heller's *Catch-22* for its navigation of paradoxical war logic and has been called the thinking-soldier's *Beetle Bailey*.[67]

"An interesting sub-category of war humor is the unintentionally comic scene or episode which often occurs in serious fiction with heavy ideological overtones. It is usually funny only to the ex-serviceman, especially one with combat experience; its humor intensifies in direct proportion to its ludicrousness."[68] Such humor is not confined to the realm of war fiction, however, as fiction is often based on fact. The ability for soldiers to find humor in the horrifying and morbid is a real aspect of coping with war. As Bruce Bairnsfather explained, "The whole of the thing [World War I] made me laugh. I could not refrain from smiling at the absurdity, the stark, fearful predicament."[69] This is not only reflected in art and literature, as in Tim O'Brien's *The Things They Carried*, when the death of a comrade who caught a bullet while urinating was described as "zapped while zipping,"[70] but also in the practice of "war porn." War porn, which Baudrillard has referred to as a "parody of violence"[71] is the collected images of death, gore, or depravity from combat zones—images taken by warriors to relieve stress and document surreal experiences, though in nonmilitary or domestic contexts they would be considered unacceptable and even criminal.[72] Such unintentional humor is mostly directed outward to the Other, or the enemy, and is part of a soldier's coping mechanism. As Mauldin explained in World War II, "He [a U.S. soldier] can grin at gruesome jokes, like seeing a German get shot in the seat of his pants, and he will stare uncomprehendingly at fragile jokes in print which would have made him rock with laughter before."[73] Because comics are drawn deliberately, truly unintentional humor is not likely, though the unintentionally funny might be found captured in a comic's frame.

Black, ironic, and satirical humor, like irrelevant humor, tends to appeal more to a civilian audience, as warriors do not often find death, unless it is the enemy's, comical.[74] So-called black humor typically refers to comedy that is somehow grotesque, macabre, sardonic, cynical, or absurd—a joke that is not funny, but is, nonetheless, life affirming.[75] War literature provides many examples of black humor, such as James Jones' *The Thin Red Line* and Kurt Vonnegut's *Mother Night*. Black humor "helps to deflate the appeal of danger" and "serves to overcome the numbness which results from repeated exposure to scenes of horror" by lowering an audience's defenses.[76]

Garry Trudeau's *Doonesbury* war comic strip is one example of black humor. Though not a warrior or a veteran, Trudeau has been described as an "artist ethnographer"[77] for basing his war-themed cartoons on extensive fieldwork in combat zones, military hospitals, and veterans' institutions, in addition to personal correspondence with Iraq War veterans. Trudeau's subject is both ugly and life affirming, covering amputations, mental trauma, death, and the people who survive it all. Trudeau says of the casualties he talks with, "In these soldiers' minds, their whole identity, who that are right now, *is* what happened to them. They *want* to tell the story.... The more they revisit it, the less power it has over them."[78] His exploration of the character B.D.'s PTSD through *Doones-bury*, particularly in the graphic novels *The Long Road Home* and *The War Within*, pushes readers to come to terms with what has happened since 9/11, with humor that is dry, metaphoric, and grim—with "hard-hitting points about the horrors and stupidities of war (including the bombing of wedding parties)."[79]

Some research has positively linked content-specific humor with education, for its ability to reduce stress and anxiety while increasing self-esteem, interest, motivation, creativity, and recall or retention.[80] It is the content-specific element that places instructive humor as a distinct category in this project, though it certainly uses tactics of light, socio-comic, and black humors. Don Sheppard's World War II cartoons for *Stars and Stripes* are one example of strips that used gag humor and social commentary to provide instruction. As a 20-year-old GI, Sheppard created the immoral and porcine Fräulein Veronica Dankeschön, who mocked the problems of life in postwar Germany and served as an army-approved reminder of the pitfalls of soldiers fraternizing with German women.[81] More recently, the Sgt. Rock series within *Opet's Odyssey* comics have offered instruction. Written by Master Sergeant Steve Opet, a reservist attached to the 10th Mountain Division during his fifteen months in Iraq, 2008–2009, *Opet's Odyssey* caricaturizes the "sometimes humourous, sometimes inane side of military life in Iraq" as based on his and his comrades' experiences.[82] The recurring character of Sgt. Rock, whose tough and bald visage is not unlike Opet's, provides friendly reminders and warnings against potentially fatal errors and carelessness, from appropriate Internet posts to proper electrical outlet usage.

Weapons of Wit

In his 1961 farewell address, President Dwight Eisenhower cautioned against the military-industrial complex—the "conjunction of an immense military establishment and a large arms industry" with "total influence—economic, political, even spiritual."[83] Beginning in 1993, international studies scholar James Der Derian began warning against the military-industrial-entertainment network (MIME-net)—the seamless production, execution, and representation of war as something distant, something virtual and technological, and something mediated.[84] The cooperation between military and entertainment industries helps recruitment, guides the behavior of current troops, and appeals to the civilian society supporting the military.[85] Such cooperation has long been in practice: the U.S. navy and the Biograph Company cooperated to bring films to audiences at the 1904 World's Fair[86]; West Point worked with director D.W. Griffith to create Civil War battle scenes in the 1915 *The Birth of a Nation*[87]; and more recently, equipment and airmen provided by the U.S. Air Force have lent

Smoking

1. No smoking in airplane at an altitude below 1000 feet.

2. No smoking during fuel transfer.

3. Never attempt to throw a lighted cigarette from the airplane. Put it out first.

Fig. 1.3: An example of cartoon art used in military training, from the 1944 B-25 Mitchell Bomber Manual.

realism to the *Iron Man* movie franchise.[88] Long before superheroes leaped from the printed page to the Silver Screen in a single bound, comics played a role in the MIME-net. "In fact, comic art was an important element in the foundation of the military-industrial complex Eisenhower described," and Iron Man is its representational hero through the blending and physical embodiment of American individualism, capitalistic enterprise, and weapons technology.[89] Even without super powers or super armaments, comics characters have held an important place within the military. For example, both Disney and Warner Brothers Studios produced cartoon training videos,[90] and the visual component of modern television meteorological reports evolved from the military's use of cartoon weather graphics for pilots.[91]

General Douglas MacArthur is credited for observing, "Whoever said the pen is mightier than the sword obviously never encountered automatic weapons." While that may be true enough, cartoons have been celebrated as "weapons of wit," capable of piercing pomposity, hitting hypocrisy, deflating depression, and skewering suffering.[92] Over the decades, comics have served multiple functions within and for military establishments, many of which relate to military morale and cohesion, consistent with the use of folklore in comics as a way of addressing audience needs and issues.[93] These functions often overlap with the various types of military humor. They provide entertainment and a break in the monotony (light humor). They offer warriors a means for venting frustrations and a way to cope with hardships (socio-comic humor). They serve as training tools (instructive humor), and help to educate the general public about the military experience (black humor). They have also acted as propaganda for militarism and recruitment, and for demoralizing the enemy. In fact, the bulk of the U.S. government's comic book output is, and has been, for the Pentagon.[94]

Comics help ease the mental and emotional burden of the military in several ways: they raise morale, they offer an outlet for venting frustrations and a means for coping, and they provide the simple escape or release of laughter. The cartoon heroine and pin-up girl "Jane" appeared regularly in Britain's *Daily Mirror* to boost morale in wartime England after the Blitz. Based on Christabel Leighton-Porte, nude model and risqué chorus girl, the curvy Jane and her dachshund Fritz were involved in daily comic strip adventures that inevitably left her scantily clad—to the delight of England's beleaguered servicemen throughout Europe. For her key role in boosting and maintaining morale, Prime Minister Winston Churchill dubbed her "Britain's Secret Weapon."[95] Similarly, the United States had "Miss Lace," in the racy *Male Call* strip by Milton Caniff—a provocative yet wholesome heroine designed expressly to bring cheer to foxholes. Lace's popularity had competition in the GI-created strip *The Wolf*, by Sgt. Leonard Sansone, featuring an anthropomorphized wolf in soldier's clothes who enjoyed admiring beautiful women.[96] During the Japanese occupation that followed the war, servicemen had the morale boosting, nearly pornographic, *Babysan* cartoons by seaman Bill Hume.[97] In less sexualized contexts, the characters and creations of Walt Disney Studios also offered a morale boost to U.S. troops with the creation of 1,200 insignias, bearing the familiar visages of Donald Duck, Mickey Mouse, Jiminy Cricket, and others, for use on planes, ships, and patches; Walt Disney himself said, "They meant a lot to the men who were fighting."[98]

Comics also are an acceptable outlet for the average soldier's pent-up antipathy.[99] For example, George Baker's World War II creation *Sad Sack* was immensely popular because it represented the frustrations and the let-downs of army life experienced by the common GI.[100] In the age of social media, this has taken on an added dimension; now, military personnel not only share the experience reflected in the comics, and share the experience of reading the comics, but also have enhanced communication potential surrounding the comics. The discussions that comics generate now traverse countries and oceans and branches through the Internet. When *Doctrine Man!!* joined Facebook, it started a firestorm of unofficial dialogue via social media about navigating the military system. The anonymous cartoonist and career army officer explains, "When I share my frustration, through the cartoon, of having worked for people who 'just didn't get it,' I have great young lieutenants and captains and great young noncommissioned officers who come online and say: 'Hey! I'm dealing with the same situation. What should I do?'"[101] The experienced cartoonist is able to have a dialogue with these officers, help them, and take their concerns back to his own superiors.

In the early 1980s, ex–Marine Tad Foster published *The Vietnam Funny Book*, filled with the cartoon drawings he created in South Vietnam in 1969. The drawings were carried back to the United States in a discarded mine pouch and sat on a shelf for eight years; they were never meant for publication. They were drawn to help Foster cope, using "humor as bait, a cushion to deal with what it was like in Nam."[102] Both humor and art are acknowledged means of managing extreme stress.[103] Fellow Vietnam-veteran Vernon Grant also used cartooning to deal with difficult situations, but in a very different way: Grant was stateside when he was chosen to take care of a table at a division banquet. Lacking the support of wives and staffs that others in charge of tables had, Grant used his artistic skills to create ten-inch caricatures of all the officers in the battalion, each accompanied by a generic wife, which he looped together

Fig. 1.4: An example of graphic narrative propaganda, "The Mischievous Twin Bears" by Bob Bindig, which appeared in the children's section of U.S.-published newspapers for Koreans.

with a fake telephone line from the commander as a display. His creativity helped to manage the daunting task—and earned him recognition from the general of the division.[104]

In a more serious context, from the Civil War to the present day, humor has helped prisoners of war, in particular, establish a sense of normalcy in a distinctly anomalous situation.[105] British Lance Bombadier Des Bettany drew hundreds of humorous cartoon sketches "to keep himself sane during his three years in the notorious [Japanese] Changi prison in Singapore [during World War II]."[106] The illustrations, done with a human-hair and bamboo paintbrush in soil and rice water on any paper scraps available, made light of the harsh conditions, imagined freedom back in England, and mocked, or fantasized revenge upon, his captors. The National Cartoonist Society has a history, dating back to World War II, of cooperating with the USO to entertain American troops by drawing funny pictures.[107] Some of these cartoonists, particularly army veteran Bruce Higdon, creator of the syndicated *Punderstatements*, have also recognized the benefits of cartooning for military families. Higdon established a monthly cartoon class for military children aged 9–12 at Fort Campbell, Kentucky, to give them something to look forward to and a way to handle their own unique experiences of familial deployment.[108]

The simple importance of pure entertainment in comics should not be underestimated, either. "Laughter and amusement are examples of human experience in war," and these transcend torment to incorporate joy. Humor is a means of "individual release and resilience, which may function as part of resistance to official discourses."[109] Research has demonstrated that laughter is energizing, healing, and relaxing.[110] In 2013 the Canadian military acknowledged the benefits of laughter by having a "Laughter Yoga" session during Mental Health Week at the Canadian Forces Base Esquimalt,[111] and since 2003 retired army colonel James L. Scott, "the Laughter Colonel," has worked to spread "laughter therapy" as a tool for national guard and army reserve families to better handle deployments.[112] Dick Wingert's World War II comic *Hubert* was popular because it was just plain funny. Hubert was a short, pudgy, disheveled GI who, along with his comrades, was fairly simple-minded and somewhat clueless, providing plenty of straight-lines and punch-lines to the European theater. "Wingert was the kind of cartoonist whose work soldiers cut out and pinned to barracks walls to laugh at again."[113]

Faced with thousands of green, but not uneducated, troops in World War II, the military had to transform its training methods—finding ways to quickly teach tedious information to anxious young men and women, explaining not only the how but also the why. Receptive to entertainment media, the government soon learned to use cartooning in educational materials.[114] In Warner Brothers' *Private SNAFU* animated training films,

Snafu died—again, and again and again—so that many GIs might live. No Christ figure in the usual sense, Snafu represented a potential threat inherent in the average GI, if he were not vigilant and did not play by the rules. Through the use of humor and outrageous situations afforded by animation, the misadventures of Private Snafu made a lasting impression on the average soldier.[115]

A similarly inept and fittingly-named character, Lester B. Boner, appeared in flight manuals as an exemplar of a mishap-prone aviation mechanic.[116] Not only were soldiers more receptive to the information presented through such entertainment, but the insider, or intergroup, humor it used could also forge and strengthen the group identity.[117] The Ministry of Propaganda and Public Education in the German Reich, under the direction of Joseph Goebbels, also developed instructional animated films for its military with both technical and ideological content.[118]

Printed comics also featured hapless and witless GIs as cautionary tales. One of the most notable among these was Will Eisner's *Private Joe Dope*, a full-paged serial resembling a traditional comic book layout, featured in *Army Motors* magazine, commissioned expressly for the purpose of teaching new recruits safety and warning them of the dangers of not following procedure. Eisner, who created *The Spirit* and is considered the father of the graphic novel, was drafted for army service in World War II and was put to work producing illustrations, posters, and comics for the entertainment and education of the troops. His bumbling Joe Dope character was later resurrected for *PS Magazine*, a publication Eisner produced for the army for more than two decades under his initiative of the American Visuals Corporation, a company dedicated to cartooning for commercial and educational purposes.[119] His art and design for *PS Magazine* encompasses Eisner's largest body of work. It was here that Eisner worked to realize the full educational and communicative potential of graphic narratives.[120] The educational benefits of comics are still recognized by the military. Merle Boward's *Top Cop*, featuring a superhero MP, was developed to promote crime prevention at Fort Meade,[121] and, around 2005, the Army Office of Information Assurance and Compliance began producing the *On Cyber Patrol* comic strip, starring Sgt. 1C John Firewall and his nemesis International Cyber Criminal, to help simplify key components of the information assurance and security regulations. The comic strip removes the jargon and uses characters to whom the average soldier can relate to help make sure soldiers understand what they need to do and what tools are available to them.[122]

The educational function of war comics is not just for soldiers, but for civilians, too. On October 10, 1965, Charlie Brown's precocious beagle Snoopy made his first appearance as a World War I Flying Ace, in Charles Schulz's comic strip *Peanuts*, determined to defeat the infamous "Red Baron." Snoopy the Flying Ace starred in more than 400 *Peanuts* strips, several animated television features, and multiple pop/novelty songs, quaffing root beer and chasing after Baron von Richthofen in his Sopwith Camel–doghouse. More than just a pop-culture icon, the Flying Ace brought the combat experience to the general public. "While Schulz believed that his most important calling was to be funny, his experience as a combat soldier—and no less his pride as a World War II veteran[—]made him mindful that serious issues of war should accurately inhabit his Flying Ace strips."[123] This accuracy was accomplished through the mention of specific locations along the Western front, correct flight equipment for the Ace, precise use of period terminology, and representations of trench warfare experiences, including "shell shock." For audiences in the 1960s, Snoopy's war adventures were a means of viewing the actions in Vietnam.[124] Snoopy was also a reminder of the sacrifices of World War II, often interacting with his "friends" and fellow "*dog*faces" Willie and Joe on Veterans' Day—which was Schulz's homage to his favorite cartoonist, fellow World War II veteran Bill Mauldin. Other war comics, however, are more direct and intentional in their education of civilians. Foster's *Vietnam Funny Book* was put into print with the hopes that it would draw Americans' attention to the "wound" of Vietnam, by encouraging "people to search for the meaning behind the drawings," which are not readily apparent to those who did not serve, in order to better understand the problems of Vietnam veterans.[125]

"The propagandistic potential for cartoons has been particularly realized during wartime, in efforts to mobilize the civilian forces and degrade the enemy on the homefront, and to demoralize the opposing soldiers on the battlefield."[126] During the First World War, President Woodrow Wilson established the Committee on Public Information (CPI) to manage news of and encourage widespread support for the war across a range of media—including comics. In 1918 the CPI released a special bulletin for cartoonists, emphasizing the importance of comics educating the public on Liberty Bonds; the bulletin requested that Liberty Bond cartooning not be directed at aesthetic or humorous value, but instead be directed as an appeal to the minds and hearts of Americans that would give readers something to consider.[127] During World War II, the Office of War Information sought ways to provide the American public with details of the war without discouraging or demoralizing the people; comics and animated cartoons fit the bill, with upbeat and patriotic themes that gave hope, offered an escape, and pushed for war contributions such as scrap collections and war bonds.[128] American propaganda comics of World War II tend to fall into four categories: spoofs of the Axis leaders, visualizations of victory, scenes of suffering, and whimsical views of military and home front life.[129] Some graphic narratives were also created in the interests of psychological operations to ingratiate American forces with indigenous populations, such as Bob Bindig's *The Mischievous Twin Bears*, a children's cartoon that was part of an effort to encourage Koreans to go back to work after years of Japanese oppression.[130] Japan also used wartime comics: optimistic family-oriented strips, single-panel humor comics that defamed the enemy, and leaflets and posters aimed at enemy troops and Asian peoples. These comics were designed to support the militaristic aims of the government by promoting unity, harmony, and productivity among Asian populations and by demoralizing the enemy with claims that wives and sweethearts in the United States and Australia were not faithful to the soldiers.[131]

Another aspect to propagandizing is the ability of comics to tell the military story. The comic *Delta Bravo Sierra*, a funny-animal (in fatigues), three-frames strip, is written by Damon Bryan Shackelford, a former officer candidate in the U.S. Army who found himself medically discharged almost immediately after finishing his training. He began by telling his and his friends' stories, "with no distinct characters or storyline." Published on the Web, the comic slowly but surely attracted followers, and other soldiers began contributing stories. "All together the comic became a strange insiders' retelling of the lives of everyday soldiers, inside jokes, and vague references to Army life ... typical of any barracks artist/cartoonist."[132] Shackelford makes no money on the strip, seeing it as a way to give back to the army by "telling the soldiers [*sic*] story in a fresh way."[133] The potential implications of telling the military story via comics are great, given the research that suggests war comics are influential in shaping ideals of heroism and masculinity as well as ideologies of war.[134]

2

Service Before Self

Military Life

You're in the army now. You're not behind the plow. You'll
never get rich, you son-of-a-bitch, you're in the army now.
—"Song of the United States Army"

Military culture is centered on combat and a shared understanding of the
preparation for and waging of war, as the reason for the organization's existence,
and is characterized by an *esprit de corps* and the warrior ethos.[1] The military
organization has three distinct features.[2] The first is the communal character
of life, strongly influenced by the degree of normative orientation of military
employees to the institutional goals and values of the military. In a strongly
institutional orientation, military life and personal life overlap with preference
given to the military, resulting in higher levels of commitment and better performance.[3] The traditional military base or garrison setting, wherein place of
work and place of residence are the same and are separated from civilian communities, fosters and nurtures the institutional outlook.[4] In the modern, occupational orientation, military personnel focus more on external, rather than
internal, activities and norms, and for the post–Cold War military,

> rapidly changing strategic assignments, mission objectives, operational partners,
> and norms governing the interaction context increasingly challenge soldiers' sta-
> ble self-conceptions. As a result, it becomes increasingly critical for soldiers to
> organize their experiences and to negotiate among central life interests. With
> increasing exposure to new roles, their self-conceptions will more and more
> reflect those roles. An integrated military identity as "peace manager"—at once
> prepared to keep and to enforce the peace—will become more potent. To the
> extent that soldiers adopt this identity, their actions will become more predictable
> and more congruent with differing mission requirements. At the same time, they
> will be less likely to experience cognitive inconsistencies that challenge their

self-conceptions and pose dilemmas that might undermine their effectiveness in accomplishing their missions.[5]

While the post–Cold War military has become increasingly occupational, there is still a stronger institutional orientation than in other professions, fields, or organizations.[6]

In addition to the officially established and imposed lifestyle and work style, informal social organizations of the enlisted personnel, developed as ways of coping with military life, control many military activities. These informal structures are inclusive, bringing in all immediate members of a unit, who live, eat, train, work, and relax together. As a result of this continuous close proximity, common attitudes develop regarding equality, cooperation, fairness, and performance standards.[7] Such solidarity is important in the face of danger, and the regulations of military life are designed to enhance group cohesion and loyalty.[8] In fact, the military is concerned not only with its basic organizational structure, but also with promoting individual and family welfare to maintain a sense of community as part of a high quality of life because community is linked with retention, commitment, readiness, and performance. Features of the military community include group symbols, rewards and honors, a common external threat, contact and proximity, and group activities.[9] With the various strategies and means of group unity, it is not surprising that "individuals who embrace the military lifestyle develop over time an increasing identification with the military as a core component of who they are, much like an ethnic identity," wherein the military image and mission are central to the group's heritage, customs, and values.[10]

The second feature of the military organization is hierarchy, which will be discussed further in the next chapter. The third feature of the military organization is discipline and control, which is closely connected to the chain of command inherent in the hierarchy. Discipline is the extent of compliance with and acceptance of rules, orders, and authority.[11] These rules are established in the common basic-training experience, and they help to explain what it means to be a "good soldier" both in and out of combat, because the military is designed to perform tasks that may never be needed, and, in combat, improvisation may be necessitated over regulation.[12] Initiation rites of degradation or mortification are used to break down civilian identities, allowing military identities to be built in their place, particularly in officer, elite unit, and special-forces training.[13] "Especially important to the performance of military tasks is that new recruits learn to overcome, channel, and above all control their emotions."[14] Military training and discipline, which has traditionally emphasized repetitive and mechanical drills[15] in conjunction with a hierarchical structure, therefore fosters stoicism, the ability to react without emotion. Stoicism allows the soldier to be ready for critical, life-threatening situations, but can also lead to a breakdown in morality.[16] How a recruit adjusts to the active military situation is dependent on his or her preconceptions of war, aggression, and military service.[17] Even beyond basic, or initial, training, an extensive amount of time is devoted to preparation. Simulations or exercises to teach, practice, and assess individual and group performance of military activities and skills are used to enable problem-solving and to familiarize personnel with environments and scenarios in which they might find themselves.[18] Warriors must consequently situate and negotiate their activities into frames of everyday ("no-duff") and/or tactical life.[19]

Graphic narratives have a significant place within these organizational features of the military by demonstrating expectations, illustrating commonality, and providing instructions for military skills. The use and usefulness of comics in the organizational culture of the military is perhaps best captured by and represented in the work of Will Eisner. Eisner's goal with *PS, The Preventative Maintenance Monthly,* which started in the 1950s, was "to effectively communicate motivational messages and no-nonsense how-to information to the individual soldier who uses or operates equipment."[20] This mission was achieved by including and integrating the troops, technical research, and the *PS* leadership and artists, who believed that using humor would promote positive emotional associations with the army's messages. Though the idea of comics being used for military education and morale purposes was not new, Eisner offered a new approach. Beginning as late as the First World War, the U.S. government used "comics with messages, stories with morals, instruction booklets aimed at adults and children, civilians and soldiers ... distributed at schools, civic events, and recruiting offices ... inserted in local newspapers and national magazines."[21] Eisner and the *PS* team, however, introduced new techniques of graphics and layout, ensured that at least half of the content was visual, and advocated the importance of laughter in learning.[22]

Sound Off

Until World War II, the American military provided a core of expertise to train a force of citizen-soldiers in the event of war. Wars were infrequent, and so the military was not designed for regular deployment and combat. In the post–Cold War era, this has changed.[23] The new warrior, according to T.R. Fehrenbach, must be trained to have pride in his flag and for obedience to his orders to do the jobs, moral or immoral, that no responsible citizen-soldier would be willing to do.[24] And yet, the experience of the soldier—citizen or professional, conscript or volunteer—has remained remarkably constant over the years. Warrior artists from the Napoleonic Wars through the present day have griped about duty assignments, bad food, bombastic officers, and absurd policies. Regardless of the circumstances surrounding their recruitment, men and women must adjust from the individual life (particularly in Western cultures) of the civilian to the communal life of the warrior. This process begins with basic training—boot camp.

As the change from militia to standing forces in the American military began during the 1940s and 1950s and into the 1960s, there was an uptick in the creation of commemorative boot-camp comic books. Ted Ritter and Bob Gadbois produced such books for the navy (1944), Marines (1949), air force (1953), and army (1965). Each follows a similar format. It opens with a nostalgic and patriotic message from an information officer in the branch and then has a fill-in-the-blank biography page for the book's owner to record such information as dates of enlistment and the beginning and end of training. The story then starts with how the book's hero joined his branch of choice, and the reader is taken through physical training, uniform fittings, health physicals, duty assignments, and barracks/camp life. The training process is gently mocked, fostering a sense of camaraderie among everyone who can sympathize with the experiences. Other authors and artists produced similar publications, such as B.J. Morris's *Hit Da Deck!* (1944), about life at a Naval Training Station, and Quarter Master 2nd Class Alex Gard's semi-autobiographical *Sailors in Boots* (1943), about new navy recruits. Similar ideas about recruitment and training hardships are also found in the works of nearly every other military graphic narrator, even when not gathered into bound keepsakes.

America's late entrance into World War I is reflected by a remarkably light-hearted view of military service in the graphic narratives, likely buoyed by the American impression of the Allies' just cause.[25] Many artists viewed enlistment as a lark or grand adventure. Foreign travel and a chance to impress ladies was a central focus of American Expeditionary Forces (AEF) cartoonists. Unlike the work of British warrior-artist Bruce Bairnsfather, which emphasizes his extensive combat experiences, many of the American warrior artists emphasized the novelty and challenges of basic training. Of these, physical training (PT), the uniform and salute, officers and bureaucracy, food and inoculations, and the pursuit of vices were paramount, and remained so throughout the subsequent century. PT, particularly push-ups, and drills, seemed to be an omnipresent feature of military life. Americans' graphic narratives of World War I highlighted "Exercise in Cadence"[26] (it would be noted nearly a century later that "political correctness is just killing cadences,"[27] which were once known for their crude and bawdy content), gas mask training,[28] Bayonet Training, and PT as "physical torture"[29] With the creation of the women's branches in the Second World War, the new group of military recruits made similar notes of the physical challenges of training.[30] And even as the century passed and the technology changed, impressions of training remain much the same. The comic strip *On Cyber Patrol* features drills with laptop computers in place of weapons[31] with an adaptation of the Marine Rifleman's Creed,[30] and another of Cyber Command Training demanding "drop and give me 20 secure ones."[33]

Dress Right, Get Dressed

The uniform is a key feature of military identity and discipline. General George S. Patton once stated, "It is absurd to believe that soldiers who cannot be made to wear the proper uniform can be induced to move forward in battle."[34] Nonetheless, it is an ongoing source of consternation for American warriors, and at least twenty artists mock some aspect of the uniform. From World War I through Korea, a major problem is the poor fit of uniforms,[35] a problem that occasionally plagues warriors into the late 20th and early 21st centuries.[36] Each generation, and each war, however, brings its own set of complaints. In World War I, the spiral leggings cause problems for many recruits, who often find themselves literally entangled in the process of dressing.[37] The overseas cap also gets bemused criticism. Captain Wallace Morgan pokes fun at the cap in an issue of *Stars and Stripes* by showing ten different, and absurd, ways it might be worn—from flattened appearances to shapes resembling horns and ducks.[38] Another *Stars and Stripes* cartoon, by James Lysle, takes aim at the overseas cap by pairing it with Roman armor in favor of a more protective helmet.[39] Abian Wallgren has his own ideas for AEF Millinery, to replace the "doomed" Campaign Hat, so that different combat roles may be distinguished by the head-dress—such as a cannon-shaped hat for artillery, a train-shaped hat for engineers, and a ship-shaped hat for Marines, or hats that may serve practical functions, such as doubling as gas masks or emergency rations.[40] In fact, Wallgren's derision for the uselessness of the entire AEF uniform is clear, with graphic narratives of both its impracticality[41] and its inability to hold up to combat maneuvers.[42] Indeed, issued uniforms, and related supplies, may often serve better uses than protection from combat and the elements. The American *Camion Cartoons* explains that the "gun makes a fine clothes hanger."[43] The Australian graphic narrative *Humorosities* asserts, "We find the shrapnel helmets very useful"... for cooking.[44] And Britain's *Fragments from France* demonstrates how the sword is useful for grilling food over a fire.[45] In the Second World War, combat helmets become useful bathing basins.[46]

In World War II, the main uniform-related concerns were poor fit and inadequate or inappropriate attire. While any World War II soldier was likely to be issued a uniform of the wrong size, as poor "Sad Sack" is, despite extensive and careful measurements,[47] it was a particular problem for female recruits—

for whom the military was unprepared. As *Winnie the WAC* proclaims, "I asked the supply sergeant for my correct size and all I got was hysterical-wild laughter!"[48] Inadequate clothing for conditions was also problematic, making the climate a harsh enemy. Bill Mauldin's "Willie and Joe" are issued leftover longjohns from the Great War, most of which do not fit.[49] During Korea, size was again the main problem. *Leatherhead* recruits are told, "It's all right if your clothes are too small—you'll lose weight in Boot Camp—and yours are too large—well, you'll probably gain a little weight."[50] In contrast to the careful, if useless, fittings of "Sad Sack's" uniform, a recruit in *Sailors in Boots* is issued one "about Size 36."[51]

In the Cold War and post–Cold War era and during its conflicts, graphic narratives focus mostly on uniform regulations—though one *Broadside* comic simply has a good laugh at the tropical attire of the U.S. Navy, with its shorts and black shoes and socks.[52] Hearkening back to the graphic narratives of World War I, several artists ridicule the individual variations in how hats are worn, subtly (or not so subtly) criticizing their practicality. *Opet's Odyssey* shows the variety of styles achieved with the patrol cap, including the "Ranger Roll," "Duckbill," "MLB," and "Wash and Wear."[53] *Power Point Ranger* does the same with the beret, illustrating such looks as "the Pirate," with the beret covering one eye; "the Cyclops," with the badge placed at the center of the forehead; and "the Princess," with the beret perched on top of the head.[54] Indeed, the broad adoption of the beret for troops in 2001 was controversial, as noted by *Private Murphy*: "Next year's uniform change to a black beret is a big issue right now.... But if you ask me, I say go with a Stetson if want a distinctive American head gear."[55] In another cartoon, Mark Baker attacks not the beret, but its wearers, with a suggestion to readers that if they do not yet know how to wear it correctly, they need to seek assistance.[56] Baker also offers guidance on proper wearing of the uniform for inspection,[57] and Steve Opet humorously reviews uniform and appearance regulations, including guidelines for boonie hats, sunglasses, cravats, gloves, bracelets, knives, socks, and boots.[58]

Other appearance regulations that make it into the graphic narratives are hairstyles and cuts, nail length and polish, jewelry,[59] insignia and patches, facial hair, and tattoos. The pride of a promotion and the earned wearing of rank insignia is a continuous theme for warrior artists.[60] The prevalence of patches is seen in a pun in the *On Cyber Patrol* educational comic strip, wherein uniform patches are mistaken for computer patches, or security fixes.[61] So important are the visual markers of rank that the newly promoted may physically swell to new proportions,[62] sprout chevrons on their foreheads,[63] or embroider insignia on their underwear.[64] Some soldiers will do anything to get a promotion. For example, *Private Breger* asks an officer playing chess, "Would the right move be worth a corporal's stripes, sir?"[65] And a Mauldin character earns a promotion

Fig. 2.1-1

Fig. 2.1: Examples of graphic narratives related to uniforms, specifically variations in wearing caps. 1. Wallace Morgan (circa 1918), 2. Steve Opet (2008), courtesy of the 10th Mountain Division and Fort Drum Museum.

Fig. 2.1-2

as enticement to play Santa Claus for the troops.[66] But woe to the person who wears the unearned insignia. Percy Crosby's World War I "Rookie" gets in trouble for wearing a general's stars because, he says, "I saw a man with them on this morning and I thought he looked awfully snappy."[67] Mark Baker's "Private Murphy" in the 1990s foolishly changes his uniform rank insignia to that of lieutenant for a Halloween costume—to the horror of his buddy.[68]

While the recruits of World War I are too young to grow moustaches,[69] the growth of facial hair to break the monotony of deployment is noted by Shel Silverstein in the Cold War, wherein a new man asks a group of soldiers all sporting handlebar moustaches, "What do you guys do for excitement around here?"[70] and by Opet with two female GIs sporting mascara moustaches to try to gain entry into the Mountain Men's Moustache Meeting Room.[71] In *Power Point Ranger*, moustaches are a sign of virility—a key feature of the warrior.[72] Facial hair regulations make for awkward humor in John Sheppard's *Blue Suiters*, wherein a square-shaped moustache "looks like Hitler. But as long as it doesn't extend past the corners of the mouth, its [sic] legal."[73] Like facial hair in the Mountain Men's Moustache club, tattoos are a sign of belonging in the military, and have been for years, despite varying regulations for inked skin,[74] even when the tattoo is a mistake. A World War II navy cartoon observes that an untattooed sailor must not have "been in long."[75] A Silverstein comic introduces readers to a GI receiving a "Dear John" letter from the woman whose face he has tattooed across his chest and abdomen.[76] *Terminal Lance* shows an impulsive new Marine, fresh out of boot camp, getting a U.S. Marine Corps insignia on his back because, he says, "I really wanted a tattoo I would never regret."[77] Mark Baker's *PV-2 Murphy* also makes a poor tattoo choice when he is inked with "airbone" instead of "airborne."[78] A soldier in a cartoon by T.H. Limb is, hopefully, stopped from a bad tattoo choice when he asks a female service member with him, "How do you think I would look with a SpongeBob tattoo?" and is told, "Lonely."[79] Good or bad, tattoos indicate group membership, as Opet indicates in a comic wherein a number of tattooed soldiers suspiciously eye the "freak" with "no ink" while stationed at Camp Victory, Iraq.[80]

During operations Enduring Freedom and Iraqi Freedom, the main focus of ridicule is the "PT," "reflective," "glow," or "safety" belt—a bright yellow strap issued for visibility during physical training. The reflective belts, repeatedly mocked by the anonymous author behind *Doctrine Man*, by virtue of their near omnipresence in his comics, even on otherwise naked soldiers[81]—not to mention by the recurring character of the Reflective Belt Mummy, who is completely wrapped in neon-yellow strips[82]—are also derisively noted in *Power Point Ranger* with an extreme version of a reflective safety uniform,[83] in *Delta Bravo Sierra* through the absurdity of wearing the belts in bed,[84] and in *Opet's Odyssey* when praise goes to a soldier for jogging with his reflective belt, even though he is foolishly doing it under the noon sun in 120-degree temperatures.[85] Other uniform features that warriors do not like include excessive battle-rattle (combat gear), overpacked rucks, and awkwardly placed ruck cables that make movement difficult.[86] On the plus side of the uniforms for operations Enduring Freedom and Iraqi Freedom, the ACUs (Army Combat Uniforms) do not need to be pressed and the boots do not need to be shined,[87] though dress uniforms may still make soldiers look like ice cream men.[88]

Say What?

Another distinct indicator of military membership is the ability to speak the military language of acronyms and jargon. Insider/outsider status is negotiated in part through the use of slang.[89] The language of the warriors, their folk slang, changes with time, deployment, and branch.[90] For example, American troops currently refer to helicopters as "birds," though the navy and Marines may call them "helos," and "choppers" is now only said in the movies. Official jargon includes the likes of the nearly 1,100 acronyms and approximately 2,000 operational terms in just the U.S. Field Manual 1–02, the army and Marine Corps' manual of operational terms and graphics.[91] Because of such excess, to the point of practical uselessness, jargon has become a recurring theme of American warrior graphic narratives since 1980. Mike Sinclair shows two soldiers looking up the words "RON" and "FEBA" in books after silently receiving the instructions, "We will move out ASAP IAW BDE SOP to LZ Grunt, where we will RON for NLT 3 days prior to RECON of FEBA BP's and LP. Any questions?"[92] Baker's *Pvt. Murphy* observes, "Sheesh. I've got a lot to learn ... starting with this foreign language," when he fails to do push-ups when ordered to "front lean and rest position. Move! You hear me! Beat your face!! Knock 'em out!!"[93] Likewise, a comic in *Go For It, Eltee!* remarks on needing "an English-Navy Navy-English Dictionary!"[94] And a John Sheppard comic needs no pithy punchline on the comic's text, "That's a rog Raven 09, didi to Bravo Zulu 102351 and RTB after Buff BDA checkout."[95]

Bob on the FOB comics are entirely about defining and illustrating military folk jargon, such as Fobbit, "one who avoids traveling off the FOB,"[96] and Geardo, "one who spends at least 50% of each paycheck (before taxes) on the latest & greatest gear."[97] The *Doctrine Man* (*DM*) comics similarly have a recurring feature of "BIF's [Bright Idea Fairy's] Compendium of Military Jargon" with humorous takes on military slang, practices, and personalities. Additionally, *DM* has a recurring character named the Termburglar, who is an army terminologist who plots new jargon and doctrine revisions from a sub–Pentagon lair, in an acknowledgement of the centrality of terminology in official military documents. Crude expressions, such as the popular "Is there a dick growing out of my forehead or something?"[98] and use of the word "balls" or "fuck" to indicate unfavorable conditions, as in "Man, I'm tired as balls,"[99] are also part of this insider-speak. Of course, it is not just the American military that has its own language. *A Piece of Cake* is an illustrated glossary of World War II Royal Air Force slang, in which comics feature quotes such as, "Don't bind! I've genned it all up, and your props will be laid on next week, so get weaving!"[100] Jargon also seems more prevalent in some branches, such as the air force, because of the lexicon of specialized terms related to the technology used, as evidenced in Bob Stevens' *Prop Wash: A Fractured Glossary of Aviation Terms*.[101]

A more controversial aspect of gaining insider status is the practice of hazing. True hazing makes only a few appearances in the graphic narratives, and they are all from the tradition-rich navy. Seaman Si is harassed by his shipmates in World War I.[102] Jeff Bacon illustrates "The 'tacking on' ceremony: no gain, no pain,"[103] in which a pin, badge, or emblem of a new milestone is punched into the chest, causing the pins to puncture the skin. Eric Thibodeau, aboard the USS *Missouri*, gives an account of WOG Day hazing,[104] or a Line-Crossing Ceremony, that often brutally commemorates a sailor's first crossing of the Equator. A number of *Pvt. Murphy's Law* comics acknowledge the less violent practice of pranks and practical jokes—especially ones in which new soldiers and even new officers are asked to get nonexistent items, such as chem-light batteries, grid squares, prop wash, and canopy lights, from supply.[105]

Administering Drugs and Food

It is not just looks and language that band together military brothers and sisters, but also the shared experiences, even the banal, and especially the unpleasant ones—such as shared "hatred" of the company bugler,[106] which is found in both the East and West, as evidenced by a Mizuki Shigeru cartoon depicting his stress as a military musician in the Japanese army during the 1940s.[107] One of the most pervasive of these experiences in the American context is getting shots—not getting shot *at*, but getting inoculations. More than twenty individual comics representing seven different wars or eras, beginning with the First World War, express humorous horror at the vaccination needle. The dreaded inoculations are even depicted on envelopes containing letters home by World War II soldiers.[108] Cartoon troops receive shots for "Smallpox, Anthrax, Chicken Pox, Measles, Mumps, Diphtheria, Yellow Fever, Swine Flu, Bird Flu, Seasonal Flu, Typhoid, Hepatitis A, B, and C, Encephalitis, Meningitis, Rotavirus, Prostate Milking, PARVO virus,"[109] plus cholera, plague,[110] and combat nerves.[111] They get shots from fanged doctors,[112] joyous medics, and pretty nurses.[113] They get shots with up to thirteen needles,[114] some so large they need three men to work them[116] or that go straight through the body and poke the next person in line.[116] Sometimes it takes multiple attempts to find a vein,[117] and sometimes a simple shot requires a tourniquet[118] or burns so much that flames can be seen on the arm.[119] For some, the scars are a mark of honor, as for *Winnie the WAC*, who brags, "This is where I got 9 shots in the arm!"[120] For others, it's something to be avoided, as for "Pvt. Murphy" who argues a vaccination conspiracy that began in the Nevada desert during the 1950s.[121] Regardless, "A Healthy Soldier is a Happy Soldier. Even soldiers need shots to keep them healthy."[122]

Unfortunately, the overall graphic narrative outlook on healthcare in the military is just as bleak as the view of vaccinations. While general camp health and hygiene seem to have improved since the Great War, which prompted graphic narratives about a lack of opportunity and ability to bathe,[123] resulting in the invention of a "Decootieizing Device,"[124] artists continue to express doubts about medical service. A Bill Mauldin cartoon from World War II claims, "There's one cure for any ill in dis man's army. Whether ya come in wid a concussion of d'brain or fallen arches, y'git a t'ermometer between ya teet,' a coupla CC pills, and report back fer duty."[125] A 1966 cartoon by Bob Stevens, reflecting on his World War II service, is more sympathetic to the doc with limited supplies and equipment, but shares Mauldin's sentiments with a depiction of an airman in foot cast, arm sling, and head bandages being told, "3 APC's every 2 hrs.... Mark for duty!"[126] Similarly, about seventy years later, *Doctrine Man* demonstrates that the treatment for decapitation is 500 mg of "Motrin."[127] During Vietnam, Jake Schuffert suggests that medics do little more than guess at ailments and cures.[128] According to Jeff Bacon, the situation may be worse in the navy; while a doctor complains bitterly, during surgery, about people saying that navy doctors aren't any good, his colleague has to remind him to put on his surgical mask.[129] This reputation may have prompted the *Brownshoes in Action* narrative "The Day the Docs Walked," which offers a light-hearted, and pun-filled, promotion of improved medical services in navy aviation.[130] Dentistry is equally suspect, as evidenced by a W.C. Pope cartoon in which a dentist cautions a patient, "Be careful when you rinse and spit ... I lost a contact!"[131] Though getting sick, or at least going on sick call, can be an expedient way to avoid duty,[132] getting treatment, however inadequate, can be a challenge. In one Mauldin comic the medic tells the patient, "You're in bad shape, man! Run over to your barrack, get your stuff together, an' be back in five minutes ready for th' ambulance,"[133] and in another, medics fight over whose case of supplies is being used to treat the combat wounded.[134] During the Korean War era, the suggestion is worse, as Eugene Packwood portrays a skull tagged "hold for treatment" in the overcrowded sick bay[135]—an illustration that seems prescient in

Fig. 2.2-1   GETTING THE "JABS"

Fig. 2.2: Examples of graphic narratives featuring inoculations. 1. Ted Stanley (1918), 2. Dorothea Byerly (1945), 3. Kevin Klein and Todd Hoelmer (1991).

the wake of the 2014 U.S. Veterans Affairs healthcare scandals in which it was revealed that patients died while waiting for treatment.[136]

Self-medication is a popular option for many warriors. Mauldin's Willie brings his wounded friend, Joe, a cognac chaser for the plasma he is receiving,[137] and the pursuit and enjoyment of alcohol, among other drugs, is a universal theme of warriors' graphic narratives. "Alcohol consumption among the world's military ... has a long history of tolerated drinking traditions and rituals."[138] In World War I, the Australian *Humorosities* shows "a dream of paradise (purely Australian)" that features alcohol,[139] the British *Fragments from France* proclaims that "the Spirit of our Troops is Excellent," whereby the spirit comes from spirits,[140] and the American *Ups and Downs of Camp Upton* shows "the Milk Line," in which troops wait for wine.[141] Prohibition in the United States is a blow to returning American troops, as indicated by Wallgren in *Stars and Stripes*.[142] During World War II, some soldiers include images of alcohol, such as beer and wine, on the envelopes they sent home,[143] and Maudlin regularly features alcohol in his cartoons because, as he writes, "Who ever heard of gittin' good mileage wit' water?"[144] Alcohol is scarcer in Korea, as suggested by a scene in which Marines scramble for a single bottle abandoned in a barn—a bottle that might be booby-trapped[145]; which may be why Roger Baker's cartoons are more likely to feature cigarette smoking, with warriors smoking as many as four at one time.[146] Beer in Vietnam, usually "BA-Me 33[qm] (Ba Muoi Ba, "beer 33"), is of poor quality—"Iffin ya hold it up to the sun 'n' look real close ya can actually see *real beer* floating in between the crud!"[147]—and for some, marijuana

Fig. 2.2-2

is preferable.[148] In operations Enduring Freedom and Iraqi Freedom, alcohol is not allowed "in country" and so a frosty mug of beer, any beer, is but a "thirsty dream."[149]

The World War I Australian *Digger Days* demonstrates, through a pairing of rum and bread, that liquor is as sustaining as food for a soldier in the field[150]—and judging by the warrior artists' depictions of the food, the liquor is understandably preferred. Both Frederick the Great and Napoleon are credited with saying, "An army marches on its stomach," in reference to forces being well fed. For some warrior artists, however, the idea of an army moving on its stomach

Fig. 2.2-3

Even soldiers need shots to keep them healthy.

is envisioned as crawling beneath combat fire,[151] rather than being amply provisioned, especially given the often meagre nutrition. Meal times are represented in the comics of the American Civil War, where "George" and his comrades sadly "lose every bean" into the fire,[152] and those of the Spanish-American War, with a depiction of dinnertime on Misery Hill.[153] The American doughboys training for World War I are always eager enough for chow[154]—an idea promoted and exploited by the Jell-O company through illustrations by *Stars and Stripes* cartoonist H.M. Stoops[155]—but the British Tommies already fighting are less than excited for hard army biscuits[156] and the invariable plum and apple jam.[157] Food-related comics are scarce in World War II, but—judging by a *Hubert* comic in which soldiers bearing plates and utensils surround a cow as one prepares to shoot her after they "milk her first"[158]—so is food.

From the Cold War on, the main feature of military food is its mysterious and unsavory qualities: hamburger made without meat[159]; meat from pack mules,[160] cavalry horses,[161] or animals with horns and bird claws[162]; beef stew from entrails[163] that may be watered down to feed more people[164]; fish caught in sewers[165]; sandwiches made of ketchup[166]; raisin cookies with things that aren't raisins and will attack if looked in the eye[167]; MREs (Meal, Ready to Eat), that are also known as "Mr. E" or "mystery,"[168] and may be forty years old[169] or are nothing but relabeled dog food cans[170]; and chow that can still be tasted thirty years after retirement.[171] In a pinch, however, "MRE crackers make excellent bullet proof vests,"[172] and thereby may help to compensate for uniform inadequacies. The only caveat to the bad food is on the FOBs (forward operating bases) of Iraq, where fast food joints can be found and DFACs (dining facilities) serve crab legs[173]—to the zeal of the FOB locust, a "migratory grazing subspecies of fobbit, often found in food courts, PX/BX, and Class I yards. FOB locusts [*sic*] grazing habits will cause them to completely empty any store, restaurant, or supply yard."[174] Such encounters are only part of the communal military lifestyle.

Not an Army of One

In a 2001 *Pvt. Murphy's Law* cartoon, Murphy watches a recruiting ad on television that declares, "I'll be the first to tell you the might of the U.S. Army doesn't lie in numbers, it lies in me. I am an Army of One." Murphy's reaction is to wonder if the "rest of us can have tomorrow off" because it "sounds to me like this guy's got things under control."[175] The military experience captured in these graphic narratives is indeed one of the many, not the one, not even of the few and proud. In fact, a recruiting comic book in 1955 urges college students to join ROTC (Reserve Officers' Training Corps) so as to not be alone and without friends on a college campus.[176] Training in World War II, "Molly Marine" "lived in a great big squadroom with 89 other girls from every state in the union. Together they worked and studied, sang and laughed."[177] Yes, camp, barracks, billet, and ship life is crowded. "Sad Sack" cannot get any room at the sink and mirror to shave and has to wear an "I tried" sign beneath his bearded face during inspection.[178] A Mauldin soldier cries out from an overcrowded sink, "Who's brushin' my teeth?"[179] Training during the Great War, Kirkland Day notes, "Indoor Army Sports is as bad as trying to find that 'haystack needle' as to find anything in a barrack."[180] This is a problem in the modern CHU (Containerized Housing Unit), too, when over-furnished with comforts of home to relieve the tedium of desert deployment.[181] Marines heading to Korea attempt to exercise on the ship deck, despite standing shoulder-pressed-to-shoulder.[182] Pvt. Murphy is surrounded by vulture-like comrades when he receives a care package from home.[183] And, as John Holmes notes in *Power Point Ranger*, "Deployment, Month 9. Familiarity breeds, first contempt, then ... violence," as a soldier in a Jeep threatens to rip the head off of his mouth-breathing Battle Buddy.[184] *Seaman Si's* comrade, Zippy, in World War I, agrees, wishing for death when Si suggests the people "who are thrown together in the same occupation get to be very much alike" and they are "like two peas in a pod."[185]

Many warrior artists make note of the numerous people they meet, sketching caricaturized likenesses.[186] One of the personality traits or types that nearly all artists encounter, or may personally possess, is the goldbrick—the slacker. A Schuffert cartoon, for example, remarks on "the biggest goof-off in the Air Force. Three separate tours in Vietnam and the only decoration he earned was an Oak Leaf Cluster to his longevity ribbon!"[187] Of course, the most famous of military goldbricks is Mort Walker's *Beetle Bailey*. When Beetle left college to join the army in 1951, he did it to escape classrooms, studies, tests, and hard-headed professors.[188] He is often seen sleeping soundly[189] or defying both orders and the laws of nature.[190] Fifty-plus years and still a private (as noted in Baker's *Sgt. Murphy*),[191] Beetle will do anything to get out of duty; breaking the "Fourth Wall" that separates the audience from the players or the real world from the fictional one, he has even used his creator Mort Walker as a scapegoat.[192] *Downrange* remarks that at Beetle's Camp Swampy they don't even know when there is a war happening.[193] And *Pope's Puns* contemplates that "if Beetle Bailey had joined the Air Force" he would sleep in the casing for the plane prop.[194] Many other artists have much more imaginative approaches to goldbricking than simply sleeping on duty, such as claiming dying relatives to receive leave,[195] enjoying the "Star Spangled Banner" as a reprieve from work,[196] using helium balloons to lighten a pack[197] or get flight pay,[198] starting rumors of buried treasure to encourage more people to dig trenches,[199] and simply looking busy to avoid actual work,[200] among many, many other amusing strategies. Herman's *Winnie the*

WAC is particularly creative at easing her workload. She sweeps dust under loose floorboards, serves all three meals in the mess at once, gets a parrot to answer roll call, and uses the company bugler to blow-dry her laundry.[201] Ironically, when cartoon warriors are not trying to get out of doing stuff, they are looking for something to do—because waiting is "the Hardest Fight of the War."[202] Boredom and tedium are relieved through sports and games such as ping-pong,[203] through gambling (Jawbone Poker,[204] stud poker,[205] care-package poker,[206] dice,[207] craps,[208] and book-making[209] have been among the favorites) and, now, through video game simulations of war.[210]

The Army-Navy Gags

Another key element of the military identity involves the association with and rivalry between different branches and divisions, each of which has a different institutional personality.[211] Branch rivalry occurs when services, each with its own interests, ideologies, and strengths, compete for resources and roles in both peacetime and wartime missions. Though long thought to be harmful to military efficiency, such competition is increasingly recognized as beneficial. "Interservice rivalry is a vivid part of American military history stretching forward from the earliest days of the Republic."[212] So vivid is the rivalry that many graphic narratives acknowledge branch specialties and inter-branch, and even inter-division, hostilities. As *Broadside* explains, when short of the recruitment quota at the end of the month, things get ugly; army recruiters claim, "Navy guys go to sea for like two years straight. Windows? You get on a ship or a sub and there *aren't* any. Ever hear of greasing?" And the navy recruiters claim, "Army guys eat *dirt* for breakfast! They don't take showers for *weeks* sometimes. Ever heard of tactical nuclear weapons?"[213]

The Marines and the air force take the brunt of the jokes. Marines tend to be portrayed as stupid and arrogant by the other branches. The Marine cry of "oorah" is labeled as "witty repartee"[214] or as "the unforgettable sound of an active mind imploding."[215] Thibodeau shows frustration with a Marine who gets the girls and then insultingly tells the sailor, "Your 'Dixie Cup's' [hat's] crooked, mate."[216] *Ricky's Tour* suggests that the Marines are spoiled when a new boot camp graduate complains about "Hell Week" because, he says, "We had to get our own cappuccinos then."[217] The air force is criticized even more harshly for being soft and pampered. An exchange between soldiers in *Delta Bravo Sierra* reveals that if leaving the army means "sleeping late, eating when you want, what you want, and not answering to anybody, anytime? ... If I'd wanted to join the Air Force I would have already done it."[215] Pilots are tauntingly called "zoomies"[219] and are said to get weapons after simulated qualifications in which they "have the enlisted shoot for us while we're at the O-club" because it is too hard to "shoot with a glass of Jeremiah Weed in your hand."[220] They even carry spare uniforms with them into the field in case they break a sweat,[221] wear sunglasses in the dark to look cool,[222] and are preoccupied with large "Breitling" watches.[223] The army is made fun of primarily in comparison to the Marines, as in a *Doctrine Man* cartoon that claims the biggest difference between the army and the Marine Corps is that "when we march in parades, kids use all five fingers to wave at the Marines,"[224] or is made fun of by the Marines, who resent soldiers' ability to wear ACUs in airports[225] and who need to do the army's dirty work even while being called "glory-hunting" by soldiers.[226] The navy is left nearly unblemished as a service, as *Private Breger in Britain* reminds peers in World War II to "salute U.S. Navy officers! They're our allies, too!"[227] Of course, rivalries happen within the branches, too. An *Incoming* cartoon shows an afterschool disagreement on an army post where the children argue, "Infantry." "Artillery." "Airborne!" "Armor."[228] Canadian cartoonist Roman Jarymowycz gets to the heart of the matter by highlighting doctrinal epistemology differences between cavalry and infantry in forces of antiquity as being practical issues of charging versus holding formations.[229]

Debriefing

The rhetorical vision of the military life is one of community, even if that community might not be perfect or always desirable. This vision is supported by the fantasy types of tradition and shared or common experiences, especially the unpleasant ones. Figure 2.3 illustrates how the fantasy themes outlined above, such as the historical continuity of training, the use of slang, hazing rituals, and rivalries to build insider status, the impracticality of uniforms, the problems with healthcare, food and duty, and the joys of alcohol build these fantasy types and the rhetorical vision of the military community. Additionally, these graphic narratives underscore not only the communal character of military life, but also the ways and means that warriors have or create for coping with group living and for beneficially adjusting to military discipline. Indeed, one of those coping mechanisms is the creation and sharing of the graphic narratives themselves, which offer perspective and sympathy for the unique challenges presented by military life. It is important to note, given the vision of community, that many of these fantasy themes are relevant to multiple countries and are remarkably consistent across time. The element of history and tradition in the military experience is vital to the idea, seen here, that the more things, such as recruitment methods and technology, change, the more things, specifically the shared lived experiences, stay the same.

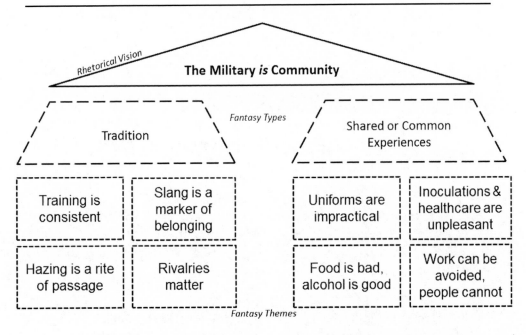

Fig. 2.3: Rhetorical vision of military life as expressed in warrior graphic narratives.

3

Kiss My Brass
Military Hierarchy

Leadership is a potent combination of strategy and character. But
if you must be without one, be without the strategy.

—General H. Norman Schwarzkopf

The formal hierarchy that exists to enact and enforce the official regulations
of the military comprises the essentially anonymous higher authorities who
decree the original orders; the commanding officer (CO) of the field, acting
through his or her adjutant and first sergeant; the CO of the technical unit; the
noncommissioned officer in charge (NCOIC) of the technical unit; and the
NCO in charge of the shifts.[1] This hierarchy is related to authoritarian ideology
and bureaucracy.[2] The officer corps, in particular, is a bureaucratic profession
and a bureaucratic organization. "Within the profession, levels of competence
are distinguished by a hierarchy of ranks; within the organization, duties are
distinguished by a hierarchy of office."[3] Enlisted personnel are part of the organizational, but not of the professional, bureaucracy. Whereas the enlisted are
specialists in the application of violence, officers are specialists in the management of violence—and in the American context, the federally funded training
of young persons for the profession of violence dates back nearly to the founding
of the United States. The vocational distinction prohibits a continuous hierarchy
within the military profession.[4] According to a post–World War II study, this
divide often leads the enlisted to initial feelings of envy toward officers, as they
yearn for the same elevated status. Then, as training and service progress, jealousy gives way to resentment for the special privileges and superior attitude of
the officer-class—an attitude that is indoctrinated through officer training
schools and commission.[5] Over time, military personnel may lose respect for
authority.[6] Thus, the bureaucratic structure influences group cohesion, using
coercion to promote or replace morale.[7]

Hierarchy and vocational distinctions influence military culture, which tends to be Janusian—divided between the battlefield and the base. Though combat and noncombat values are not mutually exclusive, and may even enhance one another,[8] the officers and enlisted on the front lines can be described as a "hot" organization, dealing with risk and crisis in life-and-death scenarios. The officers and, less so, the enlisted in headquarters and the commanders at the top of the hierarchy, on the other hand, can be described as a "cold" organization, handling the bureaucratic, corporate operations: doing the paperwork, planning the strategy, and writing the doctrine.[9] Doctrine provides a common frame of reference across the military to standardize and facilitate operations. Influenced by culture[10] and shaped by generation,[11] it links theory, history, experience, and analysis to establish beliefs about the best way to conduct military affairs.[12] Doctrine "falls between the technical details of tactics and the broad outline of grand strategy."[13] It has further been described as "the soul of warfare,"[14] a "force multiplier,"[15] "military means,"[16] "expression of a military's institutional 'belief system,'"[17] "a system of knowledge,"[18] "the intellectual foundation for ... military operations,"[19] and "fundamental principles by which military forces guide their actions in support of objectives."[20] It has also been called "only a guide"[21] and, in one instance, "troop-heavy, time-intensive, expensive."[22] In the 1980s, a U.S. army myth circulated about a Soviet general who, while planning for the potential of war with the United States, "is alleged to have declared in frustration, 'It is impossible to plan against the Americans because they don't follow their own doctrine!'"[23] More recently, doctrine has been criticized for its growing emphasis on the warrior ethos, or spirit, or culture, even while warfare is reducing the practical role of the human fighter.[24]

While graphic narratives play an educational role in fostering military identity and discipline—evidenced by many government-issued comic books that explain the history and tradition of the branches, such as navy or the national guard,[25] graphic narratives also offer an acceptable release valve for frustrations with hierarchy and regulations, and griping about or "damning" the military is an important aspect of barracks culture for warriors.[26] Comics and cartoons, along with other comedic outlets, have long offered a safe venue for dissent; parody and dissonance making criticism palatable.[27] This is especially relevant for coping with bureaucracy, as satire is, by its nature, anti-authority. It is "a hard-knuckled critique of power" that "exposes some aspect of reality to ridicule in the form of aesthetic expression" and passes judgment on perceived wrongdoing.[28] During the Cold War, particularly in the late 1950s and 1960s, a number of situation-comedy television shows in the U.S. lampooned typical military life with implicit anti-militarist themes often found in military comic strips featuring average Americans trying to muddle through armed service.[29] Parody confirms the existence of its object for mockery through exaggerated imitation of a *recognized* convention or characteristic,[30] which is why it can be so effective at undermining military authority.[31]

See Who Salutes

If the uniform is the mark of belonging and conformity, the salute is the mark of authority and hierarchy. Military courtesies are a demonstration of warriors' commitment to duty, country, and colleagues. Extension of such military courtesies is considered a key element in establishing the discipline required of transitioning from civilian to military life. The most basic of these courtesies is the salute, which is the customary way of recognizing an officer of superior rank.[32] A 1951 comic book for the U.S. Army provides soldiers with the history of and instructions for the proper salute,[33] which can cause no small amount of stress for new recruits.[34] Remembering how to salute—"you bring up your hand on hand salute and down on 'two!'"[35]—who to salute—a particular problem for poor *Seaman Si*, who saluted low ranks just for practice[36] but not the captain, because they had not been introduced[37]—and when to salute—*Winnie the WAC* salutes her major in the shower[38]—can create a lot of anxiety: "After two hours of trying to remember which to salute first—the OOD or the flag, Ensign Sampson began contemplating a hotel room."[39]

Beyond a simple reflection of military hierarchy, the salute also provides a means for expressing individual attitudes toward the system through individual manipulation of the standard rules of saluting.[40] Several artists in World War I, World War II, and OIF humorously record the individual styles of salute. In

Fig. 3.1: Examples of graphic narratives providing instruction for, or mockery of, the salute. 1. Abian Wallgren (1918), 2. Dorothea Byerly (1945), 3. Steve Opet (2008), courtesy of the 10th Mountain Division and Fort Drum Museum.

Fig. 3.1-2

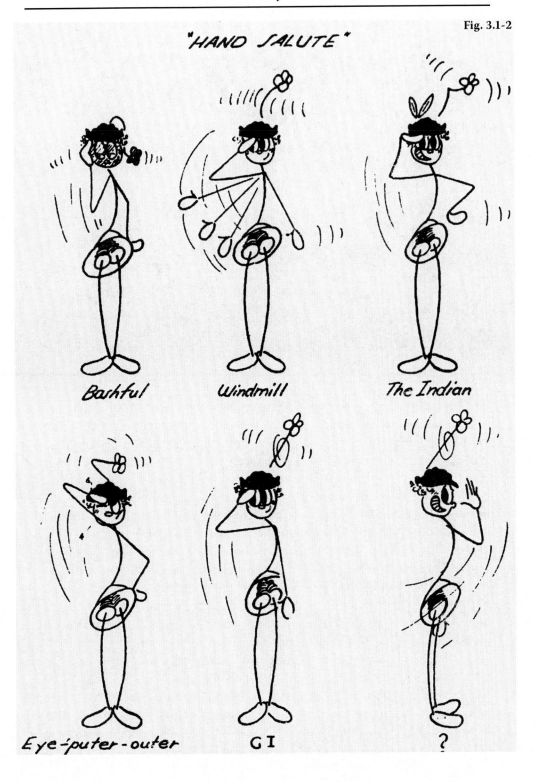

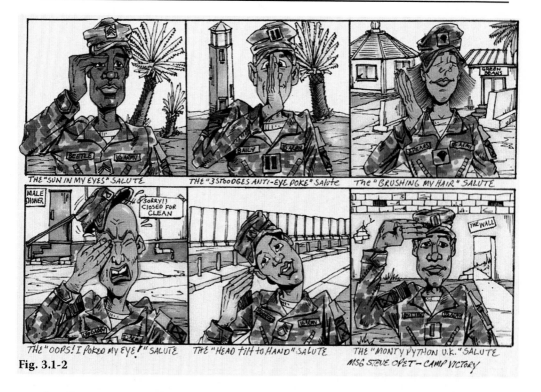

THE "SUN IN MY EYES" SALUTE   THE "3 STOOGES ANTI-EYE POKE" SALUTE   The "BRUSHING MY HAIR" SALUTE

THE "OOPS! I POKED MY EYE!" SALUTE   THE "HEAD tilt to HAND" SALUTE   THE "MONTY PYTHON U.K." SALUTE
                                                                        MSG STEVE OPET — CAMP VICTORY

Fig. 3.1-2

the Great War, Wallgren notes variations based on civilian life, such as the "Punctilious Salute," accompanied by the solicitous bow of a former head waiter; the "Old Style" tip of the hat, "not in use over here"; and the "East Side New York Style" that bends the nose. He also offers light-hearted "hints" for covering up an unnecessary salute to low-ranking personnel, for saluting two officers at once, and to "watch the position of your thumb when saluting" to ensure that thumb and nose do not come into "conspicuous proximity."[41] Dorothea Byerly of the WAVES illustrates "hand salute" variations in her World War II *Up Came a Ripple*,[42] and M.Sgt. Steve Opet's award-winning "Proper Salute" cartoon during Operation Iraqi Freedom offers such variations as the "Sun in My Eyes" salute, the "3 Stooges Anti-Eye Poke" salute, the "Brushing My Hair Salute," and the "Monty Python O.K." salute.[43] Indeed, the salute can actually be used to undermine its intended purpose of respect for superior officers, as suggested by World War II Mauldin cartoons wherein privates wait on a bike path to salute lieutenants as they ride by, because the returned salute causes them to crash,[44] or walk back and forth, saluting, in front a café when officers are eating to force an interruption of their meal.[45] Others find ways to simply avoid saluting entirely: *Private Breger in Britain* puts his arm in a sling when off duty during the Second World War,[46] and a soldier in Iraq attaches a fake arm in a permanent salute, leaving his real hands free to carry food.[47]

Officers, Not Gentlemen

Varying degrees of dislike for and frustration with officers is one of the most common and consistent themes throughout the warriors' graphic narratives, beginning with the wars of the British Empire, wherein "naval and military cartoons ... tended to favour the ordinary soldier and sailor, with many lampooning aged generals and admirals or supercilious young 'drawing-room captains' who had bought (rather than earned) their commissions."[48] An exception to this hostile trend is in the works of the Korean and Vietnam war eras, a particularly notable gap in expressions of animosity toward officers given the strong association between the Vietnam War and the intentional fratricidal or so-called "friendly-fire" practice of fragging—the assault of one's officers with the intent to kill.[49] Any possible explanation of the gap here would, however, be pure speculation, but perhaps hatred of officers was too strong to be amusing. Arrogance and undeserved privilege make up the theme of one portion of the officer-focused comics, and from this privilege stems themes of stupidity, detachment and inexperience, and mean-spiritedness—though perhaps not as mean as the military police (MPs), who are frequently found interfering with the carousing of the average serviceperson.

Graphic narrators express a sense that the privilege and entitlement of officers comes at the unfair expense of the enlisted personnel, who, by virtue of hard work and hardships, are more deserving of the perks granted to the officer class. This privilege of rank (and occasionally the privilege of staff duty) is expressed in a variety of ways—the expansive girth of officers, for example, as in Pvt. Post's paintings of the Spanish-American War[50] and in the political cartoons of Burma's 2007 "Saffron Revolution,"[51] or the cleanliness of officers compared to the raggedness of men at the front, as in the Australian *Humorosities*.[52] In fact, such personal hygiene markers became a significant point of World War II artist Bill Mauldin,[53] who earned the wrath of General Patton for portraying American GIs as unshaven and haggard. Patton had similar unfavorable feelings for Briton Bruce Bairnsfather of World War I.[54] Mauldin comments on this tension in a "Willie and Joe" comic wherein his heroes are parked in a Jeep beside a sign that proclaims they are entering the Third Army and will face fines for having no helmet, shave, buttons, tie, shine, or shampoo, "By order: Ol' Blood and Guts." As a result, the men decide to take a thousand-mile detour.[55] Indeed, according to *Beetle Bailey* cartoonist Mort Walker, "Army cartoons are often considered subversive." Not only did Patton berate Mauldin, but *Beetle Bailey* was banned twice from the *Stars and Stripes* because of Beetle's disrespect for authority and discipline,[56] W.C. Pope's *The Adventures of Arthur Awax* was challenged by a commanding officer in 1983,[57] and Mark Baker tackled an unnamed officer in a 1990s *Private Murphy's Law* cartoon by telling the offended, "Don't read it anymore, *Sir*."[58] In the tongue-in-cheek words of Pope, "The best gauge of a cartoonist's success is by the number of officers he's pissed off."[59]

The privileges that these clean, well-fed officers have, to the envy of the enlisted, include access to better food and drink,[60] gambling,[61] better lodging[62] and transportation,[63] and more leisure[64]—which is even seen in German cartoons from the Great War.[65] So ingrained is the officer's sense of privilege that in one cartoon a general remarks on a beautiful mountain vista and asks if there is a view for the enlisted men, too.[66] Moreover, not only are such indulgences kept from the enlisted, but are often available only at their expense. "Sad Sack" as a lowly World War II private is sent to the back of the line for food, movies, and the PX, but to the front of the line in combat.[67] Mauldin demonstrates that while the grunts risk their lives to take a town, the MPs stand by ready to place "off limits" signs restricting the town to officers only.[68] A central element in the Pacific World War II *senki manga* of Mizuki Shigeru is the confrontation of the lowly soldier with rigid hierarchy of the Japanese military, and the resulting disillusionment of being exploited by the system.[69] From the desert warfare of the 21st century, Jeffrey Hall tells a story of fuel rationing in which "all non-mission essential equipment must be powered down"—except for the generator that powers the captain's popcorn machine.[70] Even after World War II, a welcome-home parade for a general closes the bars to the returning enlisted men.[71] Moreover, officers may take particular enjoyment in the suffering of the enlisted, as suggested by a Vietnam cartoon in which a proclamation prohibiting senior noncoms from using "vulgar or abusive language when addressing new recruits" is seen as the loss of another "fringe benefit."[72]

That such perks are undeserved is underscored by impressions of officers' low intelligence, a perspective shared by Australians and Americans alike in World War I. A Frank Dunne *Digger Days* comic has an officer instructing a "digger" as to how to speak so as to sound like an officer. The digger replies, "This cow must think that [I'm an officer] already, 'ees just called me brainless."[73] Meanwhile, some Wallgren cartoons express the view that only hand-shakers and brown-nosers get to be officers.[74] In World War II, Mauldin depicts officers as too clueless to take cover in the midst of battle, even drawing fire by standing above the trenches while "inspirin'" the troops.[75] Decades later, Baker pokes fun at the idea that army officers are leaders with "quick minds,"[76] while Bacon similarly suggests that navy officers are indecisive—with five members of the Navy Leadership School unable to choose a place for lunch.[77] Bacon also distinguishes the kinds of surgeries necessary for different officer ranks: lobotomy for lieutenant commander, spine removal for commander, and heart removal for captain.[78] Indeed, research on incompetence in the military establishment suggests that it is usually perceived as a result of stupidity, though it is more likely the result of fourteen interrelated factors, ranging from fundamental conservatism to overreliance on brute force to belief in fate, that contribute to a "leveling down" of human capability.[79]

A related problem is that, as suggested by the immense privilege granted them, officers are seen as being out of touch. A multi-part narrative in *Downrange* talks about an annual "Q&A dinner" hosted by the general "with a group of peons to show that he's concerned about their needs," but is nothing more than a media stunt attended by shills with preset questions.[80] Occasionally a gap between officers' outlooks and the reality of the military's people and purpose is also noted. For example, both *Pvt. Murphy's Law* and *Doctrine Man* take aim at the idea of enforced morality in the army. Murphy thinks, "How stupid can this be?" when given an army values card to sign and carry with him at all times, listing the penalty of an Article 15 (non-judicial punishment), that assigns him values to live by to keep him morally straight.[81] *Doctrine Man* introduces readers to a values-oriented officer who refuses to allow movies that conflict with army values: "Somebody scheduled 'Animal House' for tonight's movie ... Nudity!! Nudity is inconsistent with Army values!! ... 'Goodfellas'...? It contains adult language!! Adult language is inconsistent with Army values!! ... 'Blackhawk Down'...? It contains graphic violence!! Graphic violence is inconsistent with Army values!!"[82] The irony, of course, is that sex and colorful language are significant components of military folk culture, and violence is the business of the military.

The perceived disconnect between enlisted personnel and officers may be related to an apparent lack of experience by officers. Bairnsfather comments on the fact that understanding between the officers and their men in World War I only began to slowly dawn when young subalterns of the field, though not the staff officers, had to share the privations of the enlisted.[83] Some graphic narratives comment on how much younger the officers are than the enlisted.[84] It is the serviceperson's practice to not call anyone "sir" who "works for a living," which is captured in a *Broadside* cartoon,[85] and so some graphic narratives look to the issue of grunts' field experience versus command's lofty ideas. This is the central idea of the currently running *Doctrine Man* (*DM*) comics, through a cast of parodic superheroes, antiheroes, and sidekicks designed to reflect particular outlooks and practices in the U.S. military. These include, among others: Doctrine Man, a "digital age hero from the analog universe"[86] with mediocre "PowerPoint" skills, who promotes the irrelevant; the blind/sightless Concept Man; the Bright Idea Fairy, an army strategist who, unlike his mythic counterpart the Good Idea Fairy (an evil creature in military lore who whispers bad advice to leaders), is a sardonic voice of reason; and his undesirable sidekick, the Ghost of Clausewitz, the floating skull of the preeminent Prussian military theorist of the Napoleonic Wars whose ideas still haunt military doctrine. Other warrior cartoonists also touch on similar ideas to *DM*. The Good Idea Fairy is found in *Delta Bravo Sierra*,[87] *Bob on the FOB*,[88] *Power Point Ranger*,[89] and *Pvt. Murphy's Law*.[90] Jabs at "PowerPoint" are found in the work of T.H. Limb, with a character whose "knowledge is only Powerpoint-deep,"[91] and Jeff Bacon, with a brief that has "absolutely no substance or value. But [has] slick graphics and animation you'll see throughout."[92]

In traditional superhero comics, costumed crusaders act to uphold the government, stand in opposition to an evil regime, or travel to an "uncivilized" location to claim it.[93] "Superheroes are routinely represented as models of right action and feeling.... Anti-heroes illustrate what thoughtful citizens concerned with justice should do."[94] Their physiques and appearance are designed to embody their ideals and environments.[95] *DM* turns this genre on its head by giving his unheroic characters superheroic trappings. The juxtaposition is a comedic but critical commentary on military leadership as being out of touch with the "boots on the ground" and with the realities of modern society. As stated in the "about" section of the *DM* Facebook page, "Doctrine is the foundation of knowledge (a good foundation NEVER changes position)," and change should be fought "every step of the way" because "tradition is fundamental (enduring traditions are unimpeded by progress)."[96]

Whether born of privilege, stupidity, or inexperience, enlisted artists agree that officers, even noncommissioned officers, have a tendency to be mean. England's Bairnsfather in World War I asks, "Do colonels eat their young?"[97] Australia's Dunne introduces readers to a sarcastic base MG instructor.[98] Meanwhile, the United States' Wallgren offers advice on "How to Be Popular Though an 'Officer.'"[99] A key feature of the naval graphic narratives *Ricky's Tour* and *Broadside* is an idea that officers relieve boredom by micromanaging and yelling at their subordinates.[100] Moreover, the military's hierarchical structure seems to ensure that everyone but the lowliest private has someone else to abuse. In the words of a *Downrange* strip, "Hooah runs downhill."[101] This is seen in *Lt. Kadish*, where "the chain-of-command in action" is depicted as individuals of one rank to the next lower pass along the message, "You *Θ©↓* wimp!!"[102] And it is seen in a "Pvt. Murphy" strip when a private first class yells at a private for not addressing him by rank, right after grumbling about the sergeant getting a power trip from having to hear his title all the time.[103]

Though "hooah runs downhill" in practice, that does not mean, however, that officers can escape expressions of antagonism in graphic narratives, which frequently offer an acceptable means for just such sentiments. In the Great War, *Seaman Si* calls his company commander "old Seaweed" and "a piece of cheese!"[104] and gels to the idea of becoming an ensign in order to "tell a C.P.O what he thinks of him"[105] A satiric advertisement in *Yank* promotes the "Little Gem Actor's Aid Kits" for acting NCOs.[106] In "Willie and Joe," men use the cover of a welcoming or victory parade in France to throw fruit and vegetables at the general's head,[107] a Pfc. tells his major, "One more crack like that an' you can't have yer job back after the war,"[108] and the nephew of the freshly-home Joe calls his Scoutmaster "a damn brass hat."[109] When the skipper falls overboard in a *Broadside* cartoon, the officer of the deck's only order is to, "Bong him off I guess,"[110] referencing the tradition of marking the entrances and exits of officers to a ship with a pipe or bell. In fact, it may just be that the officers are thought to be the real enemy of the enlisted warriors, even in war. This is certainly the perspective of World War II's "Sad Sack," who receives kindness and respect from the Japanese people and abuse from his own officers.[111] And if officers are not the enemy, then the MPs may be—as suggested by a cartoon in *Yank* in which soldiers are hiding from MPs and caution the group to not give away their position to "the enemy."[112] *Hubert* is victim to an ambush of evil-looking MPs,[113] and *Private Breger in Britain* falls victim to bureaucratic military justice when "this court finds no evidence of guilt [so] we shall let you off with a light sentence of only one month!"[114]

The Thick Red-Tape Line

Many of the same criticisms extend naturally to issues of military bureaucracy. Military bureaucracy has been called "organized anarchy" that inhibits military efficiency and success because of its reinforced ambiguities, misdirection of problems, misuse of participants, overabundance of information, excessive demands, and selectivity.[115] The inefficiency of the system is clear when *Private Breger in Britain* is ordered to "arrange these documents alphabetically and then burn them,"[116] and in *The Sad Sack* as a new "organization" takes a request for one sign through seven different desks in the same office, only to ultimately be rejected.[117] It is visible again in a scene of *Leatherhead in Korea* in which a Marine already at the front gets his draft notice during mail call,[118] and yet again in *Broadside* when a strategic planning seminar has not planned for an adequate number of seats or a sufficient amount of food.[119] Warriors have long griped about the way things are done in the military, such as the stress and workload triggered by Inspection Morning,[120] the undesirability of KP duty[121] or latrine detail,[122] the tedium of cleaning,[123] laundry regulations,[124] the constant need to line up and wait for a haircut, movie, bus,[125] or food, and the never-ending challenge of getting adequate supplies and provisions.

Purportedly, the bureaucratic structure, if used properly, is effective. An educational "Joe Dope" comic in *Army Motors* during the Second World War explains that even a private can "rakazishun" publications: "All y' gotta do is ask y'r commandin' officer! The AGO has worked long and hard to develop a

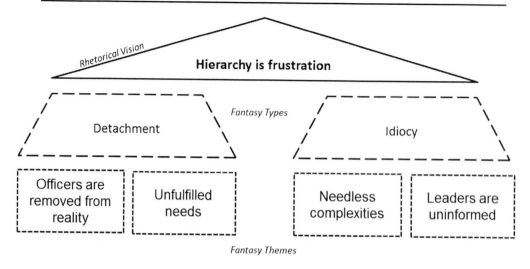

Fig. 3.2: Rhetorical vision of military hierarchy as expressed in warrior graphic narratives

system that should insure adequate distribution to every outfit.... Don't waste time writing outa channels!"[126] It never seems to work that easily, however, even for other countries. A World War I Bairnsfather cartoon, ironically labeled "The Things That Matter," is set during the September offensive of Loos; in the midst of heated combat Colonel Fitz-Shrapnel receives an urgent but situationally trivial message from General Headquarters: "Please let us know, as soon as possible, the number of tins of raspberry jam issued to you last Friday."[127] A *Lt. Kadish* strip presents the following exchange: "Hey, Lt. Bogart, what do want [sic] me to do with these radio parts? Some of them don't work." "Keep the best. Issue the rest."[128] *Power Point Ranger* tells us that supply says "NO" to every request,[129] and Thibodeau argues that even the ship store is never open.[130] Such occurrences often lead to warriors pilfering what they need, humorously demonstrated by a cartoon in *Yank* in which soldiers are taking stacks of signs that read "pilferage is sabotage" to make a tent floor.[131]

Delta Bravo Sierra (*DBS*) suggests that civilian contractors, who have picked up many of the noncombat duties that were once assigned to the enlisted, such as KP, complicate the process further. In one *DBS* strip a soldier is unable to return his IBA (Individual Body Armor) because of a hole that was there when it was issued. Moreover, the civilian contractor, who looks a lot like a devil, makes the paperwork that proves the IBA's original condition disappear.[132] (Destruction of paperwork as a means of "filing" it is also found in *Power Point Ranger* comics.[133]) Maximillian Uriarte agrees that the entire bureaucratic hierarchical "system is broken."[134] His *Terminal Lance* graphic narrative depicts that system as follows:

Here's what you need to do: Take this sheet to your battalion and have all of the shops and your command sign it.... Then you need to go into town, ask around about a guy named "Old Mackerel," he will give you a gem in exchange for sexual favors. You need the gem to get into the mines ... where you will face the Balrog of Mordor. You have to slay the beast, and carve off a piece of his horn to use in a potion ... but make sure he signs your sheet first.[135]

It does seem at times as if the bureaucrats have fun by messing with the enlisted[136] in some kind of game of fortune.[137]

Politically Comic

An issue related to the bureaucracies and hierarchies is politics. In the U.S. context, tensions exist between the First Amendment's promise of free speech for Americans and the Uniform Code of Military Justice restrictions on servicepersons' communication. At the heart of the dichotomy between public free speech and military restricted speech are concerns about discipline, battle preparedness, operation security, and military subordination to civilian control. There are, therefore, expectations regarding proper expression in the military for political neutrality, in the interest of healthy civil-military relations; maintenance of morale and loyalty, in the interest of combat preparation; control, in the interest of military efficiency; and an appearance of cohesiveness, in the interest of foreign diplomatic relations.[138] Or, as explained more simply by cartoonist Uriarte, who strives to keep his *Terminal Lance* cartoons apolitical:

There's three things you don't talk about with other Marines:

- Wives.
- Religion.
- Politics.

Why? Well, they have no place in the field or anywhere else. Why ruin good relationships with opposing political stances.[139]

It is, then, not surprising that the majority of the graphic narratives shy away from politics; but the benefit of retirement or anonymity, coupled with ambiguity of the Web 2.0 era, has allowed the occasional foray in political matters and current events, particularly in the decade of the 2010s.

In earlier eras, politics rarely made it into the comics, except for calls to "Buy Bonds"[140] or expressed hatred of enemy leaders.[141] Some exceptions include a World War I Wallgren cartoon that imagines "If All Of Us Voted This Year," to promote voting among the ranks as a responsibility,[142] and several Jake Schuffert cartoons that reference draft dodging, protesting, and avoiding combat in Vietnam[143]—fairly tame political statements in comparison to the vitriolic attacks warrior artists Holmes and Uriarte made on the 2014 prisoner exchange that freed former prisoner of war U.S. Sgt. Bowe Bergdahl. The Bergdahl event was surrounded with controversy because of the possibility that Bergdahl had deserted when he was captured and because the White House negotiated with terrorists to free him.[144] A *Terminal Lance* strip mocked the prisoner exchange with a staff sergeant requesting five Marines of Mexican heritage to be traded for a sergeant being held prisoner in Mexico because, they say, "Well, we just traded five high-profile Taliban for that shady soldier guy so clearly no one gives a shit about anything anymore."[145] *Power Point Ranger* characters, when confronted with a Taliban member yelling, "I am free to kill more Americans! OBAMA AKBAR," contemplated, "Maybe WE should desert our post and be frigging heroes."[146] *Doctrine Man*, drawn by a career army officer, ventures more cautiously into politics by using innuendo and outright silliness. One current event issue that captured his imagination was the sexually sordid court-martial of Brigadier General Jeffrey Sinclair in 2013. The married officer had an illicit three-year affair with a female captain on his staff who called him "Poppa Panda Sexy Pants."[147] *DM* had fun with both the unusual pet name[148] and Sinclair's distinctive "Foghorn Leghorn" sideburns.[149]

Debriefing

The rhetorical vision of the military hierarchy is one of frustration, wherein the lower ranks, and especially the enlisted, feel put upon and disadvantaged by a broken system—an incongruous "organized anarchy" in a culture of rigid rules and regulations, which they not only must endure but also respect, at least outwardly. This vision is supported by the strongly related fantasy types of detachment and idiocy. Figure 3.2 illustrates how the fantasy themes outlined above, such as officers' lack of experience and their removal from the reality of grunts, and the needless complexities of a system that does not, or cannot, meet the needs of its personnel, build these fantasy types and the rhetorical vision of the frustrating hierarchy. As suggested by Norman Dixon, "By now most people have become accustomed to, one might almost say blasé about, military incompetence. Like the common cold, flat feet or the British climate, it is accepted as a part of life—faintly ludicrous but quite unavoidable."[150] These graphic narratives indicate that it is not just the exalted status and privilege of superiors that can trigger feelings of jealousy and resentment toward officers, but, more importantly, the direct effect that such standing and honor have on the enlisted grunts, including inadequate provisions and increased risk. Moreover, throughout military history there has been a tendency to prefer simple explanations of incompetence to acknowledging its complex dynamic, particularly if the simple explanation, such as ignorant or evil officers, is abusive to the hierarchy.[151]

4

Frenemies
Friends and Foes

> The enemy of the moment always represented absolute evil.
> —George Orwell, *1984*

Individuals hold concepts of friends and foes as part of their identity; as part of understanding who they are and their place in society.[1] Governments use the idea of common enemies to maintain control, to reinforce dominant values, to mobilize action and allies, and to renew commitment to a common cause or ideology.[2] Enemies are heterostereotypes established by state apparatus as legitimate targets of force, sanctioning killing as honorable.[3] "In the beginning we create the enemy. Before the weapon comes the image. We *think* others to death and then invent the battle-axe or the ballistic missiles with which to actually kill them. Propaganda precedes technology."[4] Identifying antagonistic "Others" as villainous enemies, rather than rivals, emphasizes danger and necessitates military action over other forms of conflict management. The enemy becomes the antithesis of the ally, establishing a clear us-vs.-them dichotomy: We are civilized and they are uncivilized.[5] "Language about enemies is drawn from a rather small set of contradictory and ambiguous propositions that are applied regardless of whether the highlighted difference" is of ideology, ethnicity, nationality, etc.[6] Crisis rhetoric uses "decivilizing vehicles," particular *topoi* of savagery to describe the enemy in derogatory terms, its specific acts of aggression, or the scene or environment of chaos and atrocity. This reduces the chances of allies being able to identify with the Other while providing a clear scapegoat for problems and a particular target for aggression.[7]

From the perspective of the warrior, the enemy is not so simple a creature, and neither is the ally. Warriors whose first experience in a foreign land is during war do not see the country at its best, and "idealizing the absent,"[8] or being nostalgic for what he/she has left behind, can make the place, and its people, unfavorable by comparison, no matter what the situation. This problem may be compounded by the hardships of military life, for which the enemy becomes a convenient scapegoat.[9] Differences in cultures and folkways are compared hierarchically. The new and unknown are rarely as favorable and to ethnocentrics will seem even more inferior. Nation-based rivalries can arise when resources are scarce. Sentiments about the foreign people themselves are shaped by the nature of intergroup and interpersonal interactions, and "friendly interpersonal relations and hostile intergroup relations may coexist, as well as the opposite combination"[10] when one likes the "enemy" people, but not the government, or feels sympathy for the victims while disliking the culture. Warriors fighting in their home countries may see the enemy as the aggressor, simply because the intervention appears as an invasion.[11] In combat scenarios enemies are likely to be categorized by the seriousness of the perceived threat that they pose, rather than by racial, ethnic, or cultural distinctions[12]—though knowledge of the adversary culture is important to effective military operations,[13] and hatred for or dehumanization of the enemy has long been a part of combat training.[14]

Further complicating it is a society's or military's own cultural attitudes of war and race. A 2012 study by the Economic and Social Research Council found, for example, that soldiers who desecrate the bodies of the enemy dead do so because they view the enemy as different and themselves as hunters—perspectives perpetuated by social history and military traditions.[15] In fact, the Other is not always the enemy on the outside. In the United States, Afro-Americans fought in segregated military units from the colonial area through World War II. Much of this participation was unacknowledged, uncelebrated, and unrecorded. While sacrificing their lives to a nation that did not recognize them as citizens, they faced hostilities from the civilians they served, inadequate equipment, an inability to be promoted, shunning by white comrades, and rejection by the military and government in peace times. Desegregation began in the 1950s and proceeded smoothly until the Vietnam War, when the general disintegration of the military structure and culture played out not only in drug abuse and "fragging" but also in racial conflicts, which grew worse after the draft was abolished and the demographics of the military changed. In the 1980s, military leadership became more racially integrated and race relations improved. Today, the U.S. Army, in particular, is unmatched in its level of racial integration.[16] In Canada and Australia, racial and ethnic diversity in the armed forces still faces problems, as the countries deal with recruitment issues.[17]

In wartime graphic narratives, the enemy is often visually interpreted in ways that malign, belittle, or dehumanize, giving the public a way to vent their hostilities and making the task of killing the enemy easier.[18] The visual metaphors used for comic representations of the enemy are mostly the same as the enemy archetypes found in other forms of wartime propaganda.[19] "In all propaganda, the face of the enemy is designed to provide a focus for our hatred. He is the other. The outsider. The alien. He is not human. If we can only kill him, we will be rid of all within and without ourselves that is evil."[20] These archetypes represent different degrees of dehumanizing characteristics, ranging from nonhuman or bestial, to barbarian, to adversary, and encompass varying portrayals of abstractions, facelessness, demons, death, illness and madness, torturers, rapists, aggressors, megalomaniacs, criminals, and strangers.[21] Stereotyping is a key component of how such archetypes are achieved visually.[22] Stereotypes are categorical reductions of individuals or groups based on simple, widely recognized, and memorable traits, whether real or imagined. As such, stereotypes are energy- and time-saving devices that aid sense-making and reinforce group beliefs and identities.[23] In World War II–era comics and animated cartoons, for example, American artists frequently exaggerated physical attributes of Japanese to depict them as evil, emphasizing their skin tone and eye shape to give Asians a rat-like appearance.[24] During the occupation of China after the war, Chinese artists depicted the arrogance and violence of their American enemies using physical attributes of Caucasians and U.S. culture distinct from the Chinese: imposing size, obesity, hairy bodies, prominent jaws, and garish clothing.[25]

"The stereotype is an essential part of the language of comics and sequential art. In the creation of a character, physical differences help make the character recognizable to the viewer, visually unique from other characters, and 'readable' when their image, which must be repeated again and again during the course of a story unfolding, has to put in an appearance."[26] Common stereotypes involve strength or weakness, with the body being objectified to showcase particular physical attributes, which are often equated with comparable traits of personality and morality, as well as with a particular nationality.[27] In graphic narratives, stereotypes are used "to provide a means to anticipate behavior" but may also be used as a way to challenge the stereotypes themselves[28] by illustrating their absurdity or by working from an audience's accepted frame of reference to introduce new, even conflicting, ideas. Any discussion of individual or group portrayals in graphic narratives must, therefore, be cognizant of the usefulness of stereotypes as visual shorthand, as well as their presence as cultural norms or means of dissent.

Racial and ethnic stereotyping has been especially prominent in graphic narratives, even when the Other is not a wartime enemy. Following the First World War, pulps and comics reflected an American preoccupation with defining what was, and was not, American—a trend that continued into the 1950s— and race was often the essential distinction.[29] Jews, Asians, and blacks are three of the most visually abused groups in Western graphic narratives,[30] though the Irish, Nazis, and Arabs have also been frequent targets of stereotyping in comics and other pop-culture outlets.[31] Jewish stereotypes are rooted in images that began in the Middle Ages and include deviousness, avarice, skepticism, and murderousness. Asian stereotypes have often relied on subhuman or emasculated depictions, comparing both the physical and character traits of Asians to apes, monkeys, pigs, or rats, or emphasizing yellow skin, small stature, long braids, and silk clothing as effeminate. Stereotypes of blacks have generally followed one of seven types, all of which display the African race as inferior: the native, and naïve, savage (one of the most enduring stereotypes in European comics); the humble subservient; the jokester-prankster; the over-enthusiastic dreamer; the tragic temptress; the matronly and loyal subservient; and the ne'er-do-well or rebel.[32] In considering depictions of the Other in these warrior-created graphic narratives it is, therefore, important to remember that the Other is not always the antagonist.

The Other

Like other comic artists, warrior cartoonists use a number of simplistic visual cues to mark groups for easy identification, such as *Pickelhaubes* for Germans in World War I; *Stahlhelmes* for Nazis in World War II; *non la* hats for Koreans and Vietnamese; *ushankas* for communists, both Russian and Asian, as well as *papakhas* for non-communist Russians; *niqabs* and *burqas* for Muslim women; skullcaps, turbans, *keffiyeh*, and *fez* for Arabs and Muslim men, including the Turks in World War I; and Brodie helmets for allied troops in World War I and World War II. These simplistic cues are not limited to headwear and often include physical features as well. Asians drawn by Western artists are depicted in diminutive statures; the Vietnamese are often skinny, with ribs showing. Likewise, Westerners drawn by Asian artists are usually tall and heavy-set, with monstrous or grotesque variations of the "Uncle Sam" character used for Americans. Asians are also frequently depicted with prominent teeth, thick glasses, and slanted eyes—and not just by American artists. China's anti–Japanese graphic propaganda illustrates their foes with sharp, buck teeth and large noses. Until the 1960s, most Africans and African Americans are often represented with large, white lips (reminiscent of "black face" minstrel-show makeup) and broad noses. During the Second World War, Africans are commonly dressed in loincloths, with both men and women shown topless, and sporting bones in their hair, large earrings and/or particularly long ears, and necklaces and/or elongated necks. In the World Wars, Germans, especially women, are drawn by Americans as obese and fair-haired, whereas Italians were drawn as dark, hairy, and slovenly, and the French women were drawn as petite and peasant-like. Though many such depictions can be considered bigoted, there is reason to believe that they are not always intended as such—but may be the result of simply trying to capture and understand differences and new experiences. British warrior artist Bruce Bairnsfather, for example, depicts a Russian retreat as two soldiers doing *kazatskis*, or the *Kozachok*, while chanting about vodka, because he had never actually seen a Russian and so relied on a cultural stereotype, admittedly not knowing of its relative accuracy or inaccuracy.[33] Again, cultural differences are usually compared hierarchically, with the familiar taking precedence and preference over the unfamiliar.

The terminology used in reference to different racial, ethnic, or national groups tends to reflect either the vernacular of the times or a common name among a people as shorthand for referring to the entire group. For blacks, this includes: Nigger, Negro, and Coon. For Germans: Hun, Boche, Fritz/Fritzy, and Hans. For Turkish peoples, the term "Turk" is usually contextualized as an insulting epithet in itself. North Koreans and Chinese were called Brownies and Commies (Commies is also used for Soviet Russians); Vietnamese were called VC, Viet-Cong or Cong, and Charlie; and Arabs were called Sahib, Achmed, Haji, Muhammed, and Akbahr. Language patterns are also often parodied, though in many cases, particularly for European allies during the World Wars, it seems more of an effort to capture perceived reality than to ridicule, especially as American artists frequently mock American dialects and slang, too, and the American inability to properly speak other languages—such as saying "silver plate" rather than "*s'il vous plaît.*"[34] The colloquial writing of accents and dialects in this way adds a sense of realism, of capturing and conveying what and how artists hear or heard. When the language of enemy groups is parodied, however, the tone can be more demeaning. The most notable example of this is in the present-day graphic narratives of the conflicts and American deployments in Afghanistan and Iraq. The Arab languages are frequently represented as "durka durka" or "durkee durkee,"[35] a racist phrase that allegedly arose from the *South Park* television show and the 2004 film *Team America: World Police*.[36]

Pro-Living Means Anti-Enemy

Throughout many of the graphic narratives, the enemy is neither a prominent villain nor a focus of hate, despite racist or bigoted representations. As discussed in the previous chapter, officers are prominent villains of the strips—emphasized in an *Up Front* cartoon wherein a German soldier tells "Willie and Joe" that he will not interrupt their pilfering and destruction of the German officers' liquor supply,[37] and in a Frank Brandt cartoon wherein Americans are given permission by a German first sergeant to capture his commanding officer.[38] The enemy of the average military grunt is most often an inconvenience, something to be occasionally pitied and frequently evaded, rather than a villain.

In fact, studies suggest the troops who have been subjected to long-term combat will go to great lengths to avoid hostile confrontations; as long as individuals do not run away from the battle, which is a clear demonstration of cowardice among the military, other displays of fear or unwillingness to fight are tolerated.[39]

Bill Mauldin's work is particularly poignant in this regard. "Willie and Joe" express little or no animosity toward the Germans, Italians, or the Japanese. One Mauldin scene depicts a drunken Nazi soldier that no one wants to capture; the Americans get stuck with him and his café bill.[40] In another, the Americans and the Germans are singing a song together from the trenches, across the pickets.[41] Yet another demonstrates that for the men fighting, war has no winners: U.S. soldiers, stooped, dirty, unshaven, are trudging through rainy streets, flanking injured Italian soldiers; the caption, taken from actual news headlines, ironically reads, "Fresh, spirited American troops, flushed with victory, are bringing in thousands of hungry, ragged-battle-weary prisoners."[42] Several graphic narratives show the men trying to avoid the enemy entirely, such as not firing back to avoid giving away their position, including one cartoon by Sgt. Dick Wingert wherein Americans are under sniper fire and "Hubert" recommends, "Let's just ignore him and maybe he'll go away."[43] An illustration for a story in *Yank Magazine* suggests that the German soldiers and the American soldiers are actually no different, each simultaneously complaining about the other side getting them up too early in the morning.[44] A similar concept is explored in *The New Sad Sack*, as an American ransacks a Nazi bunk while a Nazi does the same to his, making their raids on each other an even draw.[45]

At its worst, the enemy is an obstacle to survival—and it is this, above all, that makes the enemy fit for destruction. In battle, rhetorician Robert Ivie notes, the enemy is neither face nor abstraction, but "the concrete, immediate, and anticipated reality of hostile, deadly fire."[46] The primary presence of the enemy in warrior comics is seen, not via representations of people, but through depictions of deadly bullets, shells, bombs, and planes. This is especially visible in the World War I work of England's Bairnsfather, who suffered what was then called "shell shock."[47] The will to survive by destruction of the enemy is perhaps most plainly captured in a Vietnam graphic narrative by Vernon Grant in which a GI tells a reporter, "I'm anti-war, anti-draft, anti-fight ... but ... I'm pro-living! So right *now* I'm anti–Viet Cong!"[48] In fact, similar sentiments are expressed, without any lightheartedness, by soldiers in the anti–Vietnam War film *Hearts and Minds*. One says, "I don't know where they [the enemy] are and that's the worst of it ... and so we just stay alive from day to day." Another observed, "I dinged him [a North Vietnamese] ... and I wanted more. And it wasn't that I wanted more for politics or anything like that, no.... I just wanted them because they were the opposition, they were the enemy."[49] It is perhaps this drive to survive that shapes the predominant psychological and physiological characteristic

Fig. 4.1-1

Fig. 4.1: Examples of graphic narratives targeting political enemies. 1. C. LeRoy Baldridge (circa 1918), 2. Sgt. "Yank" Chapman (circa 1943).

of all enemies, regardless of war or nationality: they are easily defeated. While there is more honor in defeating an enemy who is competent, depictions of an incompetent or underhanded enemy are good for morale boosts, ensuring warriors of future victory. This is especially true for warriors who have not yet seen combat, or for civilians at home, and who know the enemy only from a distance

Fig. 4.1-2

GENTLEMEN — THE
TARGET FOR TO-NITE-

or in the abstract. Additionally, because frontline troops are often fearful and unsure, depictions of such flawed characteristics in the enemy may be a projection of their own concerns and experiences.[50]

As early as the American Civil War, comics emphasized the traits of enemy failure and frailty. In the cartoons of "George" (or "Gorge") drawn by a soldier of the 44th Massachusetts Infantry, Confederates are caricaturized as poverty-stricken, poorly equipped, and starving.[51] Lt. Percy Crosby humorously makes the point in *Stars and Stripes,* during the First World War, that it is easier to kill another person when you are "crazy mad" at him,[52] and sniping Germans is referred to as "big game shooting" by Alban Butler, Jr.[53] Sketches by British artist Cpl. Douglas G. Ward, serving in India, show different "types" of Huns and Turks, including dead ones.[54] Australian artist Will Dyson depicts the Germans under the Kaiser as monkeys, dangerous only because of the "Wonders of Science" in the airplane and bomb.[55] This apishness foreshadows German depictions in the graphic narratives of the Second World War, in which Nazis are typically drunken, stupid, and/or superstitious, easily tricked by wood nymph or gremlin costumes.[56] A comical cartoon spread by Ralph Stein in *Yank Magazine,* for example, introduces a number of silly secret weapons for the invasion of Germany, such as the "Knackwurst and Sauerkraut Projector, Olfactory" to lure the enemy to American camps, and the "Wench Mortar," which would confuse the enemy by dropping "tasty babes" coated in Chanel No. 5 upon their installations.[57] (Interestingly, the common comic or cartoon depiction of Nazis as stupid differed sharply with the public perception, and enduring stereotype, of German efficiency and obedience.)[58] China similarly portrays Americans as goofy-looking and hapless in propaganda of the Korean War.[59]

The Japanese of World War II are envisioned as being much more dangerous—more likely to be sneaking up on Americans—but are also more frequently depicted as dead enemies rather than living ones. One particularly explicit graphic narrative compares the Japanese soldiers to mice, in keeping with their rat-like characteristics as found in propaganda, mainstream comic books, and animated cartoons of the era,[60] who can be lured into and electrocuted with a "better mousetrap."[61] In the following war, the North Korean army often appears as being physically beaten by the Americans, left in bruised, unconscious heaps; occasionally even being defeated by their own weather, as exaggerations show American warriors using ice as weapons.[62] Perhaps reflecting the sense of futility that accompanied the Vietnam War, enemies are more often depicted as dangerous but elusive during this era. Tad Foster labels them as "Mr. Charlie; Mr. Ingenuity and Guts,"[63] and Jake Schuffert shows them easily tricking the Americans with a Trojan Horse.[64] In more recent times, the Taliban and, to a lesser extent Iraqis, are pitted as 18th century tribesman facing off against an arsenal of modern weaponry.[65]

Overall, the enemy is typically distinct from the civilians of a country, despite the fact that in American military training and doctrine there may be no such distinction.[66] For the boots on the ground, however, graphic narratives suggest distinctions between human targets and bystanders, likely because of the perceived threat of each. During the Napoleonic Wars, Napoleon himself appears as a frequent target of ridicule by Scottish soldier and artist George Cruikshank, who is often simultaneously sympathetic to the French under Napoleon's rule.[67] In the Great War, the Kaiser is the designated villain for the English, New Zealanders, and Americans.[68] In World War II, Hitler is the frequent target (literally) shown in graphic narratives, as cleverly represented in a division Christmas card that places Hitler's face in the center of a toilet seat,[69] consistent with American public opinion that distinguished between an evil Nazi minority and a majority of innocent and beset German people.[70] China's anti–Japanese propaganda of World War II differentiates between the Japanese military and the Japanese civilians, who are shown to be victims.[71] In graphic narratives from Operation Enduring Freedom, the enemy is usually designated as the Taliban or Al Qaeda, not as Afghanistan. For example, one cartoon shows a "Taliban Crossing" sign in an area patrolled by drones, much as an American highway may be patrolled by radar-equipped police helicopters.[72]

Some graphic narratives really emphasize the ambiguity of an enemy, enemy people, and allies, both practically for warriors on the frontlines and politically for civilians on the home front. In Maximilian Uriarte's 2014 graphic novel, *The White Donkey*, two Marines can only distinguish "the good guys" in the Middle East by the glow-belts they wear.[73] In World War II, Mauldin's "Willie and Joe" tell an Italian drinking buddy, "You hear that, Ferdinand, th' invasion is over! You ain't a enemy any more."[74] In another Mauldin example, wrought with dark irony, the cashier at a small store says, "Naw—we don't hafta worry about th' owner comin' back. He was killed in Italy." The sign over the store says, "~~Hitoshi Mitsuki~~. Fruits and Vegetables. Under New Management." A sign beneath, flanked by images of the American flag reads, "Let's Keep America for *Americans*. Joe Frumage, Proprietor."[75] A strip in the *New Sad Sack* shows the private getting along far better with the Japanese people, who bestow on him signs of respect, than with his own officers, who yell at and berate him.[76]

A country's terrain and climate are frequently more hated than its people, as these things create daily hardships and discomforts for the warriors. This is seen, for example, in Shel Silverstein's *Grab Your Socks*: A scene labeled "Memory of Korea" features two soldiers talking in a barren landscape; as one gestures around him he says, "What do you mean, Where's the latrine? This IS the latrine!"[77] The bulk of human vilification appears most often with enemies who have marked physical differences and/or markedly different cultures, particularly Americans versus Asians, and Westerners versus Arabs. It is the combination of appearance with negative stereotypes and the perception of threat that propagandists rely on to foster aggression in the cause of war.[78] In fact, racist depictions of both enemies and allies are more often found in cartoons put out by the governments and other establishments, such as on postcards and stationery for letter writing to and from the troops, as in America during

World War II, and as in Russia, England, and France during the Russo-Japanese War.[79] Racial stereotypes, however, often complicate efforts to distinguish between friend and foe, as in U.S. efforts to vilify the Japanese race while praising Chinese allies during World War II. The Japanese were a prominent target of demonizing, racist cartoons, particularly on the cover of more than 500 mainstream American comic books,[80] but also, occasionally, in warriors' graphic narratives. Beyond the comparison of the Japanese to rodents or insects to be exterminated,[81] World War II graphic narratives frequently depict Pacific islanders, and the African natives—almost interchangeably—as half-naked and surreal heathens with enlarged ears, necks, heads, noses, and/or breasts, wearing grass skirts and horrific masks.[82] (Many of the nearly-naked island *women*, however, are shown to be very attractive and are the elusive romantic prey of many lonely soldiers.)[83] Several celebrate deaths of the Japanese, such as a cartoon by Frank Brandt entitled "Family Reunion in Tokyo," wherein a Japanese couple, dressed in ceremonial clothing, dine surrounded by stacks of boxes marked with the Rising Sun flag and the words "Hon Ashes of..." Yosuki, Toyama, Suki, Tujo, Jiro, Tojo, and so on.[84] Such imagery is attributed to the angry reaction of the Japanese attack on the U.S. naval base at Pearl Harbor.[85] Mauldin even includes a cartoon showing how hatred of the Japanese is fostered in basic training.[86] After the Second World War ended and the Cold War began to take shape, the people of occupied Japan, now desired as an ally by the United States, are seen in popular discourse as dependents of America—women to the masculine United States.[87] This is especially prominent in the *Babysan* cartoons of Bill Hume. "A carefree and charming girl, Babysan never forgot the acts of kindness on the part of the American. She decided, in fact, to devote herself to the cause of the American serviceman in Japan."[88] When Americans are depicted as the enemies of Asians, as in comics by China during the Korean conflict and the post–World War II occupation, they are shown not only as giant and hairy, with reptilian characteristics, but also as reckless, violent and corrupt, motivated by sexual desires, greed, and arrogance.[89]

Iraqi treachery and Muslim sexuality are the primary focus of racial and ethnic jokes made in graphic narratives of the OEF/OIF, along with mockery of language and clothing. Iraqis, particularly, are shown as untrustworthy and tenuous allies, with comics featuring double dealings by the Iraqi leadership, who make impossible demands of U.S. allies and then double-cross the Americans. One *Delta Bravo Sierra* strip, in which the Iraqis are drawn as *keffiyeh*-wearing camels and the Americans are drawn as camouflage-clad dogs (as in "dog-face" soldiers), features Iraqis laughing behind the backs of the Americans as they "agree" to use an American missile defense system only to defend themselves from Iran.[90] Similar accusations of the civilians in both Iraq and Afghanistan are alluded to in cartoon strips showing the locals posing as farmers or retailers while clearly developing IEDs (improvised explosive devices) or carrying weapons,[91] or just trying to con soldiers out of their money. And, indeed, on January 30, 2014, the *New York Times* reported on the misuse of U.S. aid money by Afghanistan.[92] Complications of friend and enemy distinctions were also officially noted in Afghanistan, particularly because of civilian casualties.[93]

The *Doctrine Man* micro-blogging that occurs alongside the comics on Facebook and Twitter feeds makes regular references to "Man Love Thursday," Thursdays being a weekend night in the Afghan calendar wherein same-sex carnal encounters among Muslim men are perceived as a common part of the weekend fun. Homosexuality, in seeming violation of the Koran in countries where Islam is otherwise strictly followed, is often seen as hypocritical and humorous by many U.S. servicepersons deployed to "the sandbox,"[94] and repeated graphic narratives in both *Doctrine Man* and *Power Point Ranger* feature gags about Muslims having same-sex or bestial intercourse.[95] Further commentary on the Muslim worldview and U.S.-Afghanistan and U.S.-Iraq relations is made in a cartoon by John Sheppard, in which bearded, *fez*-wearing men cry, "Take cover, American drones!" at the sight of witches on broomsticks over the horizon[96]; this reflects the role of the United States as the "Great Satan" in the Middle East and hints at the Americans as the enemy—or, more specifically, as evil—while also suggesting that the natives are primitive, backward, or superstitious in their thinking.

Going Native

The lyrics of an American song from the Great War ask, "How ya gonna keep 'em down on the farm, after they've seen Paree? ... They'll never want to see a rake or plow, and who the deuce can parleyvous a cow?"[97] For many of the American doughboys, the War provided them with their first, and perhaps only, opportunity to see the world. It was the first time they met people from outside their hometowns, let alone from outside their country, and many of their graphic narratives reflect their encounters with new cultures, especially that of the French. Butler, Jrs., illustrated records include multiple scenes of American troops adjusting to French ways, such as needing tickets to get bread at cafés, making one alcoholic drink last all day, using liquid saccharine instead of granulated sugar, and eating *cheval* and *escargot*.[98] Other warrior artists also consider what might happen if they took their new European sensibilities back to the United States and try to "parleyvous a cow." The work of Abian Wallgren, in particular, emphasizes the cultural changes with strips about "Yanks on the Rhein"[99] and "When We Take Our French Ways Back Home,"[100] which depict various scenes of Americans speaking French or German badly and in other situations where cultural and linguistic meanings are lost in translation. In a *Hubert* cartoon, American soldiers stationed in England are seen demonstrating stereotyped English and French habits, such as drinking tea, smoking pipes or cigarettes in holders, using monocles, and owning poodles.[101] In the words of World War II veteran and cartoonist Bob Stevens on adjusting to England, "To paraphrase a Churchillian saying, never was so little known by so many about so much ... but we learned, luv, we learned. Oh, how we learned!"[102] The French also learned much about the culture and masculine identities of their American allies.[103] Cartoons from the Pacific and China-Burma-India theaters of World War II and, later, from Vietnam tend to be bit more dubious, and racist, in adapting to native cultures, expressing preferences for a "good old-fashioned waltz" over tribal dances,[104] and claiming that too much time in the local villages result in soldiers with stretched necks and pierced ears,[105] or that too many tours in Vietnam had warriors swinging from trees in loincloths.[106] Such themes continue into the next century, as a cartoon by John Sheppard features an American veteran asking for kimchi-flavored ice cream.[107]

The children of host countries are a continuous focus of both affection and consternation, in both World Wars I and II. In the First World War many cartoonists put their pen to the cause of Europe's war orphans, though they also occasionally chronicled the difference between the cherub-faced youth featured in propaganda and the drinking, smoking, young con-artists they encountered in the streets.[108] In the Second World War, similar "undesirable" characteristics were recorded among the children of Africa and the Pacific, who beg and steal from U.S. servicemen.[109] (Even the adult natives are thought to respond better to money than to kindness.)[110] Such scenes are again noted in Operation Iraqi Freedom, with children getting candy from "the Great Satan."[111] By World War II, the fascination with local cultures was, however, stronger in the African and Pacific theaters than in the European. Indeed, the culture gap between America and the more tribal islands is acutely seen in a *Hubert* strip by Wingert wherein a convoy asks a black-face, spear-carrying native, "Which side of the road do you drive on over here, Jack?" despite there being no road, let alone no vehicles.[112] Muslims are particular oddities to the Americans, especially their habit of watching the servicemen bathe.[113] A similar lack of privacy is also encountered in the Phillipines.[114] Many soldiers, however, are still either enchanted or appalled by the habits of the French and Italians—particularly the women — and language barriers are a problem everywhere, even in England. A *Hubert* cartoon, for example, ironically has an American in a British pub remarking, "Gawsh! Dey shure does talk funny, done'dey?"[115]

The American sense of ethnocentric bewilderment or displacement is expressed by Mauldin's "Willie," as he looks around France and asks, "Did ya ever see so many furriners, Joe?"[116] and by Wingert's Hubert, who asks a British

Fig. 4.2: Examples of graphic narratives expressing ideas of adopting foreign ways during deployment. 1. Abian Wallgren (1918), 2. Frank R. Robinson (1945).

Fig. 4.2-2

"— ABOUT YOUR RUNNING DOWN TO THE NATIVE VILLAGE ALL THE TIME,
MITCHELL —"

—Cpl. Frank R. Robinson

family, "Well, how do you like it over here?"[117] Therefore, a number of cartoons for the soldiers are designed to help the new recruits successfully navigate cultural differences. The army's Information and Education Branch issued illustrated guides to "save our wandering GIs embarrassing global mistakes like offering a Moslem a can of Spam."[118] Following World War II, many American warriors discovered they had a lot to learn about the "strange and unusual country" of Japan[119]—especially if they wanted to successfully date its women, who they found to be sexy and beautiful, yet mercenary,[120] a theme that continues into present-day comics.[121] Again, the military's graphic artists contemplate what might happen when they take their newfound foreign ways back home and wear *geta* and *kimonos* and ask their families to eat on the floor.[122] Despite the charm of foreign cultures, there is also a sense of superiority. For example, a *Sad Sack* comic shows allies in the World War II Pacific theater talking cheerfully with one another—the American Sad Sack and an Asian with prominent buck fangs—until they pass by, when each makes a "pee-ew" gesture at the other's back.[123]

Strangers Among Us

Enemy images are legitimized stereotypes used for sanctioning and promoting killing and developing callous, bureaucratized violence. Heterostereotypes of animosities within a society do not carry the same weight of official authority, but they are developed from the same foundation: cultural prejudices.[124] Racism in the ranks makes infrequent but persistent appearances throughout the centuries of military comics. Its primary target is blacks, though Native Americans, the Polish, the Mexicans, the Indian, and, in the post–Vietnam era, Asians are also maligned. The author of the currently active *Terminal Lance* comic strip explains on his blog:

> Race is typically a hot issue in the Marine Corps. It's always at the top of the conversation amongst the many people-circles that inhabit the field, the tip of the comedy stick if you will. Making fun of someone's race is one of the easiest things to do, as its [sic] not exactly something you can hide from.[125]

Terminal Lance has two comics, among its first hundred, that deal specifically with race in the Marine Corps. One is on "playing the race card" and features a black man refusing to take tires to the motor pool because the Michelin Man, drawn here with a Klan hood, is white, though tires are black.[126] The other comic features an officer picturing an Asian Marine as a "Charlie" peasant.[127] Racism against the natives of a country is also present in the OEF/OIF comics, as suggested by the *Power Point Ranger* strip that shows a large, brutish American threatening ally "Haji," who is Indian rather than Arab.[128] (Similar confusion is expressed in World War I comics, wherein Americans could not tell the difference between enemy Turks and the ally Moroccans.)[129] A combination of native and foreign racism may be interpreted in the *On Cyber Patrol* training comic strips that started around 2009. Using a good-versus-evil plotline, the majority of the cyber-defenders among the U.S. forces are white (and male), such as the strip's hero Sgt. Firewall, whereas the villainous hackers are non-white, such as the strip's villain International Cyber Criminal. Going back to earlier conflicts, Shel Silverstein hints at racism in the ranks during the Korea era by showing an officer who cannot pronounce the name "Zwntszokoski"[130] and a private named "Hakim" who uses a genie in a lamp to do his latrine duty.[131]

A native of Arizona, and the son of an artilleryman who had fought in the Apache Wars, Mauldin's[132] World War II comics frequently poke fun at American Indians. In the early "Willie and Joe" comics, "Willie" speaks in broken "pidgin" English and considers a loincloth and headdress his civilian clothes.[133]

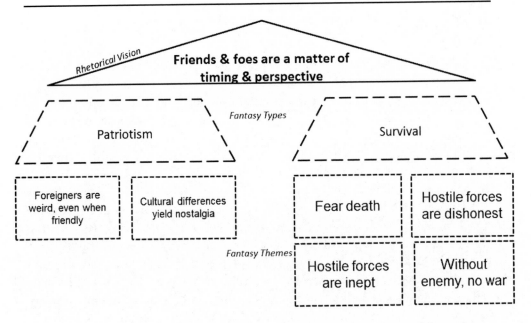

Fig. 4.3: Rhetorical vision of enemies and allies as expressed in warrior graphic narratives.

Later on, Mauldin celebrates the participation of Native Americans in the war effort,[134] as a Nazi laments, "Vot good iss it for der fuehrer to tell us god iss on our side? Der Americans haff got all der Indians!"[135] (In his postwar comics, Mauldin even comments on the taking of land from the Native Americans as ironic, given popular talk of isolationism.)[136] Night camouflage is compared to minstrel-show black-face makeup in a *Private Breger in Britain* cartoon,[137] and Sumner Grant depicts a black island native as wearing a yellow plaid zoot suit.[138] World War I features numerous comics commenting on the "Coons" that Americans encounter among ally forces. In *Camion Cartoons*, by Kirkland Day, for example, one drawing proclaims, "The Red Hats Worn by the Senegalese are Going to Make our Coons Green with Envy."[139] Another relies on particularly racist attitudes, as a black soldier explains, "Cap'n I'd done like to be xcused from this yer drill. My feets am so big dat by de time I git dem under control de company am where day am while I'se where I was!"[140] It is worth noting that black colonial people who volunteered for English service in World War I also faced racial hostility from their own countrymen,[141] though this does not strongly appear in the graphic narratives from the United Kingdom. Back to the American Civil War, Union battlefield artists, especially those fighting, express both their admiration and their reservations about the first black troops—an anomaly to witness in person.[142] "George" is less optimistic about the black troops, depicting the "First North Carolina 'Kullered' Regiment" as absurd-looking and bumbling.[143]

Debriefing

The rhetorical vision of enemies and allies developed in these comics is that, for service members, lines between friends and foes are often blurry, depending on issues of timing and perspective, both practically and conceptually. This vision comprises fantasy types focused on survival and nostalgia or patriotism. Figure 4.3 illustrates how the ideas explored in this chapter, such as cultural and racial differences and the survival instinct, build the somewhat ambiguous vision of good and evil. Overall, there is a feeling of dislike towards anyone—or anything—that jeopardizes life or makes it needlessly or excessively unpleasant, but The Enemy as The Enemy garners only apathetic responses of fury, fear, or fellowship. While bigoted expressions—whether racist, sexist, or simply ethnocentrist—exist, it is not clear that these expressions are always motivated by hostility. Instead, they may be motivated by homesickness, confusion, training, dread, or, particularly in regards to stereotypes in graphic narratives, exigency. Enemies are political creations, and the most pressing concern in combat is survival, not politics. Outside of combat, comfort and duty take precedence. In the U.S. all-volunteer army, enemies have seemingly become more political and personal to military members (even if the details about who, precisely, the enemy is are not always clear), as evidenced by American feelings of disgust and distrust toward people in Afghanistan and Iraq in the 21st century, especially as engagements in these countries extended beyond a decade.

5

Drawn Behind the Lines
Military Geography

One day it started raining, and it didn't quit for four months. We been through every kind of rain there is. Little bitty stingin' rain, and big ol' fat rain. Rain that flew in sideways. And sometimes rain even seemed to come straight up from underneath. Shoot, it even rained at night.—*Forrest Gump*

Culture and identity are deeply rooted in place, influenced by historical, geographic, and social conditions.[1] Place and space are both physical and symbolic entities. Place has a geographic location, with distinct, though elastic boundaries. It has a physical form compiled of natural or artificial objects, worked by people, at its location, which can be understood according to their manifest or latent functions. Place is interpreted and invested with meaning that captures perceived histories, ideals, dangers, or identities, and influences social behavior by reflecting cultural values and social organization.[2] Space has been alternatively perceived as an area that lacks these features and as a sphere of "coexisting heterogeneity," continuously under construction as the product of interactions.[3] Like place, space is humanized and given symbolic meaning through the experience of human purposes, and specific social groups ascribe particular values and meanings to space, such as existential dimensions of security/stress, stimulus/ennui, or status/stigma.[4]

"Militarism and military activities create spaces, places, environments and landscapes with references to a distinct moral order."[5] Military geographies are about the material and discursive control of land, involving economics, information, social order, space, environments, and landscapes. A military geography "concentrates on the influence of physical and cultural environments over political-military policies, plans, programs and combat/support operations of all types in global, regional, and local contexts."[6] The cultural factors of military geography include race, ethnicity, religions, population, social structures, language, industries, transportation, telecommunication, and military installations. Socially, place and space are significant to the military in relation to the separation of the armed forces from civilian society. As a sacrificial class—"professionals in violence"[7]—the violence they perpetuate is sequestered from the larger community.[8] They are the border-crossers, traversing the divides that distinguish the military from the civilian sphere, the borders of nations, and the boundaries of life and death. "Since violence is contagious, death-touching soldiers must be set apart. Living separately, dressing differently, they observe an ascetic vocation."[9] For example, though modern American military life resembles a middle-class existence, bases themselves tend to be in remote locations, mirroring but separated from American society.[10]

The armed forces are expressly prepared for employment in particular environments, and function below capacity outside of those environments without costly and time-consuming transitions of training, equipment, and supplies. The military operating environment comprises the physical and cultural landscape that shapes battle. The physical factors of military geography include spatial relationships, topography, geology, vegetation, bodies of water, climate/weather, daylight/darkness, and gravity/magnetism. These factors are militarily important only when related to the probable effects on a military mission. Additionally, the cultural factors of geography often introduce significant inconsistencies in areas that are physically homogenous, particularly in areas where the control of territory is connected to larger narratives of identity politics and ideology.[11] Military personnel are, therefore, trained in the art of fieldcraft—survival based on continuous analysis in regards to critical or key terrain, obstacles, cover and concealment, observation and fields of fire, and avenues of approach. Spatial relationships are the most fundamental geographic feature, involving location, size, shape and nature of land areas; here is the stage for war-theater and military pageants. Strategists see the military landscape as composed of mountains, valleys, plateaus, and plains, classified according to surface configurations, climactic labels, elevations, temperature gradients, or spheres. Frontline soldiers, trained to see a landscape in three dimensions, recognize its two-dimensional representations and understand how its elements relate as dangers and protections; they will describe the landscape as rocks, gullies, river banks, dirt, and mud, that promote or hinder comfort and convenience.[12] As a result of the lived interactions with geography, combatants often produce informal maps or representations before, during, and after a campaign, offering a first-person view of battle different from official strategy diagrams.[13]

In warfare space and time interact. "The time of day influences the combat by the difference between day and night; but the influence naturally extends further than merely to the limits of these divisions."[14] Once confined to the Earth's surface in a two-dimensional field, the advent of aircraft introduced a third dimension to war, and, later, a fourth dimension appeared when battles expanded to cyberspace. These added dimensions

> multiplied the complexity of military operations. The development of combat power *in time* and space became a perplexing new art…. But in reality, time is not the last or latest dimension. It is the first and primary dimension that commanders and leaders have had to struggle with from the dawn of history. Length, width, and height do not exist if they have no reality in time.[15]

Temporal considerations influence weapon design, strategy development, doctrine formation, force organization, and training. Effective use or even manipulation of time can overturn spatial disadvantages, and control of duration, frequency, and sequence is arguably more important to military phenomenon than length, width, or height.[16] This space-time combat perspective fits the social-historical understanding of space as geography blended with chronology, wherein space is a region that is traversed, upon which the Other are mere phenomena occupying the surface to be controlled or removed.[17]

In sequential art, space and time have both narrative and genre elements. Little attention is given to scene or place in comics studies, other than an understanding that

> the broader philosophical implication of many comics, to one extent or another is: *there is another world, which is this world.* The places that cartoonists draw are very different from the ones where readers live; every element of the comics world is created in the artist's hands. The cartoonist's image-world is a metaphorical representation of our own, though, and it can be mapped onto ours. It can even be more meaningful in some ways than an accurate depiction of our image world—the same sort of relationship that prose fiction has to reportage.[18]

Linguistically, spatial relationships are coded in six key ways: deictic shifts; distinctions between figure and ground; notions of regions, landmarks, and paths; differentiation between topological and projective locations; motion; and distinctions between the noun-based *what* and the adverb and preposition-based *where.*[19] In graphic narratives, place may also be anthropomorphized: "Links between body and location seem particularly strong in the context of the superhero, for example with reference to figures such as the Swamp Thing, who is a literal embodiment of his environment."[20] Comics can also be reduced to the spatio-topical parameters of the panels or frames. The frames give form and structure to the narrative. The margins, or gutters, often represent the passage of time, with a succession of frames establishing a rhythm.[21] The pictures and the gaps between them create an "illusion of time" and words represent sounds "which can only exist *in* time."[22] Time is represented and interpreted spatially in comics, with dialogue and action subtly out of sync in what artist Jimmy Johnson has called "comic strip space-time continuum."[23]

Weathering It Out

Preeminent Prussian military theorist Karl Von Clausewitz stated in his seminal *On War*, "Rarely has the weather any decisive influence [on combat strategy], and it is mostly only by fog that it plays a part."[24] The evidence offered in warriors' graphic narratives, however, suggests that the weather does have marked influence on the experience of combat and other military maneuvers. In fact, the military has a saying, which appears in a couple of the comics, "If it ain't rainin' we ain't trainin'!"[25] Indeed, rain has a remarkable *dampening* effect on all aspects of military life. Writing during the Civil War, "George" pities himself for having to stand guard in the rain.[26] Rain is so prevalent in the World War I experience that a Bruce Bairnsather cartoon depicts the artist on leave, recreating the atmosphere of the front for artistic inspiration, by being pelted with wind from a bellows and water from a hose.[27] Rains come on all fronts in all wars, however; so much rain that even carrier pigeons resort to dropping their messages into mail boxes[28]; so much rain that trees "leak"[29] and boots need be kept upside down over night[30]; so much rain that graphic narratives show the men marching under water while the drill sergeant shouts commands from a rowboat[31]; so much rain that it takes the shine off of boots[32]; so much rain that it falls from a cloudless sky[33]; so much rain that the animals begin lining up two-by-two.[34] It does not, however, dare to rain on generals.[35] With so much moisture, dry socks are a luxury. Bill Mauldin's Willie tells Joe, while they sit in a marsh, "Joe, yestiddy ya saved me life an' I swore I'd pay ya back. Here's me last pair o' dry socks."[36] Even a modern-day comic ironically notes a soldier standing knee-deep in water who is glad he "put on dry socks this morning."[37]

Some rain, or its frozen counterpart, snow, is perceived as a feature of the host country or of a particular base. Abian "Wally" Wallgren notes that "General Orders in Sunny France" include doing "acquatics," illustrated as marching in the rain.[38] *Hubert* observes the relativity of weather and notes that what Americans consider heavy rain, the British consider "rawther damp."[39] During the last years of the Cold War, American service in Germany was known for the wet weather. *Lt. Kadish* calls Germany "the land of castles and fests and beer and wurst and … rain."[40] Fort Drum in northern New York State has earned several graphic homages to its reputation for excessive snow and cold (a reputation that the author, who lives north of the base, can confirm is well deserved), including references in *Opet's Odyssey*,[41] *Power Point Ranger*,[42] and *Doctrine Man*.[43]

The occasional soldier chooses to see the rain cloud's silver lining. "Private Breger," bivouacking in high wind and rain, comments, "Boy, are we lucky we weren't sent to some hot and dusty place!"[44] Rain is also particularly welcomed by dirty soldiers in need of clean water. During World War II, reporters were awed by the ingenuity of Wacs in the Pacific who set water-filled helmets in the sun to warm for bathing,[45] an event captured by Vic Herman, with *Winnie the WAC* soaking in a bubble bath with her helmet as a tub.[46] In *Private Breger in Britain*, the private similarly creates a bubble bath by the rain mixing with soap in his rucksack.[47] And Vernon Grant's characters in *Stand-By One!* pray, "Oh mighty monsoon, daily washer of soiled soldiers, ... Do yer stuff for Vietnam's dirtiest fire-team!"[48]

Colder Than Hell

Rain is only one source of warriors' weather-related consternation. A Mauldin graphic narrative features a guard sweating profusely in the sun, being soaked in the rain, and shivering in the snow, until he punches his sergeant and happily lands himself *in* the guardhouse, instead of on post outside it.[49] And "Sad Sack" demonstrates the weather-related catch–22 of serving in the tropics, where one is either drenched in rain or drenched in sweat.[50] Similarly, the *New Sad Sack* goes from trembling in winter weather to trembling from contracting malaria in the tropics.[51] Temperature, or at least uncomfortable temperature, is such a prominent part of the military experience that it is often personified. Snowmen are a recurring image in the comics. Both Mauldin in World War II and Mark Baker in the OEF/OIF era suggest the use of snowman decoys to post guard on cold nights so the soldiers can go inside.[52] *Winnie the WAC* builds a snowman for a date because, she says, "Well—it's a man!"[53] Other cartoons also hint at the lifelike qualities of snowmen, particularly for warriors who may feel as cold as snowmen themselves, such as the poor World War I recruit who dreams he turns to a block of ice at 30°F,[54] and Robert Bindig's cartoon thought-bubble that develops icicles on guard duty during the Second World War.[55] A cartoon from Camp Hale, Colorado, where the 10th Mountain Division ski troops were trained in World War II, has soldiers wondering if a snowman on the mountainside is one of their men.[56] And a cartoon from Korea depicts a drunken soldier asking a snowman, "How many points you got?"[57] Cold is also graphically captured by the use of frozen stench lines (or what Mort Walker refers to as *emanata*,[58] visual cues "emanating" from the object to reveal internal conditions) coming from a trashcan; with the insignia of the 45th Infantry Division shivering in a Pine Camp, New York, Christmas; as men being frozen in formation[59]; and with the appearance of penguins.[60] Heat, on the other hand, at least in the desert warfare of OIF, is personified by Satan when temperatures in Iraq exceed 100° Fahrenheit.[61] One cartoon describes the desert experience as sticking one's "head in the oven and bak[ing] at 400 degrees for 12 hours."[62] Will Eisner also points out, "In maintenance, WEATHER is 'big'! So, get wise to the needs of your rig. Learn that metal or oil, Can be brittle or spoil. Be bold in the cold.... YOU dig??"[63]

The graphic narratives also illustrate the measures to which warriors go, or can only dream of, to combat the extreme temperatures—such as chipping in for an air conditioner with vents routed to all the pup tents,[64] or "on a 98-degree day in the Indian Ocean" retrieving the snowball "hid away 28,000 miles ago."[65] The American experience of winter in the Great War, wherein the only available fuel was an armload of green saplings, there were no gloves, and the only shoes available were three sizes too small for frozen feet, prompted a comparison to the winter at Valley Forge[66]—though trudging through bad weather was not a problem if the destination was a woman.[67] World War II graphic narratives see soldiers hugging warm artillery barrels[68] or walking in the warm exhaust behind tanks, warming their hands over cigars, or developing heat rash from wearing too many layers of clothes.[69] (Though for one soldier, trudging through knee-deep snow and high wind is less of an ordeal than the idea of being home for the birth of his baby.[70]) *Leatherhead in Korea* sleeps upside-down in his sleeping bag to keep warm.[71] In fact, Korea was so cold that cartoonists occasionally fantasize about using the weather as a weapon—such as turning puffs of frozen, icicle-like, breath into knives[72] or developing a "top secret Browny copter" that could pour water on the enemy, capturing them in blocks of ice to be picked up with a crane.[73] Other weather conditions also urge creativity among warriors. Strong winds are occasionally referenced by artists and though some, such as typhoons, pose dangers of causing deadly projectiles or forcing men overboard a ship,[74] wind can be sporting. Mauldin features troops marching into heavy winds, leaning with effort to make progress as the ranking officer proclaims, "Buck up, men—think of the fun we'll have coming back!"[75] "Sgt. Murphy" highlights this idea of fun by windsurfing in a sandstorm.[76]

Over Hill, Dale and Dusty Trail

A few graphic narratives deal directly with fieldcraft, particularly map-reading and distances travelled. A Vietnam cartoon by Jake Schuffert represents a Department of Defense briefing in which a general states, "If we defoliate, gentlemen, we're in trouble—it will turn the country into a desert, and we're not equipped nor trained for desert warfare."[77] Poor *Sad Sack* gets himself lost, even with careful attention to a map,[78] and a modern-day recruit is told that a globe is not acceptable in the map-reading course.[79] A study of letters from war demonstrates the importance of distance and space estimations in warriors' recounting of their experiences, especially in battle.[80] This attention to distance is also found in a few of the graphic narratives. The most notable of these is throughout the World War I work of Albany Butler, Jr., who has multiple scenes that include distance markers, in kilometers—each one in the shape of a tombstone.[81] One of "Private Murphy's" Laws is, "It doesn't matter if you're moving 1,000 meters or 10,000 ... It's gonna take all night!"[82] This observation points to the problems many warriors experience with the combination of geography, strategy, and leadership. Gen. John Vessey, Jr., former chairman of the Joint Chiefs of Staff, stated:

> Geographic influences were omnipresent during my service as an enlisted soldier in the Tunisian desert ... the Italian mountains ... and ... the jungles in Vietnam. Those experiences, which were very personal, had a great deal to do with the health and comfort of my comrades and myself; they affected our casualty rates and often posed more formidable challenges than the enemies we faced. I often wondered if we were "victims" of geography or "victims" of the higher command's appreciation for geography.[83]

These graphic narratives suggest that Vessey's experiences battling geography, sometimes more than the enemy, were not, and are not, uncommon. Nor was the experience of victimization at the hand of the higher command in relation to geography. Continuing the assault on officers, several cartoonists lampoon the excessive discomfort and unnecessary work warriors are put to just so officers are not inconvenienced by the weather. From World War I, Butler, Jr., records "General Summerall stalled in a snowdrift, being rescued by one of his Aides."[84] From World War II, Mauldin presents a scene of soldiers digging through waist-deep snow to get a truck out of a garage only to be told by telephone, "Division says never mind—th' colonel got tired o' waitin' an' carried th' bedroll next door himself."[85] *Private Breger in Britain* carries his colonel on his shoulders through water,[86] and, from Korea, Norval Packwood shows the Sisyphean work of a soldier digging a mountain path through the snow to the helicopter pad, clearing the pad, waiting for the officer to be dropped off ... and then having to dig the path back again because the wind from helicopter blades blew the snow back.[87]

Topographically, steep mountains and cliffs are of particular concern in warrior graphic narratives. Rock formations and hard ground introduce multiple complications to battle tactics,[88] and the risks documented in the graphic narratives include making driving difficult, as in the Alps during World War I[89]; hindering mobility, particularly with heavy equipment during World War II and Korea[90]—as one Mauldin character proclaims, "George Fielding Eliot is right. Firepower SHOULD be sacrificed for mobility"[91]; and reducing chances to stay low and take cover.[92] Another troublesome feature of topography is topsoil. All that rain the men complain about contributes to one of the most prevalent topographical foes: mud. Mud is particularly troublesome in the trenches of both world wars. During the Great War, the coming of spring meant that

Fig. 5.1: Examples of graphic narratives illustrating trench warfare. 1. Abian Wallgren (1918), 2. Frank Dunne (1918), 3. Kevin Klein and Todd Hoelmer (1991).

trenches would be flooded with water, mud, and rats.[93] Bairnsfather wryly comments that the water in the trenches was so high that there was danger of submarine torpedoes, and that the shortage of troops could be overcome by simply combing the mud for bodies (which was, in reality, filled with casualties of not only combat but also of drowning).[94] Trench warfare presented soldiers with the unappealing options of wallowing in mud and water, making movement and sleep difficult; or standing up, getting out and risking being shot.[95] And ultimately, trenches and foxholes were better than the alternative, as repeatedly suggested in dark-humor comics with men piled on top of one another in holes, shells falling all around.[96] Mud and water trigger "the Venetian walk" according Ted Stanley in World War I,[97] and several of Mauldin's World War II cartoons feature soldiers with mud-caked boots. In one such scene, Joe observes, "It aint that I mind a fifty pound pack, a ten pound rifle, an' twenty pounds o' assorted clothes an' equipment.... But when I gotta carry th' road too, I'm thru!"[98] Later, Joe decides that when he returns to civilian life he is "gonna be a perfessor on types o' European soil."[99] Oftentimes, mud is the only available means of bathing, with foxholes humorously described as "private room and bath."[100] In the Asian theaters of Korea and Vietnam, muddy waters are found not in trenches but in rice paddies through which warriors wade up to their shoulders[101] and into which men disappear if they step into a hole.[102] Vernon Grant has one of his characters solve the rice paddy problem by strapping *nón lá* (Vietnamese bamboo peasant hats) to the bottoms of his feet, allowing him to walk on the water.[103] And again, artists comment on the absurdities of command in such unfavorable conditions. A Shel Silverstein cartoon has a sergeant asking a private, both standing in ankle-deep water, "Be honest with me Parks ... Did you, or did you not shine your boots this morning?"[104]

Fig. 5.1-2

Bluey: "I'll shoot the next flamin' Tommy who asks why do they call us 'Diggers.'"

Fig. 5.1-3

DIG IN

Digging foxholes is hard work, but
they serve as protection from the enemy.

There are, nonetheless, times when warriors prefer mud to the alternatives of snow and ice (Willie and Joe, hunkered down at Alsace, fondly recall the "warm, soft mud last summer")[105] or sand, gravel, and dust. A cartoon by Daryl Talbot, for example, focuses on a soldier with a handful of sand, observing, "You know? I miss mud!"[106] In Korea, Mauldin observes that "even the mud is dusty."[107] Desert warfare has numerous geographic challenges: diverse cultural and political landscapes, vast distances, high mountains, caves, river systems, and, a particular nuisance to warriors, abrasive topsoil. Blowing sand and dust, particularly during *shamals,* is not only an uncomfortable annoyance but also reduces visibility and degrades optical information acquisition, makes air maneuvers dangerous, and damages aircraft components, weapons systems, and communication equipment.[108] Several warrior artists depict *shamals* in OEF/OIF, including Steve Opet, with a cartoon that shows a person completely covered in sand to the point of being nearly indistinguishable from the background[109]; Mark Baker, with cartoons demonstrating a comparison to an Arizona dust storm[110] and a soldier being trapped in a port-a-john by sand drifts[111]; Jeff Bacon, with a weather forecast of "partly sandy becoming mostly sandy ... with isolated sandstorms here and here"[112]; and Doctrine Man, who observes that "dust storms blow ... so to speak" while featuring a makeshift balaclava made from (dirty) underwear.[113] (Some dust-related humor is also found during the Korean conflict.)[114] Like the cold and heat, sand also inspires creativity. *Opet's Odyssey* comics have 10th Mountain soldiers returning to their snowy, ski-patrol routes by making "gravel angels" in the winter and using snowshoes to walk more easily on gravel. And in Talbot's *Laughing in Cadence,* a warrior hooks up a vacuum hose to a jet engine to clean the sand out of his tent—which is pitched in the desert.[115] A similarly futile battle against terrain is waged in the Pacific Theater of World War II by the "Sad Sack," who chops the weeds and bamboo around his tent just to have it return immediately.[116]

Revealing Concealment

The land itself is not the only geographical hazard warriors face; they also have to be concerned with what it harbors. Several accounts highlight predatory creatures encountered during combat and maneuvers. These beasts may exist only in the imagination of warriors, which is also where they pose the greatest threat. "Bogie rumors" often spread during wartime, involving fearful and fanciful tales about the enemy and its terrain as expressions of warrior anxieties.[117] A Vernon Grant graphic narrative from Vietnam even suggests that such tales are passed from one generation to another in the military, with a cartoon of two men seated on the ground, a monster creeping up behind them, as one reads a letter: "Is my Uncle a joker! ... He claims during World War II some shaggy Monster was hopping islands right along with his unit and bugging him!"[118] In the Middle East conflicts of the 21st century, camel spiders are a popular focus for bogie rumors, with stories about their size and aggressiveness offering frightful entertainment to troops.[119] Such dread is expressed in *Power Point Ranger,* wherein a soldier bombs a spider hole in Afghanistan to kill an actual spider—

"a *Taliban* spider. Nasty."[120] Octopuses capable of boarding a life raft, or even manning a helicopter,[121] and man-eating sharks are the fears of men at sea. During World War II a series of comics were used to train the men in "shark sense,"[122] and more recently the irony of being told to mind the shark watch and, simultaneously, enjoy a swim call is noted by Jeff Bacon.[123] Even as early as the Civil War, infantryman "George" draws a man-eating alligator in Carolina,[124] and a 2009 comic by Talbot shows a brawny recruit presenting an alligator to his drill sergeant—who tells him, "No pets allowed."[125] Troops deployed to jungles are warned of "Ann"—the *Anopheles* mosquito, whose "trade is dishing out Malaria"[126] and who manages to circumvent insect netting.[127] Twenty-foot-long snakes[128] that can wind around a man,[129] swallow him whole,[130] or creep up on him in sleep[131] are the bogie-creatures of Vietnam and the World War II Pacific and China-Burma-India theaters. Sumner Grant, a World War II soldier who served in Panama and Japan and illustrated the cartoon strip "FUBAR" in *The Forty-Niner*, sent several cartoons to his fiancée, drawn on envelopes, of a bugle-boy snake-charmer,[132] and Shel Silverstein, during his Korean-era service, imagines a rattlesnake as an inspection surprise for a drill sergeant.[133] Mark Baker worries about a snake biting his nose.[134] Snakes also overlap into military "pipe-dream rumors" which express wishful thinking.[135] "Snake eaters" is the nickname given to Special Ops forces, based on a 1961 demonstration by the Green Berets for President John F. Kennedy in which troops caught, prepared, and ate a snake.[136] Some cartoons express the awe of regular troops for the Special Ops and hint at the rumors, such as snake-eating, that surround these warriors. One such graphic account is of a bereted man with a wiggling snake tail hanging out of his mouth, and a soldier wearing a common camouflage cap remarks, "I thought it was an urban legend!"[137] Another shows a soldier using an air-sickness bag while watching a comrade catch, kill, and eat a snake while standing chest-deep in water.[138]

Real-life monsters are not the only thing that a landscape may hide. Topography and military tactics intersect through the use of camouflage, a topic of reverence and delight for many warriors. Foxholes and trenches may be a key source of concealment and protection from the enemy, and are the focus of not a few graphic narratives from the 1890s to the 1990s,[139] including an Australian comic that references the Australian troops' nickname of "diggers"[140]; but camouflage and disguises are the source of much more amusement. In a cartoon from World War I, Bairnsfather develops the idea of a sniper disguised as a tree to elude German pursuers. In 1927, this idea is recreated by Charlie Chaplin in the film *Shoulder Arms*,[141] and tree-costume camouflage appears again in *Private Breger in Britain*, in which the private has the misfortune of German soldiers attempting to carve their names on him[142]; in *Winnie the WAC*, who is watched while undressing by multiple sets of eyes peering from tree knotholes[143]; in

"Willie and Joe," who report no sign of the enemy, just "trees moving across the horizon at 50 mph"[144] and who have the misfortune of taking refuge in a tree that walks away[145]; and in *Cartoons for Fighters* as advice to "blend in with your background" while patrolling, with an image of a tree leaning nonchalantly on an adjacent tree.[146] A 2009 cartoon offers a Christmas-season variation on the tree-disguise theme, showing a soldier with pine boughs strapped to his helmet and a string of lights wrapped around his body.[147] Some warrior artists had even more creative camouflaging ideas during World War II, including dressing as a baby eagle to snipe from a cliff side, masquerading paratroopers as angels to deceive the enemy, tricking Germans by dressing as wood nymphs or gremlins,[148] using a wife's flowered hat as jungle camouflage,[149] engaging in psychological warfare by wearing Superman costumes,[150] and pretending to be a cow.[151] Even into the 20th century warrior artists consider camo alternatives—such as face-paint that looks like a skull "to strike fear into the heart of the enemy,"[152] scarecrows in a field,[153] "urban camo" that looks like bricks,[154] and "garrison camouflage" that simply involves the carrying of a clipboard.[155] Since 2002, concerns about camouflage, at least for American troops, have been far less fanciful, as the military has cycled through a variety of patterns while trying to fulfill competing needs of effectiveness and distinctiveness. The general perspective of the warriors themselves is that most of the patterns have been useless and dangerous.[156] The variety and perceived absurdity of the changes is lampooned by John Holmes in *Power Point Ranger* with a cartoon showing three warriors dressed in "multicam" camouflage for deployment to Africa: One is in leopard print, the next in zebra print, and the last in tiger print.[157] *Terminal Lance*'s Maximilian Uriarte takes a shot at digital camouflage with Marines of the future, who wear "digis" as historical dress uniforms, wondering, "Were they fighting wars in a *videogame*?"[158] John Sheppard offers "an alternative to traditional arctic camo" with reindeer antlers and a red nose.[159]

There is one more, very important, thing that landscape conceals—warriors relieving themselves when there are no latrines. A set of German illustrations by Albert Heim in the Great War regularly include references to toilet paper,[160] but it is not until World War II that comics truly begin addressing the logistics of toilet habits during war: "Soldiers routinely defecated in their foxholes or risked exposing themselves to fire. [A Mauldin] cartoon from May 5, 1944, is perhaps the only reference to this common indignity published in the American media during the war."[161] This cartoon is of a soldier climbing out of a foxhole under fire commenting that he wishes he "wasn't housebroke." Since World War II, bathroom humor in the American comics has become more prominent,[162] with a number of graphic narratives featuring warriors defecating in the field. Mark Baker's "Pvt. Murphy," for example, is seen going into the trees with a roll of toilet paper to "rendezvous with destiny" and seated among tall weeds reading

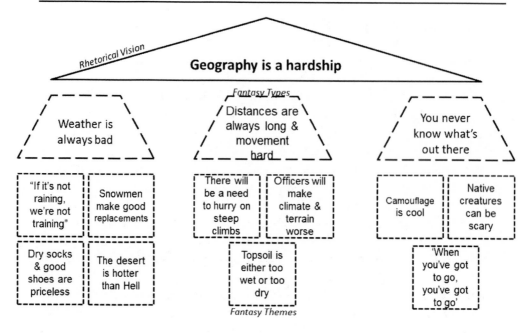

Fig. 5.2: Rhetorical vision of climate and terrain as expressed in warrior graphic narratives.

a newspaper with a shovel nearby.[163] In reference to criticisms of gender equality in the U.S. military, a *Power Point Ranger* comic illustrates concerns about urinating in the field. The graphic narrative features two male soldiers, backs to the reader, pants lowered to reveal the upper buttocks, standing behind two yellow puddles. A female soldier stands off to the side asking them to hurry up because she also needs "to piss."[164]

Love It or Leave It

In World War I, Albert Heim, commissioned by German Lieut-Gen Theodor von Wundt, "turned much of his artistic talent to creating more lighthearted vistas rather than the horrors of war,"[165] but generally, the land or location itself tends to provoke a love/hate relationship among warriors. Differences in countries and cultures tend to be compared hierarchically,[166] and homesickness can provoke negative feelings about the region of deployment. A New Zealand illustration from France in the Great War depicts a warrior, standing in the ever-present rain, looking at a street sign for "Rue Le Soliel" (*soleil*, perhaps ironically, means "sun") and "Rue des Choux," observing in a bilingual pun, "I never rued anything so much in all me blinkin' life as when I landed in this -------- place!"[167] Cartoons by Roger Baker, a Marine serving in Korea, conflate the enemy with the enemy territory, as seen in a montage of "Sketches of Korea" that include "A Gook" and a "Typical 'Gook House,'" as well as "'Papasan' King of the Rice Paddies" and a steep, baren, snowcapped mountain labeled, *"This is Ko-Re-A!"*[168] Oftentimes, too, warriors cannot appreciate the offerings of a country while engaged in combat. Mauldin's "Willie and Joe" remark that a picturesque French village has to be "either enemy or off limits,"[169] and *Leatherhead in Korea* notes, with characters driving a Jeep through heavy fire, "This here is right pretty country … first chance you get, take a look at it."[170] Mark Baker's "Pvt. Murphy" is far less impressed with the Middle East under any circumstances, disliking Baghdad even from a distance[171]—echoing an anti–France cartoon from World War II[172]—and commenting twice on garbage and pollution of the region,[173] as, too, does *Opet's Odyssey*.[174]

Debriefing

The rhetorical vision of military geography is one of hardship, with the climate and terrain often acting as enemy combatants. As General Vessey said, geographic influences have much to do with health, comfort, and survival, and troops, therefore, may feel victimized by geographic experiences.[175] This vision is supported by the fantasy types of bad weather conditions, difficult movement across long distances, and concealed dangers. Figure 5.2 illustrates how the fantasy themes outlined above, such as excessive rain, painful cold, hellish heat, irritating topsoils, camouflage, and bogie creatures, build these fantasy types and the rhetorical vision of geographic challenges. These themes are more likely to be portrayed by warrior artists through anthropomorphism, *emanata,* and *mayhemia* (visual cues of mayhem wrought on comic characters[176]) than through linguistic cues, emphasizing that geography is something that is experienced, or that "happens to" the warriors, and that it is an external force, such as an enemy, that must be confronted, or at least endured. This is made evident by a *Sad Sack* calendar in *Yank Magazine* that depicts the year as a sequence of weather to be managed—snow to clear, sun-dried dust to sweep, and rain-soaked mud to shovel.[177] Additionally, the attention to the details of climate and terrain in the graphic narratives aligns with military training in fieldcraft, which instructs warriors in attention to their surroundings and ways of managing the physical setting of maneuvers. In comparison to the enemy fantasies, discussed previously, geography, as another obstacle to survival, is often more vilified than human combatants, who are more likely to evoke sympathy from warrior artists.

6

Sex(es) in Battle
Gender and Sexuality

Nobody will ever win the battle of the sexes. There's just too much fraternizing with the enemy.—Henry Kissinger

During the Great War, countries that suffered heavy casualties, such as England, began recruiting women for combat service roles such as cooks,[1] or for temporary clerical work in army Pay Department offices.[2] In the early years of U.S. involvement in World War II, five female corps of the American military branches were established,[3] and as early as September 1942, polls indicated tremendous support for drafting unmarried women into military service, though the reality of recruitment was not as favorable.[4] Nursing was not considered a proper job for young ladies because of the menial cleaning tasks, the necessity of seeing men naked, and the knowledge of inappropriate topics such as venereal disease—and military nursing was even more distressing to families of young women.[5] Women interested in nursing or in flying could not always afford the training required as a prerequisite for service. Others found better pay and more satisfaction working in defense plants; they could not only help the war effort but could also meet their new financial responsibilities and enjoy more personal freedom than their enlisted sisters. Some were generally uninterested in undergoing the physical demands of military training and service, only to end up doing clerical or domestic work; many knew their skills were likely to be underutilized as babysitters, personal servants, or "mop commandos."[6]

The most pervasive challenge to female military recruitment, however, was public opinion. Women's families and sweethearts often disapproved of the independence and risk involved with military service. Churches denounced women's military service as antithetical and disruptive to Christian teachings. Many, males and females alike, did not believe that women were capable of military duty and would be a potentially dangerous detriment to the armed forces.

Because the primary function of the women's corps was to undertake a support role and desk duties, allowing more men to fight, some families of servicemen were angry that the women's corps put more of their sons and husbands on the frontlines. Some feared for the safety of women, because the recruits were stepping outside the protection of men. Others were worried that military training for women would disrupt the entire gendered structure of home and family, of politics, and of the economy.[7] At the least, the presence of women has disrupted the hypermasculine, sexualized, folk culture of the military that long gendered weaponry and sexed warfare.[8]

Over the years, the role of women in the military has changed—with variations in each force and each country. In general, women have moved from noncombatant roles, to combat service, to combat support, to combat, though different countries still have policies of total exclusion, partial exclusion/inclusion, or total inclusion.[9] While many Western democracies have increasingly adopted inclusionary policies that meet personnel demands and reflect diversity and gender equality, the same militaries' culture and doctrine challenge women's inclusion by emphasizing a distinctly masculine warrior spirit.[10] (This phenomenon, prominent in U.S. and Canadian contexts, is vastly different from the situation in Russia, which has long embraced a feminine warrior ethos, famously visible in the "Night Witches" pilots of World War II and World War I.[11] Gender-linked war roles are not cross-culturally consistent.[12]) Sexism is seen to be perpetuated, in part, through military folklore that idealizes, and even anthropomorphizes, the rifle and other weaponry as either phallic symbols or as women in need of special care and attention.[13] Such cultural blending of sex and power contributes to female servicepersons facing staggering obstacles to being accepted in combat duty, in avoiding and prosecuting sexual and physical assaults within their own units, and in acquiring adequate physical and mental healthcare.[14] Outside the military, American female servicepersons today, much like their World War II counterparts, still have trouble being taken seriously, despite the fact that they are often more committed to the military's goals and values than men.[15] News coverage of U.S. women warriors in Operation Iraqi Freedom, for example, tended to preference their feminine/civilian life over their masculine/warrior duties, by emphasizing relationships and children rather than rank and service.[16] This is in line with the cultural expectation that women's bodily sacrifice should be to children, not war.[17] Or it framed the ideal type of militarized femininity as traditionally subordinate or helpless (as in the case of POW Jessica Lynch) or as being in opposition to enemy masculinity (as in the Abu Ghraib abuse case).[18]

Similar challenges have plagued gays in the military, though in truth, many countries have found that integrating women into the ranks is more of a challenge than integrating openly gay personnel.[19] With the widespread creation of women's corps during World War II, there were fears that military service would turn the women into prostitutes or lesbians[20] (in fact, recent studies have indicated that self-identified lesbian or bisexual women serve in the military at rates disproportionately higher than self-identified gay or bisexual men[21]). In the United States, Britain, Canada, and Australia there had long been concern that homosexual presence and conduct in the ranks would adversely affect unit cohesion and discipline, but each country has successfully integrated openly gay personnel—with the United States being the most recent of over twenty-five countries to do so.[22]

Women also have a complex history as wartime artists, though few female warrior cartoonists could be identified, with their artwork shaped by their changing relationship to combat and war:

> For generations, men have left their homes and families to fight and die for their country and its principles while their wives, mothers, and daughters have remained safely at home, seemingly unaffected by war and violence. Men experienced war, wrote about war, photographed war, and painted war. Women, it was thought, did not. Yet a closer examination of the reality of war reveals that this was an incorrect assumption. Women in fact were directly affected by war and they expressed this impact through art.[23]

For example, when World War II started, the females in comics, both artists and characters alike, rose to the occasion. As in other industries, many women filled in for deployed men in comic creation. *Wonder Woman* came to the United States to help save democracy. So-called "Victory Girls" such as Miss America, Miss Victory, Pat Patriot, and Liberty Belle came from all walks of American life to don masks and secret identities to carry on wartime activities.[24] Other heroines in syndicated serials or single-issue publications were strictly military women, such as the mysterious War Nurse. Women illustrators often excelled at creating and drawing female characters and produced a number of wartime heroines, both costumed and quasi-military.[25] Most of these heroines were designed to appeal to men and women alike during the war years, offering new civic ideals for the women and shapely young pin-ups for the male military readership.[26]

A common complaint about the portrayal of women in comics is that appearance and sexuality is emphasized over ability, even when drawn by women. Male characters, too, however, typically have highly objectified physiques that convey their characterizations—rippling muscles for heroes, doughy or lanky bodies for villains[27]—and gay male characters are most frequently depicted as effeminate and feminized, though sometimes as hypermasculine.[28] Stereotypes are an essential part of the language of comics. Though some research has suggested that these images helped to make women in military service more socially acceptable,[29] critics have pointed to stereo- and gender-typed depictions of female military personnel as reinforcing, if not propagating, prejudices against women in the armed forces.[30] This is not surprising, given that, just as the world's militaries found it easier to incorporate gays than women into the ranks, comics have often been more empowering for queered otherness than gendered otherness.[31]

Pin-ups

American doughboys had "naughty postcards" purchased in France during World War I. American GIs had "pin-up girls" on their walls during World War II. The state-sanctioned, culturally acceptable, military-distributed photographs of provocatively, if not scantily, clad women was arguably part of the political, wartime obligation of American women to serve in support roles to the armed forces. Pin-ups provided surrogate objects of sexual desire, providing men far from home with outlets for sanctioned autoeroticism, thought to keep the soldiers aggressive and heterosexual.[32] Artist Ruge in a *Yank Magazine* cartoon pokes fun at this notion, suggesting that the men spent so much time with pin-ups as to lose interest in actual women. His comic depicts a soldier reading in bed beside an attractive and voluptuous woman, telling her, "Not now, darling. I've just come to the extra page of pin-ups."[33] They were, however, considered essential. A Bill Mauldin cartoon has soldiers paying for a chance to just look at a nudie magazine during World War II.[34] A Korean War sketch by Roger Baker suggests that only the buzz of a mosquito could distract him from looking at girly magazines.[35] And a Vernon Grant cartoon has *Playboy Magazine* being air-dropped into Vietnam.[36] Pin-ups also served as surrogate wives and sweethearts, representing the women at home the men imagined themselves protecting, and on whose behalf men said they fought.[37] As markers of virility,[38] pin-ups appeared in any medium soldiers could access: in military publications, such as *Yank Magazine*; in sexual periodicals, such as *Esquire*; on the machinery of war, particularly as "nose art"; and in the funnies pages, including characters such Miss Lace of Milton Caniff's *Male Call*.[39] The comics of warriors, not only during World War II but also before and after, reflect this attention to and appreciation for the female form, as a symbol of sex and of home and of purpose.

In the words of Mauldin's Willie, sex is "a reverint subject,"[40] so some soldiers complained that the Hollywood glamor shots of Betty Grable, Rita Hayworth, Irene Manning, Jane Russell, and their other notable contemporaries were too tame, too demure, for young men with healthy and deprived sexual appetites.[41] In the comics, the men solve this by replacing photograph reprints with living (or at least three-dimensional) women, mounted on the wall like the masthead of a ship.[42] Indeed, the pin-up is such an invasive aspect of military culture that Will Eisner uses the label as a teaching aid in his illustrated

Vietnam-era M16A manual, identifying the weapon's magazine by the feminine name "Maggie" and its firing pin as Maggie's "pin-up,"[43] befitting of the gendered and sexualized ways American military folk culture views weapons.[44] Even Willie affectionately, yet bitterly, tells his weapon, "I've given you th' best years o' me life."[45]

Pin-ups as outlets for sexual desire are, however, only seen as natural for men, not for women. Renegotiation of women's sexual identity was prompted by the World War II–era creation of the women's branches, but double standards remained and servicewomen who opted to engage in sexual relationships were considered confused by or maladjusted to military life.[46] Several comics mock female servicepersons who display images of male stars, boyfriends, or other masculine figures as somehow incongruous or otherwise unacceptable. Barsis' *They're All Yours, Uncle Sam!*, crafted through interviews with warriors, pokes fun at the pin-up boys of Wacs,[47] showing active disapproval by officers for displaying such photographs[48]; this is also seen in Barbara Bristol's semi-autobiographical *Meet Molly Marine*.[49] In fact, Vic Herman's *Winnie the WAC* frequently makes light of women's sexuality and sexual needs in the service: "Winnie's" boyfriend knits her a sweater with breast cups; she uses a helicopter to track down a date; she takes a fire extinguisher with her on a date with a GI who has just returned from eighteen months in the South Seas; she accepts multiple proposals; she uses rank to try to force a GI to marry her[50] ... all situations that belittle the female perspective in heterosexual relationships. Most recently, *Incoming! Military Cartoons* curses "female fighter jocks" for having scantily clad male, or beefcake, nose art, rather than the more traditional sexy-female, or cheesecake, nose art.[51]

Moreover, comics often emphasize an idea that female service members would, should, or, at least, could, act as objects of desire for the men. The wounded fall in love with their nurses, as seen in the works of Britain's Bruce Bairnsfather,[52] America's Abian Wallgren,[53] and New Zealand's A. Rule[54] during the Great War, and the works of America's Vernon Grant in Vietnam.[55] In the work of Herman, *Winnie the WAC* and her associates are continuously surrounded and watched by men from all branches, even while dressing; "Winnie" goes so far as to remove her shirt to attract a rescue plane.[56] Similarly, from England, a cartoon in David Langdon's *"All Buttoned Up!" A Scrapbook of R.A.F. Cartoons* shows male fighters watching a female fighter walk up stairs, clearly able to see up her uniform skirt. British fighters whistle at the female personnel in *Kiss the Girls Goodbye*.[57] A *Yank* cartoon by Ozzie St. George has a leering hulk of an MP confronting a nude, bathing Wac about being "out of uniform."[58] Leonard Sansone's *The Wolf* whistles at Wacs—and any other women.[59] *Private Breger in Britain* contrives to repeatedly embrace a Wac.[60] The idea of women as objects of sexual desire appears again in Hank Ketcham's *Half Hitch* of the

Vietnam years, with a sailor suggesting that the navy go co-ed (like colleges of the time were) and using flag signals to flirt inappropriately, and offensively, with the WAVES.[61]

More recently, the attitude has taken on a grittier and more political edge, tinged by accounts of sexual harassment and sexual abuse in the military ranks. *Power Point Ranger* (*PPR*) frequently delves into military chauvinism and has been accused, via Facebook, of sexism.[62] One of the most unambiguous *PPR* expressions of the idea that women are in the armed forces for sexual purposes is in a comic recruiting poster, flanked by women in belly-baring digis, for the military occupation specialty (MOS) of "Morale, Welfare, & Recreation Specialists" for females aged 18–29 who may also carry additional skill identifiers of "B (Bi), D (Deviant), M (Multi), P (Positional), V (Vacuum)."[63] Similarly, another *PPR* comic shows a male soldier simply telling a female soldier, "Come with me woman I have sexual needs," to which she responds, "OMG yay!"[64] With rising reports of sexual assault in the military,[65] *PPR* also highlights sexual favors as a means for women's promotion, with a female private in a camouflage bikini telling a colonel, while in a hot-tub together, "I've been practicing holding my breath. Can I earn my stripes now?"[66] Sexist humor is, apparently, particularly pronounced in the Marine Corps, where women are referred to as "wooks" and rape jokes are considered part of infantry culture.[67]

Bob on the FOB designed a comic devoted to the "hotficer, a military officer of much more than average attractiveness"; the "hotficers" are frequently unaware of their own level of attractiveness and thus "don't understand that their innocent requests for help are often viewed as cues or suggestions for inappropriate advances by other service members." The accompanying illustration is of a female officer.[68] The issue of such sexual harassment as a legitimate versus an illegitimate concern in the American military is also debated in the graphic narratives. Jeff Bacon's *Broadside* humorously suggests the reality of the issue through a male lieutenant on trial for sexual harassment telling the female judge, clerk, and jurors, "This reminds me of the joke about a lawyer and this belly-dancer...."[69] Jeffrey Hall's *Downrange*, however, hints at the possibility that reports of sexual harassment are exaggerated, with a female soldier finding amusement in harshly questioning the motivation for a health reminder for a monthly breast-cancer screening self-examination.[70]

Consistent with the general view of women as sex objects, as depicted in these graphic narratives, the warrior comics are filled with numerous tributes to the female form in ways that reveal the permissive and open, perhaps vulgar and obscene, sensibilities of military culture. For example, the bulk of illustrations of women feature large breasts, ample cleavage, round hips, and/or exposed legs—and many of those include breast-related humor. Particularly curvaceous women are found throughout Will Eisner's instructional comic books, from World War II through the mid–Cold War era.[71] Comics mock "chesty" women with big breasts[72] and flat women with small breasts[73] and "shapeless" women with an overall heftier build.[74] Firm breasts are considered "impressive"—quite literally, in a cartoon where the man is left with breast-shaped indentations on his torso from embracing a woman.[75] Naked breasts are thought to be imagined—though are made visible on the page.[76] Jiggling breasts are particularly sought after and admired.[77] The exception to this exaggerated depiction of the female form is found in *Doctrine Man* and *Downrange*, which both rely on a computer-drawn, stick-figure style. In these comics women are recognizable only through the presence of a discernible bust-line in *Doctrine Man* and longer hair in *Downrange.*

It should be noted that there is also some preoccupation with the male body, specifically the genitalia; this is noted in the newer comics. Colloquial mentions of penises are a significant part of the military culture and language,[78] such as "the big green weenie"—Marine slang for being shafted by the military through a bureaucratic inconvenience or unfair treatment. The green weenie was given literal form by Maximillian Uriarte, creator of the U.S. Marine comic strip *Terminal Lance*, with a series of cartoons depicting the giving of a neon-green dildo as a gag Christmas gift to a lieutenant.[79] *Doctrine Man* comics have an ongoing allusion to penises through recurring characters who wear codpieces, and in a remarkable strip that introduces and defines the term "Manicorn" as "a male individual who feels no shame in entering the shower in a general state of arousal," particularly when deployments limit contact with women.[80]

The Queer Question

Not all gender concerns in the military involve members of the opposite sex. In World War II, "American military officials linked the aggressiveness of the effective soldier with healthy, heterosexual desire and worried about sustaining such desire and thwarting homosexuality."[81] The aforementioned pin-ups were a significant part of the effort to "thwart" homosexuality[82] and efforts to curb the spread of sexually transmitted infections. It is suspected that gay inclinations, attitudes, and activities were hidden and repressed, often through overcompensation or exaggeration of behavioral indicators of heterosexuality, such as woman-chasing,[83] an activity heavily represented in the graphic narratives of *The Wolf* by Sansone and *Half Hitch* by Ketcham. Gays in the military are sporadically referenced in warriors' comics, and their appearance has increased since the 1990s. Two American graphic narratives from the Korean War era specifically reference recruiters asking about sexual preferences. Alex Gard, in his *Sailors in Boots* comic about basic training in the navy, presents a very young-looking recruit, who has perhaps not yet dated at all, acting shy over the question. Shel Silverstein, in *Grab Your Socks*, depicts a recruit covered in girly tattoos, thus making the question as to whether he likes women seem unnecessary.[84]

Other graphic narratives hint at homophobia. Artist Barsis alludes to the public fear of lesbians in the women's branches during the Second World War, with a male sergeant rejecting the use of a female recruit with broad shoulders, who is dressed in a pantsuit, while women in civilian skirts and dresses can be seen training in the background.[85] A *Broadside* comic strip from around 1990 features a particularly feminine winner of a cross-dressing "beauty" contest in the navy making the other sailors uncomfortable.[86] (Cross-dressing as entertainment can also be found in the World War II *Hubert* strip.)[87] Several *Power Point Ranger* graphic narratives poke fun at male sexuality and gently tease gays in the military—particularly in the navy, which has earned a mythologized stereotype of rampant homosexual activity because of the months men spent in close quarters with one another. One cartoon shows a male Marine popping out of a cake for the navy's birthday, while male sailors shout, "Take it off."[88] Another cartoon is set at a USMC birthday party where a male Marine brings a male sailor as his date because "sheep mess the dance floor."[89] Yet another shows a male sailor trying to fall asleep by counting male Marines.[90]

During the administration of U.S. president Bill Clinton, the military released an entire educational comic book devoted to the policy of Don't Ask, Don't Tell (DADT), which highlighted military prohibitions on homosexual conduct and on gay humor and sexual harassment. It is interesting to note that in this book, *Dignity and Respect*, straight soldiers, both male and female, are primarily depicted with darker skin, hair, and eye tones, whereas the soldiers who are or who might be gay are males, primarily depicted with lighter skin, blonde hair and large blue eyes—suggesting physical stereotyping of effeminate or fair features.[91] A *Doctrine Man* comic strip expresses "confusion" about the Don't Ask, Don't Tell training as "training people to become homosexuals."[92] No graphic narratives were found that deal directly with the repeal of DADT and the allowance of gays to openly serve in the U.S. military, not even in the midst of the Bradley/Chelsea Manning espionage case.[93] Such findings, or lack thereof, in the graphic narratives reflect the military folklore culture that shows support of Queer personnel by mocking it.[94]

Sexual Teases and Diseases

Studies suggest that members of the military frequently engage in high-risk sexual behaviors that both put them in jeopardy of contracting sexually transmitted infections and perpetuate a need for preventative programs.[95] Indeed, active sex-drives, risky behaviors, the threat of disease, and preventative education remain common themes in military graphic narratives, particularly those by American warriors. The Great War comics drawn by U.S. warriors, while mostly focusing on the discomforts and novelty of training, emphasize a considerable preoccupation with the "fairer sex" as many recruits illustrate dreams of impressing girls with their new uniforms and military bearing[96]— which may be why the American Expeditionary Force developed an extensive sexual continence program.[97] So, by World War II, graphic narratives that dream of women also warn of sexual dangers, extending from grotesque disease to enchanting spies.

In 1942, the British government believed it had identified a significant cause of security leaks: careless talk, especially in the company of beautiful women. The result was a propaganda poster with the edict, "Keep mum! She's not so dumb," suggesting that beauty may conceal brains.[98] A similar theme is found in more light-hearted venues, too, such as cartoons in *Yank Magazine*. One features a general insisting on personally searching a curvaceous and scantily clad woman spy,[99] and another showcases a GI dejected because his gorgeous female companion "won't talk to him until he thinks up a secret!"[100] A much more prevalent, and perhaps practical, relational concern to the average soldier, however, is spreading disease, rather than information. George Baker's "Sad Sack" is particularly concerned with safe sex, as Baker repeatedly emphasizes the need for protection, at one time donning a rubber glove to shake hands with a woman after viewing a military "sex hygiene" film[101] and at another time dashing to the "pro-station" in the midst of having an erotic dream.[102] The cautious "Sad Sack" also refuses relations with a very willing German woman, despite having been unsuccessful with ladies in every other country he has visited, because it is not

Fig. 6.1-1

Fig. 6.1: Examples of graphic narratives demonstrating means of dealing with sexual frustration during deployment. 1. SQW (1943), 2. "Doctrine Man" (2013), www.facebook.com/doctrineman.

Fig. 6.1-2

worth the fraternization fine.[103] The U.S. government itself also reinforces safe sex through cartoons, as with a comic-book-style poster "Let There Be Light" distributed by the Naval Medical Center.[104] The dangers of sexual relations with German women are particularly emphasized by cartoonist Don Sheppard in his tales of the rotund and buxom Fräulein Veronica Dankeschön a woman of loose morals whose prominent monogram of "VD" (slang for "venereal disease"—a sexually transmitted infection) serves as a continuous and not-so-subtle reminder of the menaces of involvement with German women,[105] who continued to be maligned for a heftier physical appearance well into the postwar occupation.[106]

Social disease continues to make an appearance in American comics through the Korea, Vietnam, and Desert Storm years. Much like "Sad Sack," *Leatherhead* indicates the horrific and mood-dampening effect of sex hygiene films,[107] while Vernon Grant[108] and Eric Thibodeau[109] make a point of highlighting that disease can be contracted through unprotected sex. More recently, graphic narratives have turned their attention to other sexual hardships associated with deployment—particularly seeking options for sexual release that do not involve a living female partner of the opposite sex, such as masturbation, bestiality, and same-sex encounters.

Doctrine Man is one of the most vocal of the currently ongoing comics to explore alternative sexual outlets, including masturbation—though autoeroticism is alluded to as early as World War II in the animated training film, "Coming Snafu," wherein the hapless Pvt. Snafu destroys a plane in the midst of fantasizing about a stripper, and in "Sad Sack," when the soldier requires a condom to safely continue his sexual dream. (In both of these cartoons, orgasm was suggested through the use of what Mort Walker refers to as *emanata*,[110] visual cues "emanating" from the characters that reveal internal conditions.) *Doctrine Man*'s masturbation, or "lone ranger," comics take place outside of port-a-potties or bathroom trailers on forward operating bases, with a warrior entering or leaving the latrine with a pornographic publication; onomatopoeia suggests sounds of sexual gratification originating from behind the latrine door.[111] *Terminal Lance* also highlights self-gratification with a strip entitled "The Jack Shack," which uses the format of the MasterCard commercial meme:

> Personal Protective Equipment: $5,000+
> Weapons and Gear: $5,000+
> Training a Marine: $50,000+
> Jerking off in a porta-shitter, trying to finish before passing out in 135 degree weather...
> ...Priceless.[112]

Additionally, the *Doctrine Man* strip has an occasionally recurring character that is in love with an inflatable sex doll,[113] something also hinted at in a World War II comic in which a desolate GI orders something shaped like a woman from the "The Lonely Hearts Club."[114] *Power Point Ranger* even illustrates an infantryman making a sex video with an inflatable doll in his quarters.[115] In the right weather, snowpersons may act as romantic surrogates; *Winnie the WAC* crafted a snowman during World War II[116] and a male soldier in Korea sculpted a nude and anatomically correct female snow sculpture.[117]

Another alternative for sexual gratification that is repeatedly mentioned in some of the operations Enduring Freedom and Iraqi Freedom comics is bestiality, particularly man-goat intercourse. Much of the bestiality humor is related to the racist depictions of Muslims, but it is also heralded as a reasonable, if not entirely acceptable, alternative to sex with women. This is particularly clear in a *Power Point Ranger* comic where a deployed soldier receives a sheep in the mail, to be used as a sexual partner, accompanied by a written warning for him to stay away from the "desert queens."[118] *Doctrine Man*, in a spoof on the theme song to the old television show "The Love Boat," proclaims:

> Love, exciting and new.... Come inside, I'm expecting you. Love, deployment's sweetest reward.... Let it flow, it flows back to youuuuuu!!!!
>
> The love goat, soon will be running away from you.... The love goat, promises something strange and new.... Set a course for adventure your mind on a weird romance!!
>
> Love won't hurt any more. It's a friendly smile behind a closed office door.... Yes, loooooooooovvvve, it's loooooovvvve!![119]

Though the goat often appears happy with the arrangement,[120] warriors also have the option of homosexual encounters, even if they do not identify as gay, thanks to the alleged phenomenon of "Man Love Thursday,"[121] wherein same-sex carnal encounters among Muslim men are thought to be part of weekend recreation.[122]

Another way that male warriors manage sexual frustrations and a lack of women is through lowered standards. "Beer goggles" and "deployment goggles" are repeatedly mentioned as indicators of men's willingness to date, or at least have sexual relations with, women they would find unattractive if they were not so drunk or so deprived. This phenomenon is recorded as early as World War I by Percy Crosby, who shows "how the girl next door looked" before joining the army—scrawny, shabbily dressed—and after "spending a couple months on the post"—glamorous, poised.[123] In another example, a *Stars and Stripes* cartoon from Japan/Korea shows two soldiers meeting up with two women—one tall and shapeless with a large nose and tiny eyes, the other short and squat with thick glasses and a double chin—as one soldier, ironically, says to the other, "The good lookin' one is my date," and the reader is left to wonder which woman that is.[124] *Bob on the FOB* defines deployment goggles as the

> phenomenon related to extended periods of time away from members of the opposite sex due to deployments or extended training, wherein members of the opposite sex become increasingly attractive the longer one is deployed. Very similar to "beer goggles," however, due to General Order Number One alcoholic consumption is not required for deployment goggles to work. Generally, the less time one spends on the FOB the greater the chance of deployment goggles taking effect at any given period.[125]

Uriarte, of *Terminal Lance*, extends the use of deployment goggles to his fellow female Marines, claiming that the average female Marine is not "hot" but will appear so to the men five months into deployment. Uriarte also suspects the women have their own deployment goggles when viewing their male counterparts.[126] Beer goggles, however, appear to be the more dangerous phenomenon—at least according to cartoonist Mark Baker—leading some men to want to chew off their own arms to avoid waking the "dog of a woman" they find themselves in bed with the next morning.[127]

For Love of Money

In November 2013 *Terminal Lance* started a ten-part story line, loosely spoofing *Star Wars*, entitled "Revenge of the Dependapotamus," an epic continuation of a 2010 "Myths and Legends" strip and blog entry he published on the so-called Dependapotamus:

> This creature of lore is actually quite common within the Marine Corps. Mostly found in the darkest corners of base housing, Dependapotamus may look like a predator of some kind, but it is actually defined as a parasite. Much like a tick or leach, the creature will engorge itself into gluttony through the benefits and steady paychecks offered by the unsuspecting Marine.
> While this may be a gross exaggeration of the problem, I think the Dependapotamus is mostly a product of contract marriages brought about by the broken marriage system within the military. Many unwitting Marines will bag and tag just about anything to get out of the barracks and get that fattened BAH check. Unfortunately the end result is usually this beastly creature with a few children to boot, leading to the inevitable re-enlistments to support it and its offspring, with the smell of crushed dreams and lost hope lingering in the air at the end of the night.[128]

The "Revenge" story line was reignited in 2013 with a fan-art contest held through the *Terminal Lance* Facebook page, which ultimately featured twenty-two entries illustrating Marine Corps storm-troopers, Jedi and Sith with phallic lightsabers, desert-camouflage space armor, and Jaba the Hutt–sized dependents.

While the label "Dependapotamus" is new, the experience of parasitic relationships between warriors and women has a long history documented in military comics. To the chagrin of many warriors hoping to impress ladies with their uniforms and war stories, money seems to be the driving force in soldier romances; this is succinctly captured in a "Sad Sack" comic wherein a soldier with a fifty-dollar bill pinned to his chest, rather than the poor Sad Sack with ribbons and commendations pinned to his chest, gets the girl.[129] "Willie and

Joe" encounter an "innocent" Italian woman wanting to emigrate,[130] *Hubert* is involved with an English woman attracted to the chocolate bars, cigarettes, and canned goods he brings her,[131] and soldiers from the Japanese Occupation and Korean War[132] up through the 21st century[133] encounter Japanese women with eyes for American paychecks, Green Cards, and gifts.

Power Point Ranger is also highly critical of spousal, particularly female, leeches, which artist John Holmes refers to as "barracks rats,"[134] who use sex and emotional manipulation to feed on military pay and benefits, often cheating on their deployed husbands with the mythologized "Jody," an attractive civilian man. One cheating-themed comic depicts "Tiffany Amber" heading into a sleazy motel, from a car covered in troop support and military spouse stickers.[135] Mark Baker illustrates a similar idea in a graphic narrative on a trial regarding divorce settlements and benefits between one woman and her first ex-husband from the army, her second ex-husband from the Marines, her current husband in the navy, and what readers are lead to believe will be her next husband in the air force.[136] (Such occurrences may be what spurs "Doctrine Man" to explain that the benefit of having sexual relations with a goat rather than a woman is that a goat "won't try to 'friend' you on Facebook after a romantic night."[137] This theme is repeated in a strip wherein a soldier proclaims the benefits of an inflatable girlfriend to include not writing bad checks, hanging out in the barracks while he is deployed, or complaining to the sergeant-major about him.[138]) There is little mention of military husbands, with the exceptions of a very competent character in the *Jenny* comics for military spouses, who serves as a reminder in the graphic narrative that "people always forget that over 20% of 'the troops' are female,"[139] and a *PPR* comic that depicts military husbands as "little men," easily frightened and small in stature,[140] consistent with the fears of the 1940s that personal empowerment of females in the military would disrupt the family structure and subvert men from their position as the head of the household.[141] In fact, military spouses of both genders fight a number of stereotypes in real life, with wives being thought of as uneducated, lonely gossips and husbands as incompetent, effeminate oddballs, and both being perceived as somehow lazy.[142]

G.I. Janes

Accepting women into the military was, and continues to be, a challenge in the British and American civilian and military cultures. Women were long viewed as a reason to fight, as symbols of the home and hearth to be defended, as suggested by Norval Packwood and G.C. Thomas's *Leatherhead*, wherein the Korean-War-era recruits all picture pretty girls to help them through their chores.[143] The public and widespread entrance of women into war was thought

Fig. 6.2-1

Fig. 6.2: Examples of perceptions of women in the American Services. 1. Barbara Bristol (1945), 2. Steve Opet (2008), courtesy of the 10th Mountain Division and Fort Drum Museum.

Fig. 6.2-2

to be an absurdity and an act of desperation. This sensibility is clearly expressed by Bairnsfather in commentary about the duration and desperation of World War I, by placing a woman in the trenches, much to the shock of Bert as Ol' Bill says, "I told you we'd 'ave 'em 'ere before we'd finished."[144] Even after women's branches were established in World War II, the idea of women and war was shocking, including to the servicewomen themselves, as suggested by *Winnie the WAC*, who is unsettled by a headline that says women might be drafted.[145] In fact, during World War II, cartoons in the military magazine *Hello Buddy* even mock the women in civilian employment who replaced the men serving in war.[146]

"The military services are so conspicuously a man's world that the appearance of women therein was startling. Women who joined to do a job found themselves objects of great curiosity. Suddenly they were representatives of 'womanhood.'"[147] The difficulties of gaining entrance into this so-called male domain appear and reappear in the graphic narratives, from World War II on through the present day. An Irwin Caplan cartoon in *Yank* has a Wac aid to a male general being asked by a visitor, "Is the man of the house in?"[148] A *Winnie the WAC* scene reveals confusion over how a male officer should pin a medal on a woman's rounded chest.[149] *Hubert* condescendingly tells a Wac, "Those bars don't fool me a bit—underneath it all I think you are a very charming creature!"[150] Women are turned away from the FOB's social club, the Mountain Men's Moustache Meeting, in Steve Opet's OIF-based *Opet's Odyssey* because they only have "mascara moustaches."[151] The male characters of *PPR* gripe excessively about being part of the "experiment in social engineering" of having a female squad leader in the infantry.[152] There is also an occasional expression of resentment of male warriors toward their female counterparts for what they perceive as double, or lowered, standards of behavior. The *New Sad Sack* features Wacs flirting to get what they want, at the expense of the men with whom they are stationed. *Power Point Ranger* criticizes comparatively lax regulations for women's personal grooming and appearance, with a female gunnery sergeant—sporting long, curly hair with colored stripes, large hoop earrings, excessive mascara, and long air-brushed fingernails—ironically commenting that there should be better standards.[153] As one of the few black characters seen in the *PPR* graphic narratives, this strip may also be racial commentary, particularly in light of later complaints about the army's appearance regulations being unfair to black women.[154]

Another ongoing theme in the warriors' graphic narratives is the military's inability to provide proper accommodations and resources to female personnel. Insufficient supplies for the women were an acute concern in World War II, with accounts of Wacs receiving size 18 winter bathrobes, no matter what their own size was, and Wacs in the South Pacific suffering "jungle rot" on their feet because the army had no overshoes in women's sizes.[155] Similar predicaments are captured in both Herman's *Winnie the WAC*, who is seen in baggy coveralls rolled at the ankles, and in Dorothea Byerly's autobiographical *Up Came a Ripple*, with a WAVE outfitted in sleeves too long and shoes too large.[156] Seventy years later, the military still has trouble maintaining appropriate supplies for women. *Opet's Odyssey* in OIF notes this with a comic of two women shopping in the FOB's store, unable to find facial cleansers other than men's after-shave lotions; in fact, the only female-specific product on the shelf was Chanel No. 5 perfume—both expensive and impractical.[157]

Graphic narratives by warriors similarly remark on the lack of accommodation or preparation, culturally if not practically, for women in combat. At the end of January 2014, reflection on the Pentagon's first year of integrating women into combat roles of the U.S. military was dim, with vague or mixed standards of integration across the branches and very little progress made in the Marines and army. A primary criticism was the entrance standards favored men by emphasizing strength over necessary skills.[158] The problem of women's size and strength is noted in *Opet's Odyssey* with a comic depicting a male and female soldier standing side by side with identical weapons that span the distance of the man's chest to knee and the woman's shoulder to foot. The strip's caption reads, "Hey! I'm just sayin'..."[159] The arming of women is a particularly charged issue in the United States; with guns being tied to both masculine and American identities, armed women force a reexamination of aptitudes for both citizenship and violence. "Womanhood is, after all, linked closely to sexuality; and guns— and the possibilities of violence they promise—in the hands of women whose sexuality is unregulated or unorthodox have seemed especially dangerous."[160] The perception of female sexuality as dangerous is seen repeatedly in the graphic narratives. *Winnie the WAC* uses a tank to coerce a date from a male soldier.[161] Vernon Grant features a service woman's perfume in Vietnam that is "three parts Chanel No. 5 ... two parts nerve gas."[162] John Sheppard, in *Incoming*, depicts female soldiers in target practice shooting only at the groin area of human-silhouette targets.[163] Women and weapons are also depicted as incongruous through World War II–era comics that show the women brandishing mops rather than rifles, and *PPR* comics that show them carrying lip-balm rather than a sidearm[164] or as simply being unable to carry a heavy weapon.[165]

Despite such challenges, the women warriors still earn some respect, and often the same artists that capture a cynical and chauvinistic attitude in the ranks also depict female competence. During World War II, naval efficiency increased when WAVEs replaced the men in noncombat duties, and reporters were awed by Wacs who set water-filled helmets in the sun to warm for bathing[166]—an activity light-heartedly captured in several World War II comics depicting women warriors using their helmets as bathtubs.[167] In *Meet Molly*

Marine, Bristol gives extensive acknowledgement to the various tasks performed by servicewomen to free men to fight in World War II.[168] *Power Point Ranger* admits women's competency in a strip depicting one soldier saving another during combat; the downed soldier says, "Thanks, man! I owe you my life!" and the hero, doffing the combat helmet to reveal long blonde locks, responds, "I'm just doing my job … and I'm no man."[169] *Broadside* and *Incoming!* cartoons both acknowledge women's toughness, with a higher tolerance for pain (through childbirth)[170] and for alcohol,[171] respectively. The important role of women in combat, even when women are not in officially sanctioned combat roles, is also recognized, even as early as the American Civil War, where a cartoon shows the feisty women of Fredericksburg emptying chamber pots on the heads of the Union soldiers.[172] Warrior artist Kathleen Browning in Operation Desert Storm credits American women as the deciding factor in victory over the all-male Iraqi military.[173] Mark Baker's *Pfc. Murphy* goes so far as to suggest that the debate about women in combat is hypocritical, as women have already found themselves in combat during OEF/OIF.[174] *Downrange* is equally practical, stating, "If you [a woman] want to go out there and get shot at, that's one less mission I have to go on."[175] A children's military comic, *Pvt. Joe Snuffy Goes Guard!*, highlights that men and women do the same jobs in the National Guard.[176] Cartoons and other artworks by Vietnamese military men show even

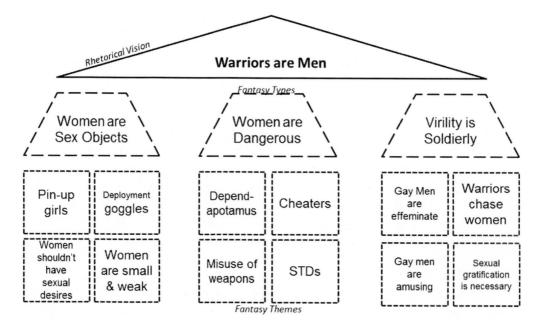

Fig. 6.3: Rhetorical vision of gender and sexuality as expressed in warrior graphic narratives.

more acceptance for women's role in not only war, but also in combat. Colonel Huy Toàn, Colonel Quang Tho, Colonel Văn Da, and battlefield artist Nguy n Van Tru all depict women in combat during the Vietnam War, armed and often side by side with men.[177]

Debriefing

The rhetorical vision of sexuality and gender expressed in these comics is that warriors are men. This vision is supported by the fantasy types of women as sex objects, women as dangerous, and virility as soldierly. Figure 6.3 illustrates how the fantasy themes outlined above, such as pin-up girls and the Dependapotamus, build these fantasy types and this hypermasculine rhetorical vision. The United States and Great Britain have both struggled with the integration of women and gays into the military. Notably, though women were permitted open enlistment decades before gays, these graphic narratives suggest that since the world wars both military and civilian culture have faced a greater challenge in accepting women of any sexual orientation, whose presence is readily visible, as viable warriors than it has the less-visible gay men, despite some discomfort about the possibility of their presence in the ranks.[178] Such themes in the warrior comics are consistent with gender and sexuality research in mainstream comic books, which suggests that comics have more easily offered queer empowerment than female empowerment.[179] Though these warrior artists acknowledge that some women are very capable soldiers, these seem to be the exception that proves, if not the rule, at least the ruling perception of women as too small and weak to offer any military service other than that of sexual gratification. Ironically, the very same objectified sexuality is also thought to make them dangerous with the weapons they are allegedly incapable of handling, with a fear that the threat they pose is to their allies rather than to the enemy.

7

Drawing Fire
Combat and Casualties

No bastard ever won a war by dying for his country. He won it by
making the other poor, dumb, bastard die for his country.

—Patton

Researchers have found many reasons why men and women choose to fight
in war, and that those motives often may change with the actual experience of
fighting. Patriotism and ideology may give way to camaraderie and loyalty, wan-
derlust and a quest for adventure may ebb with growing political awareness, and
revenge may yield a new, emerging sense of self.[1] Whatever an individual's ration-
ale for it may be, combat experience has been linked to a range of positive and
negative outcomes. Warriors report that they are better able to cope with adversity, have improved self-discipline, greater independence, a broader perspective
and greater appreciation for life's value. But they also report feelings of anxiety,
misery, and loss—emotions most frequently associated with witnessing death.[2]

All societies or organizations have measures for dealing with the dead, particularly to help the bereaved reorient themselves to the now-changed group,
providing not only reassurance but also cues for economic and social obligation.[3] Mourning is part of the "transformative effect of loss,"[4] and narratives
of death help explain the loss of life.[5] "Culturally, 'good' deaths represent ideals
enacting a symbolic victory over corporeal and social demise and the regener-
ation of life, while 'bad' ones do the opposite, leaving survivors despairing and
helpless in the face of meaninglessness or evil."[6] Religious narratives may help
to establish a "good" death, wherein an individual's life is seen to play a part in
some higher purpose.[7] In the absence of religious narratives a "heroic" death
can be achieved through an individualistic script of emotional expression and
self-sacrifice in which the dying person seeks and accepts the truth of his/her
condition or pending fate, allowing for personal growth and interpersonal rec-

onciliation. Such a script cannot be used in all kinds of death, however. Sudden death in particular does not allow the dying person to define his or her life; the social construction of death comes from the *process* of dying, and without the process, or the expectation, death is harder for people to comprehend.[8]

Death is, however, expected in the military, though its causes are varied and sudden. Therefore, the military organization must have a procedure for managing the disposal of bodies in ways that help to ensure the continuation and legitimacy of the armed forces while buoying morale in society, particularly as shared loss is a means for social and political constitution.[9] "War is one of the sovereign acts of state; and no ruling élite can ignore the issue of 'managing' patriotism."[10] Within the military the cultural script of a good death specifically involves publicly supported, combat-related activities of young persons without children, all the pomp and circumstance of formal rites of remembrance, and psychological resolution for survivors.[11] A sudden loss of life in its prime, particularly during times of crisis when dominant ideologies are made explicit and purposeful, needs to be imbued with meaning for fulfilling some greater good.[12]

Warriors themselves often make light of death and injury as a means of facing them. "Bisociation of a trivial structure on to the tragic plane" allows warriors facing the possibility of a violent end to make death itself seem insignificant, dissipating their fears.[13] One example is a paratrooper song, "Blood upon the Risers," sung to the melody of *Battle Hymn of the Republic*, which recounts a gruesome parachuting death of a rookie that involves splatters of blood, brains, and intestines as a matter of due course. The refrain is "Gory, gory, what a helluva way to die."[14] This approach to trivializing tragedy is captured by the title of the Australian Great War graphic narrative *Humorosities*—an amalgamation of "humor" and "atrocities." A skewed fatalism tends to accompany warriors' awareness of danger and risk in which, while life is desirable, death is not seen as terrible.[15] Rather than being morbid, such "gallows humor" is more often indicative of good morale.[16]

The technological advances and nature of modern, unconventional warfare has also necessitated a cultural narrative not only for combat dead but also for combat injured, due to the increased ratio of wounded to killed casualties,[17] and increased attention to the links between modern warfare and psychological effects, most notably Post-Traumatic Stress Disorder.[18] It has been suggested that adequate and appropriate training[19] can help to sustain warriors through prolonged combat, but that a disjunction between the expectations of military service, forged by veteran narratives and mass media accounts, and the experience of military service creates dissonance that may be a contributing factor to psychiatric casualties.[20] Dominant discourses emerging from 21st century war, thus, place injured bodies into frames of normalcy and triumph,[21] much like post–World War I discourse emphasized "overcoming disability" to restore prewar normalcy,[22] but injured minds still tend to be framed as abnormal and weak. Three narratives have been associated with military PTSD casualties: the *institutional* narrative structured along the parameters of the condition as described in the Diagnostic and Statistical Manual (DSM IV), an *organizational* narrative of resistance by mental health workers and advocates trying to overcome the cultural stigma associated with PTSD diagnosis and treatment, and *personal* narratives of lived experience with PTSD.[23] A fourth media-generated narrative, or frame, is also developing: one of stigma and danger.[24]

Graphic narratives, too, have ways of dealing with death. Adventure stories rely on death—especially violent or "pornographic death"—as part of the action, most particularly death of the villains, aggressors, or criminals.[25] Superhero stories are marked by death-defying and death-denying representations, though the deaths of "mere mortals" are often starting points for the rise of a hero.[26] In the last half of the 20th century, the Vietnam War, the assisted suicide movement, Do Not Resuscitate rights, cancer, AIDS, changing cultural patterns of grief, and the War on Terror pushed death more centrally into graphic narratives, not only into the immortal world of superheroes, with the cancer-caused death of Captain Marvel or the politically-charged death of Captain America— who arguable suffered from PTSD throughout the 1960s and 70s[27]—but also in the family funnies, which until the mid–1990s were untouched by mortality.[28] When death is handled in graphic narratives as something other than an action event, which is about the death itself, it is normally with attention to the impact it has on survivors or with attention to its socio-political significance.

Grin at the Grim

Historian Jay Casey writes:

Editors called upon [soldier] cartoonists to fulfill a number of tasks but the most important, in terms of recording the experiences of American arms, was their work as visual chroniclers of the reaction of common soldiers to combat. Originally included in military publications for the entertainment their work provided, cartoonists found themselves in the uncomfortable position of trying to insert humor into and draw meaning from the landscape of death that is the front in any war.[29]

Cartoonists balance realism, censorship, and humor by transferring death to the enemy and injuries to periphery, hinting at combat and allied mortality through ragged appearances, destroyed landscapes, and surreal, slapstick, fatal situations.[30] They also deal directly with mortality on a regular, if comparatively infrequent, basis.

After the extensive discussions in this book about such ordinary topics as

Fig. 7.1-1

Fig. 7.1: Examples of graphic narratives depicting ally and enemy deaths. 1. C. LeRoy Baldridge (1919), 2. Walter Mansfield (1945).

food, weather, and sex, it may seem like violence—the actual business of the military—is far removed from the graphic narratives, if not the lives, of many warriors. This, however, is not the case. Even jokes about mystery meals and wet socks are frequently told in a setting of flying bullets and bursting shells. Combat is an omnipresent aspect of warriors' graphic narratives, if not the highlight. Some graphic narratives give combat advice, such as "Always be on the lookout for good water. Dig Deep! Make the enemy keep his head down!"[31] Others touch on moments of empathy, amusement, and even humor. The combat depictions of Sgt. J.F.E. Hillen's Civil War and Pvt. Charles Johnson Post's Spanish-American War are realistic and humorless, as honest, if impressionistic, records of events including Hillen's "Charge of the Mounted Illinois," "Hooker Capturing Lookout Mountain," and "a Battle Two Miles West of Atlanta,"[32] and Post's "Bloody Ford below San Juan Hull," "The Rough Riders with their famed

"IT WAS SIMPLY A MATTER OF MAKING A BETTER MOUSE TRAP."
Fig. 7.1-2   —Pfc. Walter Mansfield

dynamite gun," and "One of our Gatling guns before the attack on San Juan Hill."[33] Other artists, however, record not so much the events of combat, but rather the bleak humor to be found in surviving it.

For some, combat seems a game. Douglas Ward depicts the Great War as a boxing match.[34] *Private Breger in Britain* plays golf caddy to a sergeant who requests, "Boy, my Thompson submachine-gun, caliber .45!"[35] *Leatherhead*s throw and catch grenades like baseballs.[36] Paper airplanes may be lightly treated as a UAV (unmanned aerial vehicle) attack.[37] And, for sailors in Operation Desert Shield, the outcome of the Super Bowl playoffs causes more tension than mounting hostilities in Iraq.[38] For others, combat is grimly ironical, at best. The World War I illustrations of American Alban Butler, Jr., downplay moments of terror through insertion of funny details such as cats, dogs, geese, and chickens running with the soldiers to the trenches during night bombing,[39] doughboys wearing gas masks running headlong into trees during a "gas discipline,"[40] men randomly firing flare guns at incoming artillery shells,[41] and helmets popping off in fear of the enemy.[42] Similarly, Clive Dixon's "The First Shell" amusingly illustrates a Scott's kilt billowing around him as he runs from a shell, while another man peeks from behind a crate of biscuits.[43] Britain's Bruce Bairnsfather also pokes fun at combat's dangers in World War I, but more through black humor, relying on sardonic puns, such as "There are times when gentlemen preferred ponds" as men jump into a water-filled hole during heavy shelling,[44] rather than charming visuals. Combat is occurring in most of Bairnsfather's work, as evidenced by bullet lines or by large shells hovering at the tops of scenes. Some cartoons, however, focus more exclusively on the experience and effects of combat, such as sitting in "live" houses waiting for the next shell to come through,[45] trying to get a haircut in the trenches[46] while bullets sing overhead, constantly having to rebuild fortifications,[47] witnessing the slow destruction of beautiful castles,[48] and repeatedly wondering, "Where did that one go?"[49] Australia's Frank Dunne is also wry about combat, suggesting that heavy fire may be bad luck brought on by a broken pocket mirror.[50] Bill Mauldin's combat comics in World War II take a similarly realistic yet sarcastic or ironic approach. In one cartoon, the proximity of the firing is demonstrated by a soldier lighting matches by holding them over the top edge of his trench.[51] In another, the men are making an amphibious landing, shells are bursting overhead and Willie requests, "Try to say sumpin' funny, Joe."[52]

As warfare has changed in the 21st century, John Holmes reminds us that not all combat is the same. In a "salute to infantrymen" he demonstrates that being in a Humvee when an IED goes off is far more terrifying than routine ground combat with 100 bloodthirsty Taliban.[53] He also argues that a Revolutionary War soldier is "tougher" and more "badass" than the present-day soldier who has all the advantages of technology.[54] John Sheppard takes this historical perspective further to state, "All Wars Suck." Here, a World War I soldier tells a World War II soldier, "Our war was the war to end all wars!" The World War II soldier tells the Vietnam soldier, "We were in the service for the duration!" And the Vietnam soldier tells the Iraq soldier, "At least your heat is a dry heat!"[55]

Death Defiance

Whether it is seen as sport, adventure, bad luck, or terror, the reality of combat is the possibility of death. A Mauldin soldier reading a French language dictionary on a ship acknowledges the worst and hopes for the best, as he explains, "If I git there without bein' sunk, an' land without gittin' shot, an' meet me a gal..."[56] Some warrior artists face their mortality by defying death in ways only possible in the surrealistic world of cartooning. From the Battle of Goldsboro in the American Civil War, "Gorge gets blown up by a shell," but is clearly able to draw a picture of it to send home.[57] An Australian digger is hit and complains, "Damn yer explosive bullets! You've gone & bust the pocket I 'ad me cigarettes in!"[58] In World War II, a *Yank* warrior's parachute fails to open ... for the second time,[59] and the British "Raff," through his training manual character Pilot Officer Prune, teaches pilots that a crash landing is good if you can walk away from it.[60] A lieutenant in Vietnam is lucky enough that "there ain't a bullet made wid yer name on it," though his entire body is seen in a bullet-hole-outline on the wall behind him.[61] "Did the round go straight through, Doc?" is what an unfortunate soldier, with a neat, round, gaping hole where his stomach should be, asks in John Sheppard's *Incoming*.[62]

Some warrior artists choose to joke about death rather than defy it. *Seaman Si*, in the midst of World War I, asks his friend, "Say, Zippy, I want to ask you about something—What do you have to be to get buried with military honors?" Zippy answers plainly, "You have to be dead!"[63] Nearly a century later, Mark Baker illustrates the macabre comedy of the airborne with repeated comics humorously portraying the risks of parachuting, including a (fabricated to prank rookies) death by electrocution in utility wires of new jumpers.[64] And *Bohica Blues,* by Chris Grant, combines jokes about uniform regulations with death by remarking of the skeletal remains of a soldier, "As long as he had his DCU [desert camouflage/combat uniform] top on, it's fine."[65] *PowerPoint Ranger* also mocks the absurdity of uniform regulations in combat with a comic strip where a soldier is hit in a firefight because he is not wearing his reflective belt.[66]

Other artists incorporate death more realistically as a matter of course, though not as a topic of focus. In the Civil War, "Gorge" depicts him and his friends returning to Newbern after the Battle of Goldsboro with canes and in tattered clothing, and a dead horse on the side of the road.[67] Hillen illustrates the "Attack of the Federal Supply Train by Rebel Cavalry," in which a Confederate corpse is visible.[68] And, from Vietnam, Tad Foster depicts a soldier reading a "Dear John" letter as he sits in the rain, bullets flying past him, with dead bodies (seen only in part) strewn about the ground.[69] There are also warrior artists who face death head on, and in so doing force their readers to face not only their mortality, but also their duty. Often, the dead of warriors' graphic narratives are likely to be the enemy, frequently represented victoriously or viciously,[70] as in *Yank* illustrator Jack Coggins' depiction of how "the once-mighty German Seventh Army crumbled and died—its funeral dirge the roar of Allied big guns."[71] A World War II illustration by Sgt. Howard Brodie, however, shows more compassion, as American infantrymen carry a Japanese prisoner on a makeshift stretcher because he wanted to die rather than walk.[72] Other regular depictions of the dead are of animals.[73] Far fewer are of comrades or superiors. Post captures the "the death of Lieutenant Ord at the capture of San Juan Hill."[74] Bairnsfather expresses grief at the loss of an officer (in contrast, somewhat, to the hostility usually shown to officers in graphic narratives).[75] In addition to drawing German casualties, one of Coggins' earliest illustrations is of American soldiers being blown up by a mine in World War II.[76] Jessica Harrison-Hall of the British Museum observes of the Vietnam War that, "Truong Hieu is one of the few Vietnamese combat artists actually to depict a casualty of war and a mid-battle scene. Such images appear to have been far more prevalent among the oeuvre of U.S. war artists."[77] For some, death representations carry added symbolic meaning. George Cruikshank portrays a skeletal Napoleon standing atop a pyramid of skulls as a dark monument to the so-called achievements of the French leader.[78] In one work by the Vietnamese cartoonist Choé, a skeleton begs for peace from the Vietnam War, with a torn hat sure to lose any offerings placed in it, even if it were not too late for the beggar to benefit from them.[79]

Regardless of who is dead, death cartoons often emphasize duty. Butler entitles his cartoon of the first Americans killed in action during World War I "Grave Responsibilities."[80] Baldridge also picks up the theme of responsibilities, quelling the discontent by showing "the first to go home"[81] and "the noncombatant"[82] as those who are dead. Brodie depicts a "burial on the spot" in *Yank*,[83] and Holmes honors responsibility to the dead with a comic that pays homage to the Old Guard at Arlington National Cemetery[84] and to a grieving widow.[85] The World War II story-manga of Japanese soldier Mizuki Shigeru conveys the importance of ties between the living and the dead in Japanese culture with episodes of soldiers collecting *katami* (memento) *ikotsu* (bones) from the deceased for their families, even going so far as to sever the fingers of a man mortally wounded but not yet dead.[86] Butler demonstrates the heroic purpose of a military death in "The Orderly Room at Valhalla," where "Buck privates from all former wars greet the latest arrival, the veteran of the FIRST Division."[87] As an Iraqi civil war looms in 2014, Holmes raises the heretical possibility of military death in vain with a comic of the ghosts of U.S. casualties from OIF remarking, "*This* is what we died for? What a waste."[88]

What Doesn't Kill You

Sometimes, death is not the worst-case scenario in war. The wounded and the traumatized continue to fight battles long after the dead are at peace. Journalist Ann Jones writes, "Sooner or later almost every American soldier comes home—on a stretcher, in a box, in an altered state of mind. Soldiers return to or fail to return to families who love them, or try to, families who recognize them, or not. Communities that help them, or can't."[89] The wounded are depicted in Post's illustrations of the aftermaths of San Juan Hill and Misery Hill during the Spanish-American War.[90] A Mauldin GI of World War II asks, "Just gimme a couple aspirin. I already got a Purple Heart."[91] An airman in *Pope's Puns* also makes a practical request: "Promise me if I get hurt, tell my mother

I had on clean underwear!!"[92] *Leatherhead in Korea* comments that when a Marine is about to go home, "The Marine is usually shot—not seriously—but shot ... or else he is hit by shrapnel, or a truck, or falls over a cliff.... Ironic as it may seem, it does, however, add a degree of prestige when he gets stateside, for then he is not only a veteran, but a wounded veteran."[93] In Vietnam, a wound could be the means to get home. A cartoon by Foster shows a warrior sticking his index finger into the path of a bullet and calling, "Doc, I'm hit!" The cartoon's caption reads, "The Trigger Finger and the Freedom Bird; *The trigger finger was the game's most valuable player. The freedom bird was the flight home. The game and the goal, was to get there.*"[94] Foster also expresses deep admiration for the "Corpsman, Medic, Doc; the nurse with balls" who enters into the heat of combat at great personal danger, to answer the cry of the wounded.[95]

Not all wounds, however, can be treated by the medic. Not all wounds are even visible to the medic. According to the National Center for PTSD and the U.S. Department of Veterans Affairs, there are four types of PTSD symptoms: re-experiencing, in which a traumatic event is relived through memories, flashbacks, and nightmares; avoidance, in which a sufferer attempts to evade situations and actions that trigger memories of a traumatic event; negative changes in beliefs or feelings, wherein a person's perspectives on self and others changes because of the trauma; and hyperarousal, wherein a person feels jittery, anxious, wary, and/or distracted. These symptoms may appear soon after a traumatic event, or may not appear until months or even years later.[96] One *Power Point Ranger* comic tackles the "crazy veteran" narrative of PTSD that many feel is circulated in the public, perpetuated by media. The setting is a college campus. A veteran with an artificial arm and leg asks a classmate if he can copy her notes for classes he will miss while at the VA getting his arm checked. She responds: "OMG, that's like, so sad that you have PTSD! OMG, we were, like, so talking about it in Diversified Cultures class yesterday, how like all of you are coming home from the war so angry and messed up in the head! Can't you just, like get over it? Let it go? So sad!" Holmes labels this comic, "Empathy rhymes with stupidity."[97]

PTSD was known as "shell shock" during the Great War; warrior artist Bairnsfather deals with re-experiencing symptoms of PTSD in his life and in his graphic narratives after being injured by a shell. He depicts "That 16-inch Sensation" as feeling chained down, literally, with a shell coming at him,[98] and says, "My dream for years to come" is of a shell landing on him.[99] Wallgren takes a much lighter and more irreverent approach to combat trauma in "Bomb, Shell and Shrapnel" in which a doughboy's "cooties" get "shell shock."[100] Maximilian Uriarte makes light of "shell shock" with a corporal suffering PTSD from witnessing the war-hardened, fraternity-party-like atmosphere of the barracks.[101] Bob Stevens is also dismissive of "combat fatigue," suggesting its symptoms are analogous to the experience of drinking "combat ration booze."[102] A particularly violent moment of re-experiencing from Vietnam is illustrated by Jake Schuffert in a cartoon showing a soldier chasing his wife out of the house with a knife and a gun because she wore black pajamas reminiscent of Vietnamese clothing.[103] Vernon Grant in Vietnam and John Holmes in operations Enduring Freedom and Iraqi Freedom both depict flashback-style re-experiences. One of *Grant's Grunts* is back home with his wife on a drive. She observes, "Herbie ... Look at that beautiful valley.... What lovely grass!... The trees are turning gold.... That stream is just too picturesque for words..." He murmurs his agreement, but is thinking to himself, "What a great spot for a couple of machine guns.... A 106 on that knoll could pick off anything on that road running parallel with the stream.... Heavy yellows and reds in the camouflage..."[104] In very similar fashion, a Holmes character is also back home with his wife in a car, and while she talks on and on, he "sees" a firefight and dead bodies around the vehicle.[105]

Avoidance is an attempt to prevent re-experiences, and can appear, at least in these graphic narratives, as closely related to negative changes in relationships. A Bairnsfather cartoon takes us years beyond World War I when "grandson Harold, aged eight, has just asked Old Bill what he did in the great war," and we see a disheveled room, furniture overturned, dishes broken, pictures crooked, with Harold hiding beneath a cloth and Old Bill standing with a chair's legs gripped menacingly in his hands.[106] Another display of violence, this one related to negative changes, is shown by Vernon Grant with a soldier who has just shot his television with his sidearm and his wife is yelling, "Those programs aren't the only thing around here that's 'sick, sick, sick!'"[107] And in the OEF/OIF era, *Doctrine Man* demonstrates violence as hyperarousal when he presents father and son sock puppets, with the son asking his dad that if he went to reverse bootcamp to readjust to civilian life, "Why do you sit on the roof at night with a deer rifle? ... you're kinda freakin' me out, Dad."[108] Wallgren, in World War I, also features symptoms of hyperarousal in "Shelling is Shocking," but as something that is comical, such as jumping in an exaggerated fashion "when some one [sic] flaps a blanket in back of you" or "when a truck buzzes up suddenly behind you" or "when a tire blows out" or "when a wine cork pops."[109]

An issue that is often related to PTSD and the emotional toll of warfare is suicide. Veterans and active duty service members may be at increased risk for suicide,[110] and the military suicide rate has, in fact, outpaced both the civilian rate of suicide and the rate of combat fatalities. In the United States, by 2011, a soldier was dying by suicide every thirty-six hours, and by 2013 the number was twice that.[111] Suicide makes very infrequent appearances in warriors' graphic narratives, but as one way that artists illustrate death, or its possibility, it is worthy to note. In World War II, a *Hubert* cartoon presents a suicide attempt because a soldier learns his girlfriend has married another man while he is at

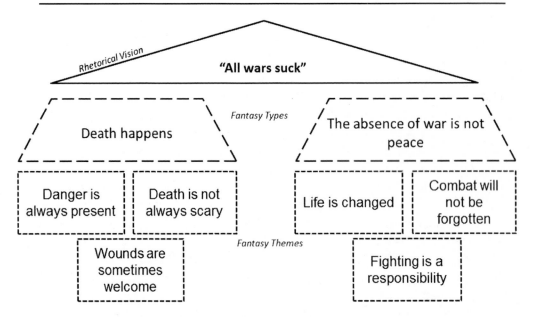

Fig. 7.2: Rhetorical vision of combat and casualties as expressed in warrior graphic narratives.

war.[112] And in Korea, Shel Silverstein presents a drill sergeant apologizing to a recruit for being hard on him while the man sits on his bunk tying a noose,[113] and a lieutenant who hangs himself when botched orders try to send him to Korea.[114] The extreme stress of military service appears in the graphic narratives in other ways, too. Mauldin's "Willie and Joe" are asked "to be a steadying influence for the replacements" of World War II, while one makes paper-doll chains and the other drinks from two bottles of liquor.[115] In Vietnam, a hunched and wrinkled old man celebrates his nineteenth birthday.[116] And, in 2010, a sailor exhibits classic reckless behavior associated with military personnel[117] when he tries to hang-glide with a truck's tow hitch to have a little fun and relaxation.[118]

Debriefing

The rhetorical vision of combat and casualties is, to quote the aforementioned cartoon by veteran John Sheppard, "All wars suck." This vision is supported by the fantasy types of death's possibility, reality, and omnipresence, and the malingering effects of war on those who fight them. Figure 7.2 illustrates how the fantasy themes outlined above, such as imminent danger, an ability to laugh at death, the potential for wounds to offer a means home (or a hero's welcome once there), the lasting emotional effects of combat, and the responsibility to others, including the dead, in battle, build these fantasy types and the rhetorical vision that all wars suck. Many of these graphic narratives use varying degrees of black humor, employing macabre jokes that are not all that funny— such as the husband attempting to kill his wife because of her pajamas, a skeletal figure watching peace slip through his grasp, or a grandfather upending a house because a child asked about the war. These comics and cartoons are, nonetheless, life affirming and part of both the coping process for combat and the mourning process for death, reaffirming commitment to the cause or to comrades and demonstrating acceptance for feelings of anxiety and loss.

8

Sillyvillians
Civil-Military Interactions

> They also serve who only stand and wait.
> —John Milton, *On His Blindness*

Civil-military relations are most frequently understood as the interaction of governmental authorities and institutions with the officer corps, but also increasingly include lower-level interactions between a public and its military in the widest range of civil society.[1] "There is a tendency for current understandings of the links between military service and civilian experience to be polarized."[2] This polarization is often viewed as military alienation from civilian leadership and society, a growing gap between the military institution and civilian society at large, increasing politicization of the military, military resistance to civilian oversight, and inappropriate political and social influence of the officers and the military institution.[3] There is not, however, a continuum stretching from military ethos on one end to civilian ethos on the other; the military's values are static and universal, while civilians' values vary individually and, as a result, tension between the professional aspirations of the military and the politics of its society can only be managed, not obliterated.[4]

Several scholars and analysts have noted a widening and corrosive gap between the general U.S. population and its military culture. Some have found that the military has started to think of itself as not only separate from but also superior to its public.[5] "In November 1999, the Triangle Institute for Security Studies found a growing disparity between the political and social views of service persons and civilians, prompting a major PBS NewsHour inquiry into the civil-military 'gap.'"[6] In the words of defense consultant and military historian Robert Goldich, "In the midst of a civilian society that is increasingly pacifistic, easygoing, and well-adjusted, the Army (career and non-career soldiers alike) remains flinty, harshly results-oriented, and emotionally extreme. The inevitable civil-military gap has become a chasm."[7] Former U.S. Defense Secretary Robert Gates and former Chairman of the Joint Chiefs of Staff Mike Mullen have criticized civilians for growing detached from the Iraq and Afghanistan wars and losing contact with those in the military.[8] There are various explanations for the civil-military gap, including the incompatibility of liberal thought, dominant in Western civilization and culture, which emphasizes individualism, with military thought, which subordinates the weaker individual to the stronger group[9]; contradictions between key premises of American civilian culture—atomization/individualism, pursuit of comfort, freedom of choice, equality, and deliberation—and the contrasting key premises of the military institution—unity, endurance, obedience, hierarchy, and readiness for violence[10]; the military's low profile of recent decades[11]; poor media coverage of military matters[12]; unrealistic ideals created by military fiction[13]; the absence of America's elite from military duty[14]; and the "undemocratic" nature of an all-volunteer force.[15]

In modern society, there is also a more personal and intimate side of civil-military relations. The military has a vested interest in the emotional support of its families, particularly since the change from a conscript to an all-volunteer force saw an increased likelihood of married enlisted soldiers.[16] "Recruitment, morale, and retention of military personnel are affected by family members' attitudes toward the military life-style."[17] Warriors' morale and outlook are positively correlated to their assessment of their families' ability to adjust to the military lifestyle, to their perception of the available support for their families, and to satisfactory communication with their families.[18] Unhappy families increase the stress of warriors, but well-adjusted families can provide support that may reduce stress and resulting illnesses in warriors.[19] The military is what is known as a "greedy institution"; its survival depends on the commitment of its members, ensured by emotional and material compensation and through normative pressures directly on the service members and indirectly on the members' families, with whom the military competes for loyalty.[20] Research clearly links family outcomes with military work demands—notably risk of service member injury or death, periodic separations, frequent relocations, foreign residence, and concerns about child education and civilian-spouse employment[21]—particularly with an all-volunteer force where the military is frequently viewed as a job more than as a duty.[22] Military attempts to socialize families to the military lifestyle and to control family behavior in line with military ideals are now the stuff of pop-culture knowledge, thanks to Tanya Biank's book *Army Wives,* and the successful television drama of the same name it inspired, with the tagline, "The Army has its code. The wives have their own."[23] In fact, such implicit family policy and the variety of services extended to the families of military personnel were developed as a reaction to the recruitment and maintenance needs of the armed forces, to ensure that families—particularly wives—would tolerate and adapt to the demands of the military lifestyle.[24]

Feelings about spousal involvement in the military vary depending on where the military spouse is and what is happening. Prior to deployment, pride in the spouse's service is common, but as deployment nears, fear and uncertainty about the logistics, the outcome, and the relationship take hold, and general satisfaction with military life becomes tinged with more negativity. During deployment, spouses must navigate the complexities of changed domestic roles and maintaining a long-distance relationship; many have to reconcile new-found independence with feelings of loneliness. The post-deployment period is marked by recognition that life and the relationship are not only different from what they were during deployment but also different from what they were pre-deployment; a period of adjustment, which includes more role changes, is needed.[25] Though the modern (American) all-volunteer military is both career and family oriented, offering service members social and material support that allows them to more easily transition into adulthood than their civilian counterparts,[26] service members still face challenges in "sustaining a dual commitment" as warrior and spouse/parent, resulting in the "civilianization" of military families through means such as increased home ownership and more spousal careers, or in the dissolution and failure of many military marriages.[27] Indeed, the endurance of the military identification is acutely apparent during the transition from military life to civilian life.[28]

Graphic narratives are no stranger to representing cultural differences, misfits, and changing identities. The most notable of such comic book storylines is Marvel's *X-Men*, with a metaphor of tolerance and acceptance for racial, sexual, ethnic, and political differences.[29] Popular culture has, likewise, treated the disabled veteran as a misfit,[30] and a number of military cartoonists have attempted to deal with this civil-military divide. Warrior-cartoonists such as Mauldin and Hume explored different facets of warriors returning from war. Mauldin looked beyond the celebrations and ticker-tape parades that followed World War II and drew "the rub between husband and wife, solider and civilian" in *Willie and Joe Back Home*, representing the resentment and bitterness Americans had toward the military, which fought the war that disrupted their lives, ignorant of the hardships the soldiers had endured.[31] Hume took a more light-hearted look at warriors of the Japanese Occupation returning to civilian life in *When We Get Back Home from Japan*, playing on how their foreign experiences would be carried over into, and color, their American lives. "Laughter ripples through the pages as they go home again, oriented but not reoriented."[32] Non-military artist Barsis particularly looked at the difficulties of transitioning from civilian to military life for female recruits in World War II in *They're All Yours Uncle Sam!* Julie Negron's strip *Jenny, the Military Spouse* offers an unprecedented graphic look at the social side of civil-military relations. Written by and for military spouses, *Jenny* highlights the peculiarities of living in a military community, from relocation issues, to shopping at the base store (BX), to dealing with other military spouses.[33]

Not That Kind of Party

Oftentimes, insider/outsider, or military/civilian, distinctions are used for humorous contrast when the focus turns to what happens when those military and civilian characteristics collide, even though, at times, it seems as if the difference between the warrior and the civilian is only uniform-deep. Several soldiers, both American and Australian, claim to be civilians simply by removing their clothes entirely,[34] by covering over their uniform with a long coat,[35] or putting on their "civies" suit—even if they do tuck the trousers into their combat boots.[36] A veteran's wife also identifies clothing as the difference between soldier and civilian when she tells her husband, "I was hopin' you'd wear your soldier suit, so I could be proud of you."[37]

Modern warrior-comics, such as John Sheppard's *Incoming*, and Daryl Talbot's *Laughing in Cadence,* frequently interject their military-focused stories with moments of military-civilian juxtaposition, such as a child asking why sailors wear bibs on the back,[38] or a sergeant singing a marching cadence as a lullaby to his sleeping child.[39] Confusion surrounding military lingo is a recurring civil-military transition topic of the graphic narratives. One of the most consistent portrayals of this references the military's use of the word "party" against the common civilian understanding of a "party." In the Second World War, *Winnie the WAC* is criticized by her sergeant for appearing in evening attire because, she says, "I thought you said it was to be a G.I. party."[40] Over fifty years later, Pvt. Murphy's drill sergeant has a "G.I. party" to welcome the new millennium, much to the disappointment of the men.[41] (A GI party is cleaning detail.) A *Pope's Puns* character is shocked that he is supposed to work at an "advanced party"[42] (which typically does preliminary reconnaissance on a mission) and an *Opet's Odyssey* soldier arrives in a toga for "TOA"[43] (which can variably refer to Time of Attack or Arrival, Tactical Operations Area, Transportation Operating Agency, Total Obligational Authority, or Transfer of Authority—among others).

Other graphic narratives and artists, most particularly Americans in World War II, also depict literal civilian translations of military terminology. Many of these make effective use of the verbal-visual combination of the graphic narrative medium by bringing the botched understandings and translations to pictorial form. *Private Breger in Britain* carries pliers with him for a "pincers movement."[44] In *Yank*, one cartoon soldier shows up with a swimsuit to join the "replacement pool,"[45] and a new "tail gunner" arrives sporting his very own tail.[46] When Mauldin's Joe starts removing his clothes out in the open, he is told, "I'm afraid you misunderstood the term, 'field stripping.'"[47] During Vietnam, Jake Schuffert shows pilots running to their posts because their commander instructs the cook to "scramble" his eggs.[48] More recently, a Steve Opet graphic narrative resembles a real "Lou LOO" of an Abbot and Costello–style routine as two soldiers try to resolve confusion over finding the LOO (the Line of Operations) or a man named Lou.[49]

Another line of jargon jokes, which first appears around the time of the Korean War, focuses on service members speaking military-ese to civilians. A Shel Silverstein comic shows a soldier talking to a woman, perhaps his wife: "... so this MP comes up to my SFC and asks to see his ID ... seems that some VIP at G-2 called the CICCQ and since the NCOIC was away on TDY the CQ checked with the OD and according to new SR, all NCOs get TPA only if..."[50] Abbreviations also cause confusion in Vietnam, as a *No Sweat* character speaks into a telephone explaining, "No, no dear, I'm not in bed, I'm in SAC, SAC, S-A-C, SAC!!!"[51] (SAC is short for Strategic Air Command.) A similar idea is seen in *Pope's Puns* with an airman boring a civilian woman with a tale: "...our last UTA was our annual BIVOUAC and our CO airlifted us TDY out of CONUS. We had to catch a hop to get back and I drove my POV home. The MRE's weren't bad either!"[52] *Half Hitch* asks over the phone, "Make up your mind.... Do you want to go dancing? Give me a simple AYE-AYE or NO answer!"[53] And *Ricky's Tour* says, "You've been at sea too long when" you ask the greeter at Walmart for "permission to come aboard."[54] The problems with translation are enhanced when an officer, accustomed to respect and acquiescence, communicates with a civilian who feels no such obligation, as seen when a general comments to his wife, "That's strange ... when I told that joke to the troops, everybody laughed."[55] Occasionally, a graphic narrative will venture into the possibilities of civilian slang slipping into military discussions, as in a Mark Baker comic where a soldier is home surrounded by his four children; while having a phone conversation with an officer he references the provisions made so the men can "go potty."[56] In another Mark Baker comic, "Sgt. Murphy" is pleased to see that his new wife has adapted to army life when she calls him to say, "I forgot to get lighter fluid when I was at the store today. Can you *square me away* and pick some up on your way home? That's all I need to be *good-to-go* for Saturday's BBQ! HOOAH?"[57] Julie Negron's *Jenny, the Military Spouse* focuses exclusively on such adjustments and learning curves in the military family.[58]

You Can't Go Home Again

Other habits besides jargon-use also have a tendency to cross from military to civilian practice, highlighting the vastly different lifestyles of the two spheres.

Part of the First World War doughboy's fascination with military life is imagining what might happen when he gets back home and brings his new military demeanor and practices with him, such as picking his teeth at the table, slurping soup, cursing,[59] saluting people on the street, waking up at 5:30 in the morning,[60] and washing his own dishes.[61] The juxtaposition of military ways in civilian settings creates humorous incongruity, whether wearing the same clothes for more than a week before washing them,[62] using signal flags to ask for more gravy at the dinner table,[63] being lonesome on an uncrowded train,[64] ordering MREs at a French restaurant,[65] requesting that a Valentine's Day card be destroyed after reading,[66] or reading a children's bedtime story in which the "three little pigs" are defended by Texas T's, HESCO Bations, an AR-15 with a red-dot scope, and air support.[67]

Though the military is, in fact, occasionally portrayed as child's play,[68] there is, nonetheless, a serious and dark side to the problems of returning to civilian life after service, and especially after a war. Beyond portrayals of PTSD, concerns about the ability of warriors to transition from combat life back to civilian life appeared in the graphic narratives as early as World War I. A sketch by England's Douglas Ward pictures a "poor old soldier" with a bum leg and a missing hand panhandling on the street.[69] In World War II, a *Hubert* cartoon shows a ragtag, filthy bunch of armed soldiers relaxing and sleeping in a barn, one commenting, "See where the folks back home are worried about how we'll fit back into civilian life."[70] For this reason, the Information and Education Division of the Army Service Forces prepared cartoon posters "to aid in teaching subjects to soldiers who are occupying enemy territory while waiting to return to the U.S."[71] But, as the *New Sad Sack* observes when he receives his discharge, the transition is complicated by housing shortages, inflation, diplomatic crises, unemployment, and the atomic rocket.[72] In World War II, Fred Levi noted how military training does not prepare a man for such tasks as changing a diaper,[73] and more recently, Maximilian Uriarte commented on the challenge of translating military service into marketable job skills when re-entering civilian life, particularly for grunts whose combat role is determined by the situation and the moment.[74]

The return of a warrior requires adjustment for the entire family. It is a relearning process for relationships, communication, problem-solving, and family roles.[75] A *Yank Magazine* cartoon illustrates this literally with a family beneath a "Welcome Home Daddy" banner being told, "I don't know what schedule you've been following, but here's the set-up for the next 30 days."[76] Over a half-century later, John Sheppard represents the point of view of the military spouse, observing, "Subtle behavior mods are required after deployment to get our Marine back to the way he was"; the dinner conversation of the particular Marine in question is, "Please pass the %*@! potatoes. Can I have some %*@! salad? Nice %*@! weather today."[77] Indeed, in the 21st century, there is extensive attention to the social and psychological fit of veterans into their civilian society. *Terminal Lance* artist Uriarte pokes fun at his own social awkwardness at returning to college: A young woman introduces herself to a veteran and asks his name. His response includes a lot of information, but no name, "Yup, just got out of the Marine Corps a couple months ago. Yup, went on two combat deployments to Iraq. Yeah I was stationed in Hawaii for a few years it was pretty awesome."[78] *Doctrine Man* repeatedly explores, and supports, the "reverse bootcamp" initiative to reintegrate veterans into civilian society. One character explains, "Dude, the signs are everywhere. We're a depraved culture. We could use the help," because, he says, "Every deployment has an impact on who you are and how you relate.... Even if you don't see a change, your family sure does, believe me."[79] Examples of the depravity include masturbating in port-o-potties, having sexual relations with a goat, and defecating in MRE boxes.[80]

Letters from Home

Civilian ties are, however, never severed. It is suggested at the beginning of the chapter that there might be an occasional tendency for warriors to view themselves as superior to civilians, as in a *Laughing in Cadence* cartoon that proclaims, "God created marines because he was disappointed in civilians."[81] But time and time again warrior artists express a desperate need to maintain their ties with home. "George," during the American Civil War, "amuses himself with a song '*Do they miss me at Home*.'"[82] In World War I and World War II, graphic narratives expressed dreams of home.[83]

More than a dozen artists, spanning a century, represent the importance of receiving letters and packages from home. Scholars have documented the

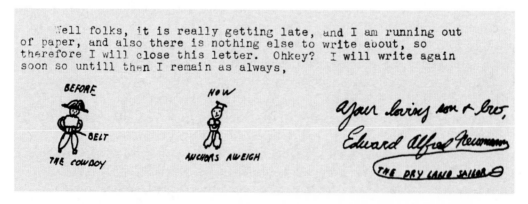

Fig. 8.1: An example of the cartoon-like sketches that appear in letters. From a 1943 letter by Edward Alfred Neumann to his family.

significant role of letter writing to warriors' identities, relational health, and morale.[84] (For graphic narratives on the practice of letter writing, see Wallgren's autobiographical angst in "From: To: Subject"[85] and his "The Complete Letter Writer."[86]) A number of artists, including Robert Bindig, Samuel Lionel Boylston, Joseph Farris, Robert Geisler, Jr., Sumner Grant, Jack Kirby, Henry Lamb, Frank. L. Mack, and William Schmitt included cartoon illustrations with letters home, and/or on their envelopes.[87] The V-Mail of World War II was often used for the creation of greeting cards sent home, as the V-Mail (or Airgraph, as it was known in England) process took full-sized messages and turned them into four-inch by five-and-a-half inch photographs for space-saving shipping; such illustrated missives may be seen on display at the Smithsonian Postal Museum and at the National Museum of American Jewish Military History.[88] Cecile Cowdery illustrated the envelopes she sent to her husband when he joined the army during World War II,[89] and Marion Gurfein sent her husband humorous, illustrated newsletters in World War II and Korea.[90] Other cartoon illustrations are regularly found in letters home, even by those without artistic talent, as a means of explanation to recipients, or as part of the stationery being used. The very premise of Edward Streeter's book series of love letters from Bill to Mabel, and the "Dere Bill" reprise by Florence Summers and Natalie Stokes, is that of cartoon-illustrated letters between a World War I rookie and his girl.[91]

Most of these graphic narratives, however, document the significant role of letter *receiving* to warriors' morale, even when stationed stateside in peacetime.[92] The most simply stated expression of this is by a soldier of the First World War through a frowning and then smiling face wearing a doughboy helmet labeled "Before & After Receiving a Letter."[93] *Seaman Si* explains that a lack of mail makes him wonder if he is still loved, and even just a single letter reassures him that he is.[94] In an illustration within a letter to his nephew during World War I, Briton Henry Lamb shows himself stopping to read missives from home even amongst the fire of combat.[95] Others also note the joy of getting letters,[96] but more vivid are depictions of the despair that comes from not having mail.[97] During World War II, Joe walks off as if to desert until Willie tells him, "I wuz just kiddin', Joe.... You got three letters!"[98] and a mail Jeep destroyed by enemy fire is a sorrowful sight to behold.[99] Decades later, poor sailor Ricky is brought to tears when he not only is the only man who does not receive a care package at mail call, but also has to take out the trash created by everyone else unpacking theirs.[100] Mail, however, is often a communal pleasure—as indicated in a 1941 cartoon by Politzer wherein a soldier is surrounded by others looking at his mail and says, "With Me Nothing Is Private—the Gang Even Opens My Postcards."[101] Indeed, reading and writing letters are activities that may be at once private and social, as recipients are often likely to share letters with associates, and writers may seek input from shared acquaintances or advice from

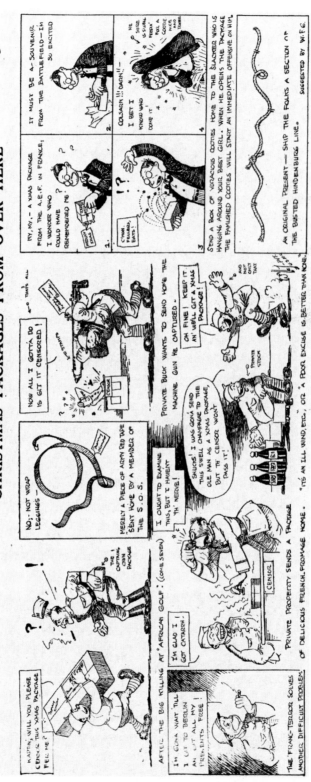

Fig. 8.2: Examples of graphic narratives showing the collision of military/war and civilian habits, specifically during holidays. 1. Abian Wallgren (1918), 2. K.F. (2007).

select others in the creation of the content.[102] This is further reflected in the graphic narratives, where not only letters but also packages, especially, are shared, whether deliberately or not, for the enjoyment of many.[103] By 2014, some artists started including social media in graphic narratives about civil-military connections—but with much more skepticism about the benefits, usually choosing to focus on warriors making fools of themselves online, as with poorly chosen "selfies" (self-photographs).[104]

If Only in My Dreams

Warriors want other comforts of home, too, such as wallpaper from back home,[105] a morning cup of coffee,[106] or fast food.[107] Such desires are often fulfilled, at least in part, through pilfering supplies or abandoned villages for curtains, rugs, even flowers.[108] The World War I cartoons of Alban Butler, Jr., frequently show flowers placed in vases made of shell casings, acknowledging the practice of "Trench Art," which turned empty munitions into vases, flatware, and other decorative pieces.[109] In cartoons, getting these domestic comforts often leads to some civil-military hilarity—as when *Private Breger* is in violation of "Articles of War inciting to Mutiny" by hanging a sign over his bed in the barracks that says, "There's no place like home," causing all the men to get weepy.[110] Or when all the men chip in on a "Little Gem—Air Cooler" for the tents.[111] Or when artist Sgt. Miller devises a pup tent with an aerial TV antennae.[112] But some of the most poignant portrayals of the connection with, and yet the distance from, civilian life appear in the graphic narratives about holidays spent in war, or even just on deployment—whether it is an Independence Day spent with ordnance instead of fireworks,[113] or an Easter celebrated with grenades instead of painted eggs.[114]

At best, warriors face the possibility of having to post guard[115] or pull KP duty for Christmas or New Year,[116] or simply not getting any rum cake because alcohol is not permitted in the Middle East—even when being delivered by Santa

Fig. 8.2-2

Claus.[117] At worst, they face a lonely and severely deprived reminder of what they left behind. The text of a World War II Christmas cartoon by Mauldin reads:

> 1. You always stayed awake late Christmas Eve, hoping to sneak a look at Santa Claus and a snort of eggnog. 2. And you were so excited in the morning you were up before dawn... 3. ...in such a hurry to get downstairs you didn't even bother to dress 4. ...but the other kids always got there first 5. Everybody admired everybody else's toys... 6. ...and scrambled to see who would get to play with them. 7. A month's grocery budget was blown on Christmas dinner 8. The sock was full of all kinds of surprises.

The associated, and yet depressingly incongruent, pictures are: 1. Posting guard. 2. Shelling. 3. Running to a trench wearing nothing but long underwear. 4. A full foxhole with no room for the last man. 5. Everyone sniffing a single bottle of Scotch. 6. A fight for the Scotch. 7. A C-ration. 8. A spider, mouse, and rocks being spilled from a sock.[118]

Most typically, though, graphic warriors express a broader mixture of seasonal joy and homesickness. As expressed by Norval Packwood, "Christmas, 1950, in Korea was not quite what most Marines had become accustomed to in the States, but the festive season was not allowed to pass without proper attention,"[119] which included using the stars off a general's staff car to top a pine tree decorated with ammunition belts, bandoliers and grenades.[120] In a pinch, during World War II, a "Very pistol will contribute th' Star of Bethlehem."[121] Drawing during Operation Desert Storm, Eric "Thib" Thibodeau expresses much the same idea in, "Spending the Holidays in the Middle East. As fun as it sounds!" The men aboard his ship, the USS *Missouri*, happily exchange gifts of lubricating oil, pipe caulking, a 9/16" wrench, a gas mask, and a new mop, because "gift-giving is tough when you're 7000 miles from the nearest 'K-Mart.'"[122] Wallgren depicts a similar concept in World War I, except for gifts sent from the frontlines to the home front with "Christmas Packages from Over Here," such as captured machine guns, voracious cooties, or "a section of the busted Hindenburg line," all wrapped in AEF red tape or spiral leggings.[123] "Doctrine Man" finds the joy of the holiday season in being alive, well, and with his fellow siblings-at-arms even when "stuck in a shithole."[124] Through it all, warriors, like those in *Private Breger in Britain*, hold on to the hope that, "Well, maybe next time we'll be back home havin' Christmas dinner with our folks an' a big tree an' presents an' a fireplace..."[125]

Just Like in the Movies?

Though the artists occasionally comment on aspects of civilian life they are forced to sacrifice,[126] one civilian mainstay for which they have little sentiment is the media. In World War I, Bruce Bairnsfather's "Old Bill" receives a stack of newspapers and other periodicals from his girl at home to cheer him up, but the headlines contain such depressing proclamations as "Allies Hurled Back with Enormous Loss" and "New Serial Horrors of War."[127] For much of the same reason, a soldier in Operation Iraqi Freedom, nearly a century later, is happy to get sequestered on jury duty so he can avoid media coverage of not only the Iraq War but also of celebrity gossip.[128]

The media are a significant part of the civil-military relationship because, as journalist Marvin Kalb asked in a post-mortem on news and foreign policy in Operation Desert Storm, "From whom, if not from the press, are the American people to get the information on which to base intelligent decision on the worthiness of a particular war, or the soundness of their government's strategies and policies, or the actual conditions on and above the fields of combat?"[129] A *Broadside* cartoon from ODS captures this very idea with a woman seated on a couch, beer or soft drink in hand, watching television, and calling out, "Normannnnn.... The war's on!..."[130] Security policy-makers think of the media-government connection as a mutual exploitation model, realizing that policy cannot be created without news organizations and that news organizations cannot cover international matters without government input.[131] Indeed, reporters are heavily reliant on the Pentagon for information in military matters, allowing the government to take significant control in shaping the news.[132] War is an "expressive activity" in which the media acts as an international conduit for information and helps to shape public opinion.[133]

Despite, or maybe because, of this, the media-military relationship is often tense.[134] Several *Pvt. Murphy's Law* graphic narratives express this tension. In one, we see Murphy and Osama bin Laden, in a split-frame, both of them reading the same newspaper and war headlines, each thinking, "I don't understand why the U.S. media gives this information away."[135] In another, "Murphy" is warned by a comrade, "Watch your six!"—though it is not an enemy combatant behind him, but a camera man from the "Liberal Media."[136] Many of the warrior artists express various levels of skepticism, disdain, bemusement, frustration, or disbelief with the news media's coverage of the war and battles in which they themselves are fighting. Jeff Bacon humorously captures this phenomenon in a comic about "a slow news day in Afghanistan," as a warrior watches TV in his tent, and sees himself on the screen watching TV in his tent, because the news camera is poked through his own window.[137]

As early as the American Civil War we get "Gorge's" view of the war news as being exaggerated for drama and home-front morale. A split-frame narrative juxtaposes the news headline, "Later from the South! A REBEL STRONGHOLD cleaned out by our Artillery!!! Our Army now able to take the Offensive!!! Stirring events on foot!!!" with his visual interpretation of the "Rebel Stronghold?"—

which is an outhouse.[138] Bill Mauldin notes similar hyperbole during World War II, contrasting a news headline about "fresh, spirited American troops, flushed with victory, [who] are bringing in thousands of hungry, ragged, battle-weary prisoners," with an image of unkempt, fatigued, and sickly American troops slouching alongside barely distinguishable POWs.[139] On the other side of the reporting spectrum, Bairnsfather in World War I remarks, "Captain Mills-Bomme's temperature cracks the thermometer on seeing his recent daring exploits described as 'On our right there is nothing to report.'"[140]

The incongruity between news reports of war and experiences of war seem to come from the arrogance of the journalists—during the Spanish-American War, Pvt. Post records an impression of newspaper publisher William Randolph Hearst on horseback reviewing the troops, as would an officer[141]—and from the public relations practices of the military and government—as Mauldin notes in World War II, "Wherever a newspaper office opens, the actors come."[141] Indeed, Mauldin's cartoons are particularly cynical about the public relations tactics of the Second World War. In one cartoon, a correspondent asks a soldier in a foxhole, "What is weighing heavier on your mind at this time … The Senate scrapping the Green-Lucas Bill, or Italy's place at the peace table?"[143] In another, a photographer tells a GI, "Congratulations. You're the 100th soldier who has posed with that bottle of Coca Cola. You can drink it."[144] In yet another, a public relations officer conducts the home-front interview for a returning soldier, telling reporters, "He thinks the food over there was swell. He's glad to be home, but he misses the thrill and excitement of battle. You may quote him."[145] And reporters are so prevalent in Korea that a cartoon by Sgt.

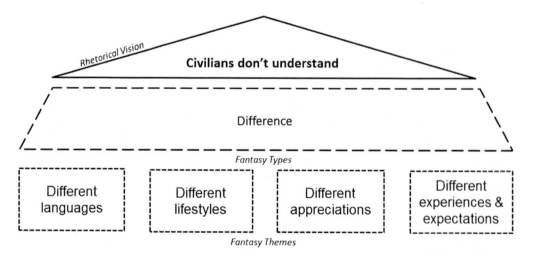

Fig. 8.3: Rhetorical vision of the civil-military relationship as expressed in warrior graphic narratives.

Kennedy from *Stars and Stripes* shows them blocking a soldier's access to the front.[146]

Warriors also note the differences between *reel* warfare and *real* warfare, in which the former is often more dangerous—though fought by better looking people.[147] Films shape civilian understanding of war and its impact on both civilians and veterans,[148] and yet warriors see little similarity between cinema and combat. Bairnsfather introduces readers to a soldier with severe injuries who ironically "went through Chateau Thierry, the Argonne, St. Mihiel, and Soissons, without a scratch. He was, however, accidentally wounded at Hollywood during the filming of No More War."[149] The television show about World War II, *Combat!*, is featured in multiple cartoons by Vernon Grant,[150] in one of which a soldier angrily shoots out the TV screen and is told, "Goonfunkle, you *Idiot! We always* lose during the first 20 minutes of 'Combat'!"[151] Decades later, Mark Baker's "Pvt. Murphy" realizes, "The Duke must have had one hell of a dentist!" when he unsuccessfully attempts to pull the pin out of a grenade with his teeth,[152] and a *Terminal Lance* cartoon compares the civilian watching a war movie and appreciating how "awesome" it is, to a Marine watching a war movie while noting all the absurd inaccuracies in it.[153]

Thanks for Nothing

Some graphic narratives comment much more directly on the civil-military gap. *Seaman Si* states in World War I, "I don't believe in complaining about the service to civilians—at that, the Navy is a fine place!"[154] And when Mark Baker's *Sgt. Murphy* in OEF/OIF is thanked by a civilian for his service, he responds, "I appreciate it, sir. But you don't have to thank me. I chose this profession."[155] While not asking for thanks, *Doctrine Man* and *Power Point Ranger* graphic narratives make repeated attempts to remind readers to recognize those fighting and those who have fought, such as "Veterans Day, 2010. Remember the men and women still fighting the longest war in America's history."[156] Others of their graphic narratives take us to scenes of mourning and remembrance in Arlington National Cemetery. Mark Baker in the modern day and Mauldin in World War II, meanwhile, comment directly on a lack of respect for service members and veterans. In his postwar "Willie and Joe" comics, Mauldin repeatedly emphasizes the difficulties facing veterans in housing,[157] employment, social life, and politics. Servicemen refuse to give veterans rides because they are civilians[158]; wives criticize their husbands for not bringing them home souvenirs from Europe[159]; and young men in uniform are told by older civilians that they "got no business discussin' serious matters."[160] More than five decades later, Mark Baker remarks on the poor pay of enlisted service members. He observes the irony of the army's decision to close the pay gap between the military and its civilian counterparts by asking, "So how much *are* civilian infantrymen making these days?"[161] Plus, he shows two men at a window for food stamps, one in uniform and one in shabby civilian clothes. The one in uniform is called a "freeloader" by the other.[162]

Debriefing

The rhetorical vision of the civil-military relationship is one of misunderstanding, wherein civilians will never be able to fully understand the military perspective, and service members will never have quite the same view of civilian life they once did. This vision is supported by the fantasy type of difference—which is the reason why civilians without any military experience are sometimes referred to as "sillyvillians," because of their seemingly silly ideas, or misconceptions, about the military life.[163] Figure 8.3 illustrates how the fantasy themes outlined above, such as different language, outlook, and experiences, build this fantasy type and the rhetorical vision of misunderstanding. This civil-military distinction is captured eloquently by Bairnsfather. In a split-frame narrative, he presents two people looking at the same moon, the civilian woman at home and the military man at war. The first observes its beauty. The second sees only its danger.[164] In sum, these graphic narratives represent the array of explanations offered for the civil-military gap, including tensions between ideals of individualism with group solidarity in the military, conflicts between the pursuit of personal comforts and freedoms with the key military premises of discipline and hierarchy, and unrealistic ideas and ideals created by media and military fiction.

Conclusion
SITREP—The Military's Rhetorical Vision

When I go home people'll ask me, "Hey Hoot, why do you do it,
man? What, you some kinda war junkie?" You know what I'll say?
I won't say a goddamn word. Why? They won't understand. They
won't understand why we do it. They won't understand that it's
about the men next to you, and that's it. That's all it is.

—*Black Hawk Down*

A SITREP is a situation report sent from one military element to another
to provide a detailed overview of its circumstances, including location, activity,
effectiveness, intelligence, logistics, status, and intentions. In civilian terms, it
is a summary. The preceding chapters have outlined the fantasy themes, types,
and rhetorical visions for various aspects of military life as found in warriors'
graphic narratives. This "situation report" will now turn to developing a meta-
rhetorical vision of the military by looking to the structural elements of symbolic
convergence and, thereby, summarizing the ideas explored throughout this
book. The communication that makes symbolic convergence—a shared worldview that promotes empathic communication—possible is a dramatizing message, creative and imaginative interpretations of the "there-and-then" that can
bring clarity to situations.[1] When such messages catch on they can spread
through lively agreement and retelling[2] and can be found through inside jokes,
such as those seen in cartoons. The elements of a dramatizing message that
build a rhetorical vision, or shared worldview, include the *dramatis personae*
(or characters) of a vision, the plotlines (or actions) of a vision, the scenes (or
the time/place setting) of a vision, the sanctioning agents (or sources of legitimacy) of a vision, and the master analogue (or righteous, social and/or pragmatic orientations) of a vision.

Rhetorical Vision Elements

By and large, the characters, and most particularly the heroes—even the unlikely ones—are "grunts," average enlisted warriors, who persevere against all odds, and usually do so with wry humor intact. These heroes, and occasional antiheroes, are alternatively patriotic, duty-bound, hapless, or beleaguered people who always try to make the best of a bad situation. They are mostly men, though there are some women heroines. In Western graphic narratives, they are also usually white, though there are some black heroes, too. The primary villains are the "brass hats," the unfeeling and somewhat clueless officers who make life difficult. Other villains are nonhuman; they are the rain, the snow, the cold, the heat, the mud, the sand, and the rocks, who make life uncomfortable. There is also the occasional villainous enemy, who can make life end.

Scenes are either of little to no significance, or are of primary significance in warriors' graphic narratives. Artists such as Mike Sinclair often have little to no scenery in the comics, placing the entire focus on the characters' words and actions. *Doctrine Man's* Anonymous often uses generic scenery—desks, water coolers, or a desert, to provide context for a comic. In graphic narratives that feature military geography or combat, however, the scene is the defining element of the dramatizing message, so much so that it becomes part of the plotline as a character, rather than just a setting.

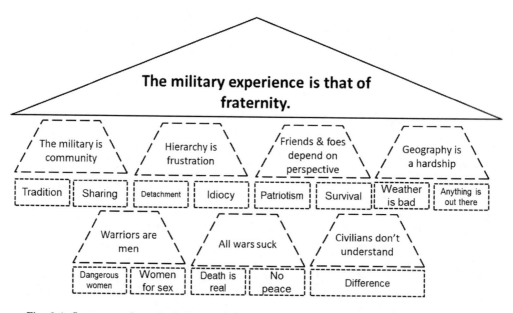

Fig. 9.1: Summary rhetorical vision of the military as expressed in warrior graphic narratives.

Simply put, the general story line in warriors' graphic narratives is daily life in the military: food, shelter, sex, health, officers, bureaucracy, weather, terrain, enemies, allies, civilians, training, combat ... and death. These are, however, but variants on a single plotline that is about the military community or family, the men and women with and for whom each warrior lives, fights, and dies. It does not matter whether those persons are close friends, obnoxious goldbricks, naïve half-wits, or even hostile officers. Nor does it really matter if they are of another gender, race, or religion, however little or poorly understood. They are all comrades at arms. The sanctioning agent is, therefore, experience—knowing firsthand what it is like to eat bad food, in the rain, sitting beside the person who today saved your life when yesterday you saved his. Because of the shrinking population who has this experience, it is all the more central to the legitimization of these messages.

The master analogue at work in these graphic narratives varies somewhat according to the individual artists. Each has a particular focus of his or her own, despite the high level of consistency in fantasy themes across the centuries. In keeping the plotlines' emphasis on people, there is a strong, underlying social orientation in the graphic narratives. The more overt orientation tends to be pragmatic, in the warriors' handling of daily difficulties, whether it is being dressed-down by an officer, staying warm in the snow, or finding sexual gratification. There is an undercurrent of righteousness that seems to naturally come with military service—duty, honor, and country. It is not, however, the overriding concern in the graphic narratives, which generally have little to do with ideology (though this is shifting in the newer graphic narratives), grunts being much more concerned with the practical matters of day-to-day life.

Warrior and Team Member

The social orientation, the importance of experience, the centrality of people in the plotlines, and the "average (GI) Joe" characters all suggest a rhetorical vision of the military that is about fraternity. In June 2014, as ISIS—the Islamic State in Iraq and Syria—pushed the newly liberated Iraq toward civil war, some veterans proclaimed, "This is not what we sacrificed for." The managing editor of the *Marine Corps Times*, Geoff Ingersoll, had a different take on it, though. In an editorial, he argued that war cannot be thought of as a transaction because there is no guaranteed outcome. Instead, he offered the perspective of a friend and fellow veteran who said, "It is our personal conduct, not strategic success which defines our sacrifices. Some who went to Iraq did so for God, others for country, but mostly we did it for the Corps ... we did it for each other."[3] A similar sentiment was echoed a month later in a blog entry entitled "Mandatory Iraq

Veteran Post" by Gary Owen, who said, "We didn't serve because it made sense. We served because of each other."[4]

The previous chapters have essentially looked at the fantasy themes of a meta-rhetorical vision—themes of culture, hierarchy, enemies, geography, gender, combat, and civilians. Figure 9.1 draws together those ideas and demonstrates how they combine and interact to form a military rhetorical vision of community, of family, of brotherhood. As the American Soldier's Creed states, "I am a warrior and a member of a team."[5] Whether facing the inconveniences of communal life, the frustrations of hierarchy, the enemy, the hardships of geography, sexual politics, combat, or the civil-military gap, warriors do it together. Even fantasies related to the Other—whether enemies, allies, women, gays, civilians, or officers—reinforce the fraternal vision of the military. The Other only becomes problematic when it threatens the military family, as with the potential for women's perceived lack of strength posing a danger in combat, unscrupulous spouses causing financial or emotional damage to brothers in arms, civilians disrespecting the military establishment, enemy combatants bringing death, or incompetent leadership making costly mistakes. Furthermore, the identification of outsiders helps to reinforce insider status or group belonging and cohesion.

Perhaps one of the most significant revelations in uncovering this rhetorical vision is its universal quality. The military experience is one of fraternity whether it is 1863, 1943, 1973, or 2013. The military experience is one of fraternity whether one volunteers or is drafted, and whether the forces are conscript or all-volunteer. The military experience is one of fraternity whether on the ground with the army, under the sea with the navy, or in the sky with the air force. The military experience is one of fraternity whether one is with American, Australian, British, Canadian, Chinese, German, Japanese, Kiwi, Korean, Vietnamese, or Yugoslavian forces. No matter who, when, or where one is in the military, the food is probably bad, lower ranks feel put upon by superiors, the enemy is politically and racially stereotyped as evil, and people die.

It is true that the face of war has changed. There has been a shift from reliance on hard power resources, such as weaponry, geography, and population, to soft power resources such as technology, education, and economy. Additionally, the military is a subsystem of its particular society and is, therefore, influenced by unique socio-economic, political, cultural, and technological forces. So ancient warriors differed from medieval warriors, who differed from modern warriors, who will differ from future warriors. But regardless of these changes, the military world exists at three basic levels that are indifferent to time or place: The individual level of the single warrior; the unit level of platoons up through branches; and the bureaucratic and industrial-technological level. War itself is constant, whether it is fought with bows or bombs or daggers or drones.

War is a *collective* activity in which a social group must be ready and willing to kill and be killed. Whether it is a conscripted force "for the duration" of a conflict or an all-volunteer peacekeeping force, its ultimate purpose is violence—even if it is violence tempered by political education, cultural empathy, and diplomacy.[6] The continuation of exertion of political will through violence contributes to the continuation of ancient military traditions shared worldwide— marching and drills, uniforms, hierarchies—which in turn contributes to the generational transcendence of military jokes and the similarities in experiences reflected in this international and intergenerational rhetorical vision of military fraternity.[7]

Endurance

The strength of the rhetorical vision is attested to through the popularity and longevity of military graphic narratives as a genre and of particular artists and series. At the writing of this conclusion, *Doctrine Man* had over 29,000 followers on Facebook and nearly 6,000 on Twitter, including General Ray Odierno, the 38th chief of staff of the U.S. Army. He has been featured in the *New York Times*.[8] *Power Point Ranger* had more than 83,000 followers on Facebook. *Terminal Lance* had more than 275,000 followers on Facebook, including General Jim Amos, 35th commandant of the Marine Corps, among its readers[9]; the creator, Maximilian Uriarte, has been profiled in *Men's Journal*.[10] *Doctrine Man* and *Delta Bravo Sierra* both won "mil-humor" awards in 2013.[11] Mort Walker was honored by the army in 2000.[12] Steve Opet has won more than fifty art awards.[13] Bill Mauldin earned a Pulitzer Prize. *Beetle Bailey,* one of the most popular comic strips in the world, has been in print for more than six decades.[14] Old Bill, Bert, and Alf, from the work of Bruce Bairnsfather, helped to raise funds for Help for Heroes, a charity supporting British service men and women from the conflicts in Afghanistan and Iraq.[15] Dorothea Byerly's *Up Came a Ripple* was republished in the mid-to-late 1990s as part of fundraising efforts for women's military service memorial in Arlington National Cemetery.[16] In 2002, Vic Herman's *Winnie the WAC* returned to duty, at the bequest of Virginia Herman, to boost morale following the events of September 11, 2001.[17] And Bill Mauldin's Willie and Joe re-upped in 2010, appearing on T-shirts to benefit Soldiers Project, a non-profit organization that provides free psychological treatment to military members and families.[18] As Maximilian Uriarte noted with a comic he did on a Katy Perry music video, "Part of me ... always tries to avoid doing pop-culture references for the mere fact that it is so fickle. In ten years, no one is going to care about Katy Perry or this video, yet this strip will still exist."[19]

The kinds of humor employed by these graphic narratives, and the hundreds of other like them, likely contribute to their popularity while not only reaffirming military fraternity but also enabling fraternal bonds. In relating to and identifying with the graphic narratives, people recognize shared hopes and fears and produce a shared cultural memory. At the outset of this book, seven distinct, if overlapping, types of humor found in or used by the military were demarcated, but a consideration of the graphic narratives that have been discussed reveals a particular blurring and blending of these humor styles. For example, a gag about a woman's figure may be irrelevant as something that has little do with life in the services, and nothing to do with war, but consideration of the "deployment goggles" phenomenon may gain a unique interpretation as a light, inside, joke. If the same sexual gag is also being told within a context of foreign deployment, it may take on a layer of serio-comic social commentary. Add a reminder about sexually transmittable infections, and it is now also instructive humor, and perhaps even black, depending on how grotesque the reminder. And, if that gag resonates with a reader's personal experience, there may also be found an individual layer of unintentional humor.

Similarly, military graphic narratives traverse the genre boundaries of the medium in ways that transcend the variables demarcating the Gold, Silver, or Bronze ages. Relying on a mix of personal experiences, shared first- and second-hand accounts, and current events, many of these graphic narratives fall somewhere between diary strips and comics journalism, with touches of editorial cartoons and the approach of the gag strip. And yet, they are also developed into full comic books and even graphic novels. It is arguably the unique military experience that enables such a nuanced mix of humor and sequential art styles within any given graphic narrative, but it is also likely related to the tradition of war cartooning and the cartoonist fraternity within the military fraternity, in which Steve Opet draws inspiration from Bill Mauldin,[20] and Mark Baker draws inspiration from Mort Walker,[22] and W.C. Pope draws inspiration from Jake Schuffert.[22]

Fantasy Variations

That the fantasy themes in the military graphic narratives bear remarkable consistency across national borders and historical periods—as well as across outlets, including government-sanctioned publications, collections not intended for publication, letters home, independent and commercial Internet services—further demonstrates the authenticity of warriors' graphic narrative expressions, beyond deliberate government attempts at education or persuasion. Such cross-national consistency, given cultural and ethnic differences in humor, further emphasizes the relative homogeneity of the military experience. Of course, there are fantasy theme and fantasy type variations within different historical periods or national situations—many of which have been mentioned throughout the analysis—along with varying emphases or areas of focus in the graphic narratives. This is consistent, as Jay Casey found, with "the course of individual involvement with the military,"[23] as evidenced by different areas of focus among artists, such as Bill Mauldin's frequent lampooning of officers, versus Hank Ketcham's usual attention to women and male-female relations. During World War I, American graphic narratives were primarily concerned with the amusement of training, whereas the British graphic narratives reflected the longer time at war with more attention to combat.

In World War II, much of the graphic narrative humor was focused on the weather and officers. During the Japanese Occupation and Korea, American cartoonists were more preoccupied with Asian cultures and women. In Vietnam, the focus became more scattered, perhaps reflecting a weakened identification with the military establishment; some focused on survival as related to both the enemy and the climate, others on banalities of daily life, especially popular culture and media, such as television, record players, and magazines. Such attention to material and cultural comforts is fitting for the first "Rock and Roll War,"[24] in which consumerism was central to the noncombat activities of military life.[25] Banalities were certainly the feature of Cold War graphic narratives—just the day-to-day bureaucracy of the military. In more recent decades, as warriors have been trained in empathy and diplomacy, and not just in violence, artists have probed military doctrine, strategy, and regulations more deeply.

Some variations are also attributable to differences in branch identity. The navy is a branch steeped in international tradition, equipped for sea, land, and air operations. It guards its independence. Graphic narratives by seaman often emphasize the distinctive lingo, hierarchy, close quarters, and unique dangers—particularly as related to shipboard technology—of naval service, alongside lighthearted nods to long-standing navy stereotypes, such as sailors with "girls in every port." The air force embodies a strategy of war related to the love of flight and flying machines. Graphic narratives by airmen, therefore, often focus on (or at least feature) planes, speed, and altitude, in addition to other things that represent flight—such as pop-culture icons like Batman and the movie *Top Gun*. The army has historically represented the idea of the citizen-soldier, with a focus on the art of war during crises. The citizen-soldier ideal is strongly represented in graphic narratives by soldiers, which make up the bulk of available warrior comics and cartoons. Soldiers' accounts tend to put the most emphasis on daily hardship or drudgery, the quirks of military culture, and civil-military transitions.[26]

Mind the Gap

While personal experience is an important feature of the rhetorical vision of the military fraternity, the messages in these graphic narratives are meaningful for civilians, too, because it helps to explain that same experience. Not only do graphic narratives and humor within the military serve training and enculturation functions; they also serve external communication functions that can benefit both the military and civilian populations. Showing pictures of deployment is easier for some veterans than just talking about it, and artwork of various kinds can ease the transition back into civilian life and help to close the civil-military gap.[27] Graphic narratives may be able to uniquely express what combat feels like.[28] The higher level of audience engagement in reading graphic narratives over other forms of media may present a distinctive means of mediated combat and deployment experience for civilians.

Though it is true that some of the humor and references are perhaps too "inside" to be readily understood by a civilian audience, the graphic narratives can show aspects of military life otherwise invisible to much of the public—most particularly, activities other than state-sanctioned killing. Indeed, letters written by soldiers during the Second World War reveal that the warriors themselves would use cartoons to help explain their experiences to loved ones at home. For example, William T. Livingston, who served from 1944 to 1946 in the army infantry with stations in the Philippines, New Guinea, and Japan, wrote to his "folks" in February 1946, "I was reading 'Up Front' by Bill Mauldin which really tells the best story of the life and thoughts of the infantryman during this war. The cartoons may seem crude to you but they really tell the actual story better than any words can. If you really want to know how we feel and what we did don't miss it. I would like to own a copy myself."[29] And Jerry Brenner, who served from 1943 to 1945 in the army artillery with stations in Europe, sent home a *Hubert* cartoon (depicting a convoy's worth of men relieving themselves along a mountain road), clipped from a newspaper or magazine in 1945.[30]

Seeing this human, noncombatant side of the military may be just the counter needed to news headlines that call veterans "ticking bombs," for whom violence and murder are a growing problem[31]—or, as the satirical military newspaper *The Duffel Blog* proclaimed, "Veterans with PTSD Linked to Everything That Could Kill Your Children."[32] That is not to say that exposure to these graphic narratives would, or should, contribute to America's banal militarism.[33] Indeed, as Stephen M. Walt pointed out, "Humor and ridicule are potent weapons when trying to keep powerful institutions under control," and a lack of popular military humor makes it harder for society to keep them in check. This function of military humor is seen in the often-subversive nature of military cartoons, an aspect underscored by the low representation of available military comics from dictatorships or military regime states. "Capable armed forces are a regrettable necessity, but treating them with excessive deference and declining to joke about their foibles makes it more likely they will be indulged rather than improved."[34] Such improvements can be to the benefit of not only civil control of the military institution, as suggested by Walt, but also to the benefit of veteran services through greater recognition and improved understanding of military experiences and their physical and emotional effects.

Casey writes: "The visual record of wartime comics deserves to see the light again, not only for what the images tell us about a certain part of the past but because much of it is still funny, if poignantly so. The work of soldier cartoonists presents a valuable area for research in that veiled social commentary, as opposed to more obvious forms of editorial comment, often informed their work."[35] Therefore, to scholars of military history or sociology, group communication, cultures, and graphic narratives, the works by these warrior artists offer valuable insights about military culture and conflicts, society, and politics. They provide us glimpses of not only the horrific and heroic, which we may find amply in literature, film, and video games, but also of the miserable and mundane, little seen in war pop-culture. Like letters, diaries, and other personal and autobiographical accounts, graphic narratives about war and the military, written and drawn by warriors, provide insight to communal experience through their culturally specific perception of the artist within an historical and collective social context. Such firsthand accounts reveal chronological facts as well as cultural awareness and self-consciousness and provide unique insight into armed conflict and the perspectives of those who experienced it.

Bravo-Zulu

The term "Bravo Zulu" originates from naval signals. Signals are letters and/or numbers and their combinations that convey particular messages. "BZ" or "Bravo Zulu" indicates "well done," and BZ messages are often given at the end of a successful mission. This BZ message is a salute to the two centuries' worth of military graphic narratives collected and considered for this volume. These graphic narratives have helped their creators and their readers navigate military life and cope with war, managing and mitigating discomfort, homesickness, loss, fear, anger, confusion, frustration, and isolation. As cartoonist Steve Opet said, "If I can get someone to crack a smile in a war zone, that makes me feel good."[36] They have also provided the servicepersons' loved ones with a means of understanding, and they offer other civilians a chance to see a different side of war and the military—the inglorious, the dull, the sensitive, and the coarse that are often excluded from news and fictions. These graphic narratives, influenced as they are by the norms and traditions of a social subgroup, limited in their circulation and their ready comprehension, further provide a pointed example of the ways in which comics' content and context are intertwined, and how they reveal particular histories and create particular communities.

Appendix
Comicography

Creator(s): 8th Route Military
Country: China
Era(s): World War II
Service: Army
Source(s): John A. Lent and Xu Ying, "Cartooning and Wartime China: Part One—1931–1945," *International Journal of Comic Art* 10, no. 1 (2008): 76–139.

Creator(s): Anonymous
Country: USA
Era(s): Operation Enduring Freedom, Operation Iraqi Freedom
Service: Army—officer
Source(s): http:www.facebook.com/doctrineman (accessed September 30, 2014); *The Further Adventures of Doctrine Man, Vol. 1* (Lexington, KY: Doctrine Man, 2013); *The Further Adventures of Doctrine Man, Vol. 2* (Bernardino, CA: Doctrine Man, 2013)

Creator(s): Al Avison
Country: USA
Era(s): Korean War
Service: unknown
Source(s): *Military Courtesy* (Harvey Comics, 1951).

Creator(s): Jeff Bacon
Country: USA
Era(s): Cold War, Operation Desert Storm, Operation Enduring Freedom, Operation Iraqi Freedom, interwar years

Service: Navy
Source(s): http://www.broadside.net (accessed March 2, 2013); *20 Years of Broadside* (Garden City, ID: Deep Water, 2006); *The Best of Broadside* (Newport News: Deep Water, 2006)

Creator(s): Bruce Bairnsfather
Country: England
Era(s): World War I
Service: Army, Capt.
Source(s): *Carry On Sergeant!* (Indianapolis: Bobbs-Merrill, 1927); Tonie Holt and Valmai Holt, eds., *The Best of Fragments from France* (South Yorkshire: Pen and Sword Military, 1998).

Creator(s): George Baker
Country: USA
Era(s): World War II
Service: Army, Sgt.
Source(s): *The Sad Sack* (New York: Simon and Schuster, 1944); *The New Sad Sack* (New York: Simon and Schuster, 1946); Sid Schapiro, ed., *I Ain't Laughing, Sir* (Stars and Stripes, 1980), 49–90; Ira Topping, ed., *The Best of YANK The Army Weekly* (New York: Arno, 1980).

Creator(s): Mark Baker
Country: USA
Era(s): Interwar years, Operation Enduring Freedom, Operation Iraqi Freedom
Service: Army

Source(s): *Private Murphy's Law* (Balti-more: United Books, 1999); *PV-2 Murphy: The Adventure Continues* (Baltimore: United Books, 2001); *Pfc. Murphy* (Baltimore: United Books, 2005); *Sgt. Murphy* (Alexandria, VA: BYRRD Enterprises, 2008).

Creator(s): Roger Baker
Country: USA
Era(s): Korean War
Service: Marines
Source(s): *USMC Tanker's Korea* (Oakland, OR: Elderberry, 2001).

Creator(s): C. Leroy Baldridge
Country: USA
Era(s): World War I
Service: Army, Pvt.
Source(s): John T. Winterich, ed., *Squads Write! A Selection of the Best Things in Prose, Verse and Cartoons from The Stars and Stripes* (New York: Harpers and Brothers, 1931); Alexander Woolcott, *The Command is Forward—Tales of the A.E.F. Battlefields as They Appeared in The Stars and Stripes* (New York: Century, 1919).

Creator(s): Barsis
Country: USA
Era(s): World War II
Service: unknown
Source(s): *They're All Yours, Uncle Sam!* (New York: Stephan Daye, 1943).

Creator(s): Des Bettany
Country: England
Era(s): World War II
Service: Army, Bomb.
Source(s): Sara Malm, "Sketches from Hell: Humorous Cartoons Drawn by British Soldier Kept as a Japanese PoW," *Daily Mail*, July 5, 2012, http://www.dailymail.co.uk/news/article-2169177/Sketches-hell-Touching-cartoons-drawn-British-soldier-years-terror-Changi-prison.html (accessed March 1, 2013).

Creator(s): Robert K. Bindig
Country: USA
Era(s): World War II
Service: Army
Source(s): Veterans History Project, American Folklife Center, Library of Congress (AFC/2001/001/32475), digital collection, http://lcweb2.loc.gov/diglib/vhp/story/loc.natlib.afc2001001.32475/artworks (accessed June 22, 2014).

Creator(s): Douglas Borgstedt
Country: USA
Era(s): World War II
Service: Sgt.
Source(s): Ira Topping, ed., *The Best of YANK The Army Weekly* (New York: Arno, 1980).

Creator(s): Samuel Lionel Boylston
Country: USA
Era(s): World War II
Service: Army Air Force, Sgt.
Source(s): Veterans History Project, American Folklife Center, Library of Congress (AFC/2001/001/1848), digital collection, http://lcweb2.loc.gov/diglib/vhp/story/loc.natlib.afc2001001.01848/ (accessed September 29, 2014).

Creator(s): Frank Brandt
Country: USA
Era(s): World War II
Service: Sgt.
Source(s): Ira Topping, ed., *The Best of YANK The Army Weekly* (New York: Arno, 1980); editor, *Cartoons for Fighters* (Washington, D.C.: Infantry Journal, 1945), 91–116.

Creator(s): Dave Breger
Country: USA
Era(s): World War II
Service: Army, Pvt.
Source(s): *Private Breger: His Adventures in Army Camp* (New York: Rand McNally, 1942); *Private Breger in Britain* (London: Pilot, 1944); "Private Breger," in *I Ain't Laughing, Sir,* ed. Sid Schapiro (Stars and Stripes, 1980).

Creator(s): Barbara Bristol
Country: USA
Era(s): World War II
Service: Marines, Pfc.
Source(s): *Meet Molly Marine* (Robert J. Weaver, 1945).

Creator(s): Kathleen A. Browning
Country: USA
Era(s): Operation Desert Storm
Service: Army
Source(s): Paula E. Calvin and Deborah A. Deacon, *American Women Artists in Wartime, 1776–2010* (Jefferson, NC: McFarland, 2011), Kindle e-book; "Mid-East Coast Girls," *Art of the American Soldier,* http://constitutioncenter.org/experience/exhibitions/past-exhibitions/art-of-the-anerican-soldier-gallery (March 4, 2013).

Creator(s): Jack Bryan
Country: USA
Era(s): World War II
Service: Army Air Force, Sgt.
Source(s): "Uniform 'Beau Brummel' Humor," eBay listing by k-townconsignments, http://www.ebay.com/itm/MILITARY-POLICE-ARMY-UNIFORM-HUMOR-POLITICAL-CARTOON-ART-MACDILL-FIELD-FLORIDA-/140943951004 (accessed October 9, 2014).

Creator(s): Johnny Bryson
Country: USA
Era(s): World War II
Service: Pvt.
Source(s): Ira Topping, ed., *The Best of YANK The Army Weekly* (New York: Arno, 1980).

Creator(s): Hal Burrows
Country: USA
Era(s): World War I
Service: Sgt.
Source(s): John T. Winterich, ed., *Squads Write! A Selection of the Best Things in Prose, Verse and Cartoons from The Stars and Stripes* (New York: Harpers and Brothers, 1931).

Creator(s): Alban B. Butler, Jr.
Country: USA
Era(s): World War I
Service: Army, Capt.
Source(s): *Training for the Trenches: A Book of Humorous Cartoons on a Serious Subject* (New York: Palmer, 1917); *"Happy Days!" A Humorous Narrative in Drawings of the Progress of American Arms, 1917–1919* (Chicago: First Division Museum at Cantigny, 2011).

Creator(s): Dorothea Byerly
Country: USA
Era(s): World War II
Service: WAVES, Y/1C
Source(s): *Up Came a Ripple* (East Orange, NJ: Greenwood, 1945).

Creator(s): Irwin Caplan
Country: USA
Era(s): World War II
Service: Sgt.
Source(s): Ira Topping, ed., *The Best of YANK The Army Weekly* (New York: Arno, 1980).

Creator(s): Ward Carroll
Country: USA
Era(s): Operation Enduring Freedom, Operation Iraqi Freedom
Service: Navy, LCdr
Source(s): "Brownshoes in Action Comix," *Approach Magazine,* http://safetycenter.navy.mil/ (accessed March 2, 2013).

Creator(s): Choé
Country: Vietnam
Era(s): Vietnam War
Service: Sgt.
Source(s): Tran Da Tu, *Writers and Artists in Vietnames Gulags with Choé's Cartoons from Vietnam* (Washington, D.C.: Century, 1990); http://www.watermargin.com/vietmain/toons/choe_art.html (accessed August 30, 2014).

Creator(s): Jack Coggins
Country: USA
Era(s): World War II
Service: Army
Source(s): David Coggins, "Jack Coggins Yank Magazine Illustrations and Articles," *Jack Banham Coggins,* October 2014, http://www.jackcoggins.info/yanklist.html.

Creator(s): Cecile Cowdery
Country: USA
Era(s): World War II
Service: military wife
Source(s): "My Personal Touch," *Reader's Digest Special Edition World War II: An Illustrated Celebration of Love Letters, Homecomings, and the American Family.* July 22, 2014: 67.

Creator(s): Percy L. Crosby
Country: USA
Era(s): World War I
Service: Army, Lieut.
Source(s): *That Rookie from the 13th Squad* (New York: Harper and Brothers, 1918); John T. Winterich, ed., *Squads Write! A Selection of the Best Things in Prose, Verse and Cartoons from The Stars and Stripes* (New York: Harpers and Brothers, 1931).

Creator(s): George Cruikshank
Country: Scotland
Era(s): Napoleonic Wars
Service: Loyal North Britons, volunteer regiment of Scots in London
Source(s): Mark Bryant, *Napoleonic Wars in Cartoons* (London: Grub Street, 2009), 16, 35–6, 63, 68, 81, 98–9, 102, 105–7, 109–15, 129–31, 134–7, 139, 145–7, 152–3, 156, and 158.

Creator(s): "Paul Crum" (Roger Pettiward)
Country: USA
Era(s): World War II
Service: Commandos
Source(s): Mark Bryant, *World War II in Comics* (London: W.H. Smith, 1989), 52, 53.

Creator(s): Kirkland H. Day
Country: USA
Era(s): World War I
Service: Army
Source(s): *Camion Cartoons* (Boston, MA: Marshall Jones, 1919).

Creator(s): Anthony Delatri
Country: USA
Era(s): World War II
Service: Pfc.
Source(s): Ira Topping, ed., *The Best of YANK The Army Weekly* (New York: Arno, 1980).

Creator(s): Clive Dixon
Country: England
Era(s): Boer War
Service: 16th Lancers, Capt.
Source(s): Mark Bryant, *Wars of Empire in Cartoons* (London: Grub Street, 2009), 125.

Creator(s): Fairfax Downey
Country: USA
Era(s): World War I
Service: Lt.
Source(s): John T. Winterich, ed., *Squads Write! A Selection of the Best Things in Prose, Verse and Cartoons from The Stars and Stripes* (New York: Harpers and Brothers, 1931).

Creator(s): O.L. Dudley
Country: USA
Era(s): World War II
Service: Cpl.
Source(s): Ira Topping, ed., *The Best of YANK The Army Weekly* (New York: Arno, 1980).

Creator(s): R.F. Duggan
Country: USA
Era(s): World War II
Service: unknown
Source(s): Donald Nijboer, *Graphic War: The Secret Aviation Drawings and Illustrations of World War II* (Ontario: Boston Mills, 2011), 34; https://www.flickr.com/photos/regierart/sets/

72157633031054732/ (accessed October 10, 2014).

Creator(s): Frank Dunne
Country: Australia
Era(s): World War I
Service: Army
Source(s): "Digger Days," Australian War Memorial, digital exhibits, http://www.awm.gov.au/exhibitions/1918 (March 27, 2013).

Creator(s): Will Dyson
Country: Australia
Era(s): World War I
Service: Australian official war artist
Source(s): Mark Bryant, *World War I in Cartoons* (London: Grub Street, 2009), 121 and 158.

Creator(s): Will Eisner
Country: USA
Era(s): World War II, Korean War, Vietnam War, Cold War
Service: Army
Source(s): "Joe Dope," *Army Motors*, http://www.jhalpe.com (accessed September 18, 2011); "Joe Dope," in *Cartoons for Fighters*, Frank Brandt, ed. (Washington, D.C.: Infantry Journal, 1945); Eddie Campbell, ed., *P.S Magazine: The Best of the Preventative Maintenance Monthly* (New York: Abrams ComicArts, 2011); Department of the Army, *Troubleshooting Equipment in Combat Units* (Washington, D.C.: U.S. Government Printing Office, 1973); *The M561/M792 GAMA Goat: Operation and Preventative Maintenance* (Department of the Army, 1979); *The M16A1 Rifle: Operation and Preventative Maintenance* (Washington, D.C.: U.S. Government Printing Office, 1969).

Creator(s): K.F.
Country: USA
Era(s): Operation Enduring Freedom, Operation Iraqi Freedom
Service: Army
Source(s): "On Cyber Patrol," Army Office of Information Assurance and Compliance—http://ciog6.army.mil/OnCyberPatrol/OCPComics/tabid/129/Default.aspx (accessed June 30, 2013).

Creator(s): Jaro Fabry
Country: USA
Era(s): World War II
Service: Pvt.
Source(s): Ira Topping, ed., *The Best of YANK The Army Weekly* (New York: Arno, 1980).

Creator(s): Joseph Farris
Country: USA
Era(s): World War II
Service: Army
Source(s): *A Soldier's Sketchbook from the Front Lines of World War II* (Washington, D.C.: National Geographic, 2011).

Creator(s): Leslie J. Feingold
Country: USA
Era(s): World War II
Service: Army[?]
Source(s): "ZOOT: In Action," National Museum of American Jewish Military History, digital exhibits. http://nmajmh.pastperfect-online.com/34213cgi/mweb.exe?request=record;id=4638B7D4-BFA8–435B-9963–002086834533;type=101 (accessed September 29, 2014).

Creator(s): Ian Fenwick
Country: England
Era(s): World War II
Service: Special Air Service
Source(s): Mark Bryant, *World War II in Cartoons* (London: W.H. Smith, 1989), 29, 100, 101.

Creator(s): Thomas Flannery
Country: USA
Era(s): World War II
Service: Pfc.
Source(s): Ira Topping, ed., *The Best of YANK The Army Weekly* (New York: Arno, 1980).

Creator(s): Tad Foster
Country: USA
Era(s): Vietnam War
Service: Marines
Source(s): *The Vietnam Funny Book: An Antidote to Insanity* (Novato, CA: Presidio, 1980).

Creator(s): Alex Gard
Country: USA
Era(s): World War II
Service: Navy, QM/2c
Source(s): *Sailors in Boots* (New York: Charles Scribner's Sons, 1943).

Creator(s): Art Gates
Country: USA
Era(s): World War II
Service: Cpl.
Source(s): Ira Topping, ed., *The Best of YANK The Army Weekly* (New York: Arno, 1980).

Creator(s): Theodor Seuss Geisel
Country: USA
Era(s): World War II
Service: Army
Source(s): *Starve the Squander Bug,* UNT Digital Library, http://digital. library.unt.edu/ark:/67531/metadc138/ (accessed October 10, 2014); *This Is Ann,* with Munro Leaf (War Department, 1943).

Creator(s): Robert G. Geisler, Jr.
Country: USA
Era(s): Vietnam War
Service: Marines, Cpl.
Source(s): Veterans History Project, American Folklife Center, Library of Congress (AFC/2001/001/76576), manuscripts.

Creator(s): "George"
Country: USA—Union States
Era(s): American Civil War
Service: 44th Massachusetts Infantry
Source(s): Robert E. Bronner, *The Soldier's Pen* by Robert E. Bronner (New York: Hill and Wang, 2006).

Creator(s): Chris Grant
Country: USA
Era(s): Operation Enduring Freedom, Operation Iraqi Freedom
Service: Army Reserve, SSgt.
Source(s): Jason Chudy, "Reservist's Cartoons Detail Burdens of Desert Deployment" *Stars and Stripes*, August 9, 2004, http://www.stripes.com/news/ reservist-s-cartoons-detail-burdens-of-desert-deployment-1.22605 (accessed March 3, 2013).

Creator(s): Sumner Grant
Country: USA
Era(s: World War II
Service: Army, Pfc.
Source(s): Veterans History Project, American Folklife Center, Library of Congress (AFC/2001/001/20970), digital collection, http://lcweb2.loc.gov/ diglib/vhp/story/loc.natlib. afc2001001,20970/ (accessed May 2, 2014).

Creator(s): Vernon Grant
Country: USA
Era(s): Vietnam War
Service: Army
Source(s): *Stand-by One!* (Hong Kong: Dublin Associates, 1969); "Grant's Grunts," *Pacific Stars and Stripes* archives.

Creator(s): Marion Reh Gurfein
Country: USA
Era(s): World War II
Service: military spouse
Source(s): "The Goofein Journal," Veterans History Project, American Folklife Center, Library of Congress (AFC/2001/001/799), digital collection, http://lcweb2.loc.gov/diglib/vhp/story/ loc.natlib.afc2001001.00799/artworks (accessed September 30, 2014).

Creator(s): Jeffrey Hall
Country: USA
Era(s): Operation Enduring Freedom, Operation Iraqi Freedom

Service: Air National Guard, SSgt.
Source(s): *Downrange*, http://www.military.com/cartooncontent/0,14763,Hall_Index,00.html (accessed March 1, 2013); *Downrange*, http://www.military-quotes.com/military-cartoons.htm (accessed March 1, 2013);

Creator(s): Cecil L. Hartt
Country: Australia
Era(s): World War I
Service: Corpl.
Source(s): *Humorosities by an Australian Soldier* (London: Australian Trading and Agencies, n.d.)

Creator(s): Albert Heim
Country: Germany
Era(s): World War I
Service: commissioned by Lieut-Gen Theodor von Wundt, 26th Division
Source(s): Ann Gripper, "Heim Front: German Artist's World War I Cartoons Up for Auction," *Mirror*, March 15, 2012, http://www.mirror.co.uk/news/uk-news/world-war-i-cartoons-by-albert-heim-761412 (accessed March 2, 2013).

Creator(s): Vic Herman
Country: USA
Era(s): World War II
Service: Army, Cpl.
Source(s): *Winnie the WAC* (Philadelphia: David McKay, 1945).

Creator(s): Frank Hewitt
Country: USA
Era(s): World War II
Service: Pfc.
Source(s): Ira Topping, ed., *The Best of YANK The Army Weekly* (New York: Arno, 1980).

Creator(s): J.F.E. Hillen
Country: USA, Union States
Era(s): American Civil War
Service: Army, Sgt.
Source(s): Harry L. Katz and Vincent Virga, *Civil War Sketch Book: Drawings*

from the Battlefront (New York: W.W. Norton, 2012).

Creator(s): Holcomb
Country: USA
Era(s): World War I
Service: Army
Source(s): *Ups and Downs ... of Camp Upton* (New York: Bescardi, 1917).

Creator(s): John F. Holmes
Country: USA
Era(s): Operation Enduring Freedom, Operation Iraqi Freedom
Service: Army, Sgt.
Source(s): *Power Point Ranger, Vol. 1* (New York: World Audience, 2012); *FM 1.0 Counter Boredom Operations: Power Point Ranger Comics 1–170* (Amazon Digital Services, 2014), Kindle e-book; *FM 2.0 Field Expedient Practical Joking: Power Point Ranger Comics 171–340* (Amazon Digital Services, 2014), Kindle e-book; *FM 3.0 Secret Squirrel Stuff: Power Point Ranger Comics 341–510* (Amazon Digital Services, 2014), Kindle e-book; *Grunts: Downrange with Corporal Thog and Specialist Roy* (Think On Productions, 2014), Kindle e-book; http://www.pptranger.net/comics/ (accessed August 17, 2014); https://facebook.com/Powerpointranger (accessed August 17, 2014).

Creator(s): Bill Hume (and John Annarino)
Country: USA
Era(s): Japanese Occupation
Service: Navy
Source(s): *Babysan: A Private Look at the Japanese Occupation* (Tokyo: Kasuga Boeki, 1953); *When We Get Back Home from Japan* (Tokyo: Kyoya, 1953); *Babysan's World: The Humne'n Slant on Japan* (Rutland, VT: Charles E. Tuttle, 1954).

Creator(s): Roman Jarymowycz
Country: Canada
Era(s): unknown, modern
Service: LtCol

Source(s): *Cavalry from Hoof to Track* (Westport, CT: Praeger, 2008); *Rendezvous 81*, eBay listing by superpetmuffin, http://www.ebay.com/itm/ Canadian-Military-Comic-Cartoon-Art-1981-RV-Signed-CH-Belzile-LGC-DR-Baker-MGC-/111384909823?pt=LH_ DefaultDomain_2&hash= item19ef0ed7ff (accessed October 9, 2014).

Creator(s): "Jon" (W.J.P. Jones)
Country: Wales
Era(s): World War II
Service: Eighth Army, England
Source(s): Mark Bryant, *World War II in Cartoons* (London: W.H. Smith, 1989), 137.

Creator(s): Mike Jones
Country: USA
Era(s): Operation Enduring Freedom, Operation Iraqi Freedom
Service: Navy
Source(s): *Ricky's Tour*, http://www. military.com/cartooncontent/ 0,14763,Jones_Index,00.html, 2005–2007. (accessed March 1, 2013).

Creator(s): Al Kaelin
Country: USA
Era(s): World War II
Service: Sgt.
Source(s): Ira Topping, ed., *The Best of YANK The Army Weekly* (New York: Arno, 1980).

Creator(s): Hugh Kennedy
Country: USA
Era(s): World War II
Service: Sgt.
Source(s): Ira Topping, ed., *The Best of YANK The Army Weekly* (New York: Arno, 1980).

Creator(s): Hank "Dennis the Menace" Ketcham
Country: USA
Era(s): Vietnam War
Service: Navy

Source(s): *Half Hitch* (Greenwich, CT: Fawcett, 1970).

Creator(s): Kim Sung-hwan
Country: Korea
Era(s): Korean War
Service: Ministry of Defense
Source(s): Andrew Salmon, "A Cartoonist at War: 'Gobau's' Korea, 1950," *The Asia-Pacific Journal* 28, no. 3 (2009): http://japanfocus.org/-andrew-salmon/ 3186 (accessed March 2, 2013).

Creator(s): Kevin Kline and Tood M. Hoelmer
Country: USA
Era(s): Interwar Years, Operation Desert Storm
Service: National Guard, Sgts.
Source(s): *Pvt. Joe Snuffy Goes Guard!* (Washington, D.C.: National Guard Bureau, 1991).

Creator(s): Joseph Kramer
Country: USA
Era(s): World War II
Service: Pfc.
Source(s): Ira Topping, ed., *The Best of YANK The Army Weekly* (New York: Arno, 1980).

Creator(s): Henry Lamb
Country: England
Era(s): World War I
Service: Fusiliers
Source(s): Imperial War Museum, digital archives, http://www.iwm.org.uk/ collections/item/object/1030005166 (August 11, 2014).

Creator(s): Sidney Landi
Country: USA
Era(s): World War I
Service: Sgt.
Source(s): Ira Topping, ed., *The Best of YANK The Army Weekly* (New York: Arno, 1980).

Creator(s): David Langdon
Country: England

Era(s): World War II
Service: Royal Air Force
Source(s): *All Buttoned Up!: A Scrapbook of R.A.F. Cartoons* (London: Sylvan, n.d.); Jenny Nicholson, *Kiss the Girls Goodbye* (London: Hutchinson); C.H. Ward-Jackson, *It's a Piece of Cake or R.A.F. Slang Made Easy* (1945).

Creator(s): Fred Levi
Country: USA
Era(s): World War II
Service: Army[?]
Source(s): National Museum of American Jewish Military History, digital exhibits. http://nmajmh.pastperfect-online.com/34213cgi/mweb.exe?request=record;id=7A3D5B4C-D21C-4054-AF00–578601797908;type=101 (accessed September 29, 2014).

Creator(s): T.H. Limb
Country: USA
Era(s): Operation Enduring Freedom, Operation Iraqi Freedom
Service: Army
Source(s): personal e-mail correspondence with the curator of the 10th Mountain Division and Fort Drum Museum, February 15, 2013.

Creator(s): Frank Mack
Country: USA
Era(s): World War II
Service: Pvt.
Source(s): Ira Topping, ed., *The Best of YANK The Army Weekly* (New York: Arno, 1980).

Creator(s): Walter Mansfield
Country: USA
Era(s): World War II
Service: Pvt.
Source(s): Ira Topping, ed., *The Best of YANK The Army Weekly* (New York: Arno, 1980).

Creator(s): Robert McClelland Martin
Country: USA
Era(s): World War II

Service: Army, Lt.
Source(s): Veterans History Project, American Folklife Center, Library of Congress (AFC/2001/001/479), digital collection, http://lcweb2.loc.gov/diglib/vhp/story/loc.natlib.afc2001001.00479/ (accessed September 29, 2014).

Creator(s): Bill Mauldin
Country: USA
Era(s): World War II, Korean War
Service: Army
Source(s): *Up Front* (New York: W.W. Norton, 2000); *Bill Mauldin in Korea* (New York: W.W. Norton. 1952); Todd DePastino, ed., *Willie and Joe the World War II Years* (Seattle: Fantagraphics, 2011); Todd DePastino, ed., *Willie and Joe Back Home* (Seattle: Fantagraphics, 2011).

Creator(s): Ernest Maxwell
Country: USA
Era(s): World War II
Service: Cpl.
Source(s): Ira Topping, ed., *The Best of YANK The Army Weekly* (New York: Arno, 1980).

Creator(s): Albert J. Merrifield
Country: USA
Era(s): Operation Enduring Freedom, Operation Iraqi Freedom
Service: Sgt.
Source(s): *Bob on the FOB*, https://www.facebook.com/bobonthefobcomics (accessed July 21, 2013).

Creator(s): Ted Miller
Country: USA
Era(s): World War II
Service: Sgt.
Source(s): Ira Topping, ed., *The Best of YANK The Army Weekly* (New York: Arno, 1980).

Creator(s): Wallace Morgan
Country: USA
Era(s): World War I
Service: Cpt.

Source(s): John T. Winterich, ed., *Squads Write! A Selection of the Best Things in Prose, Verse and Cartoons from The Stars and Stripes* (New York: Harpers and Brothers, 1931).

Creator(s): B.J. Morris
Country: USA
Era(s): World War II
Service: unknown
Source(s): *Hit Da Deck!* (Boston: Libbie, 1944).

Creator(s): Robert Mullan
Country: Canada
Era(s): unknown, modern
Service: MCpl
Source(s): Canadian Military Project, http://www.rootsweb.ancestry.com/~canmil/cartoons/ (accessed October 6, 2014); http://www.oocities.org/hollywood/theater/7041/humour.html (accessed October 6, 2014).

Creator(s): Julie L. Negron
Country: USA
Era(s): Operation Enduring Freedom, Operation Iraqi Freedom
Service: military spouse
Source(s): *PCSing.... It's a Spouse Thing!: The First Few Years of "Jenny, The Military Spouse," A Comic Strip for, by and about Life as a Military Spouse* (Lulu/JulieNegron, 2005–2010)

Creator(s): Bill Newcombe
Country: USA
Era(s): World War II
Service: Sgt.
Source(s): Ira Topping, ed., *The Best of YANK The Army Weekly* (New York: Arno, 1980).

Creator(s): Jack Niles and Jim Dye
Country: USA
Era(s): European Occupation
Service: unknown
Source(s): *Mox Nix: Cartoons About Your Tour in Europe* (Kassel, Germany: Hessische Druck and Verlogsonstalt, 1952).

Creator(s): Steve Opet
Country: USA
Era(s): Operation Iraqi Freedom
Service: Army Reserves, MSgt.
Source(s): *Opet's Odyssey,* 10th Mountain Division and Fort Drum Museum, https://www.facebook.com/FortDrum Museum (accessed March 1, 2013).

Creator(s): Norval Eugene Packwood
Country: USA
Era(s): Korean War
Service: Marines, Cpl.
Source(s): *Leatherhead: The Story of Marine Corps Boot Camp* (Quantico: Marine Corps Association, 1951); *Leatherhead in Korea* (Quantico: Marine Corps Gazette, 1952).

Creator(s): Joseph V. Parrino
Country: USA
Era(s): Cold War
Service: Army, Cpl.
Source(s): Veterans History Project, American Folklife Center, Library of Congress (AFC/2001/001/626), digital collection, http://lcweb2.loc.gov/diglib/vhp-stories/loc.natlib.afc2001001.00626/ (September 2, 2014).

Creator(s): Perce Pearce
Country: USA
Era(s): World War I
Service: Navy
Source(s): *Seaman Si* (Great Lakes Bulletin, 1918).

Creator(s): Charles Pearson
Country: USA
Era(s): World War II
Service: Sgt.
Source(s): Ira Topping, ed., *The Best of YANK The Army Weekly* (New York: Arno, 1980).

Creator(s): Politzer
Country: USA
Era(s): World War II
Service: unknown
Source(s): Park Kendall, *Gone with the*

Draft: Love Letters of a Trainee (New York: Grosset and Dunlap, 1941).

Creator(s): Michael Ponce De Leon
Country: USA
Era(s): World War II
Service: Pvt.
Source(s): Ira Topping, ed., *The Best of YANK The Army Weekly* (New York: Arno, 1980).

Creator(s): W.C. Pope
Country: USA
Era(s): Cold War, Interwar Years, Operation Desert Storm, Operation Enduring Freedom, Operation Iraqi Freedom
Service: Air Force Reserve
Source(s): *Above and Beyond: Pope's Puns 2 and Other Air Force Cartoons* (Herkimer, NY: W.C. Pope Studio, 1991–2009); "Pope's Puns," *Citizen Airman*, http://www.citamn.afrc.af.mil (accessed June 16, 2014); "Pope's Puns," http://www.popespuns.com (accessed August 17, 2014); "Pope's Puns," http://www.military.com/NewContent/0,13190,Pope_Index,00.html (accessed March 1, 2013).

Creator(s): Charles Johnson Post
Country: USA
Era(s): Spanish-American War
Service: Army, Pvt.
Source(s): *The Little War of Private Post: The Spanish-American War Seen Up Close* (Lincoln, NE: University of Nebraska Press, 1999).

Creator(s): "Raff" (Bill Hooper)
Country: England
Era(s): World War II
Service: Royal Air Force
Source(s): Mark Bryant, *World War II in Cartoons* (London: W.H. Smith, 1989), 113.

Creator(s): Hans Raum
Country: Germany
Era(s): World War I
Service: unknown

Source(s): "Scenes at Bad Kissingen Military Camp," eBay listing by star515, http://www.ebay.com/itm/Germany-Bad-Kissingen-Military-Camp-Four-ca-1910s-Comics-Cartoons-Watercolors-/231289333520?pt=Art_Drawings&hash=item35d9eb2710 (accessed October 9, 2014).

Creator(s): Ted Ritter and Rob Gadbois
Country: USA
Era(s): World War II, Korean War, Vietnam War, Cold War
Service: unknown
Source(s): *Bet Your Boots: The Story of Recruit Training* (New York: Victoria, 1944); *Boots and Boondocks: The Story of Marine Boot Camp* (New York: Victoria, 1949); *Off We Go: The Story of Air Force Basic Military Training* (New York: Victoria, 1953); *You've Had It: The Story of Basic Training* (New York: Victoria, 1965).

Creator(s): Frank Robinson
Country: USA
Era(s): World War II
Service: Cpl.
Source(s): Ira Topping, ed., *The Best of YANK The Army Weekly* (New York: Arno, 1980).

Creator(s): Jack Ruge
Country: USA
Era(s): World War II
Service: Cpl.
Source(s): Ira Topping, ed., *The Best of YANK The Army Weekly* (New York: Arno, 1980).

Creator(s): Leo Salkin
Country: USA
Era(s): World War II
Service: PhoM3c
Source(s): Ira Topping, ed., *The Best of YANK The Army Weekly* (New York: Arno, 1980).

Creator(s): Leonard Sansone
Country: USA

Era(s): World War II
Service: Sgt.
Source(s): *The Wolf* (New York: United, 1945).

Creator(s): Damon Bryan Schackelford
Country: USA
Era(s): Operation Enduring Freedom, Operation Iraqi Freedom
Service: Army
Source(s): *Delta Bravo Sierra. Rally Point: Vol. 1, Year 1, 2008* (Lexington, KY: www.deltabravosierra.com, 2008); *Delta Bravo Sierra,* http://www.delta bravosierra.com (accessed February 27, 2013).

Creator(s): "Jake" Schuffert
Country: USA
Era(s): Vietnam War
Service: Air Force
Source(s): *"No Sweat" ... More 'n More* (Washington, D.C.: Army Times, 1970).

Creator(s): William Schmitt
Country: USA
Era(s): World War II
Service: Army
Source(s): "These are actual envelopes sent home containing letters," http://www.488thportbattalion.org/Envelopes.html (accessed March 4, 2014).

Creator(s): Ron Searle
Country: England
Era(s): World War II
Service: Royal Engineers
Source(s): Mark Bryant, *World War II in Cartoons* (London: W.H. Smith, 1989), 53, 128.

Creator(s): Don Sheppard
Country: USA
Era(s): World War II
Service: Army
Source(s): "Speaking of Pictures.... GI's Blowzy Frauleins Hurt Germans' Feelings," *Life Magazine,* June 17, 1946, 12–3.

Creator(s): John Sheppard
Country: USA
Era(s): Operation Enduring Freedom, Operation Iraqi Freedom
Service: Air Force
Source(s): *Incoming! Military Cartoons* (Hoschton, GA: ShepArt Studios, 2007–2011); *"Blue Suiters": Cartoons of the USAF* (Hoschton, GA: ShepArt Studios, 2013).

Creator(s): Hal Sherman
Country: USA
Era(s): World War II
Service: unknown
Source(s): "Original Comic Illustration," eBay listing by leedel, http://www.ebay.com/itm/Hal-Sherman-Original-Comic-World-War-2-Military-Cartoon-No-1-of-Set-/181542306687?pt=Art_ Drawings&hash=item2a44c3c37f (accessed October 9, 2014)

Creator(s): Mizuki Shigeru
Country: Japan
Era(s): World War II, Japanese Occupation
Service: Imperial Japanese Army
Source(s): Roman Rosenbaum, "Mizuki Shigeru's Pacific War," *International Journal of Comic Art* vol. 10, no. 2 (2008): 354–379.

Creator(s): Shel Silverstein
Country: USA
Era(s): Korean War, Cold War
Service: Army
Source(s): *Take Ten.... A Collection of Cartoons* (Tokyo: Pacific Stars and Stripes, 1955); *Grab Your Socks* (New York: Ballantine, 1956).

Creator(s): Mike Sinclair
Country: USA
Era(s): Cold War
Service: unknown
Source(s): "Lt. Kadish," *I Ain't Laughing, Sir,* ed. Sid Schapiro (Stars and Stripes, 1980), 117–134.

Creator(s): Thomas R. "Ozzie" St. George
Country: USA
Era(s): World War II
Service: Army, Cpl.
Source(s): *C/O Postmaster* (New York: Thomas Y. Crowell, 1943); Ira Topping, ed., *The Best of YANK The Army Weekly* (New York: Arno, 1980).

Creator(s): "Ted" Stanley
Country: USA
Era(s): World War I
Service: Army
Source(s): *Perils of a Private: Sketches of Camp Life* (Boston: Small, Maynard, 1918).

Creator(s): Ralph Stein
Country: USA
Era(s): World War II
Service: Pvt.
Source(s): Ira Topping, ed., *The Best of YANK The Army Weekly* (New York: Arno, 1980).

Creator(s): Bob Stevens
Country: USA
Era(s): World War II (reflected), Korean War, Vietnam War, Cold War
Service: Air Force
Source(s): *"There I Was..." 25 Years* (Blue Ridge Summit, PA: TAB, 1992); *More There I Was ...* (Fallbrook, CA: Aero, 1974); *"There I Was.... Flat on My Back"* (Fallbrook, CA: Aero, 1975); *Prop Wash: A Fractured Glossary of Aviation Terms* (Fallbrook, CA: Village, 1983).

Creator(s): H.M. Stoops
Country: USA
Era(s): World War I
Service: A.E.F.
Source(s): *Inked Memories of 1918* (LeRoy, NY: Jell-O, 1924); John T. Winterich, ed., *Squads Write! A Selection of the Best Things in Prose, Verse and Cartoons from The Stars and Stripes* (New York: Harpers and Brothers, 1931).

Creator(s): Edward Streeter and G. William Breck

Country: USA
Era(s): World War I
Service: Lieut.
Source(s): *Love Letters of Bill to Mable; Comprising "Dere Mable," "Thats Me All Over, Mable," "Same Old Bill, Eh Mable!"* (New York: Frederick A. Stokes, 1918, 1919).

Creator(s): Florence Elizabeth Summers and Natalie Stokes
Country: USA
Era(s): World War I
Service: Military spouses
Source(s): *Dere Bill: Mable's Love Letters to Her Rookie* (New York: Frederick A. Stokes, 1918, 1919).

Creator(s): Daryl Talbot
Country: USA
Era(s): Operation Enduring Freedom, Operation Iraqi Freedom
Service: Marines
Source(s): *Laughing in Cadence: Dress Right Dress Military Cartoons* (Stillwater, OK: New Forums, 2009).

Creator(s): Eric Thibodeau
Country: USA
Era(s): Operation Desert Storm
Service: Navy
Source(s): http://ericthibodeau.com/uss_missouri.htm (accessed March 3, 2013).

Creator(s): Huy Toàn
Country: Vietnam
Era(s): Vietnam War
Service: Col.
Source(s): Jessica Harrison-Hall, *Vietnam Behind the Lines: Images from the War, 1965–1975* (Chicago, IL: Art Media Resources, 2002); http://www.dogmacollection.com/artists/vietnamese-propaganda-artists.html (accessed August 30, 2014); http://ml-review.ca/AllianceIssues/A2004/VietPaintings.html (accessed August 30, 2014).

Creator(s): unknown
Country: USA

Era(s): World War I
Service: A.E.F.
Source(s): "First World War Soldier's Hand-Drawn Cartoon Attached to Letter," http://www.swansongrp.com/picdocs/wwitoon.html (accessed June 26, 2013).

Creator(s): unknown
Country: USA
Era(s): interwar years, Operation Enduring Freedom
Service: Army
Source(s): *Dignity and Respect: A Training Guide on Homosexual Conduct Policy* (Department of the Army, 2001).

Creator(s): unknown
Country: USA
Era(s): Cold War
Service: Army
Source(s): *Komrad Ivan* (Fort Benning, GA: U.S. Government Printing Office, 1979).

Creator(s): unknown
Country: USA
Era(s): World War II
Service: Navy
Source(s): *Let There Be Light,* National Museum of American Jewish Military History, digital exhibit, http://nmajmh.pastperfect-online.com/34213cgi/mweb.exe?request=record;id=A79E7004–8B9B-44C2-BA54–427539373183;type=101 (accessed September 29, 2014).

Creator(s): unknown
Country: USA
Era(s): World War II
Service: Air Force
Source(s): "Navigator Gooney," in Donald Nijboer, *Graphic War: The Secret Aviation Drawings and Illustrations of World War II* (Ontario: Boston Mills, 2011), 236.

Creator(s): unknown
Country: USA
Era(s): World War II

Service: unknown
Source(s): "Original Cartoon Drawing," eBay listing by forbunnysakes, http://www.ebay.com/itm/Original-World War II-Patriotic-Humor-ONE-OF-A-KIND–Solder-Art-Pen-Ink-Drawing-/251580750115? (accessed July 2, 2014).

Creator(s): unknown
Country: USA
Era(s): Vietnam War
Service: National Guard
Source(s): *Ready Then Ready Now* (Washington, D.C.: Office of Public Affairs, National Guard Bureau, 1965).

Creator(s): unknown
Country: USA
Era(s): Cold War
Service: Army, ROTC
Source(s): *Time of Decision* (Harvy Comics, 1955).

Creator(s): Maximilian Uriarte
Country: USA
Era(s): Operation Enduring Freedom, Operation Iraqi Freedom
Service: Marines
Source(s): *The White Donkey* (2014): http://www.maximilianu.com/portfolio/terminal-lance-the-white-donkey/ (accessed November 1, 2014); *Terminal Lance: #1–100 Compilation* (Korea: Veterans Expeditionary Media, 2011); *Terminal Lance Head Call: The First 100 MarineTimes Strips* (Amazon Digital Services, 2013), Kindle e-book; *Terminal Lance,* http://terminallance.com (accessed October 1, 2014); *Terminal Lance,* https://www.facebook.com/terminallance (accessed July 22, 2014).

Creator(s): F.V.
Country: Australia
Era(s): World War II
Service: unknown
Source(s): "Cartoon Album," eBay listing by mazelbooks, http://www.ebay.com/itm/World War II-Original-MANUSCRIPT-Cartoon-Album-MILI-

TARY-NEW-GUINEA-DARWIN-
/131314126079?PT=AU_Antiquarian_C
ollectable_Books&hash=item1e92ee8cff
(accessed October 9, 2014).

Creator(s): various
Country: USA
Era(s): World War II
Service: assorted
Source(s): Ira Topping, ed., *The Best of
YANK The Army Weekly* (New York:
Arno, 1980).
Creator(s): various
Country: USA
Era(s): World War II
Service: American Services and civilian
publications
Source(s): *Hello Buddy: Comics of War,*
"Sold by a Disabled Veteran" (New York:
Service Men's Magazine); *Hello Buddy:
Comics of War,* eBay listing by aces_100,
http://www.ebay.com/itm/VINTAGE-
HELLO-BUDDY-COMICS-OF-WAR-
FACTS-OF-SERVICES-BY-SERVICE-
MENS-MAGAZINE-/400360196067
(accessed October 10, 2014).

Creator(s): various
Country: USA
Era(s): World War II
Service: assorted
Source(s): Sid Schapiro, ed., *I Ain't Laugh-
ing, Sir* (Stars and Stripes, 1980), 49–90

Creator(s): various
Country: USA
Era(s): World War II, Japanese Occupa-
tion, Korean War
Service: assorted
Source(s): *Out of Line: A Collection of
Cartoons from Pacific Stars and Stripes*
(Tokyo: Toppon, 1952).

Creator(s): various
Country: USA
Era(s): World War II
Service: civilian magazines
Source(s): R.M. Barrows, ed., *The Ser-
geant Is a Jerk* (Chicago: Book Produc-
tion Industries, 1944).

Creator(s): various
Country: New Zealand
Era(s): World War I
Service: B.E.F.
Source(s): *Shell Shocks, by New Zealan-
ders in France* (London: Jarrold and
Sons, 1916).

Creator(s): various
Country: USA
Era(s): Vietnam
Service: Army
Source(s): Vietnam Graffiti Project, *Viet-
nam Graffiti* (2009–2010): http://www.
vietnamgraffiti.com/walker-graffiti
(accessed October 28, 2014).

Creator(s): Mort Walker
Country: USA
Era(s): Cold War
Service: Army
Source(s): *50 Years of Beetle Bailey* (New
York: NBM, 2000).

Creator(s): Abian A. "Wally" Wallgren
Country: USA
Era(s): World War I
Service: Marines, Pvt.
Source(s): *Wally: His Cartoons of the
A.E.F.* (Stars and Stripes, 1919); "Wally,"
Stars and Stripes, Library of Congress
digital archives, http://memory.loc.gov/
phpdata/issuedisplay.php?collection=
sgpsas&aggregate=sgpsas (accessed
March 3, 2013); John T. Winterich, ed.,
*Squads Write! A Selection of the Best
Things in Prose, Verse and Cartoons
from The Stars and Stripes* (New York:
Harpers and Brothers, 1931).

Creator(s): Douglas C. Ward
Country: England
Era(s): World War I
Service: Army in India, Cpl.
Source(s): *Topical Sketches,* Irvin De-
partment of Rare Books and Special
Collections, Digital Collections,
http://library.sc.edu/digital/collec-
tions/rts.html (accessed March 6,
2013).

Creator(s): Jim Weeks
Country: USA
Era(s): World War II
Service: Sgt.
Source(s): Ira Topping, ed., *The Best of YANK The Army Weekly* (New York: Arno, 1980).

Creator(s): R.D. Whitcomb
Country: USA
Era(s): World War I
Service: Army, 1st Cavalry
Source(s): *Military Cartoons* (Douglas, AZ: RD Whitcomb, 1916).

Creator(s): Sidney D. White
Country: USA
Era(s): World War II
Service: Army
Source(s): Veterans History Project, American Folklife Center, Library of Congress (AFC/2001/001/31890), digital collection, http://lcweb2.loc.gov/diglib/vhp-stories/loc.natlib.afc2001001.31890/artworks (accessed September 2, 2014).

Creator(s): Dick Wingert
Country: USA
Era(s): World War II
Service: Army
Source(s): *Hubert* (London: Love and Malcomson, 1944); "Hubert," *I Ain't Laughing, Sir,* ed. Sid Schapiro (Stars and Stripes, 1980), 91–116; Frank W. Maresca, *A Soldier's Odyssey: To Remember Our Past as It Was* (Trafford, 2012).

Creator(s): Tom Zibelli
Country: USA
Era(s): World War II
Service: Pfc.
Source(s): Ira Topping, ed., *The Best of YANK The Army Weekly* (New York: Arno, 1980).

Creator(s): Milos Zubec
Country: Yugoslavia
Era(s): World War II
Service: POW, registered with the Canadian Army
Source(s): Mark Bryant, *Cartoons of World War II* (London: W.H. Smith, 1989), 128

Notes

Preface

1. Barsis, *They're All Yours, Uncle Sam!* (New York: Stephen Daye, 1943).

2. Vic Herman, *Winnie the WAC* (Philadelphia, PA: David McKay, 1945).

3. See: Tony Isabella, *1,000 Comic Books You Must Read* (Iola, WI: Krause, 2009; Kindle e-book), loc. 1165.

4. David Hajdu, *The Ten-Cent Plague: The Great Comic-Book Scare and How It Changed America* (New York: Picador, 2009); Trina Robbins, *A Century of Women Cartoonists* (Northampton, MA: Kitchen Sink, 1993); Bradford W. Wright, *Comic Book Nation: The Transformation of Youth Culture in America* (Baltimore, MD: Johns Hopkins University Press, 2001).

5. Barbara Bristol, *Meet Molly Marine* (N.p.: Robert J. Weaver, 1945.).

6. Dorothea Byerly, *Up Came a Ripple* (East Orange, NJ: Greenwood, 1945).

7. Tonie Holt and Valmai Holt, "Introduction to the 'BB4H4H' Edition of Best of Fragments from France," in *The Best of Fragments from France* by Bruce Bairnsfather, ed. Tonie Holt and Valmai Holt (South Yorkshire, UK: Pen and Sword Military, 2009), 4.

8. Todd DePastino, *Bill Mauldin: A Life Up Front* (New York: W.W. Norton, 2008).

9. AP, "Sometimes Funny Stuff Happens, Even in Iraq," *New Zealand Herald*, January 17, 2009.

10. "W.C. Pope," *Military.com*, no date, http://www.military.com/NewContent/0,13190,Pope_Index,00.html (accessed March 1, 2013).

11. Jason Chudy, "Reservist's Cartoons Detail Burdens of Desert Deployment," *Stars and Stripes*, August 9, 2004, http://www.stripes.com/news/reservist-s-cartoons-detail-burdens-of-desert-deployment-1.22605 (accessed March 13, 2013).

12. Stephen M. Walt, "Two Chief Petty Officers Walk into a Bar...," *Foreign Policy*, April 7, 2014, http://www.foreignpolicy.com/articles/2014/04/07/why_cant_we_make_fun_of_the_military_anymore, para. 1–2.

13. Walt, "Two Chief Petty Officers." Also: Thomas D. Beamish, Harvey Molotch, and Richard Flacks, "Who Supports the Troops? Vietnam, the Gulf War, and the Making of Collective Memory," *Social Problems* 42, no. 3 (1995): 344–60.

14. Walt, "Two Chief Petty Officers," para. 15.

15. Keith Yellin, *Battle Exhortation: The Rhetoric of Combat Leadership* (Columbia, SC: University of South Carolina Press, 2008).

16. Susan L. Carruthers, "No One's Looking: The Disappearing Audience for War," *Media, War and Conflict* 1, no. 1 (2008): 70–6.

Introduction

1. Douglas Wolk, *Reading Comics: How Graphic Novels Work and What They Mean* (Cambridge, MA: Da Capo, 2007), Kindle e-book: loc. 979.

2. Robert C. Harvey, *The Art of the Funnies: An Aesthetic History*. Studies in Popular Culture (Jackson, MS: University Press of Mississippi, 1994), 4.

3. Thomas Milton Kemnitz, "The Cartoon as a Historical Source," *Journal of Interdisciplinary History* 4, no. 1 (1973): 81–93; Wolk, *Reading Comics*.

4. Neil Cohn, "Un-Defining 'Comics': Separating the Cultural from the Structural in Comics," *International Journal of Comic Art* 7, no. 2 (2005): 236.

5. Scott McCloud, *Understanding Comics: The Invisible Art* (New York: HarperPerennial, 1993), 8.

6. Jon Pérez Laraudogoitia, "The Comic as Binary Language: An Hypothesis on Comic Structure," *Journal of Quantitative Linguistics* 15, no. 2 (2008): 111–35; Jon Pérez Laraudogoitia, "The Composition and Structure of the Comic," *Journal of Quantitative Linguistics* 16, no. 4 (2009): 327–53.

7. As quoted in Mort Walker, *The Lexicon of Comicana* (Lincoln, NE: iUniverse.com, 2000): 10.

8. Wolk, *Reading Comics*.

9. Thierry Groensteen, *The System of Comics* (1999, trans. Bart Beaty and Nick Nguyen; Jackson, MS: University Press of Mississippi, 2007).

10. Wolk, *Reading Comics*.

11. Dale Jacobs, "Beyond Visual Rhetoric: Multimodal Rhetoric and Newspaper Comic Strips," *International Journal of Comic Art* 9, no. 1 (2007):

502–14; J. Maggio, "Comics and Cartoons: A Democratic Art-Form." *PS: Political Science and Politics* 40, no. 2 (2007): 237–9; Joseph Witek, *Comic Books as History: The Narrative Art of Jack Jackson, Art Spiegelman, and Harvey Pekar* (Jackson, MS: University Press of Mississippi, 1989); Harvey, *Art of the Funnies*; McCloud, *Understanding Comics*.

12. Wolk, *Reading Comics*, loc. 987.

13. Randy Duncan and Matthew J. Smith, *The Power of Comics: History, Form and Culture* (New York: Continuum, 2009); David Carrier, "Caricature," in *A Comic Studies Reader*, ed. Jeet Heer and Kent Worcester (Jackson, MS: University Press of Mississippi, 2009), 105–15; Robert C. Harvey, "Comedy at the Juncture of Word and Image: The Emergence of the Modern Magazine Gag Cartoon Reveals the Vital Blend," in *The Language of Comics Word and Image*, Studies in Popular Culture, ed. Robin Varnum and Christina T. Gibbons (Jackson, MS: University Press of Mississippi, 2001), 75–106; Robert C. Harvey, "How Comics Came to Be: Through the Juncture of Word and Image from Magazine Gag Cartoons to Newspaper Strips: Tools for Critical Appreciation Plus Rare, Seldom Witnessed Historical Facts," in *A Comic Studies Reader*, ed. Jeet Heer and Kent Worcester (Jackson, MS: University Press of Mississippi, 2009), 25–45.

14. See: Cohn, "Un-Defining 'Comics'"; also: Jeet Heer and Kent Worcester, "Introduction," in *A Comic Studies Reader*, ed. Jeet Heer and Kent Worcester (Jackson, MS: University Press of Mississippi, 2009), xi–xv; Duncan and Smith, *Power of Comics*.

15. Arthur Asa Berger, *Li'l Abner: A Study in American Satire*, Studies in Popular Culture (New York: University Press of Mississippi, 2006).

16. David Kunzle, *Father of the Comic Strip: Rodolphe Töpffer* (Jackson, MS: University Press of Mississippi, 2007).

17. Jerry Robinson, *The Comics: An Illustrated History of Comic Strip Art 1895–2010* (1974; Milwaukie, OR: Dark Horse, 2011); Harvey, *Art of the Funnies*.

18. Arthur Asa Berger, *The Comic-Stripped American: What Dick Tracy, Blondie, Daddy Warbucks, and Charlie Brown Tell Us About Ourselves* (New York: Walker, 1972).

19. Harvey, *Art of the Funnies*; Walker, *Lexicon of Comicana*.

20. Lucy Shelton Caswell, "Comic Strips," in *History of Mass Media in the United States: An Encyclopedia*, ed. Margaret A. Blanchard (London, UK: Routledge, 1998), 150–2.

21. Walker, *Lexicon of Comicana*.

22. James Geller (Jay) Black, "Amoozin' but Confoozin': Comic Strips as a Voice of Dissent in the 1950s," *ETC: A Review of General Semantics* 66, no. 4 (2010): 460–77; Harvey, *Art of the Funnies*.

23. Dick Ahles, "His Roots Still Local, Beetle Bailey Turns 50," *New York Times*, September 3, 2000, http://www.nytimes.com/2000/09/03/nyregion/his-roots-still-local-beetle-bailey-turns-50.html (accessed July 9, 2013).

24. Isaac Cates, "The Diary Comic," in *Graphic Subjects: Critical Essays on Autobiography and Graphic Novels*, ed. Michael A. Chaney (Madison,

WI: University of Wisconsin Press, 2011; Kindle e-book).

25. Kent Worcester, "Symposium—The State of the Editorial Cartoon: Introduction," *PS: Political Science and Politics* 40, no. 2 (2007): 223; also Kemnitz, "The Cartoon as a Historical Source."

26. Charles Press, *The Political Cartoon* (Toronto, ON: Associated University Presses Ltd., 1981); Julie Davis, "Power to the Cubicle-Dwellers: An Ideological Reading of *Dilbert*," in *Comics and Ideology* vol. 2, Popular Culture Everyday Life, ed. Matthew P. McAllister, Edward H. Sewell, Jr., and Ian Gordon (New York: Peter Lang, 2009), 275–300.

27. Matthew J. Shaw, "Drawing on the Collections," *Journalism Studies* 8, no. 5 (2007): 742–54.

28. Ernest G. Bormann, Jolene Koester, and Janet Bennett, "Political Cartoons and Salient Rhetorical Fantasies: An Empirical Analysis of the '76 Presidential Campaign," *Communication Monographs* 45, no. 4 (1978): 317–29; Michael A. DeSousa and Martin J. Medhurst, "Political Cartoons and American Culture: Significant Symbols of Campaign 1980," *Studies in Visual Communication* 8 (1982): 84–97; Ruth Thibodeau, "From Racism to Tokenism: The Changing Face of Blacks in *New Yorker* Cartoons," *Public Opinion Quarterly* 53, no. 4 (1989): 483–94.

29. Linus Abraham, "Effectiveness of Cartoons as a Uniquely Visual Medium for Orienting Social Issues," *Journalism and Communication Monographs* 11, no. 2 (2009): 117–65.

30. Denise Teodora Ioniță, Andrade Victoria Suciu, Mihaela Suhalitca, and Oana Voitovici, "Political Cartoons," *Journal of Media Research* 3, no. 11 (2011): 28–44; Juana I. Marín-Arrese, "Cognition and Culture in Political Cartoons," *Intercultural Pragmatics* 5, no. 1 (2008): 1–18; DeSousa and Medhurst, "Political Cartoons and American Culture."

31. Frank L. Cioffi, "Disturbing Comics: The Disjunction of Word and Image in the Comics of Andrzej Mleczko, Ben Katchor, R. Crumb, and Art Spiegelman," in *The Language of Comics Word and Image*, Studies in Popular Culture, ed. Robin Varnum and Christina T. Gibbons (Jackson, MS: University Press of Mississippi, 2001), 97–122; Black, "Amoozin' but Confoozin.'"

32. Amy Kiste Nyberg, "Comic Books," in *History of Mass Media in the United States: An Encyclopedia*, ed. Margaret A. Blanchard (London, UK: Routledge, 1998), 149–50.

33. Manny Farber, "Comic Strips," in *Arguing Comics: Literary Masters on a Popular Medium*, ed. Jeet Heer and Kent Worcester (Jackson, MS: University Press of Mississippi, 2009), 91–3; Bradford W. Wright, *Comic Book Nation: The Transformation of Youth Culture in America* (Baltimore, MD: Johns Hopkins University Press, 2001); Duncan and Smith, *Power of Comics*; Witek, *Comic Books as History*.

34. David Hajdu, *The Ten-Cent Plague: The Great Comic-Book Scare and How It Changed America* (New York: Picador, 2009).

35. Wolk, *Reading Comics*; Wright, *Comic Book Nation*.

36. Stephen Krensky, *Comic Book Century: The History of American Comic Books* (Minneapolis, MN: Twenty-First Century, 2008); Paul Lopes,

Demanding Respect: The Evolution of the American Comic Book (Philadelphia, PA: Temple University Press, 2009); Wolk, *Reading Comics*.

37. Lopes, *Demanding Respect*.

38. Lopes, *Demanding Respect*; Wolk, *Reading Comics*.

39. DiPaolo, *War, Politics and Superheroes*.

40. For more on these genres see Duncan and Smith, *Power of Comics*.

41. Sol M. Davidson, "The Funnies' Neglected Branch: Special Purpose Comics," *International Journal of Comic Art* 7, no. 2 (2005): 340–57.

42. Joan Stewart Ormrod, "Graphic Novels," in *Encyclopedia of Contemporary British Culture*, ed. Peter Childs and Mike Storry (London, UK: Routledge, 1999), 236–7.

43. Michael A. Chaney, "Introduction," in *Graphic Subjects: Critical Essays on Autobiography and Graphic Novels*, ed. Michael A. Chaney (Madison, WI: University of Wisconsin Press, 2011), Kindle e-book; Wolk, *Reading Comics*.

44. Elisabeth El Rafaie, *Autobiographic Comics: Life Writing in Pictures* (Jackson, MS: University Press of Mississippi, 2012).

45. Amy Kiste Nyberg, "Theorizing Comics Journalism," *International Journal of Comic Art* 8, no. 2 (2006): 98–112; Amy Kiste Nyberg, "Comics Journalism: Drawing on Words to Picture the Past in *Safe Area Goražde*," in *Critical Approaches to Comics: Theories and Methods*, ed. Matthew J. Smith and Randy Duncan (New York: Routledge, 2012), 116–28; Kristian Williams, "The Case for Comics Journalism: Artist-Reporters Leap Tall Conventions in a Single Bound," *Columbia Journalism Review*, March/April 2005, 51–5.

46. Eldad Nakar, "Memories of Pilots and Planes: World War II in Japanese *Manga*, 1957–1967," *Social Science Japan Journal* 6, no. 1: 57–76; Dru Pagliassotti, Kazumi Nagaike and Mark McHarry, "Editorial: Boys' Love Manga Special Section," *Journal of Graphic Novels and Comics* 4, no. 1 (2013): 1–8; Setsu Shigematsu, "Dimensions of Desire: Sex, Fantasy, and Fetish in Japanese Comics," in *Themes and Issues in Asian Cartooning: Cute, Cheap, Mad, and Sexy*, ed. John A. Lent (Bowling Green, OH: Bowling Green State University Popular Press, 1999), 127–64; Kanako Shiokawa, "Cute but Deadly: Women and Violence in Japanese Comics," in *Themes and Issues in Asian Cartooning: Cute, Cheap, Mad, and Sexy*, ed. John A. Lent (Bowling Green, OH: Bowling Green State University Popular Press, 1999), 93–126; K. Yoshimura, "Essei Manga no Tokucho," in *Manga no Kyokasho*, ed. I. Shimizu, T. Akita, T. Naiki, and K. Yoshimura (Kyoto: Rinkawa Shoten, 2008), 196–8, as summarized in Akiko Sugawa-Shimada, "Rebel with Causes and Laughter for Relief: 'Essay Manga' of Tenten Hosokawa and Rieko Saibara, and Japanese Female Readership," *Journal of Graphic Narratives and Comics* 2, no. 2 (2011): 169–85.

47. Russell W. Belk, "Material Values in the Comics: A Content Analysis of Comic Books Featuring Themes of Wealth," *Journal of Consumer Research* 14 (1987): 26–42; Arthur Asa Berger, "Comics and Culture," *Journal of Popular Culture* 5, no. 1 (1971): 164–77; Carla B. Howery, "*Get Real*

Comics Reveal a Sociological Touch," *Footnotes*, February 2007, http://www.asanet.org/footnotes/feb00/fn07.html; Rebecca Wanzo, "The Superhero: Meditations on Surveillance, Salvation, and Desire," *Communication and Critical/Cultural Studies* 6, no. 1 (2009): 93–7; Black, "Amoozin' but Confoozin.'"

48. Wolk, *Reading Comics*, loc. 375.

49. Jon Hogan, "The Comic Book as Symbolic Environment: The Case of Iron Man," *ETC: A Review of General Semantics* 66, no. 2 (2009): 199–214.

50. Karin Kukkonen, "Popular Cultural Memory: Comics, Communities and Context Knowledge," *Nordicom Review* 29, no. 2 (2008): 261–73; Benjamin Woo, "The Android's Dungeon: Comic-Bookstores, Cultural Spaces, and the Social Practices of Audience," *Journal of Graphic Novels and Comics* 2, no. 2 (2011): 125–36; Wolk, *Reading Comics*.

51. Kelley J. Hall and Betsy Lucal, "Tapping into Parallel Universes: Using Superhero Comic Books in Sociology Courses," *Teaching Sociology* 27 (January 1999): 60–6.

52. Examples: Stergios Botzakis, "'To Be Part of the Dialogue': American Adults Reading Comic Books," *Journal of Graphic Novels and Comics* 2, no. 2 (2011): 113–23; Kerry Cheesman, "Using Comics in the Science Classroom," *Journal of College Science Teaching* 35, no. 4 (2006): 48–51; Mark Crilley, "Getting Student to Write Using Comics," *Teacher Librarian* 37, no. 1 (2009): 28–31; Virginia Gerde and R. Spencer Foster, "X-Men Ethics: Using Comic Books to Teach Business Ethics," *Journal of Business Ethics* 77, no. 3 (2008): 227–30; Katharine H. Hutchinson, "An Experiment in the Use of Comics as Instructional Material," *Journal of Educational Sociology* 23, no. 4 (1949): 236–45; Bridget M. Marshall, "Comics as Primary Sources: The Case of Journey into Mohawk Country," in *Comic Books and American Cultural History*, ed. Matthew Pustz (New York: Continuum, 2012), 26–39; Jessamyn Neuhaus, "How Wonder Woman Helped My Students 'Join the Conversation': Comic Books as Teaching Tools in a History Methodology Course," in *Comic Books and American Cultural History*, ed. Matthew Pustz (New York: Continuum, 2012), 11–25; Cord Scott, "The 'Good' Comics: Using Comic Books to Teach History," *International Journal of Comic Art* 8, no. 1 (2006): 546–61; Hall and Lucal, "Tapping into Parallel Universes."

53. E.H. Gombrich, *The Image and the Eye: Further Studies in the Psychology of Pictorial Representation* (London, UK: Phaidon, 1982); Harvey, *Art of the Funnies*; Kunzle, *Father of the Comic Strip*; Wolk, *Reading Comics*.

54. Examples: Richard Scully and Marian Quartly, "Using Cartoons as Historical Evidence," in *Drawing the Line: Using Cartoons as Historical Evidence*, ed. Richard Scully and Marian Quartly (Clayton, Australia: Monash University ePress, 2009), 01.1–01.13; Shaw, "Drawing on the Collections." Also: William W. Savage, Jr., *Comic Books and America, 1945–1954* (Norman, University of Oklahoma Press, 1990); Marshall, "Comics as Primary Sources"; Wright, *Comic Book Nation*.

55. Jason Dittmer, *Captain America and the Nationalist Superhero* (Philadelphia, PA: Temple

University Press, 2013); John E. Moser, "Madmen, Morons, and Monocles: The Portrayal of the Nazis in *Captain America*," in *Captain America and the Struggle of the Superhero*, ed. Robert C. Weiner (Jefferson, NC: McFarland, 2009), 24–35; DiPaolo, *War, Politics and Superheroes*; Wanzo, "The Superhero."

56. Nick Thorkelson, "Cartoons Against the Axis: World War II Bonds Cartoons from the Terry-D'Alessio Collection. Sandy Schecter with Special Thanks to Hilda Terry and Art Spiegelman. New York City, NY: Museum of Comic and Cartooning Art, October 8, 2005-February 6, 2006," *International Journal of Comic Art* 8, no. 1 (2006): 591.

57. Lucy Shelton Caswell, "Drawing Swords: War in American Editorial Cartoons," *American Journalism* 21, no. 2 (2004): 13–45.

58. Harry L. Katz and Vincent Virga, *Civil War Sketchbook: Drawings from the Battlefront* (New York: W.W. Norton, 2012); Shaw, "Drawing on the Collections."

59. Daniel J. Leab, "Cold War Comics," *Columbia Journalism Review*, Winter 1965, 42–7.

60. Leonard Rifas, "Cartooning and Nuclear Power: From Industry Advertising to Activist Uprising and Beyond," *PS: Political Science and Politics* 40, no. 2 (2007): 255–60.

61. Lynn Spigel, *Welcome to the Dreamhouse: Popular Media and Postwar Suburbs* (Durham, NC: Duke University Press, 2001).

62. Teodora Carabas, "Tales Calculated to Drive You MAD: The Debunking of Spies, Superheroes, and Cold War Rhetoric in Mad Magazine's 'SPY vs SPY,'" *Journal of Popular Culture* 40, no. 1 (2007): 4–24.

63. Jeff McLaughlin, "9–11–01: Truth, Justice and Comic Books," *International Journal of Comic Art* 8, no. 1 (2006): 412–25; Kristiaan Versluys, "Art Spiegelman's *In the Shadow of No Towers*: 9–11 and the Representation of Trauma," *MFS Modern Fiction Studies* 52, no. 4 (2006): 980–1003.

64. For critical considerations of such comics, see Dieter De Bruyn, "Patriotism of Tomorrow? The Commemoration and Popularization of the Warsaw Rising through Comics," *Slovo* 22, no. 2 (2010): 46–65; Annette Matton, "From Realism to Superheroes in Marvel's *The 'Nam*," in *Comics and Ideology* vol. 2, Popular Culture Everyday Life, ed. Matthew P. McAllister, Edward H. Sewell, Jr., and Ian Gordon (New York: Peter Lang, 2009), 151–76; Witek, *Comic Books as History*.

65. Martin Barker and Roger Sabin, "'Doonesbury Does Iraq': Garry Trudeau and the Politics of an Anti-War Strip"; *Journal of Graphic Novels and Comics* 3, no. 2 (2012): 127–42; Julianne H. Newton, "Trudeau Draws Truth," *Critical Studies in Media Communication* 24, no. 1 (2007): 81–5.

66. Todd DePastino, *Bill Mauldin: A Life Up Front* (New York: W.W. Norton, 2008); Richard Harwell, *Margaret Mitchell's Gone with the Wind Letters 1936–1949* (New York: Macmillan, 1976).

67. Janis L. Edwards and Carol K. Winkler, "Representative Form and the Visual Ideograph: The Iwo Jima Image in Editorial Cartoons," *Quarterly Journal of Speech* 83 (1997): 289–310; Christopher Kent, "War Cartooned/Cartoon War: Matt Morgan and the American Civil War in *Fun* and *Frank Leslie's*

Illustrated Newspaper," *Victorian Periodicals Review* 36, no. 2 (2003): 153–81; David R. Spencer, "Visions of Violence: A Cartoon Study of America and War," *American Journalism* 21, no. 2 (2004): 47–78; David R. Spencer, "The Press and the Spanish American War Political Cartoons of the Yellow Journalism Age," *International Journal of Comic Art* 9, no. 1 (2007): 262–80; Fred Vultee, "Dr. FDR and Baby War: The World Through Chicago Political Cartoons Before and After Pearl Harbor," *Visual Communication Quarterly* 14 (Summer 2007): 158–75; Caswell, "Drawing Swords."

68. Michael A. Chaney, "The Animal Witness of the Rwandan Genocide," in *Graphic Subjects: Critical Essays on Autobiography and Graphic Novels*, ed. Michael A. Chaney (Madison, WI: University of Wisconsin Press, 2011), Kindle e-book; Dieter DeBruyn, "Patriotism of Tomorrow? The Commemoration and Popularization of the Warsaw Rising through Comics," *Slovo* 22, no. 2 (2010): 46–65; Allen Douglas and Fedwa Malti-Douglas, "From the Alergian War to the Armenian Massacres: Memory, Trauma, and Medicine in *Petit Polio* of Farid Boudjellal," *International Journal of Comic Art* 10, no. 2 (2008): 282–307; Pascal Lefèvre, "The Unresolved Past: Repercussions of World War II in Belgian Comics," *International Journal of Comic Art* 9, no. 1 (2007): 296–310; Esther MacCallum-Stewart, "The First World War and British Comics," *University of Sussex Journal of Contemporary History* 6 (2003): 1–18; Eldad Nakar, "Memories of Pilots and Planes: World War II in Japanese *Manga*, 1957–1967," *Social Science Japan Journal* 6, no. 1: 57–76; Kees Ribbens, "World War II in European Comics: National Representations of Global Conflict in Popular Historical Culture," *International Journal of Comic Art* 12, no. 1 (2010): 1–33; Roman Rosenbaum, "Motomiya Hiroshi's *The Country Is Burning*," *International Journal of Comic Art* 9, no. 1 (2007): 591–601; Joseph Witek, "Comic Books as History: The First Shot at Fort Sumter," in *Comic Books as History: The Narrative Art of Jack Jackson, Art Spiegelman, and Harvey Pekar* (Jackson, MS: University Press of Mississippi, 1989), 13–47.

69. Alexander Clarkson, "Virtual Heroes: Boys, Masculinity and Historical Memory in War Comics 1945–1995," *THYMOS: Journal of Boyhood Studies* 2, no. 2 (2008): 175–85; Travis Langley, "Freedom Versus Security: The Basic Human Dilemma from 9/11 to Marvel's *Civil War*," *International Journal of Communication* 11, no. 1 (2009): 426–35; Annette Matton, "From Realism to Superheroes in Marvel's *The 'Nam*," in *Comics and Ideology* vol. 2, ed. Matthew P. McAllister, Edward H. Sewell, Jr., and Ian Gordon, Popular Culture Everyday Life (New York: Peter Lang, 2009), 151–76; Adam Riches, *When the Comics Went to War* (Edinburgh, UK: Mainstream, 2009); Cord Scott, "The Return of the War Comic: A Revival of Military Themes and Characters in Comic Books," *International Journal of Comic Art* 10, no. 2 (2008): 649–59; Brian Swafford, "The Death of Captain America: An Open-ended Allegorical Reading of Marvel Comics' *Civil War* Storyline," *International Journal of Comic Art* 10, no. 2 (2008): 632–48; Joseph Witek, "The Dream of

Total War: The Limits of a Genre," *Journal of Popular Culture* 30, no. 2 (1996): 37–45.

70. Michael Birdwell, "'Oh, You Thing from Another World, You': How Warner Bros. Animators Responded to the Cold War (1948–1980)," *Film and History* 31, no. 1 (2001): 34–9; Teodora Carabas, "Tales Calculated to Drive You MAD: The Debunking of Spies, Superheroes, and Cold War Rhetoric in Mad Magazine's 'SPY vs SPY,'" *Journal of Popular Culture* 40, no. 1 (2007): 4–24; Robert Genter, "'With Great Power Comes Great Responsibility': Cold War Culture and the Birth of Marvel Comics," *Journal of Popular Culture* 40, no. 6 (2007): 953–78; Daniel J. Leab, "Cold War Comics," *Columbia Journalism Review*, Winter 1965, 42–7; Kristin L. Matthews, "The ABCs of *Mad* Magazine: Reading, Citizenship, and Cold War America," *International Journal of Comic Art* 8, no. 2 (2006): 248–68; Kristin L. Matthews, "A Mad Proposition in Postwar America," *Journal of American Culture* 30, no. 2 (2007): 212–21; Peter Salisbury, "Giles's Cold War: How Fleet Street's Favourite Cartoonist Saw the Conflict," *Media History* 12, no. 2 (2006): 157–75.

71. Martin Barker and Roger Sabin, "'Doonesbury Does Iraq': Garry Trudeau and the Politics of an Anti-War Strip," *Journal of Graphic Novels and Comics* 3, no. 2 (2012): 127–42; Jamie Egolf, "Political Commentary and Dissent in the Tapestry and Cartoon Strip," *International Journal of Comic Art* 11, no. 2 (2009): 432–46; Nancy Hudson-Rodd and Sundar Ramanathaiyer, "Cartooning the Iraq War: No Laughing Matter," *International Journal of Comic Art* 8, no. 1 (2006): 532–45; Julianne H. Newton, "Trudeau Draws Truth," *Critical Studies in Media Communication* 24, no. 1 (2007): 81–5; Stefanie Wichhart, "Propaganda and Protest: Political Cartoons in Iraq During the Second World War," in *Drawing the Line: Using Cartoons as Historical Evidence*, ed. Richard Scully and Marian Quartly (Clayton, Australia: Monash University ePress, 2009), 08.1–08.21.

72. Nicole Devarenne, "'A Language Heroically Commensurate with His Body': Nationalism, Fascism, and the Language of the Superhero," *International Journal of Comic Art* 10, no. 1 (2008): 48–54; Marc DiPaolo, *War, Politics and Superheroes: Ethics and Propaganda in Comics and Film* (Jefferson, NC: McFarland, 2011); Jason Dittmer, "Fighting for Home: Masculinity and the Constitution of the Domestic in *Tales of Suspense* and *Captain America*," in *Heroes of Film, Comics and American Culture: Essays on Real and Fictional Defenders of Home*, ed. Lisa M. Detora (Jefferson, NC: McFarland, 2009, Kindle e-book); Jason Dittmer, *Captain America and the Nationalist Superhero* (Philadelphia, PA: Temple University Press, 2013); Ryan Edwardson, "The Many Lives of Captain Canuck: Nationalism, Culture, and the Creation of a Canadian Comic Book Superhero," *Journal of Popular Culture* 37, no. 2 (2003): 184–201; Mitra C. Emad, "Reading Wonder Woman's Body: Mythologies of Gender and Nation," *Journal of Popular Culture* 39, no. 6 (2006): 954–84; A. David Lewis, "The Militarism of American Superheroes After 9/11," in *Comic Books and American Cultural History: An Anthology*, ed. Matthew

Pustz (New York: Continuum, 2012), 223–36; Ronald C. Thomas, Jr., "Hero of the Military-Industrial Complex: Reading Iron Man through Burke's Dramatism," in *Heroes of Film, Comics and American Culture: Essays on Real and Fictional Defenders of Home*, ed. Lisa M. Detora (Jefferson, NC: McFarland, 2009, Kindle e-book), chapter 8.

73. Harry Amana, "The Art of Propaganda: Charles Alston's World War II Editorial Cartoons for the Office of War Information and the Black Press," *American Journalism* 21, no. 2 (2004): 79–111; Ivana Dobrivojevic, "Cartoons as a Powerful Propaganda Tool: Creating the Images of East and West in the Yugoslav Satirical Press," in *Drawing the Line: Using Cartoons as Historical Evidence*, ed. Richard Scully and Marian Quartly (Clayton, Australia: Monash University ePress, 2009), 10.1–10.16; Janusz Kaźmierczak, "Raymond Williams and Cartoons: From Churchill's Cigar to Cultural History," *International Journal of Comic Art* 7, no. 2 (2005): 147–63; Cord Scott, "Written in Red, White, and Blue: A Comparison of Comic Book Propaganda from World War II and September 11," *Journal of Popular Culture* 40, no. 2 (2007): 325–43; Matthias Schneider, "Der Fuehrer's Animation—Animation and Propaganda in the German Reich," trans. Annette Gentz, *International Journal of Comic Art* 6, no. 2 (2004): 172–81; Fredrik Strömberg, *Comic Art Propaganda* (New York: St. Martin's Griffin, 2010).

74. Adam Cathcart, "Atrocities, Insults, and 'Jeep Girls': Depictions of the U.S. Military in China, 1945–1949," *International Journal of Comic Art* 10, no. 1 (2008): 140–54; William B. Hart II and Fran Hassenchal, "Culture as Persuasion: Metaphor as Weapon," in *Bring 'Em On: Media and Politics in the Iraq War*, ed. Lee Artz and Yahya R. Kamalipour (Lanham, MD: Rowman and Littlefield, 2005), 85–100; Hubertus F. Jahn, "Kaiser, Cossacks, and Kolbasniks: Caricatures of the German in Russian Popular Culture," *Journal of Popular Culture* 31, no. 4 (1998): 109–22; Robert MacDougall, "Red, Brown and Yellow Perils: Images of the American Enemy in the 1940s and 1950s," *Journal of Popular Culture* 32, no. 4 (1999): 59–75; John E. Moser, "Madmen, Morons, and Monocles: The Portrayal of the Nazis in *Captain America*," in *Captain America and the Struggle of the Superhero*, ed. Robert C. Weiner (Jefferson, NC: McFarland, 2009), 24–35.

75. Jay Casey, "The Dynamics of Quiet Heroism and Invisible Death in American Soldier Cartoons of the World Wars," *International Journal of Comic Art* 9, no. 1 (2007): 281–95; Jay Casey, "'What's So Funny?' The Finding and Use of Soldier Cartoons from the World Wars as Historical Evidence," in *Drawing the Line: Using Cartoons as Historical Evidence*, ed. Richard Scully and Marian Quartly (Clayton, Australia: Monash University ePress, 2009), 07.1–07.23; Stephen E. Kercher, "Cartoons as 'Weapons of Wit': Bill Mauldin and Herbert Block Take on America's Postwar Anti-Communist Crusade," *International Journal of Comic Art* 7, no. 2 (2005): 311–20; John A. Lent and Xu Ying, "Cartooning and Wartime China: Part One—1931–1945," *International Journal of Comic Art* 10, no. 1 (2008): 76–139; Carmen Moran, "Allies Cartoon Humor in

World War II: A Comparison of 'Willie and Joe' and 'Bluey and Curley,'" *International Journal of Comic Art* 6, no. 2 (2004): 431–45; Roman Rosenbaum, "Mizuki Shigeru's Pacific War," *International Journal of Comic Art* 10, no. 2 (2008): 354–79; Scott R. Schoner, "A Survey of Doughboy Humor in World War I," *International Journal of Comic Art* 9, no. 2 (2007): 288–315.

76. Michael Birdwell, "Technical Fairy First Class? Is This Any Way to Run an Army?: Private SNAFU and World War II," *Historical Journal of Film, Radio, and Television* 25, no. 2 (2005): 203–12; David H. Culbert, "Walt Disney's Private Snafu: The Use of Humor in World War II Army Films," *Prospects* 1 (October 1976): 81–96; Cord Scott, "'Frankly, Mac, This "Police Action" Business Is Going Too Damn Far!': Armed Forces Cartoons during the Korean Conflict" (paper presented at the Korean War Conference: Commemorating the 60th Anniversary, hosted by the Victoria College/University of Houston-Victoria Library, June 24–26, 2010).

77. See discussion in: Lydia Fish, "Informal Communication Systems in the Vietnam War: A Case Study in Folklore, Technology and Popular Culture," *New Directions in Folklore* 7 (2003): http://hdl.handle.net/2022/6907.

78. Witek, "Dream of Total War."

79. Casey, "What's So Funny," 07.3.

80. Ibid., 07.1.

81. See: Will Eisner, *Graphic Storytelling and Visual Narrative* (New York: Norton, 2008); Winfried Nöth, "Narrative Self-Reference in a Literary Comic: M.-A. Mathieu's *L'Origine*," *Semiotica* 165–1/4 (2007): 173–90; Robert C. Harvey, *The Art of the Funnies: An Aesthetic History*, Studies in Popular Culture (Jackson, MS: University Press of Mississippi, 1994); Douglas Wolk, *Reading Comics: How Graphic Novels Work and What They Mean* (Cambridge, MA: Da Capo, 2007).

82. Harvey, *Art of the Funnies*, 9.

83. Martin J. Medhurst and Michael A. DeSousa, "Political Cartoons as Rhetorical Form: A Taxonomy of Graphic Discourse," *Communication Monographs* 48 (1981): 197–236.

84. Denise M. Bostdorff, "Making Light of James Watt: A Burkean Approach to the Form and Attitude of Political Cartoons," *Quarterly Journal of Speech* 73 (1987): 43–59; Dori Moss, "The Animated Persuader," *PS: Political Science and Politics* 40, no. 2 (2007): 241–4. Also see: Thomas, Jr., "Hero of the Military-Industrial Complex."

85. Examples: Francis E. Barcus, "A Content Analysis of Trends in Sunday Comics 1900–1959," *Journalism Quarterly* 38, no. 2 (1961): 171–80; Russell W. Belk, "Material Values in the Comics: A Content Analysis of Comic Books Featuring Themes of Wealth," *Journal of Consumer Research* 14 (1987): 26–42; Arthur Asa Berger, *The Comic-Stripped American: What Dick Tracy, Blondie, Daddy Warbucks, and Charlie Brown Tell Us About Ourselves* (New York: Walker, 1972); Leo Bogart, "Comic Strips and their Adult Readers," in *Mass Culture: The Popular Arts in America*, ed. Bernard Rosenberg and David M. White (Glencoe, IL: Free Press, 1957), 189–98; Harold H. Kassarjian, "Social Values and the Sunday Comics: A Content Analysis," in *Advances in Consumer Research* vol. 10, ed. Richard P. Bagozzi and Alice M. Tybout (Ann Arbor, MI: Association for Consumer Research, 1983), 434–8; Harold H. Kassarjian, "Males and Females in the Funnies: A Content Analysis," in *Personal Values and Consumer Psychology*, ed. Robert E. Pitts, Jr., and Arch G. Woodside (Lexington, MA: Lexington, 1984), 87–109; Lyle W. Shannon, "The Opinions of Little Orphan Annie and Her Friends," in *Mass Culture: The Popular Arts in America*, ed. Bernard Rosenberg and David M. White (Glencoe, IL: Free Press, 1957), 212–7; Susan Spiggle, "Measuring Social Values: A Content Analysis of Sunday Comics and Underground Comix," *Journal of Consumer Research* 13 (1986): 100–13.

86. Tim Blackmore, "*300* and Two: Frank Miller and Daniel Ford Interpret Herodotus's Thermopylae Myth," *International Journal of Comic Art* 6, no. 2 (2004): 325–49; Ian Gordon, "Nostalgia, Myth, and Ideology: Visions of Superman at the End of the 'American Century,'" in *Comics and Ideology* vol. 2, Popular Culture Everyday Life, ed. Matthew P. McAllister, Edward H. Sewell, Jr., and Ian Gordon (New York: Peter Lang, 2009), 177–94.

87. Examples: Casey Brienza, "Producing Comics Culture: A Sociological Approach to the Study of Comics," *Journal of Graphic Novels and Comics* 1, no. 2 (2010): 105–19; Karin Kukkonen, "Popular Cultural Memory: Comics, Communities and Context Knowledge," *Nordicom Review* 29, no. 2 (2008): 261–73; Matthew P. McAllister, Edward H. Sewell, Jr., and Ian Gordon, eds., *Comics and Ideology* vol. 2. Popular Culture Everyday Life (New York: Peter Lang, 2009); Karen McGrath, "Gender, Race, and Latina Identity: An Examination of Marvel Comics' *Amazing Fantasy* and *Araña*," *Atlantic Journal of Communication* 15, no. 4 (2007): 268–83; J. Gavin Paul, "Ashes in the Gutter: 9/11 and the Serialization of Memory in DC Comics' *Human Target*," *American Periodicals* 17, no. 2 (2007): 208–27; Matthew Pustz, ed., *Comic Books and American Cultural History* (New York: Continuum, 2012).

88. Kenneth Alan Adams and Lester Hill, Jr., "Protest and Rebellion: Fantasy Themes in Japanese Comics," *Journal of Popular Culture* 25, no. 1 (1991): 99–127; William L. Benoit, Andrew A. Klyukovski, John P. McHale, and David Airne, "A Fantasy Theme Analysis of Political Cartoons on the Clinton-Lewinsky-Starr Affair," *Critical Studies in Media Communication* 18, no. 4 (2001): 377–94; Janis L. Edwards and Huey-Rong Chen, "The First Lady/First Wife in Editorial Cartoons: Rhetorical Visions Through Gender Lenses," *Women's Studies in Communication* 23, no. 3 (2000): 367–91; Bormann, Koester, and Bennett, "Political Cartoons."

89. Ernest G. Bormann, "The Symbolic Convergence Theory of Communication: Applications and Implications for Teachers and Consultants," *Journal of Applied Communication Research* 10, no. 1 (1982): 51.

90. Ernest G. Bormann, "Symbolic Convergence Theory and Communication in Group Decision Making," in *Communication and Group Decision Making*, 2nd ed., ed. Randy Y. Hirokawa and Mar-

shall Scott Poole (Thousand Oaks, CA: Sage, 1996), 81–113; Bormann, "Applications and Implications."

91. Ernest G. Bormann, "Fantasy and Rhetorical Vision: The Rhetorical Criticism of Social Reality," *Quarterly Journal of Speech* 58 (1972): 396–407; Bormann, Koester, and Bennett, "Political Cartoons."

92. See: T. Brunyé, G. Riccio, J. Sidman, A. Darowski, and F.J. Diedrich, "Enhancing Warrior Ethos in Initial Entry Training," *Proceedings of the Human Factors and Ergonomics Society Annual Meeting* 50, no. 25 (2006): 2634–37; Charles A. Cotton, "Commitment in Military Systems," in *Legitimacy and Commitment in the Military*, ed. Thomas C. Wyatt and Reuven Gal (New York: Greenwood, 1990), 47–66; Andrew King, "The Word of Command: Communication and Cohesion in the Military," *Armed Forces and Society* 32, no. 4 (2006): 493–512; Peggy McClure and Walter Broughton, "Measuring the Cohesion of Military Communities," *Armed Forces and Society* 26, no. 3 (2000): 473–87; G.L. Siebold, "The Essence of Military Group Cohesion," *Armed Forces and Society* 33, no. 2 (2007): 286–95.

93. Example: Dawn O. Braithwaite, Paul Schrodt, and Jody Koenig, "Symbolic Convergence Theory: Communication, Dramatizing Messages, and Rhetorical Visions in Families," in *Engaging Theories in Family Communication*, ed. Dawn O Braithwaite and Leslie A. Baxter (Thousand Oaks, CA: Sage, 2006), 146–61.

94. Example: Bradley G. Jackson, "A Fantasy Theme Analysis of Peter Senge's Learning Organization," *Journal of Applied Behavioral Science* 36, no. 2 (2000): 193–209.

95. Examples: Margaret Duffy, "High Stakes: A Fantasy Theme Analysis of the Selling of Riverboat Gambling in Iowa," *Southern Communication Journal* 62 (1997): 117–32; Margaret Duffy, "Web of Hate: A Fantasy Theme Analysis of the Rhetorical Vision of Hate Groups Online," *Journal of Communication Inquiry* 27, no. 3 (2003): 291–312; Linda Putnam, Shirley A. Van Hoeven, and Connie A. Bullis, "The Role of Rituals and Fantasy Themes in Teachers' Bargaining," *Western Journal of Speech Communication* 55 (1991): 85–103; David. L. Rarick, Mary B. Duncan, David G. Lee and Laurinda W. Porter, "The Carter Persona: An Empirical Analysis of the Rhetorical Visions of Campaign '76," *Quarterly Journal of Speech* 63, no. 3 (1977): 258–73.

96. Ernest G. Bormann, John F. Cragan, and Donald C. Shields, "In Defense of Symbolic Convergence Theory: A Look at the Theory and Its Criticisms After Two Decades," *Communication Theory* 4, no. 4 (1994): 259–94; also: Bormann, "Rhetorical Criticism of Social Reality."

97. Ernest G. Bormann, Roxann L. Knutson, and Karen Musolf, "Why Do People Share Fantasies? An Empirical Investigation of a Basic Tenet of the Symbolic Convergence Communication Theory," *Communication Studies* 48, no. 3 (1997): 254–76.

98. John F. Cragan and Donald C. Shields, *Symbolic Theories in Applied Communication Research: Bormann, Burke, and Fisher* (Cresskill, NJ: Hampton, 1995); Bormann, "Rhetorical Criticism of Social Reality."

99. Ernest G. Bormann, "Fantasy and Rhetorical Vision: Ten Years Later," *Quarterly Journal of Speech* 68 (1982): 288–305; Bormann, "Rhetorical Criticism of Social Reality."

100. Bormann, Cragan and Shields, "In Defense," 276.

101. Donald C. Shields and C. Thomas Preston, Jr., "Fantasy Theme Analysis in Competitive Rhetorical Criticism," *National Forensic Journal* 3 (1985): 102–15.

102. Bormann, "Applications and Implications," 52.

103. Ernest G. Bormann, John F. Cragan, and Donald C. Shields, "An Expansion of the Rhetorical Vision Component of the Symbolic Convergence Theory: The Cold War Paradigm Case," *Communication Monographs* 63, no. 1 (1996): 1–28; Bormann, "Rhetorical Criticism of Social Reality"; Bormann, "Applications and Implications"; Cragan and Shields, *Symbolic Theories*; Bormann, Cragan and Shields, "In Defense."

104. Cragan and Shields, *Symbolic Theories*; Shields and Preston, Jr., "Fantasy Theme Analysis."

105. Roderick P. Hart, "Cultural Criticism," in *Modern Rhetorical Criticism*, 2nd ed. (Boston, MA: Allyn and Bacon, 1997), 231–58.

106. Sonja K. Foss, "Fantasy-Theme Criticism," in *Rhetorical Criticism: Exploration and Practice*, 2nd ed. (Prospect Heights, IL: Waveland, 1996), 121–64.

107. Cheryl Broom and Susan Avanzino, "The Communication of Community Collaboration: When Rhetorical Visions Collide," *Communication Quarterly* 58, no. 4 (2010): 480–501.

108. Casey, "What's So Funny," 07.2.

109. A Funny Thing Happened Back in Vietnam, *Pacific Stars and Stripes*, February 19, 1981, 7.

Chapter 1

1. Graham Chapman, John Cleese, Terry Gilliam, Eric Idle, Terry Jones and Michael Palin, *The Complete Monty Python's Flying Circus: All the Words, Vol. 1* (New York: Pantheon, 1989).

2. Craig Zelizer, "Laughing Our Way to Peace or War: Humour and Peacebuilding," *Journal of Conflictology* 1, no. 2 (2010): 1–9, E-journal.

3. John T. Winterich, ed., *Squads Write! A Selection of the Best Things in Prose, Verse and Cartoons from the Stars and Stripes* (New York: Harper and Brothers, 1931); in Ira Topping, ed., *The Best of Yank the Army Weekly, 1942–1945* (New York: Arno, 1980), vol. 2, no. 25, 11.

4. Homer Litzenberg, "Preface," in *Leatherhead in Korea*, by SSGT Norval E. Packwood, Jr. (Quantico, VA: Marine Corps Gazette, 1952), 2.

5. Blane Anderson, "Humor and Leadership," *Journal of Organizational Culture, Communications and Conflict* 9, no. 1 (2005): 137–44; Brigadier J. Nazareth, *Psychology of Military Humour* (Olympia Fields, IL: Lancer, 2008); Eric J. Romero and Kevin W. Cruthirds, "The Use of Humor in the Workplace," *Academy of Management Perspectives* 20, no. 2 (2006): 58–69.

6. Carol Burke, "Marching to Vietnam," *Journal of American Folklore* 102, no. 406 (1989): 424–41.

7. Samuel A. Stouffer, Edward A. Suchman, Leland C. Devinney, Shirley A. Star, and Robin M. Williams, Jr., *The American Soldier: Adjustment During Army Life* (Princeton, NJ: Princeton University Press, 1949).

8. That? Humor in the Literature of the Second World War," *Journal of American Culture* 12, no. 3 (1989): 11.

9. Nazareth, *Psychology of Military Humour.*

10. Ibid., 107.

11. Nazareth, *Psychology of Military Humour*; also see: Bruce Bairnsfather, *Carry On Sergeant!* (Indianapolis, IN: Bobbs-Merrill, 1927).

12. Nazareth, *Psychology of Military Humour.*

13. Jon Grinspan, "Laugh During Wartime," *New York Times*, January 9, 2012, http://opinionator. blogs.nytimes.com/2012/01/09/laugh-during-wartime/ (accessed July 6, 2013).

14. Mark Bryant, *Napoleonic Wars in Cartoons* (London, UK: Grubb Street, 2009).

15. Mark Bryant, *Wars of Empire in Cartoons* (London, UK: Grubb Street, 2009).

16. Jon Grinspan, "'Sorrowfully Amusing': The Popular Comedy of the Civil War," *Journal of the Civil War* 1, no, 3 (2011): Kindle e-journal, loc. 86.

17. Ibid.

18. For example, see Baird Jarman, "The Graphic Art of Thomas Nast: Politics and Propriety in Postbellum Publishing," *American Periodicals* 20, no. 2 (2010): 156–89.

19. Grinspan, "Sorrowfully Amusing," loc. 110.

20. Cameron C. Nickels, *Civil War Humor* (Jackson, MS: University Press of Mississippi, 2010).

21. Lucy Shelton Caswell, "Drawing Swords: War in American Editorial Cartoons," *American Journalism* 21, no. 2 (2004): 13–45; David R. Spencer, "The Press and the Spanish American War," *International Journal of Comic Art* 9, no. 1 (2007): 262–80.

22. Scott R. Schoner, "A Survey of Doughboy Humor in World War I," *International Journal of Comic Art* 9, no. 2 (2007): 288–315.

23. Tonie Holt and Valmai Holt, "Introduction to the 'BB4H4H' Edition of Best of Fragments from France," in *The Best of Fragments from France*, by Capt. Bruce Bairnsfather, ed. Tonie Holt and Valmai Holt (South Yorkshire, UK: Pen and Sword Military, 2009); Grinspan, "Sorrowfully Amusing."

24. Jay Casey, "'What's So Funny?' The Finding and Use of Soldier Cartoons from the World Wars as Historical Evidence," in *Drawing the Line: Using Cartoons as Historical Evidence*, ed. Richard Scully and Marian Quartly (Clayton, Australia: Monash University ePress, 2009), 07.4.

25. Daily Mail Reporter, "What a Lovely War: Cartoons of Life on the First World War Frontline Unearthed (and There's Not a Filthy Trench in Sight)," *Mail Online*, March 11, 2012, http://www. dailymail.co.uk/news/article-2113408/Humorous-German-cartoons-life-frontline-World-War-I-unearthed-theyre-funny.html (accessed March 2, 2013).

26. Allen Douglas, *War, Memory, and the Politics of Humor: The Canard Enchaîné and World War I* (Berkeley, CA: University of California Press, 2002); Paul Fussell, *The Great War and Modern Memory: The Illustrated Edition* (New York: Sterling, 2009).

27. Charles Skilling, "Kilroy Was Here," *Western Folklore* 22, no. 4 (1963): 276–7.

28. W.N. Davis, "Foreword," in *Wits of War: Unofficial GI Humor History of World War II*, by Edwin J. Swineford (Fresno, CA: Kilroy Was Here, 1989), v.

29. Sabrina Tavernise, "As Fewer American Serve, Growing Gap Is Found Between Civilians and Military," *New York Times*, November 24, 2011, http://www.nytimes.com/ 2011/11/25/us/civilian-military-gap-grows-as-fewer-americans-serve.html (accessed June 20, 2013).

30. Carol Burke, "Military Speech," *New Directions in Folklore* 7 (2003): http://hdl.handle.net/ 2022/6905; Richard Allen Burns, "'This Is My Rifle, This Is My Gun...': Gunlore in the Military," *New Directions in Folklore* 7 (2003): http://hdl.handle. net/2022/6906; Ben Zweibelson, "Building Another Tower of Babel: Why Acronyms are Ruining Shared Military Understanding," *Small Wars Journal*, May 7, 2013, http://smallwarsjournal. com/jrnl/art/building-another-tower-of-babel; also see: Gordon L. Rottman, *FUBAR: Soldier Slang of World War II* (New York: Metro, 2007).

31. John A. Lent, "Cartooning, Public Crises, and Conscientization: A Global Perspective," *International Journal of Comic Art* 10, no. 1 (2008): 352–86; Nick Thorkelson, "Cartoons Against the Axis: World War II Bonds Cartoons from the Terry-D'Alessio Collection. Sandy Schecter with Special Thanks to Hilda Terry and Art Spiegelman. New York City, NY: Museum of Comic and Cartooning Art, October 8, 2005-February 6, 2006," *International Journal of Comic Art* 8, no. 1 (2006): 591–4.

32. John A. Lent and Xu Ying, "Cartooning and Wartime China: Part One—1931–1945," *International Journal of Comic Art* 10, no. 1 (2008): 76–139.

33. Matthias Schneider, "Der Fuehrer's Animation: Animation and Propaganda in the German Reich," trans. Annette Gentz, *International Journal of Comic Art* 6, no. 2 (2004): 172–81.

34. Peter Aichinger, *The American Soldier in Fiction, 1880–1963: A History of Attitudes Toward Warfare and the Military Establishment* (Ames, IA: Iowa State University Press, 1975).

35. Catherine Merridale, "Culture, Ideology and Combat in the Red Army, 1939–45," *Journal of Contemporary History* 41, no. 2 (2006): 305–24.

36. Cord Scott, "'Frankly, Mac, This "Police Action" Business Is Going Too Damn Far!' Armed Forces Cartoons During the Korean Conflict" (paper presented at the Korean War Conference: Commemorating the 60th Anniversary, hosted by the Victoria College/University of Houston-Victoria Library June 24–26 2010).

37. Lydia Fish, "Informal Communication Systems in the Vietnam War: A Case Study in Folklore, Technology and Popular Culture," *New Directions in Folklore* 7 (2003): http://hdl.handle.net/2022/6907, e-journal.

38. Burke, "Marching to Vietnam."

39. Lt. Col. Martin Heuer, "Personal Reflections on the Songs of Army Aviators in the Vietnam War,"

New Directions in Folklore 7 (2003): http://hdl.handle.net/2022/6909.

40. Les Cleveland, "Songs of the Vietnam War: An Occupational Folk Tradition," *New Directions in Folklore* 7 (2003): http://hdl.handle.net/2022/6908, para. 16.

41. Lee Anderson, *Battle Notes: Music of the Vietnam War* (Superior, WI: Savage, 2003).

42. The Vietnam Graffiti Project, "The Graffiti," *Vietnam Graffiti* (2009–2010): http://www.vietnamgraffiti.com/the-graffiti.

43. "Grants Heroes," *Pacific Stars and Stripes* (August 25, 1968): 6; David Harris, "Cartoons and More Cartoons," *Cantabrigia*, February 22, 2007, http://blogs.wickedlocal.com/ cambridge/2007/02/22/cartoons-and-more-cartoons/#axzz2YZ6QvdYh (accessed July 5, 2013); Jason Thompson, "PULPman Profiles: Vernon Grant," *PULP: The Manga Magazine* 5, no. 12 (2001): archived at http://web.archive.org/web/20041020025320/www.pulp-mag.com/archives/5.12/pulpman.shtml.

44. Richard L. Graham, *Government Issue: Comics for the People, 1940s-2000s* (New York: Abrams Comicarts, 2011).

45. Teodora Carabas, "Tales Calculated to Drive You MAD: The Debunking of Spies, Superheroes, and Cold War Rhetoric in *Mad Magazine's* 'SPY vs SPY,'" *Journal of Popular Culture* 40, no. 1 (2007): 4–24; Kristin L. Matthews, "The ABCs of *Mad* Magazine: Reading, Citizenship, and Cold War America," *International Journal of Comic Art* 8, no. 2 (2006): 248–68.

46. Christine Scodari, "Operation Desert Storm as 'Wargames': Sport, War, and Media Intertextuality," *Journal of American Culture* 16, no. 1 (1993): 1–5.

47. Riikka Kuusisto, "Heroic Tale, Game, and Business Deal? Western Metaphors in Action in Kosovo," *Quarterly Journal of Speech* 88, no. 2 (2002): 50–68.

48. Sean Zwagerman, "A Day That Will Live in Irony: September 11 and the War on Humor," in *The War on Terror and American Popular Culture: September 11 and Beyond*, ed. Andrew Schopp and Matthew B. Hill (Cranbury, NJ: Rosemont, 2009).

49. Grimaldi, "Is There Humor in Afghanistan?" *The Public Manager* 30, no. 4 (2001): 55–6; William B. Hart II and Fran Hassenchal, "Culture as Persuasion: Metaphor as Weapon," in *Bring 'Em On: Media and Politics in the Iraq War*, ed. Lee Artz and Yahya R. Kamalipour (Lanham, MD: Rowman and Littlefield, 2005).

50. Giselinde Kuipers, "'Where Was King Kong When We Needed Him?' Public Discourse, Digital Disaster Jokes, and the Functions of Laughter After 9/11," *Journal of American Culture* 28, no. 1 (2005): 70–84; Zwagerman, "A Day That Will Live in Irony."

51. Andrew Paul Williams, Justin D. Martin, Kaye D. Trammell, Kristen Landreville, and Chelsea Ellis, "Late-Night Talk Shows and War: Entertaining and Informing through Humor," *Journal of Global Mass Communication* 3, no. 1–4 (2010): 131–38.

52. For example: Kara Ballenger-Browning and Douglas C. Johnson, "Key Facts on Resilience," *Naval Center for Combat and Operational Stress Control*, http://www.med.navy.mil/sites/nmcsd/nccosc/heal thProfessionalsV2/reports/Documents/resilience TWPFormatted2.pdf; Jeni Tyson, "Compassion Fatigue in the Treatment of Combat-Related Trauma During Wartime," *Clinical Social Work* 35, no. 3 (2007): 183–92.

53. Graham, *Government-Issue.*

54. Waldmeir, "What's Funny About That," 11.

55. Robert C. Harvey, *The Art of the Funnies: An Aesthetic History*, Studies in Popular Culture (Jackson, MS: University Press of Mississippi, 1994), 203.

56. Quoted in: Stephanie Newton, "Bailey Strip Gets Attitude Adjustment," in *Mort Walker Conversations*, Conversations with Comic Artists, ed. Jason Whiton (Jackson, MS: University Press of Mississippi, 2005, 170; also: Dick Ahles, "His Roots Still Local, Beetle Bailey Turns 50," *New York Times*, September 3, 2000, http://www.nytimes.com/2000/ 09/03/nyregion/ his-roots-still-local-beetle-bailey-turns-50.html (accessed July 9, 2013); Jason Whiton, ed., *Mort Walker Conversations* (Jackson, MS: University Press of Mississippi, 2005); Harvey, *Art of the Funnies.*

57. Waldmeir, "What's Funny About That," 11.

58. See: Scott, "Frankly, Mac."

59. Virginia Herman, "Forward," in *Winning the WAC: The Return of a World War II Favorite* by Cpl. Vic Herman (Encinitas, CA: KNI, Inc./Virginia Herman, 2002), 1; Carole Landis, "Forward," in *Winnie the WAC*, by Cpl. Vic Herman (Philadelphia, PA: David McKay, 1945), 1–4; Dolly Maw, "Herman's Hacienda," *San Diego Magazine*, July 1971, 68–9, 91, and 94.

60. Julie L. Negron, *PCSing.... It's a Spouse Thing!* (N.p.: Lulu.com/JulieNegron, 2010), 3.

61. In: Negron, *PCSing.*

62. Waldmeir, "What's Funny About That," 14.

63. "Drawing from Experience," *Stars and Stripes*, 50th Anniversary Special Edition (April 18, 1992): 33.

64. Carmen Moran, "Allies Cartoon Humor in World War II: A Comparison of 'Willie and Joe' and 'Bluey and Curley,'" *International Journal of Comic Art* 6, no. 2 (2004): 431–45; Casey, "What's So Funny."

65. Todd DePastino, *Bill Mauldin: A Life Up Front* (New York: W.W. Norton, 2008).

66. Moran, "Allies Cartoon Humor."

67. Kevin McComack, "Doctrine Man Assists Military Men and Women Laugh at Life," *Kevin McComack Blogspot*, December 5, 2010, http://kevinmccomack.blogspot.com/2010/12/ doctrine-man-assists-military-men-and.html (accessed March 1, 2013); Thom Shanker, "Masked Military Man Is Superhero for Troops"; *New York Times*, November 18, 2010, http://www.nytimes.com/ 2010/11/19/us/19pentagon.html (accessed November 9, 2012); Clint VanWinkle, "Doctrine Man!! Saving the World Without a Plan," *Command Posts*, June 19, 2012, http://www.commandposts.com/2012/06/doctrine-man-saving-the-world-wihout-a-plan/ (accessed September 22, 2013).

68. Waldmeir, "What's Funny About That," 16.

69. Bairnsfather, *Carry On Sergeant*, 31.

70. Tim O'Brien, *The Things They Carried* (1990; Boston, MA: Mariner, 2009), 16.

71. Jean Baudrillard, "War Porn," trans. Paul A.

Taylor, *International Journal of Baudrillard Studies* 2, no. 1 (2005): http://www.ubishops.ca/baudrillard studies/vol2_1/ Taylor.htm/.

72. Mathis Chiroux, "Is Our Military Addicted to 'War Porn'?" *Huffington Post,* January 15, 2012, http://www.huffingtonpost.com/matthis-chiroux/is-our-military-addicted-_b_1206537.html (accessed July 9, 2013); John Rico, "Why Soldiers Take Photos," *Salon,* April 22, 2012, http://www.salon.com/2012/04/23/why_soldiers_take_photos/; see also: Nathan Roger, "Abu Ghraib Abuse Images: From Perverse War Trophies Through Internet Based War Porn to Artistic Representations and Beyond," *At the Interface/Probing the Boundaries* 75 (2011): 121–38.

73. Bill Mauldin, *Up Front* 1945 (New York: W.W. Norton, 2000), 34.

74. Waldmeir, "What's Funny About That."

75. Patrick O'Neill, "The Comedy of Entropy: The Contexts of Black Humour," *Canadian Review of Comparative Literature* 10, no. 2 (1983): 145–66.

76. Aichinger, "American Soldier in Fiction," 97.

77. Hal Foster, *The Return of the Real: The Avant-Garde at the End of the Century* (Cambridge, MA: MIT Press, 1996).

78. Quoted in: Gene Weingarten, "Doonesbury's War" *Washington Post,* October 22, 2006, http://www.washingtonpost.com/wp-dyn/content/article/2006/10/20/AR2006102000446.html (accessed July 7, 2013), para. 12.

79. Martin Barker and Roger Sabin, "'Doonesbury Does Iraq': Garry Trudeau and the Politics of an Anti-War Strip," *Journal of Graphic Novels and Comics* 3, no. 2 (2012): 140; also Julianne H. Newton, "Trudeau Draws Truth," *Critical Studies in Media Communication* 24, no. 1 (2007): 81–5.

80. Ronald A. Berk, "Student Ratings of 10 Strategies for Using Humor in College Teaching," *Journal on Excellence in College Teaching* 7, no. 3 (1996): 71–92; Jean M. Civikly, "Humor and the Enjoyment of College Teaching," in *Communicating in College Classrooms,* ed. Jean M. Civikly (San Francisco, CA: Jossey-Bass, 1986); Bernard J. Dodge and Allison Rossett, "Heuristic for Humor in Instruction," *Performance and Instruction* 21, no. 4 (1982): 11–32; Deborah J. Hill, *Humor in the Classroom: A Handbook for Teachers* (Springfield, IL: Charles C. Thomas, 1988); Avner Ziv, "The Influence of Humorous Atmosphere on Divergent Thinking," *Contemporary Educational Psychology* 8, no. 1 (1983): 68–75; Avner Ziv, "Teaching and Learning with Humor: Experiment and Replications," *Journal of Experimental Education* 57, no. 1 (1988): 5–15.

81. "Drawing from Experience."

82. AP, "Sometime Funny Stuff Happens, Even in Iraq," *New Zealand Herald,* January 19, 2009.

83. Dwight D. Eisenhower, "Military-Industrial Complex Speech, 1961," *The Avalon Project,* no date, http://avalon.law.yale.edu/20th_century/eisenhower001.asp.

84. James Der Derian, *Virtuous War: Mapping the Military-Industrial-Media-Entertainment Network,* 2nd ed. (New York: Routledge, 2009).

85. Rebecca Keegan, "The U.S. Military's Hollywood Connection," *Los Angeles Times,* August 21, 2011, http://articles.latimes.com/2011/aug/21/entertainment/la-ca-military-movies-20110821 (accessed June 17, 2013).

86. Lawrence Suid, *Guts and Glory: The Making of the American Military Image* (Lexington, KY: University Press of Kentucky, 2002).

87. Katharine Q. Seelye, "When Hollywood's Big Guns Come Right from the Source," *New York Times,* June 10, 2002, http://www.nytimes.com/2002/06/10/us/when-hollywood-s-big-guns-come-right-from-the-source.html (accessed July 3, 2013).

88. Donna Miles, "Edwards Team Stars in 'Ironman' Superhero Movie," *U.S. Department of Defense,* May 2, 2007, http:// www.defense.gov/news/news article.aspx?id= 33023; Donna Miles, "Military, Hollywood Team Up to Create Realism, Drama on Big Screen," *U.S. Department of Defense,* June 8, 2007, http://www.defense.gov/News/Newsarticle.aspx?ID= 46352.

89. Ronald C. Thomas, Jr., "Hero of the Military-Industrial Complex: Reading Iron Man Through Burke's Dramatism," in *Heroes of Film, Comics and American Culture: Essays on Real and Fictional Defenders of Home,* ed. Lisa M. Detora (Jefferson, NC: McFarland, 2009, Kindle e-book), loc. 2040.

90. Michael Birdwell, "Technical Fairy First Class? Is This Any Way to Run an Army?: Private SNAFU and World War II," *Historical Journal of Film, Radio, and Television* 25, no. 2 (2005): 203–12; Walton Rawls, *Disney Dons Dogtags: The Best of Disney Military Insignia from World War II* (New York: Abbeville, 1992).

91. Roger Turner, "Laughing at the Weather? The Serious World of Weather Cartoons," *History of Science Society Newsletter,* January 2009, http://www.hssonline.org/publications/ Newsletter2009/January2009Turner.html.

92. Stephen E. Kercher, "Cartoons as 'Weapons of Wit': Bill Mauldin and Herbert Block Take on America's Postwar Anti-Communist Crusade," *International Journal of Comic Art* 7, no. 2 (2005): 311–20; also see: Reneé Klish, *Art of the American Soldier: Documenting Military History Through Artists' Eyes and in Their Own Words* (Washington, D.C.: Center of Military History, 2011).

93. Amanda Carson Banks and Elizabeth Wein, "Folklore and the Comic Book: The Traditional Meets the Popular," *New Directions in Folklore* 2 (1998): http://hdl.handle.net/2022/ 7218.

94. Graham, *Government Issue.*

95. Ali Kefford, "The Original GI Jane" (reprinted from "A Strip for Victory"), *Skylighters* (n.d.), http://www.skylighters.org/jane.

96. R.C. Harvey, *Milton Caniff's Male Call: The Complete Newspaper Strips: 1942–1946* (Neshannock, PA: Hermes, 2011); Sgt. Leonard Sansone, *The Wolf* (New York: United, 1945).

97. Bill Hume and John Annarino, *Babysan: A Private Look at the Japanese Occupation* (Tokyo: Kasuga Boeki, 1953), 6.

98. Quoted in: Rawls, *Disney Dons Dogtags,* front cover.

99. Jay Casey, "The Dynamics of Quiet Heroism and Invisible Death in American Soldier Cartoons of the World Wars," *International Journal of Comic Art* 9, no. 1 (2007): 281–95.

100. Wartime S&S, "Yank Cartoons on Sale," *Stars and Stripes*, April 17, 1982, 9; Casey, "What's So Funny?"

101. Quoted in: Shanker, "Masked Military Man," para. 10.

102. A Funny Thing Happened Back in Vietnam, *Pacific Stars and Stripes*, February 19, 1981, 7.

103. Bill Briggs, "Unmasking the Agony: Combat Troops Turn to Art Therapy," NBCNewswww, May 24, 2013, http://usnews.nbcnews.com/_news/2013/05/26/18471262-unmasking-the-agony-combat-troops-turn-to-art-therapy?lite (accessed May 27, 2013); Varick A. Chittenden, "'These Aren't Just My Scenes': Shared Memories in a Vietnam Veteran's Art," *Journal of American Folklore* 102, no. 406 (1989): 412–23; Genie Joseph, "Laughter Is Best Medicine for Military Families," *U.S. Army*, April 15, 2011, http://www.army.mil/article/55071/Laughter_is_best_medicine_for_ military_ families/.

104. Thompson, "PULPman Profiles"

105. John E. Deaton, S. William Berg, Milton Richlin, and Alan J. Litrownik, "Coping Activities in Solitary Confinement of U.S. Navy POWs in Vietnam"; *Journal of Applied Social Psychology* 7, no. 3 (1977): 239–57; Linda D. Henman, "Humor as a Coping Mechanism: Lessons from POWs," *Humor* 14, no. 1 (2001): 83–94; J.E. Nardini, "Survival Factors in American Prisoners of War of the Japanese," *American Journal of Psychiatry* 109, no. 4 (1952): 241–8; Nickels, *Civil War Humor*.

106. Sara Malm, "Sketches from Hell: Humorous Cartoons Drawn by British Soldier Kept as a Japanese PoW for Three Years in Changi Prison," *Daily Mail*, July 5, 2012, http://www. dailymail.co.uk/news/article–2169177/Sketches-hell-Touching-cartoons-drawn-British-soldier-years-terror-Changi-prison.html (accessed March 1, 2013), para. 2.

107. Rick Schindler, "Cartoonists Draw Smiles from Troops on USO Tour," TODAYwww, November 11, 2011, http://www.today.com/id/45255297/ns/today-today_books/t/cartoonists-draw-smiles-troops-uso-tour/ (accessed July 19, 2013).

108. Christian Pelusi, "Cartoonist Bruce Higdon Draws Military Kids to His USO Fort Campbell Classes," *USO News*, August 27, 2012, http://www.uso.org/bruce-higdon-cartoon-class-fort-campbell/.

109. Katherine E. Brown and Elina Penttinen, "'A "Sucking Chest Wound" Is Nature's Way of Telling You to Slow Down...' Humour and Laughter in War Time," *Critical Studies on Security* 1, no, 1 (2013): 124–6.

110. Mary I. Huntley, "Take Time for Laughter," *Creative Nursing* 15, no. 1 (2009): 39–42; Mary Huntley and Edna Thayer, *A Mirthful Spirit: Embracing Laughter for Wellness* (Edina, MN: Beaver's Pond, 2007); C.W. Metcalf and Roma Felible, *Lighten Up: Survival Skills for People Under Pressure* (Menlo Park, CA: Addison-Wesley, 1992); Joseph, "Laughter Is Best Medicine."

111. "Laughter Yoga in the Canadian Military," *Laughter Yoga International*, May 23, 2013, http://www.laughteryoga.org/news/news_details/441.

112. Luis Martinez, "'Laughing Colonel' Helps Troops Cope," ABC News, January 13, 2006, http://abcnews.go.com/U.S./IraqCoverage/story?id=1504555#.UdhzJm2G6So (accessed July 19, 2013).

113. Andy Rooney, "War, Cartoons and Death for Ex-Striper Wingert," *Stars and Stripes Europe*, March 6, 1994, 9.

114. David H. Culbert, "Walt Disney's Private Snafu: The Use of Humor in World War II Army Films," *Prospects* 1, October (1976): 81–96; Frank Brandt, ed., *Cartoons for Fighters* (Washington, D.C.: Infantry Journal, 1945); Graham, *Government Issue*.

115. Birdwell, "Technical Fairy First Class," 203–4.

116. Donald Nijboer, *Graphic War: The Secret Aviation Drawings and Illustrations of World War II* (Ontario, ON: Boston Mills, 2011).

117. Srdjan Vucetic, "Identity Is a Joking Matter: Intergroup Humor in Bosnia," *Spaces of Identity* 4, no. 2 (2004): 7–34.

118. Matthias Schneider, "Der Fuehrer's Animation."

119. "Biography: The Army Years and PS Magazine," *WillEisner.com*, no date, http://www. willeisner.com/biography/5-the-army-years.html; "Biography: Spirited Work," *WillEisner.com*, no date, http://www.willeisner.com/biography/3-spirited-work.html.

120. Paul E. Fitzgerald, *Will Eisner and PS Magazine: An Ongoing Legacy of Nitty Gritty Laughs and Deadly Serious How-To Comics for Generations of America's Warriors* (Fincastle, VA: Fitzworld.com, 2009).

121. Jim Lea, "The GI's World as Soldier's Pencil Sees It," *Pacific Stars and Stripes*, August 28, 1977, 11.

122. C. Todd Lopez, "'Sergeant Firewall' Promotes Information Assurance," *The Mountaineer*, August 19, 2010, A5.

123. Jeffrey S. Reznick, "*Snoopy as the World War I Flying Ace*. Jane O'Cain. Produced by the Charles M. Schulz Museum and Research Center and toured by ExhibitsUSA. College Park, MD: College Park Aviation Museum, Aug. 30-Nov. 30, 2008," *International Journal of Comic Art* 11, no. 1 (2009): 554.

124. Reznick, "Snoopy as the World War I Flying Ace."

125. "A Funny Thing Happened Back in Vietnam."

126. Lent, "Cartooning, Public Crises."

127. Committee on Public Information, Bureau of Cartoons, Bulletin No. 16, September 28, 1919, 1–2 (http://historymatters.gmu.edu/d/5052/).

128. Cord Scott, "Written in Red, White, and Blue: A Comparison of Comic Book Propaganda from World War II and September 11," *Journal of Popular Culture* 40, no. 2 (2007): 325–43.

129. Thorkelson, "Cartoons Against the Axis."

130. Robert K. Bindig memoirs, Veterans History Project, AFC/2001/001/32475, American Folklife Center, Library of Congress.

131. Lent, "Cartooning, Public Crises."

132. Damon Bryan Shackelford, *Delta Bravo Sierra: Rally Point: Vol. 1, Year 1, 2008*, www.deltabravosierra.us, 2008, 6.

133. Shackelford, *Delta Bravo Sierra*, back cover.

134. See, for example: Alexander Clarkson, "Virtual Heroes: Boys, Masculinity and Historical Memory in War Comics 1945–1995," *Thymos: Journal of*

Boyhood Studies 2, no. 2 (2008): 175–85; Joseph Witek, "The Dream of Total War: The Limits of a Genre," *Journal of Popular Culture* 30, no. 2 (1996): 37–45.

Chapter 2

1. Les Cleveland, "Songs of the Vietnam War: An Occupational Folk Tradition," *New Directions in Folklore* 7 (2003): http://hdl.handle.net/2022/6908; Karen D. Davis and Brian McKee, "Women in the Military: Facing the Warrior Framework," in *Challenge and Change in the Military: Gender and Diversity Issues*, ed. Franklin C. Pinch, Allister T. MacIntyre, Phyllis Browne and Alan C. Okros (Kingston, ON: Canadian Defence Academy Press, 2006), 52–75; Karen O. Dunivin, "Military Culture: Change and Continuity," *Armed Forces and Society* 20, no. 4 (1994): 531–47; Williamson Murray, "Does Military Culture Matter?" *Foreign Policy Research Institute* 43, no. 1 (1999): 134–51.

2. Kurt Lang, "Military Organizations," in *Handbook of Organizations*, ed., John G. March (Chicago, IL: Rand McNally, 1965), 838–78. For more on military structure, see: Gerhard Kümmel, "A Soldier Is a Soldier Is a Soldier!? The Military and Its Soldiers in an Era of Globalization," in *Handbook of the Sociology of the Military*, ed. Giuseppe Caforio (New York: Springer, 2006), 417–33.

3. Charles C. Moskos, "Institutional and Occupational Trends in Armed Forces," in *The Military: More Than Just a Job?*, ed. Charles C. Moskos and Frank R. Wood (Washington, D.C.: Pergamon-Brassey's, 1988), 15–26; also see: Arie Shirom, "On Some Correlates of Combat Performance," *Administrative Science Quarterly* 21 (1976): 419–32.

4. Morris Janowitz, *The Professional Soldier: A Social and Political Portrait* (New York: Free Press, 1960).

5. Volker Franke, *Preparing for Peace: Military Identity, Value Orientations, and Professional Military Education* (Westport, CT: Praeger, 1999).

6. Joseph Soeters, "Value Orientations in Military Academies: A Thirteen Country Study," *Armed Forces and Society* 24, no. 1 (1997): 7–32.

7. Anonymous, "Informal Social Organization in the Army," *American Journal of Sociology* 51, no. 5 (1946): 365–70; John Hockey, *Squaddies: Portrait of a Subculture* (Exeter, UK: Exeter University Press, 1986).

8. Janowitz, *The Professional Soldier*.

9. Collette Van Laar, *Increasing a Sense of Community in the Military: The Role of Personnel Support Programs* (Santa Monica, CA: RAND, 1999).

10. James G. Daley, "Understanding the Military as an Ethnic Identity," in *Social Work Practice in the Military*, ed. James G. Daley (Binghamton, NY: Hawthorn, 1999), 291–306.

11. Ben Shalit, *The Psychology of Conflict and Combat* (New York: Praeger, 1988).

12. Howard Brotz and Everett Wilson, "Characteristics of Military Society," *American Journal of Sociology* 51, no. 5 (1946): 371–5; Morris Janowitz, *Sociology and the Military Establishment* (New York:

Russell Sage Foundation, 1959); Thomas M. McCloy and William H. Clover, "Value Formation at the Air Force Academy," in *The Military: More Than Just a Job?*, ed. Charles C. Moskos and Frank R. Wood (Washington, D.C.: Pergamon-Brassey's, 1988), 129–49.

13. Joseph L. Soeters, Donna J. Winslow, and Alise Weibull, "Military Culture," in *Handbook of the Sociology of the Military*, ed. Giuseppe Caforio (New York: Springer, 2006), 237–54. Also see: Eyal Ben-Ari, *Mastering Soldiers: Conflict, Emotion, and the Enemy in an Israeli Military Unit*, New Directions in Anthropology, vol. 10 (New York: Berghahn, 1998); Janowitz, *Sociology and the Military Establishment*.

14. Soeters, Winslow and Weibull, "Military Culture," 251.

15. Janowitz, *Sociology and the Military Establishment*.

16. Lt. Lucian Grigorescu, *Camouflaged Emotions: Stoicism in the Military* (Quantico, VA: United States Marine Corps, Command and Staff College, 2009).

17. Robert A. Clark, "Aggressiveness and Military Training," *American Journal of Sociology* 51, no. 5 (1946): 423–32; August B. Hollingshead, "Adjustment to Military Life," *American Journal of Sociology* 51, no. 5 (1946): 439–47.

18. Janowitz, *Sociology and the Military Establishment*.

19. Anne Irwin, "The Problem of Realism and Reality in Military Training Exercises," in *New Directions in Military Sociology*, ed. Eric Oullet (Whitby, ON: De Sitter, 2005), 93–133.

20. Paul E. Fitzgerald, *Will Eisner and PS Magazine: An Ongoing Legacy of Nitty Gritty Laughs and Deadly Serious How-To Comics for Generations of America's Warriors*, Fitzworld.com, 2009, 10.

21. Richard L. Graham, *Government Issue: Comics for the People, 1940s-2000s* (New York: Abrams Comicarts, 2011), 11–2.

22. Fitzgerald, *Will Eisner and PS Magazine*.

23. Robert L. Goldich, "American Military Culture from Colony to Empire," *Daedalus, the Journal of the American Academy of Arts and Sciences* 140, no. 3 (2011): 58–74.

24. T.R. Fehrenbach, *This Kind of War: The Classic Military History of the Korean War*, 50th Anniversary Edition (New York: Open Road Integrated Media, 2014, Kindle e-book).

25. See: Anonymous, "America's Entrance into the War," *The Round Table: The Commonwealth Journal of International Affairs* 7, no. 27 (1917): 491–514.

26. Alban B. Butler, Jr., *Training for the Trenches: A Book of Humorous Cartoons on a Serious Subject* (New York: Palmer, 1917).

27. Mark Baker, *PV-2 Murphy the Adventure Continues: A "Pvt. Murphy's Law" Collection* (Baltimore, MD: United Books, 2001), 26.

28. Percy L. Crosby, *That Rookie from the 13th Squad* (New York: Harper and Brothers, 1918), n.p.; Ted Stanley, *Perils of a Private: Sketches of Camp Life* (Boston, MA: Small, Maynard, 1918), n.p.

29. Holcomb, *Ups and Downs ... of Camp Upton...* (New York: Bescardi, 1917), n.p.

30. Dorothea Byerly, *Up Came a Ripple* (East Orange, NJ: Greenwood, 1945), n.p.; Barbra E. Bristol, *Meet Molly Marine* (N.p.: Robert J. Weaver, 1945).

31. K.F., *On Cyber Patrol*, Army Office of Information Assurance and Compliance, http://ciog6. army.mil/OnCyberPatrol/OCPComics/tabid/129/ Default.aspx, September 1, 2008.

32. The creed begins: "This is my rifle. There are many like it, but this one is mine. It is my life. I must master it as I must master my life."

33. K.F., *On Cyber Patrol*, Army Office of Information Assurance and Compliance, http://ciog6. army.mil/OnCyberPatrol/OCPComics/tabid/129/ Default.aspx, April 1, 2010.

34. Gerald Astor, *Terrible Terry Allen: Combat General of World War II—The Life of an American Soldier* (New York: Presidio, 2003), 157.

35. For examples: Kirkland Day, *Camion Cartoons* (Boston, MA: Marshall Jones, 1919), n.p.; Stanley, *Perils of a Private*, n.p.; Holcomb, *Ups and Downs*, n.p.

36. For example: Baker, *PV-2 Murphy*, 5.

37. Crosby, *That Rookie*, n.p.; Wallgren, in *Squads Write! A Selection of the Best Things in Prose, Verse, and Cartoons from The Stars and Stripes*, ed. John T. Winterich (New York: Harper and Brothers, 1931), 62.

38. Wallace Morgan, in: Winterich, *Squads Write*, 132.

39. James C. Lysle, in: Winterich, *Squads Write*, 133.

40. Abian A. Wallgren *Wally: His Cartoons of the A.E.F.* (NP: Stars and Stripes, 1919), "Spring Suggestions for A.E.F. Millinery."

41. Ibid., "To the Committee on Uniforms."

42. Ibid., "Fashions at the Front."

43. Day, *Camion Cartoons*, n.p.

44. Cecil L. Hartt, *Humorosities by an Australian Soldier* (London, EC: Australian Trading and Agencies, n.d.), n.p.

45. Bruce Bairnsfather, *The Best of Fragments from France*, ed. Tonie Holt and Valmai Holt (South Yorkshire, UK: Pen and Sword Military, 1998), 16.

46. Vic Herman, *Winnie the WAC* (Philadelphia, PA: David McKay, 1945), n.p..

47. George Baker, *The Sad Sack* (New York: Simon and Schuster, 1944), "The Uniform."

48. Herman, *Winnie the WAC*.

49. Bill Mauldin, *Willie and Joe the World War II Years*, ed. Todd DePastino (Seattle, WA: Fantagraphics, 2011), 17.

50. Norval Eugene Packwood, *Leatherhead: The Story of Marine Corps Boot Camp* (Quantico, VA: Marine Corps Association, 1951), 13.

51. Alex Gard, *Sailors in Boots* (New York: Charles Scribner's Sons, 1943), n.p.

52. Jeff Bacon, *The Best of Broadside: A Humorous Look at Life in the Navy* (Newport News, VA: Deep Water, 1992), n.p.

53. Steve Opet, *Opet's Odyssey*, https://www. facebook.com/photo.php?fbid=154764967917709& set=a.154761024584770.32717.137174599676746& type=3&theater.

54. John Holmes, *Power Point Ranger* online, http://ryogahouse.wordpress.com/2011/06/12/ army-makes-patrol-cap-defeault-headgear-for-acu-and-sewing-on-of-badges-optional/.

55. Baker, *PV-2 Murphy*, 41.

56. Mark Baker, *Pfc. Murphy: Private Murphy's Law Book* (Baltimore, MD: United Books, 2005), 25.

57. Mark Baker, *Private Murphy's Law* (Baltimore, MD: United Books, 1999), 86.

58. Opet, *Opet's Odyssey*, https://www.facebook. com/photo.php?fbid=154763271251212&set=a.1547 61024584770.32717.137174599676746&type= 3&theater.

59. Holmes, *Power Point Ranger* online, https:// www.facebook.com/photo.php?fbid=686254311397 575&set=a.686251228064550.1073741851.1132561 55364063&type=3&theater.

60. For examples: Byerly, *Up Came a Ripple*, n.p.; Mauldin *Willie and Joe*, 51; Baker, *PV-2 Murphy*, 9; Mark Baker, *Sgt. Murphy: A "Pvt. Murphy's Law" Collection* (Alexandria, VA: Byrrd Enterprises, 2008), n.p.

61. K.F., *On Cyber Patrol*, Army Office of Information Assurance and Compliance, http://ciog6. army.mil/OnCyberPatrol/OCPComics/tabid/129/ Default.aspx, November 6, 2010.

62. Wallgren, in: Winterich, *Squads Write*, 3.

63. Bob Abramowitz cartoon in *Yank* 2, no. 1 (June 25, 1943): 18 (reprinted in Ira Topping, ed., *The Best of YANK The Army Weekly* [New York: Arno, 1980]).

64. Herman, *Winnie the WAC*, n.p.

65. Dave Breger, *Private Breger: His Adventures in Army Camp* (New York: Rand McNally, 1942), "Orderly."

66. Mauldin, *Willie and Joe*, 219.

67. Crosby, *That Rookie*, n.p.

68. Baker, *PV-2 Murphy*, 40.

69. Stanley, *Perils of a Private*, n.p.

70. Shel Silverstein, *Take Ten…. A Collection of Cartoons* (Tokyo: Pacific Stars and Stripes, 1955), n.p.

71. Opet, *Opet's Odyssey*, https://www.facebook. com/photo.php?fbid=154764731251066&set=a. 154761024584770.32717.137174599676746&type= 3&theater.

72. Holmes, *Power Point Ranger* online, http:// www.pptranger.net/comics/2012–11–04-mustache_ movember.

73. John Sheppard, *"Blue Suiters": Cartoons of the USAF* (Hoschton, GA: ShepArt Studios, 2013), 55.

74. See discussions in: Nate Rawlings, "Tat-us Quo: Despite Strict New Army Rules Other Branches Keep Tattoo Policies Intact," *Time*, September 26, 2013, http://nation.time.com/2013/09/ 26/tat-us-quo-despite-strict-new-army-rules-other-branches-keep-tattoo-policies-intact/; Michelle Tan, "Army May Ease Tattoo Policy," *USA Today*, August 21, 2014, http://www.usatoday.com/story/news/ nation/2014/08/21/army-may-ease-tattoo-policy-for-officers/14416091/ (accessed October 1, 2014).

75. Leo Salkin cartoon in *Yank* 2, no. 1 (June 25, 1943): 14 (reprinted in Ira Topping, ed., *The Best of YANK The Army Weekly* [New York: Arno, 1980]).

76. Shel Silverstein, *Grab Your Socks* (New York: Ballantine, 1956), 77.

77. Maximilian Uriarte, *Terminal Lance: #1–100 Compilation* (Veterans Expeditionary Media, 2011), 70.

78. Baker, *PV-2 Murphy*, 66–8.

79. T.H. Limb, personal correspondence, February 15, 2013.

80. Opet, *Opet's Odyssey*, https://www.facebook.com/photo.php?fbid=154764094584463&set=a.154761024584770.32717.137174599676746&type=3&theater.

81. For examples: Anonymous, *The Further Adventures of Doctrine Man!! Vol. 2* (San Bernardino, CA: Doctrine Man, 2013), 60; Anonymous, *Doctrine Man* online, https://www.facebook.com/photo.php?fbid=780247935341693&set=a.169913026375190.35223.110598432306650&type=3&theater.

82. For example: Anonymous, *Doctrine Man Vol. 2*, 65.

83. Holmes, *Power Point Ranger* online, http://blog.predatorbdu.com/2012/03/power-point-ranger-safety-first.html.

84. Damon Bryan Shackelford, *Delta Bravo Sierra. Rally Point: Vol. 1, Year 1, 2008*, www.deltabravosierra.com, 2008, 31.

85. Opet, *Opet's Odyssey*, https://www.facebook.com/photo.php?fbid=154764021251137&set=a.154761024584770.32717.137174599676746&type=3&theater.

86. Baker, *PV-2 Murphy*, 24–25 and 33.

87. Baker, *Sgt. Murphy*, n.p.

88. Anonymous, *The Further Adventures of Doctrine Man!! Vol. 1* (Lexington, KY: Doctrine Man, 2013), 2.

89. Angus Gillespie, "Sea Service Slang: Informal Language of the Navy and Coast Guard," in *Warrior Ways: Explorations in Modern Military Folklore*, ed. Eric A. Eliason and Tad Tuleja (Logan, UT: Utah State University Press, 2012), 116–36.

90. Ben Brody, "U.S. Military Lingo: The (Almost) Definitive Guide," *NPR*, December 4, 2013: http://www.npr.org/blogs/parallels/2013/12/04/248816232/u-s-military-lingo-the-almost-definitive-guide (accessed June 6, 2014).

91. Mark Patton, "Wordsmiths Take Aim at Simplifying Acronyms for Army," *Stars and Stripes*, August 14, 2011, http://www.stripes.com/news/wordsmiths-take-aim-at-simplifying-acronyms-for-army-1.152177 (accessed September 22, 2013).

92. Mike Sinclair, "Lt. Kadish," in *I Ain't Laughing, Sir: 40 Years of GI Humor from Stars and Stripes and Yank Magazine*, ed. Sid Schapiro (Stars and Stripes, 1982), 127.

93. Baker, *Private Murphy's Law*, 12.

94. Bruce Higdon, *Go for It, Eltee* (Murfreesboro, TN: R.S. Redditt and Associates, 1982), n.p.

95. John Sheppard, *Incoming! Military Cartoons* (Hoschton, GA: ShepArt Studios, 2007–2011), 82.

96. A.J. Merrifield, *Bob on the FOB*, http://www.bouhammer.com/2009/08/bob-on-the-fob-fobbit/.

97. Merrifield, *Bob on the FOB*, http://infothread.org/Weapons%20and%20Military/bob%20on%20the%20fob.jpg.

98. Uriarte, *Terminal Lance*, 19.

99. "Ernie" Sorrell Ernest, cartoon publicly shared through Facebook, March 14, 2014.

100. C.H. Ward-Jackson, *It's a Piece of Cake or R.A.F. Slang Made Easy*, illustrations by David Langdon (N.p.: n.p., 1945), 33.

101. Bob Stevens, *Prop Wash: A Fractured Glossary of Aviation Terms* (Fallbrook, CA: Village, 1983).

102. Perce Pearce, *Seaman Si* (N.p.: Great Lakes Bulletin, 1918), 53 and 55.

103. Bacon, *Best of Broadside*, n.p.

104. Eric Thibodeau, http://ericthibodeau.com/uss_missouri.htm.

105. Baker, *Private Murphy's Law*, 59; Baker, *Pfc. Murphy*, 38–39; Baker, *PV-2 Murphy*, 23.

106. Douglas G. Ward, *Topical Sketches* (Irvin Department of Rare Books and Special Collections, Digital Collections: http://library.sc.edu/digital/collections/rts.html 1915–1916), 20; Sumner Grant creative works, December 1944, Veterans History Project, AFC/2001/001/20970, American Folklife Center, Library of Congress, http://lcweb2.loc.gov/diglib/vhp/story/loc.natlib.afc2001001.20970/.

107. See: Roman Rosenbaum, "Mizuki Shigeru's Pacific War," *International Journal of Comic Art* 10, no. 2 (2008): 354.

108. Robert K. Bindig artworks, 18 May 1945, Veterans History Project, AFC/2001/001/32475, American Folklife Center, Library of Congress, http://lcweb2.loc.gov/diglib/vhp/story/loc.natlib.afc2001001.32475/artworks; Grant, "Creative Works," June 1944, December 1944, and 28 July 1945, http://lcweb2.loc.gov/diglib/vhp/story/loc.natlib.afc2001001.20970/.

109. Anonymous, *Doctrine Man Vol. 2*, 45.

110. Vernon Grant, *Stand-by One!* (Hong Kong: Dublin, 1969), n.p.

111. Jake Schuffert, *"No Sweat" ... More 'n More* (Washington, D.C.: Army Times, 1970), 8.

112. Baker, *The Sad Sack*, "Shots."

113. Leonard Sansone, *The Wolf* (New York: United, 1945), n.p.

114. John Holmes, *Power Point Ranger, Vol. 1* (New York: World Audience, 2012), 42.

115. Crosby, *That Rookie*, n.p.

116. Packwood, *Leatherhead*, 24.

117. W.C. Pope, *Above and Beyond: Pope's Puns 2 and Other Air Force Cartoons* (Herkimer, NY: W.C. Pope, 2009), 48.

118. Thomas Flannery cartoon in *Yank* 2, no. 32 (January 28, 1944): 24 (reprinted in *The Best of YANK The Army Weekly*, ed. Ira Topping, [New York, NY: Arno, 1980]).

119. Pope, *Above and Beyond*, 79.

120. Herman, *Winnie the WAC*, n.p.

121. Baker, *Private Murphy's Law*, 6.

122. Kevin Kline and Todd M. Hoelmer, *Pvt. Joe Snuffy Goes Guard!* (Washington, D.C.: National Guard Bureau, 1991), n.p.

123. Alexander Woolcott, *The Command Is Forward: Tales of the A.E.F. Battlefields as They Appeared in The Stars and Stripes*, ill. C. LeRoy Baldridge (New York: Century, 1919), 22; Wallgren, *Wally*, "Well, It's More Than the Turks Get."

124. Wallgren, in: Winterich, *Squads Write*, 177.

125. Mauldin, *Willie and Joe*, 23.

126. Bob Stevens, *"There I Was..." 25 Years* (Blue Ridge Summit, PA: TAB, 1992), 33.

127. Anonymous, *Doctrine Man Vol. 1*, 50.

128. Schuffert, *No Sweat*, 107.

129. Bacon, *Best of Broadside*, n.p.

130. Ward Carroll, "Brownshoes in Action Comix," *Approach*, January–February 2010, 33.

131. Pope, *Above and Beyond*, 78.

132. Dick Wingert, "Hubert," in *I Ain't Laughing, Sir: 40 Years of GI Humor from Stars and Stripes and Yank Magazine*, ed. Sid Schapiro (N.p.: Stars and Stripes, 1982), 43; Hank Ketcham, *Half Hitch* (Greenwich, CT: Fawcett, 1970), n.p.

133. Mauldin, *Willie and Joe*, 231.

134. Ibid., 257.

135. Packwood, *Leatherhead*, 42.

136. See, for example: Richard Simon, "More Details from Audit of VA Healthcare Scandal Expected Monday," *LATimes*, June 6, 2016: http://www.latimes.com/nation/la-na-va-healthcare-audit-texas-20140606-story.html (accessed June 7, 2014).

137. Mauldin, *Willie and Joe*, 419.

138. Genevieve M. Ames, Carol B. Cunradi, Roland S. Moore, and Pamela Stern, "Military Culture and Drinking Behavior Among U.S. Navy Careerists," *Journal of Studies on Alcohol and Drugs* 68, no. 3 (2007): 336. Also see: Larry H. Ingraham, *The Boys in the Barracks: Observations on American Military Life* (Philadelphia, PA: Institute for the Study of Human Issues, 1984).

139. Hartt, *Humorosities*, n.p.

140. Bairnsfather, *Best of Fragments from France*, 26.

141. Holcomb, *Ups and Downs*, n.p.

142. Wallgren, in: Winterich, *Squads Write*, 284.

143. Grant, "Creative Works," September 1944 and November 1944, http://lcweb2.loc.gov/diglib/vhp/story/loc.natlib.afc2001001.20970/; William Schmitt, "Envelopes sent Home," at http://www.488thportbattalion.org/Envelopes.html.

144. Mauldin, *Willie and Joe*, 438.

145. Norval Eugene Packwood, *Leatherhead in Korea* (Quantico, VA: Marine Corps Gazette, 1952), 26.

146. Roger G. Baker, *USMC Tanker's Korea: The War in Photos, Sketches and Letters Home* (Oakland, OR: Elderberry, 2001), 24.

147. Grant, *Stand-By One*, n.p.

148. Tad Foster, *The Vietnam Funny Book: An Antidote to Insanity* (Novato, CA: Presidio, 1980), "Thai Weed and Time Out." Also see: Grant, *Stand-By One*, n.p.

149. Chris Grant, *Bohica Blues*, in "Reservist's Cartoons Detail Burdens of Desert Deployment," *Stars and Stripes*, by Jason Chudy, August 9, 2004, http://www.stripes.com/news/reservist-s-cartoons-detail-burdens-of-desert-deployment-1.22605.

150. Frank Dunne, *Digger Days*, Australian War Memorial, http://trove.nla.gov.au/version/44131648.

151. Ward, *Topical Sketches*, at http://library.sc.edu/digital/collections/rts.html, 17; Bairnsfather, *Best of Fragments from France*, 66–7.

152. In: Robert E. Bronner, *The Soldier's Pen* (New York: Hill and Wang, 2006), 51.

153. Charles Johnson Post, *The Little War of Private Post: The Spanish-American War Seen Up Close* (Lincoln, NE: University of Nebraska Press, 1999), 181.

154. Stanley, *Perils of a Private*, "Every Man for Himself"; Butler, *Training for the Trenches*, "How to Load Fast and Full."

155. H.M. Stoops, *Inked Memories of 1918* (LeRoy, NY: Jell-O, 1924).

156. Ward, *Topical Sketches*, at http://library.sc.edu/digital/collections/rts.html, 28.

157. Bairnsfather, *Best of Fragments from France*, 84.

158. Dick Wingert, *Hubert* (London, UK: Love and Malcomson, 1944), 34.

159. Silverstein, *Grab Your Socks*, 17.

160. In: *Out of Line: A Collection of Cartoons from Pacific Stars and Stripes* (Tokyo: Toppon, 1952), n.p.

161. Anon., in: *Out of Line*, n.p.

162. Miller, in: *Out of Line*, n.p.

163. Baker, *PV-2 Murphy*, 58.

164. Schuffert, *No Sweat*, 109.

165. Ibid., 70.

166. Jeffrey Hall, *Downrange*, "Chow Hall," http://www.military.com/cartooncontent/0,14763,Downrange_072605,00.html.

167. Shackelford, *Delta Bravo Sierra*, 11.

168. Baker, *Private Murphy's Law*, 37–8.

169. Shackelford, *Delta Bravo Sierra*, 23.

170. Maximilian Uriarte, "Like a Dog," *Terminal Lance* online, http://terminallance.com/2014/09/02/terminal-lance-like-a-dog-marine-corps-times/.

171. Higdon, *Go for It Eltee*, n.p.

172. Pope, *Above and Beyond*, 38.

173. Baker, *Sgt. Murphy*, n.p.

174. Merrifield, *Bob on the FOB*, http://www.bouhammer.com/2009/10/bob-on-the-fob-fob-locust/.

175. Baker, *Pfc. Murphy*, 37.

176. Unknown, *Time of Decision* (Harvey Comics, 1955), in Richard L. Graham, *Government Issue: Comics for the People, 1940s-2000s* (New York, NY: Abrams Comicarts, 2011), 59–69.

177. Bristol, *Meet Molly Marine*, n.p.

178. Baker, *The Sad Sack*, "Morning Shave."

179. Mauldin, *Willie and Joe*, 176.

180. Day, *Camion Cartoons*, n.p.

181. Opet, *Opet's Odyssey*, https://www.facebook.com/photo.php?fbid=154762311251308&set=a.154761024584770.32717.137174599676746&type=3&theater.

182. Packwood, *Leatherhead in Korea*, 9.

183. Baker, *Private Murphy's Law*, 21.

184. John Holmes, *FM 3.0 Secret Squirrel Stuff: Power Point Ranger Comics 341–510* (NP: Amazon Digital Services, 2014, Kindle e-book), loc. 13.

185. Pearce, *Seaman Si*, 63.

186. See, for examples: Alban B. Butler, Jr., *"Happy Days!" A Humorous Narrative in Drawings of the Progress of American Arms, 1917–1919* (Chicago, IL: First Division Museum at Cantigny, 2011), 102 and 103; 1940s era soldier, "Original Cartoon Drawing," http://www.ebay.com/itm/Original-World War II-Patriotic-Humor-ONE-OF-A-KIND-Soldier-Art-Pen-Ink-Drawing-/251580750115?; Day, *Camion Cartoons*, "Cross Section of Our Last Billet"; Holcomb, *Ups and Downs*, np; Unknown, "A Peep in a Y.M.C.A. Hut—and Some Characters," *Shell Shocks: By the New Zealanders in France* (London: Jarrold

and Sons, 1916), 44. Also see: Albert Heim, in: Ann Gripper, "Heim Front: German Artist's World War I Cartoons up for Auction," *Mirror Online*, March 15, 2013, http://www.mirror.co.uk/news/uk-news/world-war-i-cartoons-by-albert-heim-761412.

187. Schuffert, *No Sweat*, 7.

188. Mort Walker, *50 Years of Beetle Bailey* (New York: NBM, 2000), 10.

189. Walker, *50 Years*, 82.

190. Ibid., 123.

191. Baker, *Sgt. Murphy*, n.p.

192. Walker, *50 Years*, 125.

193. Hall, *Downrange*, "Camp Swampy," http://www.military.com/cartooncontent/0,14763,Downrange_060718,00.html.

194. W.C. Pope, *Pope's Puns*, "Beetle Bailey," http://www.military.com/cartooncontent/0,14763,Pope_060811,00.html.

195. Hartt, *Humorosities*, n.p.

196. Stanley, *Perils of a Private*, "When the 'Star-Spangled Banner' Is Unusually Welcome."

197. Breger, *Private Breger*, "Full-Pack Drill."

198. Pope, *Pope's Puns*, "Flight Pay," http://www.military.com/cartooncontent/0,14763,Pope_082604,00.html.

199. Mauldin, *Willie and Joe*, 226.

200. Merrifield, *Bob on the FOB*, http://www.bouhammer.com/2009/10/bob-on-the-fob-hard-lurker/.

201. Herman, *Winnie the WAC*, n.p.

202. Baldridge, in: Winterich, *Squads Write*, 32.

203. Grant, "Creative Works," September 1944 at http://lcweb2.loc.gov/diglib/vhp/story/loc.natlib.afc2001001.20970/.

204. R.D. Whitcomb, *Military Cartoons* (Douglas, AZ: RD Whitcomb, 1916), n.p.

205. Holcomb, *Ups and Downs*, n.p.

206. Hall, *Downrange*, "Care Package Poker," http://www.military.com/cartooncontent/0,14763,Downrange_052605,00.html.

207. Grant, "Creative Works," May 1944, June 1944, September 1944, October 1944, and 27 November 1945, http://lcweb2.loc.gov/diglib/vhp/story/loc.natlib.afc2001001.20970/.

208 Dave Breger, *Private Breger in Britain* (London, UK: Pilot, 1944), 130.

209. Mauldin, *Willie and Joe*, 15.

210. K.F., *On Cyber Patrol*, Army Office of Information Assurance and Compliance, http://ciog6.army.mil/OnCyberPatrol/OCPComics/tabid/129/Default.aspx, September 4, 2007, and March 1, 2010; Uriarte, *Terminal Lance*, 7 and 29; Opet, *Opet's Odyssey*, https://www.facebook.com/photo.php?fbid=154762607917945&set=a.154761024584770.32717.137174599676746&type=3&theater.

211. See: Carl H. Builder, *The Masks of War: American Military Styles in Strategy and Analysis* (Baltimore, MD: Johns Hopkins University Press, 1989).

212. Don M. Snider, "The U.S. Military in Transition to Jointness: Surmounting Old Notions of Interservice Rivalry," *Airpower Journal*, Fall 1996, 16.

213. Bacon, *Best of Broadside*, n.p.

214. Ibid., n.p.

215. Anonymous, *Doctrine Man Vol. 2*, 56.

216. Thibodeau, at http://ericthibodeau.com/uss_missouri.htm.

217. Mike Jones *Ricky's Tour*, "Recruit Resort," http://www.military.com/cartooncontent/0,14763,Jones_102805,00.html.

218. Shackelford, *Delta Bravo Sierra*, 34.

219. Sinclair, "Lt. Kadish," in *I Ain't Laughing, Sir*, 133.

220. Anonymous, *Doctrine Man Vol. 2*, 55.

221. Holmes, *Power Point Ranger*, 98.

222. Anonymous, *Doctrine Man Vol. 2*, 57.

223. Ibid., 62.

224. Anonymous, *Doctrine Man* online, https://www.facebook.com/DoctrineMan/photos/pb.110598432306650.-2207520000.1412183437./835331446500008/?type=3&theater.

225. Uriarte, *Terminal Lance*, 53.

226. Packwood, *Leatherhead in Korea*, 28 and 29.

227. Breger, *Private Breger in Britain*, 89.

228. Sheppard, *Incoming*, 146.

229. Roman Jarymowycz, *Cavalry from Hoof to Track* (Westport, CT: Praeger, 2008, Kindle e-book), loc. 1260.

Chapter 3

1. Anonymous, "Informal Social Organization in the Army," *American Journal of Sociology* 51, no. 5 (1946): 365–70.

2. Joseph L. Soeters, Donna J. Winslow, and Alise Weibull, "Military Culture," in *Handbook of the Sociology of the Military*, ed. Giuseppe Caforio (New York: Springer, 2006), 237–54.

3. Samuel P. Huntington, *The Soldier and the State: The Theory and Politics of Civil-Military Relations* (Cambridge, MA: Belknap Press of Harvard University Press, 1957), 16.

4. Volker Franke, *Preparing for Peace: Military Identity, Value Orientations, and Professional Military Education* (Westport, CT: Praeger, 1999); Morris Janowitz, *The Professional Soldier: A Social and Political Portrait* (New York: Free Press, 1960); Huntington, *The Soldier and the State*.

5. Ralph Lewis, "Officer-Enlisted Men's Relationships," *American Journal of Sociology* 52, no. 5 (1947): 410–19.

6. Donald T. Campbell, and Thelma H. McCormack, "Military Experience and Attitudes Toward Authority," *American Journal of Sociology* 62, no. 5 (1957): 482–90.

7. Morris Janowitz, *Sociology and the Military Establishment* (New York: Russell Sage Foundation, 1959); Soeters, Winslow and Weibull, "Military Culture."

8. Franke, *Preparing for Peace*.

9. Soeters, Winslow and Weibull, "Military Culture."

10. Stephen Peter Rosen, "Military Effectiveness: Why Society Matters," *International Security* 19, 4 (1995): 5–31.

11. Jonathan M. Acuff, "Generational Analysis and the Evolution of Military Doctrine and Strategy," in *Theory and Application of the "Generation" in*

International Relations and Politics, ed. Brent J. Steele and Jonathan M. Acuff (New York: Palgrave Macmillan, 2012), 177–202.

12. Dennis Drew and Don Snow, *Making Strategy: An Introduction to National Security Processes and Problems* (Maxwell Air Force Base, AL: Air University Press, 1988).

13. Deborah D. Avant, "The Institutional Sources of Military Doctrine: Hegemons in Peripheral Wars," *International Studies Quarterly* 37 (1993), 410.

14. Julian Corbett, *Naval and Military Essays* (Cambridge, UK: Cambridge University Press, 1914), 24.

15. Geoffrey Sloan, "Military Doctrine, Command Philosophy and the Generation of Fighting Power: Genesis and Theory," *International Affairs* 88, 2 (2012): 243.

16. Barry Posen, *The Sources of Military Doctrine* (Ithaca, NY: Cornell University Press, 1984), 13.

17. Aaron P. Jackson, *The Roots of Military Doctrine* (N.p.: Combat Studies Institute Press, 2013), 1.

18. Josef Teboho Ansorge, "Spirits of War: A Field Manual," *International Political Sociology* 4 (2010): 362.

19. Purdue Libraries, *Military Doctrine: A Reference Handbook* (Brownbag Presentation, November 4, 2009), slide 2.

20. AAP-6, *The NATO Glossary of Terms and Definitions* (Brussels: NATO, 1989).

21. Thomas E. Hanson, "Forward," in *The Roots of Military Doctrine* by Aaron P. Jackson (N.p.: Combat Studies Institute Press, 2013), iii.

22. Elisabeth Bumiller, "West Point Is Divided on a War Doctrine's Fate," *New York Times*, May 27, 2012, http://www.nytimes.com/2012/05/28/world/at-west-point-asking-if-a-war-doctrine-was-worth-it.html (accessed September 22, 2013), para. 2.

23. Hanson, "Forward," iii.

24. Karen D. Davis and Brian McKee, "Women in the Military: Facing the Warrior Framework," in *Challenge and Change in the Military: Gender and Diversity Issues*, ed. Franklin C. Pinch, Allister T. MacIntyre, Phyllis Browne and Alan C. Okros (Winnipeg, CA: Canadian Forces Leadership Institute, 2004), 52–75.

25. See examples in: Richard L. Graham, *Government Issue: Comics for the People, 1940s–2000s* (New York: Abrams Comicarts, 2011), 52–57.

26. Larry H. Ingraham, *The Boys in the Barracks: Observations on American Military Life* (Philadelphia, PA: Institute for the Study of Human Issues, 1984).

27. Frank L. Cioffi, "Disturbing Comics: The Disjunction of Word and Image in the Comics of Andrzej Mleczko, Ben Katchor, R. Crumb, and Art Spiegelman," in *The Language of Comics Word and Image*, Studies in Popular Culture, ed. Robin Varnum and Christina T. Gibbons, 97–122 (Jackson, MS: University Press of Mississippi, 2001); James Eric Black, "Amoozin' but Confoozin': Comic Strips as a Voice of Dissent in the 1950s," *ETC: A Review of General Semantics* 66, no. 4 (2010): 460–77.

28. Jeffrey P. Jones, *Entertaining Politics*, 2nd ed. (Lanham, MD: Rowman and Littlefield, 2010): 83 and 238.

29. Lisa M. Mundey, *American Militarism and Anti-Militarism in Popular Media, 1945–1970* (Jefferson, NC: McFarland, 2012).

30. Keith Yellin, *Battle Exhortation: The Rhetoric of Combat Leadership* (Columbia, SC: University of South Carolina Press, 2008), 70 and 72.

31. Mundey, *American Militarism*.

32. Theodore Layton Bailey, *Military Courtesy* (New York: Review, 1919); Dept. of the Army, *Foundations of Leadership MSL II*, revised ed. (New York: Pearson Custom, 2008).

33. Al Avison, *Military Courtesy* (Harvey Comics, 1951), 51.

34. For examples: Percy L. Crosby, *That Rookie from the 13th Squad* (New York: Harper and Brothers, 1918); Kirkland H. Day, *Camion Cartoons* (Boston, MA: Marshall Jones, 1919); "Ted" Stanley, *Perils of a Private: Sketches of Camp Life* (Boston, MA: Small, Maynard, 1918), n.p.

35. Crosby, *That Rookie*, n.p.

36. Perce Pearce, *Seaman Si* (N.p.: Great Lakes Bulletin, 1918), 11.

37. Ibid., 22.

38. Vic Herman, *Winnie the WAC* (Philadelphia, PA: David McKay, 1945), n.p.

39. Jeff Bacon, *The Best of Broadside: A Humorous Look at Life in the Navy* (Newport News, VA: Deep Water, 1992), n.p.

40. Alexandra Jaffe, "Saluting in Social Context," *Journal of Applied Behavioral Science* 24, no. 3 (1988): 263–75.

41. Abian A. Wallgren *Wally: His Cartoons of the A.E.F.* (N.p.: Stars and Stripes, 1919), 9.

42. Dorothea J. Byerly, *Up Came a Ripple* (East Orange, NJ: Greenwood, 1945), n.p.

43. Steve Opet, *Opet's Odyssey*, https://www.facebook.com/photo.php?fbid=15476458125 1081&set=a.154761024584770.32717.13717459967 6746&type=3&theater.

44. Bill Mauldin, *Willie and Joe the World War II Years*, ed. Todd DePastino (Seattle, WA: Fantagraphics, 2011), 67.

45. Mauldin, *Willie and Joe*, 70.

46. Dave Breger, *Private Breger in Britain* (London, UK: Pilot, 1944), 16.

47. Opet, *Opet's Odyssey*, https://www.facebook.com/photo.php?fbid=154763154584557&set=a.154 761024584770.32717.137174599676746&type=3& theater.

48. Mark Bryant, *Wars of Empire in Cartoons* (London, UK: Grubb Street, 2009), 9.

49. George Lepre, *Fragging: Why U.S. Soldiers Assaulted Their Officers in Vietnam* (Lubbock, TX: Texas Tech University Press, 2011).

50. Charles Johnson Post, *The Little War of Private Post: The Spanish-American War Seen Up Close* (Lincoln, NE: University of Nebraska Press, 1999), 53.

51. Lisa Brooten, "Political Cartoons and Burma's Transnational Public Sphere," in *Southeast Asian Cartoon Art: History, Trends and Problems*, ed. John A. Lent (Jefferson, NC: McFarland, 2014, Kindle e-book), chapter 7.

52. Cecil L. Hartt, *Humorosities by an Australian Soldier* (London, EC: Australian Trading and Agencies, n.d.), n.p.

53. For example, see: Mauldin, *Willie and Joe*, 463.

54. Todd DePastino, *Bill Mauldin: A Life Up Front* (New York: W.W. Norton, 2008).

55. Mauldin, *Willie and Joe*, 565.

56. Mort Walker, "Forward," in *Above and Beyond: Pope's Puns and Other Air Force Cartoons*, by W.C. Pope (Herkimer, NY: WC Pope Studio, 2009), 3.

57. W.C. Pope, "Introduction," in *Above and Beyond: Pope's Puns and Other Air Force Cartoons*, by W.C. Pope (Herkimer, NY: WC Pope Studio, 2009), 4–5.

58. Mark Baker, *Private Murphy's Law* (Baltimore, MD: United Books, 1999), 54.

59. Pope, "Introduction," 4.

60. Irwin Tousler in *Yank* 4, no. 28 (December 28, 1945): 22 (reprinted in *The Best of YANK The Army Weekly*, ed. Ira Topping [New York: Arno, 1980]); George Baker, *The Sad Sack* (New York: Simon and Schuster, 1944), "Officers Only"; Eric Thibodeau, at http://ericthibodeau.com/uss_missouri.htm.

61. Irwin Caplan cartoon in *Yank* 2, no. 1 (June 25, 1943): 32 (reprinted in *The Best of YANK The Army Weekly*, ed. Ira Topping [New York: Arno, 1980]).

62. Mauldin, *Willie and Joe*, 363.

63. Ibid., 527.

64. Maximilian Uriarte, *Terminal Lance: #1–100 Compilation* (Veterans Expeditionary Media, 2011), 72.

65. Albert Heim, in: Ann Gripper, "Heim Front: German Artist's World War I Cartoons up for Auction," *Mirror Online*, March 15, 2013, http://www.mirror.co.uk/news/uk-news/world-war-i-cartoons-by-albert-heim-761412.

66. Mauldin, *Willie and Joe*, 479.

67. George Baker, *The New Sad Sack* (New York: Simon and Schuster, 1946), "Always Dissatisfied"; also see: Baker, *Sad Sack*, "First Come-First Served."

68. Mauldin, *Willie and Joe*, 290.

69. See: Roman Rosenbaum, "Mizuki Shigeru's Pacific War," *International Journal of Comic Art* 10, no. 2 (2008): 361.

70. Jeffrey Hall, *Downrange*, "Popcorn," http://www.military.com/cartooncontent/0,14763,Downrange_060924,00.html.

71. Mauldin, *Willie and Joe*, 627.

72. Jake Schuffert, *"No Sweat" ... More 'n More* (Washington, D.C.: Army Times, 1970), 136.

73. Frank Dunne, *Digger Days*, Australian War Memorial, http://nla.gov.au/nla.pic-vn4306092.

74. Wallgren, "Why Were You Only a Private?" *Stars and Stripes*, February 28, 1919: 7; Wallgren, *Wally*, 13.

75. Mauldin, *Willie and Joe*, 522.

76. Mark Baker, *Sgt. Murphy: A "Pvt. Murphy's Law" Collection* (Alexandria, VA: Byrrd, 2008), n.p.

77. Jeff Bacon, *20 Years of Broadside* (Garden City, ID: Deep Water, 2006), 30.

78. Ibid., 5.

79. Norman F. Dixon, *On the Psychology of Military Incompetence* (New York: Random House eBooks, 2011, Kindle e-book), loc. 203.

80. Hall, *Downrange*, "Second Helping," http://

www.military.com/cartooncontent/0,14763,Downrange_101105,00.html.

81. Mark Baker, *PV-2 Murphy the Adventure Continues: A "Pvt. Murphy's Law" Collection* (Baltimore, MD: United, 2001), 11.

82. Anonymous, *The Further Adventures of Doctrine Man!! Vol. 1* (Lexington, KY: Doctrine Man, 2013), 58.

83. Bruce Bairnsfather, *The Best of Fragments from France*, ed. Tonie Holt and Valmai Holt (South Yorkshire, UK: Pen and Sword Military, 1998), 27.

84. Ernest Maxwell cartoon in *Yank* 4, no. 28 (December 28, 1945): 23 (reprinted in *The Best of YANK The Army Weekly*, ed. Ira Topping [New York: Arno, 1980]); Shel Silverstein, *Grab Your Socks* (New York: Ballantine, 1956), 51.

85. Bacon, *20 Years of Broadside*, 83.

86. Anonymous, *Doctrine Man Vol. 1*, 1.

87. Damon Bryan Shackelford, *Delta Bravo Sierra. Rally Point: Vol. 1, Year 1, 2008*, www.deltabravosierra.com, 2008, 12.

88. A.J. Merrifield, *Bob on the FOB*, http://rokdrop.com/2008/06/06/bob-on-the-fobs-creature-gallery/.

89. John Holmes, *Power Point Ranger, Vol. 1* (New York: World Audience, 2012), 55.

90. Baker, *Sgt. Murphy*, n.p.

91. T.H. Limb, personal correspondence, February 15, 2013.

92. Bacon, *20 Years of Broadside*, 37.

93. Marc DiPaolo, *War, Politics and Superheroes: Ethics and Propaganda in Comics and Film*. Jefferson, NC: McFarland, 2011.

94. Rebecca Wanzo, "The Superhero: Meditations on Surveillance, Salvation, and Desire," *Communication and Critical/Cultural Studies* 6, no. 1 (2009): 93.

95. Nicole Devarenne, "'A Language Heroically Commensurate with His Body': Nationalism, Fascism, and the Language of the Superhero," *International Journal of Comic Art* 10, no. 1 (2008): 48–54; Julia Round, "London's Calling: Alternate Worlds and the City as Superhero in Contemporary British-American Comics," *International Journal of Comic Art* 10, no. 1 (2008): 24–31.

96. Doctrine Man: About, *Facebook*, https://www.facebook.com/DoctrineMan/info.

97. Bruce Bairnsfather, *Carry On Sergeant* (Indianapolis, IN: Bobbs-Merrill, 1927), 100.

98. Dunne, *Digger Days*, Australian War Memorial, http://nla.gov/au/nla.pic-vn4306090.

99. Wallgren, *Wally*, 23.

100. Mike Jones, *Ricky's Tour*, http://www.military.com/cartooncontent/0,14763,Jones_070418,00.html

101. Hall, *Downrange*, "Hooah," http://www.military.com/cartooncontent/0,14763,Downrange_032206,00.html.

102. Mike Sinclair, "Lt. Kadish," in *I Ain't Laughing, Sir: 40 Years of GI Humor from Stars and Stripes and Yank Magazine*, ed. Sid Schapiro (Stars and Stripes, 1982), 121.

103. Baker, *Private Murphy*, 57.

104. Pearce, *Seaman Si*, 34.

105. Ibid., 50.

106. Charles Luchsinger cartoon in *Yank* 3, no. 42 (April 6, 1945): 22 (reprinted in *The Best of YANK The Army Weekly*, ed. Ira Topping [New York: Arno, 1980]).

107. Mauldin, *Willie and Joe*, 476.

108. Ibid., 347.

109. Bill Mauldin, *Willie and Joe Back Home*, ed. Todd DePastino (Seattle, WA: Fantagraphics, 2011), 4.

110. Bacon, *20 Years of Broadside*, 55.

111. Baker, *New Sad Sack*, "The Enemy."

112. Irwin Caplan cartoon in *Yank* 3, no. 42 (April 6, 1945): 24 (reprinted in *The Best of YANK The Army Weekly*, ed. Ira Topping [New York: Arno, 1980]).

113. Dick Wingert, *Hubert* (London, UK: Love and Malcomson, 1944), 57.

114. Breger, *Private Breger in Britain*, 88.

115. Alan Ned Sabrosky, James Clay Thompson, and Karen A. McPherson, "Organized Anarchies: Military Bureaucracy in the 1980s," *Journal of Applied Behavioral Science* 18, no. 2 (1982): 137–53.

116. Breger, *Private Breger in Britain*, 20.

117. George Baker cartoon in *Yank* 3, no. 41 (March 30, 1945): 1 (reprinted in *The Best of YANK The Army Weekly*, ed. Ira Topping [New York: Arno, 1980]).

118. Norval Eugene Packwood, *Leatherhead in Korea* (Quantico, VA: Marine Corps Gazette, 1952), 65.

119. Bacon, *20 Years of Broadside*, 44.

120. Day, *Camion Cartoons*, n.p.

121. Wallgren, "Conscientious Objectors," *Stars and Stripes*, August 30, 1918: 7.

122. Sumner Grant creative works, September 1944, Veterans History Project, AFC/2001/001/20970, American Folklife Center, Library of Congress, http://lcweb2.loc.gov/diglib/vhp/story/loc.natlib.afc2001001.20970/.

123. Baker, *Private Murphy*, 16.

124. Opet, *Opet's Odyssey*, https://www.facebook.com/photo.php?fbid=154762044584668&set=a.154761024584770.32717.137174599676746&type=3&theater.

125. Tom Zibelli cartoon in *Yank* 3, no. 2 (June 30, 1944): 22 (reprinted in *The Best of YANK The Army Weekly*, ed. Ira Topping [New York: Arno, 1980]).

126. Will Eisner, "Joe Dope," *Army Motors* 6, no. 4 (July 1945): 117.

127. Bairnsfather, *Best of Fragments from France*, 18.

128. Sinclair, "Lt. Kadish," in *I Ain't Laughing*, 123.

129. Holmes, *Power Point Ranger*, 40.

130. Thibodeau, http://ericthibodeau.com/uss_missouri.htm.

131. Ozzie St. George cartoon in *Yank* 4, no. 16 (October 5, 1945): 24 (reprinted in *The Best of YANK The Army Weekly*, ed. Ira Topping [New York: Arno, 1980]).

132. Shackelford, *Delta Bravo Sierra*, 9.

133. Holmes, *Power Point Ranger* online, https://www.facebook.com/photo.php?fbid=6862514713 97859&set=pb.113256155364063.-2207520000.1403547664.&type=3&theater.

134. Uriarte, *Terminal Lance*, 18.

135. Ibid., 37.

136. Bacon, *Best of Broadside*, n.p.

137. Douglas G. Ward, *Topical Sketches* (Irvin Department of Rare Books and Special Collections, Digital Collections: http://library.sc.edu/digital/collections/rts.html 1915–1916), 51.

138. Cathy Parker, *Freedom of Expression in the American Military: A Communication Modeling Analysis* (New York: Praeger, 1989).

139. Maximilian Uriarte, *Terminal Lance Head Call: The First 100 MarineTimes Strips* (Amazon Digital Services, 2013, Kindle e-book), loc. 1295.

140. For example: David Langdon, *All Buttoned Up!: A Scrapbook of R.A.F. Cartoons* (London, UK: Sylvan, n.d.), 36–7.

141. For example: LeRoy Baldridge, in *Squads Write! A Selection of the Best Things in Prose, Verse, and Cartoons from The Stars and Stripes*, ed. John T. Winterich (New York: Harper and Brothers, 1931), 207.

142. Wallgren, *Wally*, "If All of Us Voted This Year."

143. Schuffert, *No Sweat*, 13, 145, and 157.

144. Julian E. Barnes, Jennifer Levitz and Dion Nissenbaum, "U.S. Official: Sgt. Bowe Bergdahl Has Declined to Speak to His Family," *Wall Street Journal*, June 8, 2014, http://online.wsj.com/articles/u-s-official-sgt-bowe-bergdahl-has-declined-to-speak-to-his-family-1402242356 (accessed June 10, 2014).

145. Maximilian Uriarte, *Terminal Lance* online, http://terminallance.com/2014/06/03/terminal-lance-conversion-rate/.

146. John Holmes, *Power Point Ranger* online, https://www.facebook.com/photo.php?fbid=75061 7758294563&set=a.113279995361679.11895.11325 6155364063&type=1&theater.

147. Craig Whitlock, "Sordid Details Spill Out in Rare Court Martial of a General," *Washington Post*, August 14, 2013, http://www.washingtonpost.com/world/national-security/sordid-details-spill-out-in-rare-court-martial-of-a-general/2013/08/14/f6c89c 68–008d-11e3-a661–06a2955a5531_story.html (accessed June 10, 2014).

148. Anonymous, *Doctrine Man* online, https://www.facebook.com/photo.php?fbid=63371364999 5123&set=a.169913026375190.35223.1105984323 06650&type=3&theater.

149. Anonymous, *Doctrine Man* online, https://www.facebook.com/photo.php?fbid=78949310441 7176&set=a.169913026375190.35223.11059843 2306650&type=3&theaterom/photo.php?fbid=750 617758294563&set=a.113279995361679.11895.113 256155364063&type=1&theater.

150. Dixon, *On the Psychology of Military Incompetence*, loc. 161.

151. Ibid.

Chapter 4

1. Vamik D. Volkan, *The Need to Have Enemies and Allies: From Clinical Practice to International Relationships* (Northvale, NJ: Jason Aronson, 1988).

2. Murray Edelman, *Constructing the Political*

Spectacle (Chicago, IL: University of Chicago Press, 1988), 66; Sam Keen, *Faces of the Enemy: Reflections of the Hostile Imagination* (San Francisco, CA: Harper and Row, 1986); Debra Merskin, "The Construction of Arabs as Enemies: Post–9/11 Discourse of George W. Bush," in *Bring 'Em On: Media and Politics in the Iraq War*, ed. Lee Artz and Yahya R. Kamalipour (Lanham, MD: Rowman and Littlefield, 2005), 121–38; Kurt R. Spillman and Kati Spillman, "Some Sociobiological and Psychological Aspects of 'Images of the Enemy,'" in *Enemy Images in American History*, ed. Ragnhild Fiebig-von Hase and Ursula Lehmkuhl (Providence, RI: Berghahn, 1997), 43–64.

3. Ulrich Beck, "The Sociological Anatomy of Enemy Images: The Military and Democracy After the End of the Cold War," in *Enemy Images in American History*, ed. Ragnhild Fiebig-von Hase and Ursula Lehmkuhl (Providence, RI: Berghahn, 1997), 65–87. For more on state-sanctioned killing and warfare see: Carolyn Marvin and David W. Ingle, *Blood Sacrifice and the Nation: Totem Rituals and the American Flag* (Cambridge: Cambridge University Press, 1999).

4. Keen, *Faces of the Enemy*.

5. Robert L. Ivie, "Images of Savagery in American Justifications for War," *Communication Monographs* 47 (1980): 279–94; Robert L. Ivie, *Democracy and America's War on Terror*, Rhetoric, Culture, and Social Critique (Tuscaloosa, AL: University of Alabama Press, 2005).

6. Edelman, *Constructing the Political Spectacle*, 74.

7. Benjamin R. Bates, "Audiences, Metaphors, and the Persian Gulf War," *Communication Studies* 55, no. 3 (2004): 447–63; Jason A. Edwards, "Defining the Enemy for the Post-Cold War World: Bill Clinton's Foreign Policy Discourse in Somalia and Haiti," *International Journal of Communication* 2 (2008): 830–47; Robert L. Ivie, "Democracy, War, and Decivilizing Metaphors of American Insecurity," in *Metaphorical World Politics*, ed. Francis A. Beer and Christ'l De Landtsheer (East Lansing, MI: Michigan State University Press, 2004), 75–90.

8. W. Edgar Gregory, "The Idealization of the Absent," *American Journal of Sociology* 51, no. 1 (1944): 53–4.

9. Henry Elkin, "Aggressive and Erotic Tendencies in Army Life," *American Journal of Sociology* 51, no. 5 (1946): 408–13.

10. Daniel Glaser, "The Sentiments of American Soldiers Abroad Toward Europeans," *American Journal of Sociology* 51, no. 5 (1946): 438.

11. Konrad Kellen, *Conversations with Enemy Soldiers in Late 1968/Early 1969: A Study of Motivation and Morale*, prepared for the Office of the Assistant Secretary of Defense/International Security Affairs and the Advanced Research Projects Agency (Santa Monica, CA: RAND, 1970).

12. Eyal Ben-Ari, *Mastering Soldiers: Conflict, Emotion, and the Enemy in an Israeli Military Unit*, New Directions in Anthropology, vol. 10 (New York: Berghahn, 1998).

13. Montgomery McFate, "The Military Utility of Understanding Adversary Culture," *Joint Force Quarterly* 38 (2005): 42–8.

14. Cord Scott, "'Frankly, Mac, This "Police Action" Business Is Going Too Damn Far!' Armed Forces Cartoons during the Korean Conflict," Paper presented at the Korean War Conference: Commemorating the 60th Anniversary, hosted by the Victoria College/University of Houston-Victoria Library June 24–26 2010: 4; William B. Brown, "It Means Something: The Ghosts of War," in *Storytelling Sociology: Narrative as Social Inquiry*, ed. Ronald J. Berger and Richard Quinney (Boulder, CO: Lynne Rienner, 2005), 245–63.

15. ESRC, "Soldiers Who Desecrate the Dead See Themselves as Hunters," *Economic and Social Research Council*, 2012, http://www.esrc.ac.uk/news -and-events/press-releases/21182/ Soldiers_who_de secrate_the_dead_see_themselves_as_hunters.aspx.

16. John Sibley Butler, "Race Relations in the Military," in *The Military: More Than Just a Job?*, ed. Charles C. Moskos and Frank R. Wood (Washington, D.C.: Pergamon-Brassey's, 1988), 15–26; Sherie Mershon and Steven Schlossman, *Foxholes and Color Lines: Desegregating the U.S. Armed Forces* (Baltimore, MD: Johns Hopkins Press, 1998); Charles C. Moskos and John Sibley Butler, *All That We Can Be: Black Leadership and Racial Integration the Army Way* (New York: Basic, 1996); David R. Segal, *Recruiting for Uncle Sam: Citizenship and Military Manpower Policy* (Lawrence, KS: University Press of Kansas, 1989).

17. For a more complete discussion, see: Christian Leuprecht, "Demographics and Diversity Issues in Canadian Military Participation," in *Challenge and Change in the Military: Gender and Diversity Issues*, ed. Franklin C. Pinch, Allister T. MacIntyre, Phyllis Browne and Alan C. Okros (Kingston, Canada: Canadian Defence Academy Press, 2006), 122–46; Christina Silk, Rachelle Boyle, Annie Bright, Merilyn Bassett, and Nicola Roach, *The Case for Cultural Diversity in Defence*, Report for the Defence Equity Organisation of the Australian Defence Organisation, 2000, http://www.defence.gov.au/fr/reports/ CulturalDiversity.pdf; Donna J. Winslow, Lindy Heinecken, and Joseph L. Soeters, "Diversity in the Armed Forces," in *Handbook of the Sociology of the Military*, ed. Giuseppe Caforio (New York: Springer, 2006), 299–310.

18. Lucy Shelton Caswell, "Drawing Swords: War in American Editorial Cartoons," *American Journalism* 21, no. 2 (2004): 13–45; Joan L. Conners, "Hussein as Enemy: The Persian Gulf War in Political Cartoons," *Harvard International Journal of Press/Politics* 3, no. 3 (1998): 96–114; Michael A. DeSousa, "Symbolic Action and Pretended Insight: The Ayatollah Khomeini in U.S. Editorial Cartoons," in *Rhetorical Dimensions in Media: A Critical Casebook*, ed. Martin J. Medhurst and Thomas W. Benson (Dubuque, IA: Kendall/Hunt, 1984), 204–30; William B. Hart II and Fran Hassenchal, "Dehumanizing the Enemy in Editorial Cartoons," in *Communication and Terrorism: Public and Media Responses to 9/11*, ed. Bradley S. Greenberg (Cresskill, NJ: Hampton, 2002), 123–51; William B. Hart II and Fran Hassenchal, "Culture as Persuasion: Metaphor as Weapon," in *Bring 'Em On: Media and Politics in the Iraq War*, ed. Lee Artz and Yahya R. Kamalipour

(Lanham, MD: Rowman and Littlefield, 2005), 85–100.

19. "Episode 4: Demonising and Dehumanising the Enemy," *Deconstructing Propaganda: World War II Comic Book Covers*, YouTube video, posted by "DWilt55," May 2, 2011, http://youtu.be/poPnVcgp aYk (accessed March 13, 2013).

20. Keen, *Faces of the Enemy*, 16.

21. Robert L. Ivie, "Metaphor and the Rhetorical Invention of Cold War 'Idealists,'" *Communication Monographs* 54 (1987): 165–82; Keen, *Faces of the Enemy*.

22. Fredrik Strömberg, *Comic Art Propaganda* (New York: St. Martin's Griffin, 2010).

23. Homi K. Bhabha, *The Location of Culture* (London, UK: Routledge, 1994); Stuart Hall, "The Spectacle of the 'Other,'" in *Representation: Cultural Representation and Signifying Practices*, ed. Stuart Hall (London, UK: Sage, 1997), 223–79; Craig McGarty, Vincent Y. Yzerbyt, and Russel Spears, "Social, Cultural, and Cognitive Factors in Stereotype Formation," in *Stereotypes as Explanations: The Formation of Meaningful Beliefs About Social Groups*, ed. Craig McGarty, Vincent Y. Yzerbyt, and Russel Spears (Cambridge, UK: Cambridge University Press, 2002), 1–15; Russell Spears, "Four Degrees of Stereotype Formation: Differentiation by Any Means Necessary," in *Stereotypes as Explanations: The Formation of Meaningful Beliefs About Social Groups*, ed. Craig McGarty, Vincent Y. Yzerbyt, and Russel Spears (Cambridge, UK: Cambridge University Press, 2002), 127–56.

24. See Cord Scott, "Written in Red, White, and Blue: A Comparison of Comic Book Propaganda from World War II and September 11," *Journal of Popular Culture* 40, no. 2 (2007): 325–43.

25. Adam Cathcart, "Atrocities, Insults, and 'Jeep Girls': Depictions of the U.S. Military in China, 1945–1949," *International Journal of Comic Art* 10, no. 1 (2008): 140–54. Also, see cartoons in *Kang Mei yuan Chao bao jia wei man hua ji*, by Shi Wen lian mei shu xie (Guangzhou, China: Xin Hua shu dian hua nan zong fen dian, 1951; archived at the Digital Collections at the Center for Research Libraries, http://ecollections.crl.edu/cdm4/document.php?CISOROOT=/hunters&CISOPTR=11973).

26. Will Eisner, *Expressive Anatomy for Comics and Narrative: Principles and Practices from the Legendary Cartoonist* (New York: Norton, 2008), 145.

27. For more on these ideas, see: Nicole Devarenne, "'A Language Heroically Commensurate with His Body': Nationalism, Fascism, and the Language of the Superhero," *International Journal of Comic Art* 10, no. 1 (2008): 48–54; Mitra C. Emad, "Reading Wonder Woman's Body: Mythologies of Gender and Nation," *Journal of Popular Culture* 39, no. 6 (2006): 954–84; Karen McGrath, "Gender, Race, and Latina Identity: An Examination of Marvel Comics' *Amazing Fantasy* and *Araña*," *Atlantic Journal of Communication* 15, no. 4 (2007): 268–83; Eisner, *Expressive Anatomy*.

28. David A. Beronä, "Worldless Comics: The Imaginative Appeal of Peter Kuper's *The System*," in *Critical Approaches to Comics: Theories and Methods*, ed. Matthew J. Smith and Randy Duncan (New York: Routledge, 2012), 21; Strömberg, *Comic Art Propaganda*; Christina M. Knopf, "'Hey Soldier, Your Slip Is Showing': Militarism vs. Femininity in World War II Comic Pages and Books," in *Ten Cent War*, ed. James Kimble and Trisha Goodnow (Jackson, MS: University Press of Mississippi, forthcoming).

29. Nathan Vernon Madison, *Anti-Foreign Imagery in American Pulps and Comic Books, 1920–1960* (Jefferson, NC: McFarland, 2013).

30. Strömberg, *Comic Art Propaganda*.

31. Richard L. Graham, *Government Issue: Comics for the People, 1940s-2000s* (New York: Abrams Comicarts, 2011); Merskin, "Construction of Arabs"; Strömberg, *Comic Art Propaganda*.

32. Strömberg, *Comic Art Propaganda*.

33. Bruce Bairnsfather, *Carry On Sergeant* (Indianapolis, IN: Bobbs-Merrill, 1927), 104.

34. Alban B. Butler, Jr., *Happy Days!* (Oxford, UK: Osprey, 2011), 17.

35. For example, see: Anonymous, *The Further Adventures of Doctrine Man!! Vol. 2* (San Bernardino, CA: Doctrine Man, 2013), 126.

36. See: ITS Crew, "Military Acronyms, Terminology and Slang Reference," Imminent Threat Solutions, January 5, 2012, http://www.itstactical.com/intellicom/language/military-acronymstermino logy-and-slang-reference/; Gary Johnston, "durka durka," *Urban Dictionary*, October 29, 2004, http://www.urbandictionary.com/define.php?term=durka %20durka (accessed January 5, 2014).

37. Bill Mauldin, *Willie and Joe the World War II Years*, ed. Todd DePastino (Seattle, WA: Fantagraphics, 2011), 539.

38. Frank Brandt cartoon in *Yank* 3, no. 2 (July 7, 1944): 17 (reprinted in *The Best of YANK The Army Weekly*, ed. Ira Topping [New York: Arno, 1980]).

39. Randall Collins, *Violence: A Micro-Sociological Theory* (Princeton, NJ: Princeton University Press, 2008).

40. Mauldin, *Willie and Joe*, 297.

41. Ibid., 375.

42. Ibid., 487.

43. In: Frank W. Maresca, *A Soldier's Odyssey: To Remember Our Past as It Was* (N.p.: Trafford, 2012), 566.

44. In: *Yank* 2, no. 32 (January 28, 1944): 11 (reprinted in *The Best of YANK The Army Weekly*, ed. Ira Topping [New York: Arno, 1980]).

45. George Baker, *The New Sad Sack* (New York: Simon and Schuster, 1946), "Raid."

46. Robert L. Ivie, *Dissent from War* (Bloomfield, CT: Kumarian, 2007), 35.

47. See: Tonie Holt and Valmai Holt, eds., *The Best of Fragments from France by Capt. Bruce Bairnsfather* (South Yorkshire, UK: Pen and Sword Military, 2009), 12.

48. Vernon Grant, *Stand-by One!* (Hong Kong: Dublin Associates, 1969), n.p.

49. *Hearts and Minds*, directed by Peter Davis (1974; Criterion Collection), YouTube video, posted by "Sao Vàng," August 22, 2012, http://youtube/1d2ml82lc7s.

50. Collins, *Violence*.

51. In: Robert E. Bronner, *The Soldier's Pen* (New York: Hill and Wang, 2006), 158.

52. Percy Crosby cartoon, in: John T. Winterich, ed. *Squads Write! A Selection of the Best Things in Prose, Verse, and Cartoons from The Stars and Stripes* (New York: Harper and Brothers, 1931), 140.

53. Butler, *Happy Days*, 54.

54. Douglas G. Ward, *Topical Sketches* (Irvin Department of Rare Books and Special Collections, Digital Collections: http://library.sc.edu/digital/collections/rts.html 1915–1916), 7.

55. In: Mark Bryant, *World War I in Cartoons* (London, UK: Grubb Street, 2009), 121.

56. Dave Breger, *Private Breger in Britain* (London, UK: Pilot, 1944), 75 and 144.

57. Ralph Stein cartoon in *Yank* 2, no. 1 (June 25, 1943): 6–7 (reprinted in *The Best of YANK The Army Weekly*, ed. Ira Topping [New York: Arno, 1980]).

58. Michaela Hönicke, "'Know Your Enemy': American Wartime Images of Germany, 1942–1943," in *Enemy Images in American History*, ed. Ragnhild Fiebig-von Hase and Ursula Lehmkuhl (Providence, RI: Berghahn, 1997), 231–78.

59. Shi Wen lian mei shu xie, *Kang Mei yuan Chao bao jia wei man hua ji* (Guangzhou, China: Xin Hua shu dian hua nan zong fen dian, 1951), 1 and 3.

60. See, for example: Strömberg, *Comic Art Propaganda*.

61. Mansfield cartoon in *Yank* 3, no. 42 (April 6, 1945): 24 (reprinted in *The Best of YANK The Army Weekly*, ed. Ira Topping [New York: Arno, 1980]).

62. For example: Norval Eugene Packwood, *Leatherhead in Korea* (VA: Marine Corps Gazette, 1952), 52–3.

63. Tad Foster, *The Vietnam Funny Book: An Antidote to Insanity* (Novato, CA: Presidio, 1980), n.p.

64. Jake Schuffert, *"No Sweat" ... More 'n More* (Washington, D.C.: Army Times, 1970), 21.

65. For example: John F. Holmes, *Power Point Ranger, Vol. 1* (New York: World Audience, 2012), 72.

66. For example, FM100–5 made clear statements of antipathy specifically against civilians of enemy nations during the World War I and World War II years, while more recent versions of FM100–5 are vaguer. See: Bruce McKeever, "Framing the Enemy: A Study of American Military Training in Modern War" (paper presented at the Eastern Sociological Society, Baltimore, MD, February 2014).

67. For example, see: Mark Bryant, *Napoleonic Wars in Cartoons* (London, UK: Grubb Street, 2009), 111.

68. See: Baldridge cartoons in: Winterich, *Squads Write*, 34 and 207; Ward, *Topical Sketches*, 66; W.J. Calthrop, "Father William," *Shell Shocks: By the New Zealanders in France* (London: Jarrold and Sons, 1916), 25.

69. Sgt. "Yank" Chapman, "Season's Greetings From the Oldest Fortress Group Overseas," in Robert McClelland Martin Collection (AFC/2001/001/479), Veterans History Project, American Folklife Center, Library of Congress, http://lcweb2.loc.gov/diglib/vhp/story/loc.natlib.afc2001001.00479/pageturner?ID=pm0001001&page=4.

70. Hönicke, "Know Your Enemy."

71. In: John A Lent and Xu Ying. "Cartooning and Wartime China: Part One—1931–1945," *International Journal of Comic Art* 10, no. 1 (2008): figures on 27, 95.

72. John Sheppard, *"Blue Suiters": Cartoons of the USAF* (Hoschton, GA: ShepArt Studios, 2013), 39.

73. Maximilian Uriarte, *The White Donkey* (2014), http://www.maximilianu.com/portfolio/terminal-lance-the-white-donkey/.

74. Mauldin, *Willie and Joe*, 294.

75. Bill Mauldin, *Willie and Joe Back Home*, ed. Todd DePastino (Seattle, WA: Fantagraphics, 2011), 40.

76. Baker, *New Sad Sack*, "The Enemy."

77. Shel Silverstein, *Grab Your* Socks (New York: Ballantine, 1956), 38–9.

78. Ragnhild Fiebig-von Hase, "Introduction," in *Enemy Images in American History*, ed. Ragnhild Fiebig-von Hase and Ursula Lehmkuhl (Providence, RI: Berghahn, 1997), 1–40; David J. Finlay, Ole R. Holsti, and Richard R. Fagen, *Enemies in Politics* (Chicago, IL: Rand-McNally, 1967); Ivie, *Dissent from War*.

79. American examples of such World War II cartoon imagery can be found throughout the Library of Congress's Veterans' History Project archives, such as in the Joseph Ingram Gurfein Collection (AFC/2001/001/25846), Veterans History Project, American Folklife Center, Library of Congress, and the Albert J. Webb Collection (AFC/2001/001/1005), Veterans History Project, American Folklife Center, Library of Congress. Russian, French, and English examples may be seen in: John Dower, *Yellow Promise/Yellow Peril: Foreign Postcards of the Russo-Japanese War* (Massachusetts Institute of Technology, 2008), digital book at http://ocw.mit.edu/ans7870/21f/21f.027/yellow_promise_yellow_peril/yp_essay03.html, "Cartoon Adversaries."

80. "Episode 9: Images of the Enemy, Japan," *Deconstructing Propaganda: World War II Comic Book Covers*, YouTube video, posted by "DWilt55," October 1, 2013, http://youtu.be/tId_EcrkDOQ.

81. Edmund P. Russell III, "'Speaking of Annihilation' Mobilizing for War Against Human and Insect Enemies, 1914–45," *Journal of American History* 82 (1996): 1505–29.

82. Sallows cartoon in *Yank* 1, no. 39 (March 19, 1943): 24; Douglas Borgstedt cartoon in *Yank* 2, no. 28 (December 31, 1943): 21; Frank R. Robinson cartoon in *Yank* 3, no. 47 (May 11, 1945): 24; Charles Pearson cartoon in *Yank* 4, no. 28 (December 28, 1945): 23 (all reprinted in *The Best of YANK The Army Weekly*, ed. Ira Topping [New York: Arno, 1980]).

83. See, for example: Frank Brandt cartoon in *Yank* 2, no. 1 (June 25, 1943): 19, and Ned Hilton cartoon in *Yank* 2, no. 1 (June 25, 1943): 32 (reprinted in *The Best of YANK The Army Weekly*, ed. Ira Topping [New York: Arno, 1980]). Also: Sumner Grant creative works, August 1944, Veterans History Project, AFC/2001/001/20970, American Folklife Center, Library of Congress, http://lcweb2.loc.gov/diglib/vhp/story/loc.natlib.afc2001001.20970/; Sidney White, "Ah, Fruit," Veterans History Project, AFC/2001/001/31890, American Folklife Center, Library of Congress, http://lcweb2.loc.gov/diglib/

vhp-stories/loc.natlib.afc2001001.31890/artworks; F. V., *Australian Army Second World War Cartoon Album*, "We Don't Get Much Sport Up Here," http://www.ebay.com/itm/World War II-Original-MANU SCRIPT-Cartoon-Album-MILITARY-NEW-GUINEA-DARWIN-/131314126079?pt=AU_Antiquarian_Collectable_Books&hash=item1e92ee8cff.

84. Frank Brandt cartoon in *Yank* 2, no. 25 (December 10, 1943): 15 (reprinted in *The Best of YANK The Army Weekly*, ed. Ira Topping [New York: Arno, 1980]).

85. "Episode 9: Images of the Enemy, Japan."

86. Mauldin, *Willie and Joe*, 178.

87. Naoka Shibusawa, *America's Geisha Ally: Reimagining the Japanese Enemy* (Cambridge, MA: Harvard University Press, 2006, Kindle e-book).

88. Bill Hume and John Annarino, *Babysan: A Private Look at the Japanese Occupation* (Tokyo: Kasuga Boeki, 1953), 7. Also see: Bill Hume, *Babysan's World: The Hume'n Slant on Japan* (Rutland, VT: Charles E. Tuttle, 1954).

89. See discussions in: Cord, "Frankly, Mac," 5; Cathcart, "Atrocities, Insults, and 'Jeep Girls.'" For example: Shi Wen lian mei shu xie, *Kang Mei yuan Chao bao jia wei man hua ji*, 2.

90. Damon Bryan Shackelford, *Delta Bravo Sierra. Rally Point: Vol. 1, Year 1*, 2008, www.deltabravosierra.com, 2008, 20. For similar themes, also see: Anonymous, *Doctrine Man Vol. 2*, 64, 73, 77, 116, 119, 122, and 138.

91. Holmes, *Power Point Ranger*, 82.

92. Matthew Rosenberg and Azam Ahmed, "U.S. Aid to Afghans Flows on Despite Warnings of Misuse," *New York Times*, January 30, 2014, http://www.nytimes.com/2014/01/30/world/asia/report-says-afghanistan-cant-be-trusted-to-prevent-misuse-of-us-aid.html (accessed January 31, 2014).

93. J. Alexander Thier and Azita Ranjbar, "Killing Friends, Making Enemies: The Impact and Avoidance of Civilian Casualties in Afghanistan," *United States Institute of Peace Briefing*, July 2008, http://www.usip.org/sites/default/files/resources/USIP_0708_2.PDF.

94. Bouhammer, "And You Thought I Was Lying About Man-Love Thursdays," *Bouhammer's Blog*, January 28, 2010, http://www.bouhammer.com/2010/01/and-you-thought-i-was-lying-about-man-love-thursdays/ (accessed December 29, 2013); Bouhammer, "Their Thursday Night is Our Saturday Night," *Bouhammer's Afghan and Military Blog*, July 18, 2006, http://www.bouhammer.com/2006/07/their-thursday-night-is-our-saturday-night/ (accessed December 29, 2013); Fox News, "Afghan Men Struggle with Sexual Identity, Study Finds," FoxNews.com, January 28, 2010, http://www.foxnews.com/politics/2010/01/28/afghan-men-struggle-sexual-identity-study-finds/ (accessed December 29, 2013).

95. Anonymous, *The Further Adventures of Doctrine Man!! Vol. 2* (Lexington, KY: Doctrine Man, 2013), 145; Holmes, *Power Point Ranger*, 19, 27, 29, and 90.

96. Sheppard, *Blue Suiters*, 35.

97. Michael Duffy, "Vintage Audio—How Ya Gonna Keep 'Em Down on the Farm," FirstWorld-War, August 22, 2009, http://www.firstworldwar.com/audio/howyagonna.htm.

98. Butler, *Happy Days*, 17, 18, 20, 22, 30, 66, and 74.

99. Abian Wallgren, *Wally: His Cartoons of the A.E.F.* (N.p.: Stars and Stripes, 1919), "Yanks on the Rhein."

100. Ibid., "When We Take Our French Ways Back Home."

101. Wingert, *Hubert*, 46.

102. Bob Stevens, *"There I Was..." 25 Years* (Blue Ridge Summit, PA: TAB, 1992), 21.

103. Thierry Terret, "American Sammys and French *Poilus* in the Great War: Sport, Masculinities and Vulnerability," *International Journal of the History of Sport* 28, nos. 3–4 (2011): 351–71.

104. Douglas Borgstedt cartoon in *Yank* 2, no. 28 (December 31, 1943): 21 (reprinted in *The Best of YANK The Army Weekly*, ed. Ira Topping [New York: Arno, 1980]).

105. Frank Robinson cartoon in *Yank* 3, no. 47 (May 11, 1945): 24 (reprinted in *The Best of YANK The Army Weekly*, ed. Ira Topping [New York: Arno, 1980]).

106. Schuffert, *No Sweat*, 128.

107. John Sheppard, *Incoming! Military Cartoons* (Hoschton, GA: ShepArt Studios, 2007–2011), 140.

108. In: Winterich, *Squads Write*, 116, 120, 125, and 268; Butler, *Happy Days*, 17.

109. George Baker, *The Sad Sack* (New York: Simon and Schuster, 1944), "Shine"; Baker, *The New Sad Sack*, "Food for Feed."

110. Baker, *Sad Sack*, "The Native."

111. Jeff Bacon, *20 Years of Broadside* (Garden City, ID: Deep Water, 2006), 49.

112. Wingert, *Hubert*, 1.

113. Mauldin, *Willie and Joe*, 278.

114. Baker, *New Sad Sack*, "Sightseers."

115. Wingert, *Hubert*, 8.

116. Mauldin, *Willie and Joe*, 468.

117. Wingert, *Hubert*, 4.

118. In: Frank Brandt, ed., *Cartoons for Fighters* (Washington, D.C.: Infantry Journal, 1945), n.p.

119. Bill Hume and John Annarino, *When We Get Back Home from Japan* (Tokyo: Kyoya, 1953), 3.

120. Hume and Annarino, *Babysan*.

121. Holmes, *Power Point Ranger*, 44.

122. Hume and Annarino, *When We Get Back Home from Japan*.

123. Baker, *New Sad Sack*, "Allied Harmony."

124. Randall Collins, "Three Faces of Cruelty: Towards a Comparative Sociology of Violence," *Theory and Society* 1, no. 4 (1974): 415–40; Beck, *The Sociological Anatomy*.

125. Maximillian Uriarte, *Terminal Lance #1–100 Compilation* (Korea: Veterans Expeditionary Media, 2011), 8.

126. Ibid., 8.

127. Ibid., 52.

128. Holmes, *Power Point Ranger*, 24.

129. Butler, *Happy Days*, 70.

130. Silverstein, *Grab Your Socks*, 91.

131. Ibid., 37.

132. Todd DePastino, *Bill Mauldin: A Life Up Front* (New York: W.W. Norton, 2008).

133. Mauldin, *Willie and Joe*, 27, 130.

134. Of the 3,600-plus Navajos who served in World War II, only 420 were "Code Talkers" in six Marine Corps divisions; they used speech as a weapon of precision, combining their own language with about 400 code words of their own, throughout the Asian-Pacific Theater, coding and decoding messages faster, and more securely, than the military's black box. See: Bruce Watson, *The Navajo Code Talkers* (Pune, India: New World City, 2011).

135. Mauldin, *Willie and Joe*, 282.

136. Bill Mauldin, *Willie and Joe Back Home*, 45.

137. Breger, *Private Breger in Britain*, 15.

138. Grant, "Creative Works," September 1944, http://lcweb2.loc.gov/diglib/vhp/story/loc.natlib.afc2001001.20970/.

139. Kirkland H. Day, *Camion Cartoons* (Boston, MA: Marshall Jones, 1919), 19.

140. Ibid., 29.

141. Jacqueline Jenkinson, "'All in the Same Uniform'? The Participation of Black Colonial Residents in the British Armed Forces in the First World War," *Journal of Imperial and Commonwealth History* 40, no. 2 (2012): 207–30.

142. In: Harry L. Katz and Vincent Virga, *Civil War Sketch Book: Drawings from the Battlefront* (New York: W.W. Norton, 2012), 86 and 145.

143. In: Bonner, *The Soldier's Pen*, 195.

Chapter 5

1. Homi K. Bhabha, *The Location of Culture* (London, UK: Routledge, 1994); Donal Carbaugh, *Situating Selves: The Communication of Social Identities in American Scenes* (Albany, NY: State University of New York Press, 1996); John Urry, "The Sociology of Space and Place," in *The Blackwell Companion to Sociology*, ed. Judith R. Blau (Malden, MA: Blackwell, 2004), 3–15.

2. Stanley D. Brunn, Harri Andersson, and Carl T. Dahlma, "Landscaping for Power and Defence," in *Landscapes of Defence*, ed. John R. Gold and George Revill (Harlow, UK: Prentice Hall, 2000), 68–84; Thomas F. Gieryn, "A Space for Place in Sociology," *Annual Review of Sociology* 26 (2000): 463–96; Ernest J. Green, "The Social Functions of Utopian Architecture," *Utopian Studies* 4, no. 1 (1993): 1–13; Robert K. Merton, *Social Theory and Social Structure*, rev. ed. (Glencoe, IL: Free Press, 1957).

3. Doreen Massey, *For Space* (Los Angeles, CA: Sage, 2005), 9. Also, Gieryn, "A Space for Place."

4. David Ley, *A Social Geography of the City* (New York: HarperCollins, 1983).

5. Rachel Woodward, *Military Geographies* (Malden, MA: Blackwell, 2004), 3.

6. John M. Collins, *Military Geography for Professionals and the Public* (Washington, D.C.: Brassey's, 1998; Kindle e-book), loc. 228. Also, Woodward, *Military Geographies*.

7. Morris Janowitz, *The Professional Soldier: A Social and Political Portrait* (New York: Free Press, 1960).

8. See: Mary Douglas, *Purity and Danger* (London, UK: Routledge, 1966).

9. Carolyn Marvin and David W. Ingle, *Blood Sacrifice and the Nation: Totem Rituals and the American Flag* (Cambridge, UK: Cambridge University Press, 1999), 100. Also see Joseph L. Soeters, Donna J. Winslow, and Alise Weibull, "Military Culture," in *Handbook of the Sociology of the Military*, ed. Giuseppe Caforio (New York: Springer, 2006), 237–54.

10. Eliot Cohen, "The Military," in *Understanding America: The Anatomy of an Exceptional Nation*, ed. Peter H. Schuck and James Q. Wilson (New York: Public Affairs, 2008), 247–74.

11. Mark W. Corson, "Operation Iraqi Freedom: Geographic Considerations for Desert Warfare," in *Military Geography from Peace to War*, ed. Eugene J. Palka and Francis A. Galgano (New York: McGraw-Hill, 2005), 149–80; Peter Shirlow, "Fundamentalist Loyalism: Discourse, Resistance and Identity Politics," in *Landscapes of Defence*, ed. John R. Gold and George Revill (Harlow, UK: Prentice Hall, 2000), 85–101; Nigel J. Thrift and Dean K. Forbes, "A Landscape with Figures: Political Geography with Human Conflict," *Political Geography Quarterly* 2, no. 3 (1983): 247–64; Collins, *Military Geography*.

12. Collins, *Military Geography*; Woodward, *Military Geographies*.

13. William Cartwright, "An Investigation of Maps and Cartographic Artefacts of the Gallipoli Campaign 1915: Military, Commercial and Personal," *Geospatial Visualisation* XIV (2013): 19–40.

14. Carl Von Clausewitz, *On War*, ed. Frederic Natusch Maude, trans. James John Graham (1832; n.p.: Amazon Digital Services, 2011; Kindle e-book), loc. 2947.

15. Robert R. Leonhard, *Fighting by Minutes: Time and the Art of War* (Westport, CT: Praeger, 1994), 3. Also see: Christina M. Knopf and Eric J. Ziegelmayer, "Fourth Generation Warfare and the U.S. Military's Social Media Strategy: Promoting the Academic Conversation," *Air and Space Power Journal—Africa and Francophonie* 4 (2012): 3–22.

16. Leonhard, *Fighting by Minutes*.

17. Massey, *For Space*.

18. Douglas Wolk, *Reading Comics: How Graphic Novels Work and What They Mean* (Cambridge, MA: Da Capo, 2007; Kindle e-book), loc. 2180.

19. David Herman, "Spatial Reference in Narrative Domains," *Text* 21, no. 4 (2001): 515–41.

20. Julia Round, "London's Calling: Alternate Worlds and the City as Superhero in Contemporary British-American Comics," *International Journal of Comic Art* 10, no. 1 (2008): 26.

21. Thierry Groensteen, *The System of Comics*, trans. by Bart Beaty and Nick Nguyen (1999; Jackson, MS: University Press of Mississippi, 2007).

22. Scott McCloud, *Understanding Comics: The Invisible Art* (New York: HarperPerennial, 1993), 95.

23. Jimmy Johnson, *Arlo and Janis*, daily comic strip, July 10, 2013, http://www.gocomics.com/arloandjanis/2013/07/10 (accessed July 10, 2013).

24. Clausewitz, *On War*, loc. 2955.

25. Maximilian Uriarte, *Terminal Lance: #1–100 Compilation* (Korea: Veterans Expeditionary Media, 2011), 104; Mark Baker, *PV-2 Murphy the Adventure Continues: A "Pvt. Murphy's Law" Collection* (Baltimore, MD: United Books, 2001), 34.

26. In: Frank W. Maresca, *A Soldier's Odyssey: To Remember Our Past as It Was* (N.p.: Trafford, 2012), 51.

27. Bruce Bairnsfather, *The Best of Fragments from France*, ed. Tonie Holt and Valmai Holt (South Yorkshire, UK: Pen and Sword Military, 1998), 103.

28. Fred Schwab cartoon in *Yank* 3, no. 2 (June 30, 1944): 22 (reprinted in *The Best of YANK The Army Weekly*, ed. Ira Topping [New York: Arno, 1980]).

29. Bill Mauldin, *Willie and Joe the World War II Years*, ed. Todd DePastino (Seattle, WA: Fantagraphics, 2011), 486.

30. Ibid., 497.

31. Norval Eugene Packwood, *Leatherhead: The Story of Marine Corps Boot Camp* (Quantico, VA: Marine Corps Association, 1951), 30.

32. Robert R. Mullan, "Military Cartoons," *Canadian Military Project*, http://www.rootsweb.ancestry.com/~canmil/cartoons/cartoon3.htm.

33. Mark Baker, *Sgt. Murphy: A "Pvt. Murphy's Law" Collection* (Alexandria, VA: Byrrd, 2008), n.p.

34. Daryl Talbot, *Laughing in Cadence: Dress Right Dress Military Cartoons* (Stillwater, OK: New Forums, 2009), 19.

35. Jake Schuffert, *"No Sweat" ... More 'n More* (Washington, D.C.: Army Times, 1970), 63.

36. Mauldin, *Willie and Joe*, 357.

37. Talbot, *Laughing in Cadence*, 39.

38. Wallgren, "General Orders in Sunny France," *Stars and Stripes*, February 22, 1918, 7.

39. Dick Winger, *Hubert* (London, UK: Love and Malcomson, 1944), 21.

40. Mike Sinclair, "Lt. Kadish," in *I Ain't Laughing, Sir: 40 Years of GI Humor from Stars and Stripes and Yank Magazine*, ed. Sid Schapiro (N.p.: Stars and Stripes, 1982), 131.

41. Steve Opet, *Opet's Odyssey*, https://www.facebook.com/photo.php?fbid=154765824584290&set=a.154761024584770.32717.137174599676746&type=3&theater.

42. John Holmes, *Power Point Ranger* online, https://www.facebook.com/photo.php?fbid=68244 5958445077&set=a.681933538496319.1073741849.113256155364063&type=3&theater.

43. Anonymous, *Doctrine Man* online, https://www.facebook.com/photo.php?fbid=68997447436 9040&set=pb.110598432306650.-2207520000.1 397854136&type=3&theater.

44. Dave Breger, *Private Breger: His Adventures in Army Camp* (New York: Rand McNally, 1942), "Bivouac."

45. Doris Weatherford, *American Women and World War II* (Edison, NJ: Castle, 2008).

46. Vic Herman, *Winnie the WAC* (Philadelphia, PA: David McKay, 1945), n.p. Also: Leonard Sansone, *The Wolf* (New York: United, 1945), n.p.

47. Dave Breger, *Private Breger in Britain* (London, UK: Pilot, 1944), 79.

48. Vernon Grant, *Stand-by One!* (Hong Kong: Dublin Associates, 1969), n.p.

49. Mauldin, *Willie and Joe*, 216.

50. George Baker, *The Sad Sack* (New York: Simon and Schuster, 1944), "Tropics."

51. George Baker, *The New Sad Sack* (New York: Simon and Schuster, 1946), "Change of Climate."

52. Mark Baker, *Pfc. Murphy: Private Murphy's Law Book* (Baltimore, MD: United Books, 2005), 35; Mauldin, *Willie and Joe*, 220.

53. Herman, *Winnie the WAC*, n.p.

54. Ted Stanley, *Perils of a Private: Sketches of Camp Life* (Boston, MA: Small, Maynard, 1918), "A Night Mare at 30° Below."

55. Robert K. Bindig artworks, 4 March 1945, Veterans History Project, AFC/2001/001/32475, American Folklife Center, Library of Congress, 1945, http://lcweb2.loc.gov/diglib/vhp/story/loc.natlib.afc2001001.32475/artworks.

56. Dick Ericson cartoon in *Yank* 2, no. 28 (December 31, 1943): 22 (reprinted in *The Best of YANK The Army Weekly*, ed. Ira Topping [New York: Arno, 1980]).

57. Al Summers cartoon in *Out of Line: A Collection of Cartoons from Pacific Stars and Stripes* (Tokyo: Toppon, 1952), n.p.

58. Mort Walker, *The Lexicon of Comicana*, iUniverse.com, 2000, 28–9.

59. Mauldin, *Willie and Joe*, 224, 219, 155, 223 and 251.

60. W.C. Pope, *Pope's Puns*, http://www.citamn.afrc.af.mil/shared/media/ggallery/hires/AFG-111115–002.jpg.

61. Anonymous, *The Further Adventures of Doctrine Man!! Vol. 2* (San Bernardino, CA: Doctrine Man, 2013), 52; Opet, *Opet's Odyssey*, https://www.facebook.com/photo.php?fbid=154762957917910&set=a.154761024584770.32717.137174599676746&type=3&theater.

62. Jeffrey Hall, *Downrange*, "Sponsor," http://www.military.com/cartooncontent/0,14763,Downrange_070202,00.html.

63. Will Eisner, "Joe's Dope Sheet" (PS, no. 115, 1962) in *P.S Magazine: The Best of the Preventative Maintenance Monthly*, ed. Eddie Campbell (New York: Abrams ComicArts, 2011), 234–5.

64. Mauldin, *Willie and Joe*, 107.

65. Jeff Bacon, *The Best of Broadside: A Humorous Look at Life in the Navy* (Newport News, VA: Deep Water, 1992), n.p.

66. Alban B. Butler, Jr., *Happy Days!* (Oxford, UK: Osprey, 2011), 24 and 26.

67. Stanley, *Perils of a Private*, "It Makes a Difference."

68. Breger, *Private Breger in Britain*, 76.

69. Mauldin, *Willie and Joe*, 223, 530 and 560.

70. Ibid., 45.

71. Norval Eugene Packwood, *Leatherhead in Korea* (VA: Marine Corps Gazette, 1952), 44.

72. Packwood, *Leatherhead in Korea*, 52–3.

73. C. Miller cartoon in *Out of Line: A Collection of Cartoons from Pacific Stars and Stripes* (Tokyo: Toppon, 1952), n.p.

74. Packwood, *Leatherhead in Korea*, 10–11.

75. Mauldin, *Willie and Joe*, 173.

76. Baker, *Sgt. Murphy*, n.p.

77. Schuffert, *No Sweat*, 76.

78. Baker, *Sad Sack*, "Lost."

79. Talbot, *Laughing in Cadence*, 69.

80. Christina M. Knopf, "Sense-Making and Map-Making: War Letters as Personal Geographies," *NANO* 6 (2014): http://www.nanocrit.com/issues/6-

2014/sense-making-map-making-war-letters-personal-geographies.

81. For example: Butler, *Happy Days*, 43–45.

82. Mark Baker, *Private Murphy's Law* (Baltimore, MD: United Books, 1999), 84.

83. John W. Vessey Jr., "Preface," in *Military Geography for Professionals and the Public*, ed. John M. Collins (Washington, D.C.: Brassey's, 1998; Kindle e-book), loc. 159.

84. Butler, *Happy Days*, 23.

85. Mauldin, *Willie and Joe*, 224.

86. Breger, *Private Breger in Britain*, 34.

87. Packwood, *Leatherhead in Korea*, 72.

88. See the discussion in: Jon C. Malinowski, "Peleliu: Geographic Complications of Operation Stalemate," in *Military Geography from Peace to War*, ed. Eugene J. Palka and Francis A. Galgano (New York: McGraw-Hill, 2005), 91–112.

89. Bairnsfather, *Best of Fragments from France*, 129.

90. Packwood, *Leatherhead in Korea*, 64.

91. Mauldin, *Willie and Joe*, 265.

92. Packwood, *Leatherhead in Korea*, 50; Mauldin, *Willie and Joe*, 317.

93. Butler, *Happy Days*, 40. Also: Abian A. Wallgren, *Wally: His Cartoons of the AEF* (N.p.: Stars and Stripes, 1919), "Ruff on Rats."

94. Bairnsfather, *Best of Fragments from France*, 51 and 120.

95. Bairnsfather, *Best of Fragments from France*, 65; Mauldin, *Willie and Joe*, 386.

96. For examples: Bairnsfather, *Best of Fragments from France*, 7; Butler, *Happy Days*, 88 and 89; Baker, *Sad Sack*, "Deplorable Conditions," "Rest"; Baker, *New Sad Sack*, "Peace at Last."

97. Stanley, *Perils of a Private*, "Signs of Spring No. 2."

98. Mauldin, *Willie and Joe*, 41, 21, 232 and 558.

99. Ibid., 494.

100. Baker, *New Sad Sack*, "First Class Accommodations." Also see: Dick Wingert, "Hubert," in *I Ain't Laughing, Sir: 40 Years of GI Humor from Stars and Stripes and Yank Magazine*, ed. Sid Schapiro (N.p.: Stars and Stripes, 1982), 34; Mauldin, *Willie and Joe*, 420.

101. Vernon Grant, "Grant's Grunts," *Pacific Stars and Stripes*, February 23, 1969: 16.

102. Packwood, *Leatherhead in Korea*, 14.

103. Grant, *Stand-By One*, n.p.

104. Shel Silverstein, *Grab Your Socks* (New York: Ballantine, 1956), 80.

105. Mauldin, *Willie and Joe*, 570.

106. Talbot, *Laughing in Cadence*, 30.

107. Bill Mauldin, *Bill Mauldin in Korea* (New York: W.W. Norton, 1952), 62.

108. Eugene J. Palka, "Operation Enduring Freedom: The Military Geographic Challenges of Afghanistan," in *Military Geography from Peace to War*, ed. Eugene J. Palka and Francis A. Galgano (New York: McGraw-Hill, 2005), 321–42; Corson, "Geographic Considerations for Desert Warfare."

109. Opet, *Opet's Odyssey*, https://www.facebook.com/photo.php?fbid=154762271251312&set=a.154761024584770.32717.137174599676746&type=3&theater.

110. Baker, *Pfc. Murphy*, 71.

111. Baker, *Sgt. Murphy*, n.p.

112. Jeff Bacon, *20 Years of Broadside* (Garden City, ID: Deep Water, 2006), 42.

113. Anonymous, *Doctrine Man Vol. 2*, 63.

114. Shel Silverstein, *Take Ten.... A Collection of Cartoons* (Tokyo: Pacific Stars and Stripes, 1955).

115. Talbot, *Laughing in Cadence*, 49.

116. Baker, *New Sad Sack*, "Jungle Chore."

117. Robert H. Knapp, "A Psychology of Rumor," *The Public Opinion Quarterly* 8, no. 1 (1944): 22–37; Justin M. Oswald, "Know Thy Enemy: Camel Spider Stories Among U.S. Troops in the Middle East," in *Warrior Ways: Explorations in Modern Military Folklore*, ed. Eric A. Eliason and Tad Tuleja (Boulder, CO: Utah State University Press, 2012), 38–57.

118. Grant, *Stand-by One*, n.p.

119. Oswald, "Know Thy Enemy."

120. John F. Holmes, *Power Point Ranger, Vol. 1* (New York: World Audience, 2012), 85.

121. Schuffert, *No Sweat*, 41.

122. Frank Brandt, ed., *Cartoons for Fighters* (Washington, D.C.: Infantry Journal, 1945), "Shark Sense."

123. Bacon, *Best of Broadside*, n.p.

124. In: Robert E. Bronner, *The Soldier's Pen* (New York: Hill and Wang, 2006), 41.

125. Talbot, *Laughing in Cadence*, 11.

126. Theodor Seuss Geisel and Munro Leaf, *This Is Ann* (N.p.: War Department, 1943).

127. Thomas R. St. George, *C/O Postmaster* (New York: Thomas Y. Crowell, 1943), 180.

128. Vernon Grant, "Grant's Grunts," *Pacific Stars and Stripes*, February 23, 1969: 16.

129. Tad Foster, *The Vietnam Funny Book: An Antidote to Insanity* (Novato, CA: Presidio, 1980), np; Grant, *Stand-By One*, n.p.

130. Charles Pearson cartoon in *Yank* 3, no. 3 (July 7, 1944): 24 (reprinted in *The Best of YANK The Army Weekly*, ed. Ira Topping [New York: Arno, 1980]).

131. Sidney White, "Dream About to Be Shattered," Veterans History Project, AFC/2001/001/31890, American Folklife Center, Library of Congress, http://lcweb2.loc.gov/diglib/vhp-stories/loc.natlib.afc2001001.31890/artworks/.

132. Sumner Grant creative works, May 1944 and August 1944, Veterans History Project, AFC/2001/001/20970, American Folklife Center, Library of Congress, http://lcweb2.loc.gov/diglib/vhp/story/loc.natlib.afc2001001.20970/.

133. Silverstein, *Take Ten*, n.p.

134. Baker, *PV-2 Murphy*, 37.

135. Knapp, "A Psychology of Rumor."

136. Rebecca Onion, "The Snake-Eaters and the Yards," *Slate*, November 27, 2013, http://www.slate.com/articles/news_and_politics/american_military_history/2013/11/the_green_berets_and_the_montagnards_how_an_indigenous_tribe_won_the_admiration.html.

137. John Sheppard, *Incoming! Military Cartoons* (Hoschton, GA: ShepArt Studios, 2007–2011), 31.

138. Baker, *PV-2 Murphy*, 56.

139. Kevin Kline and Todd M. Hoelmer, *Pvt. Joe Snuffy Goes Guard!* (Washington, D.C.: National

Guard Bureau, 1991), "Dig In"; Bill Mauldin, *Up Front*, 1945 (New York: W.W. Norton, 2000), 15; Herman, *Winnie the WAC*, n.p.; Talbot, *Laughing in Cadence*, 78 and 80; Baker, *Pvt. Murphy's Law*, 64; Bairnsfather, *Best of Fragments from France*, 17; Butler, *Happy Days*, 46 and 47; Charles Johnson Post, *The Little War of Private Post: The Spanish-American War Seen Up Close* (Lincoln, NE: University of Nebraska Press, 1999), 244.

140. Frank Dunne, *Digger Days*, Australian War Memorial, http://www.awm.gov.au/exhibitions/1918/soldier/tommy.asp.

141. Bairnsfather, *Best of Fragments from France*, 43.

142. Breger, *Private Breger in Britain*, 39.

143. Herman, *Winnie the WAC*, n.p.

144. Mauldin, *Willie and Joe*, 71.

145. Ibid., 199.

146. Brandt, *Cartoons for Fighters*, "Tips on Patrolling."

147. Talbot, *Laughing in Cadence*, 12.

148. Breger, *Private Breger in Britain*, 25, 27, 75, and 144.

149. Sidney White, "Illustration for Camouflage Manual, Gowan Field [Spring 1943]," Veterans History Project, AFC/2001/001/31890, American Folklife Center, Library of Congress, http://lcweb2.loc.gov/diglib/vhp-stories/loc.natlib.afc2001001.31890/artworks/.

150. Johnny Bryson cartoon in *Yank* 3, no. 2 (June 30, 1944): 24 (reprinted in *The Best of YANK The Army Weekly*, ed. Ira Topping [New York: Arno, 1980]).

151. Mauldin, *Willie and Joe*, 73.

152. Baker, *Pvt. Murphy's Law*, 65.

153. Sheppard, *Incoming*, 116.

154. Pope, *Pope's Puns*, "New Camo," http://www.military.com/cartooncontent/0,14763,Pope_021005,00.html.

155. Maximilian Uriarte, *Terminal Lance Head Call: The First 100 MarineTimes Strips* (N.p.: Amazon Digital Services, 2013; Kindle e-book), loc. 1235.

156. David W. Brown, "The Irresponsibility Stupid and Dangerous Camouflage Patterns of the U.S. Military," *The Week*, January 22, 2013, http://theweek.com/article/index/238909/the-irresponsibly-stupid-and-dangerous-camouflage-patterns-of-the-us-military.

157. Holmes, *Power Point Ranger*, 46.

158. Maximilian Uriarte, "Past Tense Dress," *Terminal Lance* online, http://terminallance.com/2014/07/22/terminal-lance-335-past-tense-dress/.

159. Sheppard, *Incoming*, 11.

160. See: Ann Gripper, "Heim Front: German Artist's World War I Cartoons up for Auction," *Mirror Online*, March 15, 2013, http://www.mirror.co.uk/news/uk-news/world-war-i-cartoons-by-albert-heim-761412.

161. Todd DePastino, *Bill Mauldin: A Life Up Front* (New York: W.W. Norton, 2008), 164.

162. Bathroom gags are seen in: Kathleen A. Browning, "Mid East Coast Girls, Supply Finally Came Through!" http://constitutioncenter.org/experience/exhibitions/past-exhibitions/art-of-the-anerican-soldier-gallery; Anonymous, *The Further*

Adventures of Doctrine Man!! Vol. 1 (Lexington, KY: Doctrine Man, 2013), 99; *John Holmes, Grunts: Downrange with Corporal Thog and Specialist Roy* (N.p.: Think On Productions, 2104; Kindle e-book), loc. 13; Uriarte, *Terminal Lance*, 36.

163. Baker, *PV-2 Murphy*, 60 and 62. Also see: Foster, *Vietnam Funny Book*.

164. Holmes, *Power Point Ranger* online, https://www.facebook.com/photo.php?fbid=643388795684127&set=a.507071605982514.112846.1132561553 64063&type=3&theater.

165. In: Gripper, "Heim Front."

166. Daniel Glaser, "The Sentiments of American Soldiers Abroad Toward Europeans," *American Journal of Sociology* 51, no. 5 (1946): 438.

167. Thompson, "RUE-FUL," *Shell Shocks: By the New Zealanders in France* (London: Jarrold and Sons, 1916), 51.

168. Roger G. Baker, *USMC Tanker's Korea: The War in Photos, Sketches and Letters Home* (Oakland, OR: Elderberry, 2001), 63.

169. Mauldin, *Willie and Joe*, 481.

170. Packwood, *Leatherhead in Korea*, 17.

171. Baker, *Pfc. Murphy*, 77.

172. Thomas Flannery cartoon in *Yank* 3, no. 3 (July 7, 1944): 24 (reprinted in *The Best of YANK The Army Weekly*, ed. Ira Topping [New York: Arno, 1980]).

173. Baker, *Sgt. Murphy*, n.p.

174. Opet, *Opet's Odyssey*, https://www.facebook.com/photo.php?fbid=154761121251427&set=a.154761024584770.32717.137174599676746&type=3&theater.

175. Vessey, "Preface."

176. Walker, *The Lexicon on Comicana*, 60.

177. George Baker cartoon in *Yank* 2, no. 28 (December 31, 1943): 24 (reprinted in *The Best of YANK The Army Weekly*, ed. Ira Topping [New York: Arno, 1980]).

Chapter 6

1. Gwyn Harries-Jenkins, "Institution to Occupation to Diversity: Gender in the Military Today," in *Challenge and Change in the Military: Gender and Diversity Issues*, ed. Franklin C. Pinch, Allister T. MacIntyre, Phyllis Browne and Alan C. Okros (Kingston, Canada: Canadian Defence Academy Press, 2006), 26–51.

2. John Black, "War, Women and Accounting: Female Staff in the UK Army Pay Department Offices, 1914–1920," *Accounting, Business and Financial History* 16, no. 2 (2006): 195–218.

3. Between 1942 and July 1943, the Women's Army Auxiliary Corps (WAAC, later shortened to WAC), the Women Accepted for Volunteer Emergency Service (the Navy WAVES), the Semper Paratus—Always Ready (SPARS) division of the Coast Guard, the women's Marines, and the Women's Airforce Service Pilots (WASPs) were established.

4. Doris Weatherford, *American Women and World War II* (Edison, NJ: Castle, 2008); Emily Yellin, *Our Mothers' War: American Women at Home*

and at the Front During World War II (New York: Free Press, 2004).

5. Rosemary Neidel-Greenlee and Evelyn Monahan, *And If I Perish: Frontline U.S. Army Nurses in World War II* (New York: Knopf, 2003); Edith M. Stern, "Nurses Wanted: A Career Boom," *Survey Graphic*, February 1942, 79 and 179.

6. Weatherford, *American Women*.

7. Leisa D. Meyer, *Creating GI Jane: Sexuality and Power in the Women's Army Corps During World War II* (New York: Columbia University Press, 1996); Weatherford, *American Women*; Yellin, *Our Mothers' War*. Also see: Barabara Freidman, "'The Soldier Speaks': *Yank* Coverage of Women and Wartime Work," *American Journalism* 22, no, 2 (2005): 63–82.

8. Mildred McAfee Horton, "Women in the United States Navy," *American Journal of Sociology* 51, no. 5 (1946): 448–50; Susanna Trnka, "Living a Life of Sex and Danger: Women, Warfare, and Sex in Military Folk Rhymes," *Western Folklore* 54, no. 3 (1995): 232–41.

9. Marina Nuciari, "Women in the Military: Sociological Arguments for Integration," in *Handbook of the Sociology of the Military*, ed. Giuseppe Caforio (New York: Springer, 2006), 279–98; Harries-Jenkins, "Institution to Occupation to Diversity."

10. Karen D. Davis and Brian McKee, "Women in the Military: Facing the Warrior Framework," in *Challenge and Change in the Military: Gender and Diversity Issues*, ed. Franklin C. Pinch, Allister T. MacIntyre, Phyllis Browne and Alan C. Okros (Kingston, Canada: Canadian Defence Academy Press, 2006), 52–75; Laura C. Prividera and John W. Howard III, "Masculinity, Whiteness, and the Warrior Hero: Perpetuating the Strategic Rhetoric of U.S. Nationalism and the Marginalization of Women," *Women and Language* 29, no. 2 (2006): 29–37; Orna Sasson-Levy, "Constructing Identities at the Margins: Masculinities and Citizenship in the Israeli Army," *The Sociological Quarterly* 43, no. 3 (2002): 357–83.

11. Kristal L.M. Alfonso, *Femme Fatale: An Examination of the Role of Women in Combat and the Policy Implications for Future American Military Operations*, Drew Papers no. 5 (Maxwell Airforce Base, AL: Air University Press, 2009).

12. Joshua A. Goldstein, *War and Gender: How Gender Shapes the War System and Vice Versa* (Cambridge, UK: Cambridge University Press, 2001).

13. For examples, see: Richard Allen Burns, "'This Is My Rifle, This Is My Gun...': Gunlore in the Military," *New Directions in Folklore* 7 (2003): http://hdl.handle.net/2022/6906; Trnka, "Living a Life of Sex and Danger."

14. Jordan Cuddemi, "'Siblings in Service': Women Veterans Discuss Challenges, Camaraderie," *Valley News*, January 24, 2014, http://www.vnews.com/news/townbytown/hartford/10334804-95/siblings-in-service-women-veterans-discuss-challenges-camaraderie (accessed January 24, 2014); Jan Goodwin, "The VA Health-Care System's Dishonorable Conduct," *Good Housekeeping*, March 2010, 160–6, 218–22; Evelyn M. Monahan and Rosemary Neidel-

Greenlee, *A Few Good Women: America's Military Women from World War I to the Wars in Iraq and Afghanistan* (New York: Anchor, 2011). Note: Though military women have a greater chance of being sexually assaulted than men, in the U.S. military the majority of sexual assault victims are men, usually by men, who often do not report the incidences because of shame or homophobia, particularly before the repeal of "Don't Ask, Don't Tell," which banned openly gay persons serving. See: James Dao, "In Debate over Military Sexual Assault, Men Are Overlooked Victims," *New York Times*, June 23, 2013, http://www.nytimes.com/2013/06/24/us/in-debate-over-military-sexual-assault-men-are-overlooked-victims.html (accessed July 24, 2013).

15. Patricia Shields, "Sex Roles in the Military," in *The Military: More Than Just a Job?*, ed. Charles C. Moskos and Frank R. Wood (Washington, D.C.: Pergamon-Brassey's, 1988), 99–114.

16. Laura C. Prividera and John W. Howard III, "Masculinity, Whiteness, and the Warrior Hero: Perpetuating the Strategic Rhetoric of U.S. Nationalism and the Marginalization of Women," *Women and Language* 29, no. 2 (2006): 29–37.

17. Carolyn Marvin and David W. Ingle, *Blood Sacrifice and the Nation: Totem Rituals and the American Flag* (Cambridge, UK: Cambridge University Press, 1999).

18. Laura Sjoberg, "Agency, Militarized Femininity and Enemy Others," *International Feminist Journal of Politics* 9, no. 1 (2007): 82–101.

19. Bernard D. Rostker, Susan D. Hosek, and Mary E. Valana, "Gays in the Military," *RAND Review*, Spring 2011, http://www.rand.org/pubs/periodicals/rand-review/issues/2011/spring/gays.html/.

20. Meyer, *Creating GI Jane*; Weatherford, *American Women*; Yellin, *Our Mothers' War*.

21. Rostker, Hosek and Valana, "Gays in the Military."

22. Elisabeth Bumiller, "One Year Later, Military Says Gay Policy Is Working," *New York Times*, September 19, 2012, http://www.nytimes.com/2012/09/20/us/dont-ask-dont-tell-anniversary-passes-with-little-note.html/ (accessed January 26, 2014); Nathaniel Frank, *Gays in Foreign Militaries 2010: A Global Primer* (Santa Barbara, CA: University of California, 2010), http://www.palmcenter.org/files/FOREIGNMILITARIESPRIMER2010FINAL.pdf/; Rostker, Hosek and Valana, "Gays in the Military."

23. Paula E. Calvin and Deborah A. Deacon, *American Women Artists in Wartime, 1776–2010* (Jefferson, NC: McFarland, 2011; Kindle e-book), loc. 71.

24. Mike Madrid, *Supergirls: Fashion, Feminism, and Fantasy, and the History of Comic Book Heroines* (Minneapolis, MN: Exterminating Angel, 2009).

25. David Hajdu, *The Ten-Cent Plague: The Great Comic-Book Scare and How It Changed America* (New York: Picador, 2009); Trina Robbins, *A Century of Women Cartoonists* (Northampton, MA: Kitchen Sink, 1993); Bradford W. Wright, *Comic Book Nation: The Transformation of Youth Culture in America* (Baltimore, MD: Johns Hopkins University Press, 2001).

26. Hajdu, *The Ten-Cent Plague*.

27. Karen McGrath, "Gender, Race, and Latina Identity: An Examination of Marvel Comics' *Amazing Fantasy* and *Araña*," *Atlantic Journal of Communication* 15, no. 4 (2007): 268–83; Douglas Wolk, *Reading Comics: How Graphic Novels Work and What They Mean* (Cambridge, MA: Da Capo, 2007; Kindle e-book).

28. Jeffrey P. Dennis, "Gay Content in Newspaper Comics," *Journal of American Culture* 35, no. 4 (2012): 304–14; Rob Lendrum, "Queering Super-Manhood: The Gay Superhero in Contemporary Mainstream Comic Books," *Journal for the Arts, Sciences, and Technology* 2, no. 2 (2004): 69–73; Mark J. McLelland, "The Love Between 'Beautiful Boys' in Japanese Women's Comics," *Journal of Gender Studies* 9 (2000): 13–25.

29. Christina M. Knopf, "'Hey, Soldier, Your Slip Is Showing': Militarism Versus Femininity in World War II Comic Pages and Books," in *Ten Cent War*, ed. James Kimble and Trisha Goodnow (Jackson, MS: University Press of Mississippi, forthcoming).

30. Laura Browder, *Her Best Shot: Women and Guns in America* (Chapel Hill, NC: University of North Carolina Press, 2006); Meyer, *Creating GI Jane*.

31. Courtney Lee Weida, "Wonderi(ing) Women: Investigating Gender Politics and Art Education within Graphica," *Visual Culture and Gender* 6 (2011): 97–107.

32. Henry Elkin, "Aggressive and Erotic Tendencies in Army Life," *American Journal of Sociology* 51, no. 5 (1946): 408–13; Robert B. Westbrook, "'I Want a Girl, Just Like the Girl That Married Harry James': American Women and the Problem of Political Obligation in World War II," *American Quarterly* 42, no. 4 (1990): 587–614.

33. Cpl. Ruge cartoon in *Yank* 2, no. 1 (June 25, 1943): 13 (reprinted in *The Best of YANK The Army Weekly*, ed. Ira Topping [New York: Arno, 1980]).

34. Bill Mauldin, *Willie and Joe the World War II Years*, ed. Todd DePastino (Seattle, WA: Fantagraphics, 2011), 20.

35. Roger G. Baker, *USMC Tanker's Korea: The War in Photos, Sketches and Letters Home* (Oakland, OR: Elderberry, 2001), 37.

36. Vernon Grant, *Stand-by One!* (Hong Kong: Dublin Associates, 1969), n.p.

37. Westbrook, "I Want a Girl."

38. Elkin, "Aggressive and Erotic Tendencies."

39. R.C. Harvey, *Milton Caniff's Male Call: The Complete Newspaper Strips: 1942–1946* (Neshannock, PA: Hermes, 2011).

40. Mauldin, *Willie and Joe*, 504.

41. Westbrook, "I Want a Girl."

42. Dick Winger, *Hubert* (London, UK: Love and Malcomson, 1944), 3; M/Sgt. Jack Lovell cartoon in *Yank* 3, no. 2 (June 30, 1944): 24 (reprinted in *The Best of YANK The Army Weekly*, ed. Ira Topping [New York: Arno, 1980]).

43. Will Eisner, *The M16A1 Rifle: Operation and Preventative Maintenance* (Washington, D.C.: U.S. Government Printing Office, 1969), 26–7.

44. Trnka, "Living a Life of Sex and Danger."

45. Mauldin, *Willie and Joe*, 506.

46. Meyer, *Creating GI Jane*.

47. The use of "Wac" herein indicates the female servicemember herself, as opposed to "WAC," which indicates the service branch.

48. Barsis, *They're All Yours, Uncle Sam!* (New York: Stephan Daye, 1943), n.p.

49. Barbara E. Bristol, *Meet Molly Marine* (N.p.: Robert J. Weaver, 1945), n.p.

50. Vic Herman, *Winnie the WAC* (Philadelphia, PA: David McKay, 1945), n.p.

51. John Sheppard, *Incoming! Military Cartoons* (Hoschton, GA: ShepArt Studios, 2007–2011), 94.

52. Bruce Bairnsfather, *The Best of Fragments from France*, ed. Tonie Holt and Valmai Holt (South Yorkshire, UK: Pen and Sword Military, 1998), 115.

53. Wallgren, "SK IN HOSP (IN LINE OF BEAUTY)," *The Stars and Stripes*, April 19, 1918, 7.

54. A. Rule, "'In Blighty!' A Thing We Dream About," *Shell Shocks: By the New Zealanders in France* (London: Jarrold and Sons, 1916), 29.

55. Grant, *Stand-By One*, n.p.

56. Herman, *Winnie the WAC*, n.p.

57. Jenny Nicholson and David Langdon, *Kiss the Girls Goodbye* (London: Hutchinson, c. 1944), 73.

58. Sgt. Ozzie St. George cartoon in *Yank* 4, no. 28 (December 28, 1945): 23 (reprinted in *The Best of YANK The Army Weekly*, ed. Ira Topping [New York: Arno, 1980]).

59. Leonard Sansone, *The Wolf* (New York: United, 1945).

60. Dave Breger, *Private Breger in Britain* (London, UK: Pilot, 1944), 61.

61. Hank Ketcham, *Half Hitch* (Greenwich, CT: Fawcett, 1970), n.p.

62. *Power Point Ranger* Facebook page discussion thread, January 15, 2014, https://www.facebook.com/Powerpointranger.

63. John F. Holmes, *Power Point Ranger, Vol. 1* (New York: World Audience, 2012), 31.

64. John Holmes, *Power Point Ranger* online, https://www.facebook.com/photo.php?fbid=68625 1994231140&set=a.686251228064550.1073741851.113256155364063&type=3&theater.

65. Meredith Clark, "Landmark Year for Military Sex Assault Reform Ends with Spike in Reports," MSNBC.com, December 28, 2013/January 12, 2014, http://www.msnbc.com/melissa-harris-perry/big-jump-reports-military-sex-assault (accessed February 10, 2014).

66. Holmes, *Power Point Ranger*, 33. Also see: Holmes, *Power Point Ranger* online, https://www.facebook.com/photo.php?fbid=686251861397820&set=a.686251228064550.1073741851.1132561553 64063&type=3&theater.

67. See: Brian Adam Jones, "The Sexist Facebook Movement the Marine Corps Can't Stop," *Task and Purpose*, August 20, 2014: http://taskandpurpose.com/sexist-facebook-movement-marine-corps-cant-stop/.

68. A.J. Merrifield, *Bob on the FOB*, https://www.facebook.com/photo.php?fbid=10151506427 809860&set=pb.44533969859.-2207520000.1391 800599.&type=3&theater.

69. Jeff Bacon, *20 Years of Broadside* (Garden City, ID: Deep Water, 2006), 70.

70. Jeffrey Hall, *Downrange*, "Mail," http://www.military.com/cartooncontent/0,14763,Downrange_060830,00.html.

71. See: Eddie Campbell, ed., *P.S Magazine: The Best of the Preventative Maintenance Monthly* (New York: Abrams ComicArts, 2011); Department of the Army, *Troubleshooting Equipment in Combat Units* (Washington, D.C.: U.S. Government Printing Office, 1973); Will Eisner, *The M561/M792 GAMA Goat: Operation and Preventative Maintenance* (Department of the Army, n.d.).

72. Shel Silverstein, *Grab Your* Socks (New York: Ballantine, 1956), 22–3. Also: Jack Niles and Jim Dye, *Mox Nix: Cartoons About Your Tour in Europe* (Kassel, Germany: Hessische Druck and Verlogsonstalt, 1952, 43.

73. Silverstein, *Grab Your Socks*, 84.

74. Silverstein, *Grab Your Socks*, 98. Also: Holmes, *Power Point Ranger* online, http://www.pptranger.net/comics/2012–08–14-climb_to_glory; Fred Levi, "Sailors on dock with girls—copied from postcard," National Museum of American Jewish Military History, http://nmajmh.pastperfect-online.com/34213cgi/mweb.exe?request=record;id=7A3D5B4C-D21C-4054-AF00-578601797908;type=101.

75. Cpl. Troelstrup Clark, FEN cartoon featured in *Out of Line: A Collection of Cartoons from Pacific Stars and Stripes* (Tokyo: Toppon, 1952), n.p.

76. Sgt. Ted Miller cartoon in *Yank* 3, no. 41 (March 30, 1945): 24 (reprinted in *The Best of YANK The Army Weekly*, ed. Ira Topping [New York: Arno, 1980]). Also, Bristol, *Meet Molly Marine*, n.p.

77. Grant, *Stand-By One*, n.p. Also, Nordstrom cartoon featured in *Out of Line: A Collection of Cartoons from Pacific Stars and Stripes* (Tokyo: Toppon, 1952), n.p.

78. See discussion in: Maximilian Uriarte, *Terminal Lance: #1–100 Compilation* (Korea: Veterans Expeditionary Media, 2011), 36

79. Ibid., 95–7.

80. Anonymous, *The Further Adventures of Doctrine Man!! Vol. 1* (Lexington, KY: Doctrine Man, 2013), 78.

81. Westbrook, "I Want a Girl." Also see: Elkin, "Aggressive and Erotic Tendencies in Army Life."

82. John D'Emilio and Estelle Freedman, *Intimate Matters: A History of Sexuality in America* 3rd ed. (Chicago, IL: University of Chicago Press, 2012; Kindle e-book).

83. Elkin, "Aggressive and Erotic Tendencies in Army Life."

84. Silverstein, *Grab Your Socks*, 4.

85. Barsis, *They're All Yours*, n.p.

86. Jeff Bacon, *The Best of Broadside: A Humorous Look at Life in the Navy* (Newport News, VA: Deep Water, 1992), n.p.

87. Wingert, *Hubert*, 29.

88. John Holmes, *FM 2.0 Field Expedient Practical Joking: Power Point Ranger Comics 171–340* (NP: Amazon Digital Services, 2014; Kindle e-book), loc. 8.

89. Holmes, *Power Point Ranger* online, http://www.pptranger.net/comics/2012–11–10-usmc_birthday.

90. John Holmes, *FM 1.0 Counter Boredom Operations: Power Point Ranger Comics 1–170* (N.p.: Amazon Digital Services, 2014; Kindle e-book), loc. 6.

91. Unknown, *Dignity and Respect: A Training Guide on Homosexual Conduct Policy* (Washington, D.C.: Department of the Army, 2001).

92. Anonymous, *Doctrine Man Vol. 1*, 59.

93. Manning leaked hundreds of thousands of classified documents while serving in the U.S. Army. A closeted gay man under the Don't Ask, Don't Tell policy, while serving his sentence for espionage, Manning declared himself to be a female who would undergo hormone therapy as soon as possible. For additional background on the case, see, for example, Adam Gabbatt, "'I am Chelsea Manning,' Says Jailed Solider Formerly Known as Bradley," *The Guardian*, August 22, 2013, http://www.theguardian.com/world/2013/aug/22/bradley-manning-woman-chelsea-gender-reassignment (accessed February 17, 2014).

94. Mickey Weems, "Taser to the 'Nads: Brutal Embrace of Queerness in Military Practice," in *Warrior Ways: Explorations in Modern Military Folklore*, ed. Eric A. Eliason and Tad Tuleja (Boulder, CO: Utah State University Press, 2012), 139–60.

95. See: Cherrie B. Boyer, Mary-Ann B. Shafer, Richard A. Shaffer, Stephanie K. Brodine, Stanley I. Ito, Debra L. Yniguez, Dana M. Benas, and Julius Schachter, "Prevention of Sexually Transmitted Diseases and HIV in Young Military Men: Evaluation of a Cognitive-Behavioral Skills-Building Intervention," *Sexually Transmitted Diseases* 28, no. 6 (2001): 349–55; John D. Malone, Kenneth C. Hyams, Richard E. Hawkins, Trueman W. Sharp, and Fredric D. Daniell, "Risk Factors for Sexually-Transmitted Diseases Among Deployed U.S. Military Personnel," *Sexually Transmitted Diseases* 20, no. 5 (1993): 294–8.

96. For examples, see: Percy L. Crosby, *That Rookie from the 13th Squad* (New York: Harper and Brothers, 1918); Kirkland H. Day, *Camion Cartoons* (Boston, MA: Marshall Jones, 1919); Ted Stanley, *Perils of a Private: Sketches of Camp Life* (Boston, MA: Small, Maynard, 1918).

97. Fred D. Baldwin, "No Sex, Please, We're American," *HistoryClub*, April 29, 2014: http://history.scout.com/story/1387336-no-sex-please-were-american?s=155.

98. The National Archives, "Propaganda: Home Front," *The Art of War*, of http://www.national archives.gov.uk/theartofwar/prop/home_front/INF3_0229.htm.

99. Pvt. Ralph Stein cartoon in *Yank* 1, no. 1 (June 17, 1942): 17 (reprinted in *The Best of YANK The Army Weekly*, ed. Ira Topping [New York: Arno, 1980]).

100. Pvt. F.A. Bernard cartoon in *Yank* 1, no. 39 (March 19, 1943): 22 (reprinted in *The Best of YANK The Army Weekly*, ed. Ira Topping [New York: Arno, 1980]).

101. George Baker, *The Sad Sack* (New York: Simon and Schuster, 1944), "Sex Hygiene."

102. George Baker, *The New Sad Sack* (New York: Simon and Schuster, 1946), "Dream."

103. Ibid., "The Worm Turns, Reluctantly."

104. Unknown, *Let There Be Light*, National

Museum of American Jewish Military History, http://nmajmh.pastperfect-online.com/34213cgi/mweb.exe?request=record;id=A79E7004–8B9B-44C2-BA54–427539373183;type=101.

105. "Speaking of Pictures.... GI's Blowzy Frauleins Hurt Germans' Feelings," *Life Magazine*, June 17, 1946, 12–3; "Drawing from Experience," *Stars and Stripes*, 50th Anniversary Special Edition, April 18, 1992, 32–33.

106. Niles and Dye, *Mox Nix*, 15.

107. Norval Eugene Packwood, *Leatherhead: The Story of Marine Corps Boot Camp* (Quantico, VA: Marine Corps Association, 1951), 90.

108. Grant, *Stand-By One*, n.p.

109. Eric Thibodeau, http://ericthibodeau.com/uss_missouri.htm.

110. Mort Walker, *The Lexicon of Comicana* (Lincoln, NE: iUniverse.com, 2000), 28–9.

111. Anonymous, *Doctrine Man Vol. 1*, 23.

112. Uriarte, *Terminal Lance*, 89.

113. Anonymous, *Doctrine Man Vol. 1*, 67, 69, 88 and 150.

114. Pvt. SQW cartoon in *Yank* 2, no. 1 (June 25, 1943): 18 (reprinted in *The Best of YANK The Army Weekly*, ed. Ira Topping [New York: Arno, 1980]).

115. Holmes, *Power Point Ranger* online, https://www.facebook.com/photo.php?fbid=693041387385534&set=a.681933538496319.1073741849.113256155364063&type=1&theater.

116. Herman, *Winnie the WAC*, n.p.

117. Sgt. Frank Miller cartoon featured in *Out of Line: A Collection of Cartoons from Pacific Stars and Stripes* (Tokyo:, 1952), n.p.

118. Holmes, *Power Point Ranger*, 61.

119. Anonymous, *Doctrine Man Vol. 1*, 79.

120. Ibid., 33 and 114.

121. Anonymous, *Doctrine Man Vol. 1*, 31; Anonymous, *The Further Adventures of Doctrine Man!! Vol. 2* (San Bernardino, CA: Doctrine Man, 2013), 46.

122. Bouhammer, "And You Thought I Was Lying About Man-Love Thursdays," *Bouhammer's Blog*, January 28, 2010, http://www.bouhammer.com/2010/01/and-you-thought-i-was-lying-about-man-love-thursdays/ (accessed December 29, 2013); Bouhammer, "Their Thursday Night Is Our Saturday Night. *Bouhammer's Afghan and Military Blog*, July 18, 2006, http://www.bouhammer.com/2006/07/their-thursday-night-is-our-saturday-night/ (accessed December 29, 2013); Fox News, "Afghan Men Struggle with Sexual Identity, Study Finds," FoxNews.com, January 28, 2010, http://www.foxnews.com/politics/2010/01/28/afghan-men-struggle-sexual-identity-study-finds/ (accessed December 29, 2013).

123. Crosby, *That Rookie*.

124. Al Summers cartoon in: *Out of Line: A Collection of Cartoons from Pacific Stars and Stripes* (Tokyo: Toppon, 1952), n.p.

125. Merrifield, *Bob on the FOB*, http://simhq.com/forum/files/usergals/2011/02/full-881–5994–36717_409217654859_44533969859_4277224_3431957_n.jpg. (Note: General Order Number 1 delineates prohibited activities for soldiers. "FOB" is short for Forward Operating Base.)

126. Uriarte, *Terminal Lance*, 76.

127. Mark Baker, *Private Murphy's Law* (Baltimore, MD: United Books, 1999), 92–3; Mark Baker, *PV-2 Murphy the Adventure Continues: A "Pvt. Murphy's Law" Collection* (Baltimore, MD: United Books, 2001), 88; Mark Baker, *Pfc. Murphy: Private Murphy's Law Book* (Baltimore, MD: United Books, 2005), 49; Holmes, *Power Point Ranger*, 41.

128. Uriarte, *Terminal Lance*, 61. Also: Maximillian Uriarte, *Terminal Lance* online, http://terminallance.com/2010/08/06/terminal-lance-56-myths-and-legends-ii-the-dependapotamus/.

129. Baker, *Sad Sack*, "Impressed."

130. Mauldin, *Willie and Joe*, 291.

131. Wingert, *Hubert*, 52.

132. Bill Hume and John Annarino, *Babysan: A Private Look at the Japanese Occupation* (Tokyo: Kasuga Boeki, 1953), 31, 35, 57, 83 and 95.

133. Holmes, *Power Point Ranger*, 44.

134. Holmes, *Power Point Ranger* online, http://www.pptranger.net/comics/2012–07–25-barracks_rat_trap. Note: "Barracks rat" is part of Marine Corps slang and refers to a woman with a reputation for dating multiple Marines.

135. Holmes, *Power Point Ranger*, 67. Also see: Holmes, *Power Point Ranger* online, http://www.pptranger.net/comics/2011–08–14–2330_hours.

136. Mark Baker, *Sgt. Murphy: A "Pvt. Murphy's Law" Collection* (Alexandria, VA: Byrrd, 2008), n.p.

137. Anonymous, *Doctrine Man Vol. 2*, 72.

138. Anonymous, *Doctrine Man* online, https://www.facebook.com/photo.php?fbid=727983493901471&set=a.169913026375190.35223.110598432306650&type=1&theater.

139. Julie L. Negron, *PCSing.... It's a Spouse Thing!: The First Few Years of "Jenny, The Military Spouse," A Comic Strip for, by and about Life as a Military Spouse* (N.p.: Lulu/JulieNegron, 2005–2010), n.p. Note: The 20-percent figure referenced in the comic likely refers to the women in the U.S. Air Force, as *Jenny* is an Air Force–focused comic. The overall percentage of women in active duty service in the American military is closer to 15 percent. See: CNN Staff, "By the Numbers: Women in the U.S. Military," CNN.com, January 24, 2013, http://www.cnn.com/2013/01/24/us/military-women-glance/ (accessed February 28, 2014).

140. Holmes, *Power Point Ranger* online, https://www.facebook.com/photo.php?fbid=686251651397841&set=a.686251228064550.1073741851.113256155364063&type=3&theater.

141. Meyer, *Creating GI Jane*.

142. See: Amy Bushatz, "Top Ten MilSpouse Stereotypes We Hate the Most," SpouseBuzz.com, August 16, 2014, http://spousebuzz.com/blog/2014/08/top-10-military-spouse-stereotypes-we-hate-the-most.html (accessed August 26, 2014); Guest Bloggers, "Top 10 Worst ManSpouse Stereotypes," SpouseBuzz.com, August 30, 2014, http://spousebuzz.com/blog/2014/08/top-10-male-military-spouse-stereotypes-we-hate-the-most.html (accessed October 2, 2014).

143. Packwood, *Leatherhead*, 40.

144. Bairnsfather, *Best of Fragments from France*, 110. This strip also does a pun on gunpowder and

women's powder, further suggesting the irony in the idea of women soldiers.

145. Herman, *Winnie the WAC*, n.p.

146. As seen in images available in an eBay listing, http://www.ebay.com/itm/VINTAGE-HELLO-BUDDY-COMICS-OF-WAR-FACTS-OF-SERVICES-BY-SERVICE-MENS-MAGAZINE-/400360196067.

147. Mildred McAfee Horton, "Women in the United States Navy," *American Journal of Sociology* 51, no. 5 (1946): 449.

148. Sgt. Irwin Caplan cartoon in *Yank* (July 7, 1944), 24 (reprinted in *The Best of YANK The Army Weekly*, ed. Ira Topping [New York: Arno, 1980]).

149. Herman, *Winnie the WAC*, n.p.

150. Wingert, *Hubert*, 36.

151. Steve Opet, *Opet's Odyssey*, https://www.facebook.com/photo.php?fbid=154764731251066&set=a.154761024584770.32717.137174599676746&type=3&theater.

152. Holmes, *Power Point Ranger* online, https://www.facebook.com/photo.php?fbid=68625165 8064507&set=a.686251228064550.1073741851.113 256155364063&type=3&theater.

153. Holmes, *Power Point Ranger* online, https://www.facebook.com/photo.php?fbid=6862543113 97575&set=a.686251228064550.1073741851.1132 56155364063&type=3&theater.

154. Helene Cooper, "Army's Ban on Some Popular Hairstyles Raises Ire of Black Female Soldiers," *New York Times*, April 20, 2014, http://www.nytimes.com/2014/04/21/us/politics/armys-ban-on-some-popular-hairstyles-raises-ire-of-black-female-soldiers.html (accessed October 11, 2014).

155. Weatherford, *American Women and World War II*.

156. Dorothea Byerly, *Up Came a Ripple* (East Orange, NJ: Greenwood, 1945), n.p.

157. Opet, *Opet's Odyssey*, https://www.facebook.com/photo.php?fbid=154762474584625&set=a.154761024584770.32717.137174599676746&type=3&theater.

158. Stars and Stripes, "Military's Progress on Women in Combat Criticized," Military.com, January 31, 2014, http://www.military.com/daily-news/2014/01/31/militarys-progress-on-women-in-combat-criticized.html (accessed February 2, 2014).

159. Opet, *Opet's Odyssey*, https://www.facebook.com/photo.php?fbid=154761817918024&set=a.154761024584770.32717.137174599676746&type=3&theater.

160. Browder, *Her Best Shot*, 12.

161. Herman, *Winnie the WAC*, n.p.

162. Vernon Grant, "Grant's Grunts," *Pacific Stars and Stripes*, March 16, 1969, 16.

163. Sheppard, *Incoming*, 19.

164. Holmes, *Power Point Ranger*, 21.

165. Holmes, *Power Point Ranger* online, https://www.facebook.com/photo.php?fbid=686254374 730902&set=a.686251228064550.1073741851.113256155364063&type=3&theater.

166. Weatherford, *American Women and World War II*.

167. Herman, *Winnie the WAC*, n.p.; Sansone, *The Wolf*, n.p.

168. Bristol, *Meet Molly Marine*.

169. Holmes, *Power Point Ranger*, 77.

170. Bacon, *20 Years of Broadside*, 90.

171. Sheppard, *Incoming*, 16.

172. In: Robert E. Bronner, *The Soldier's Pen* (New York: Hill and Wang, 2006), 171.

173. In: Paula E. Calvin and Deborah A. Deacon, *American Women Artists in Wartime, 1776–2010* (Jefferson, NC: McFarland, 2011), 171.

174. Baker, *Pfc. Murphy*, 91 and 92.

175. Hall, *Downrange*, "Mortal Combat," http://www.military.com/cartooncontent/0,14763,Down range_070605,00.html.

176. Kevin Klien and Todd M. Hoelmer, *Pvt. Joe Snuffy Goes Guard!* (Washington, D.C.: National Guard Bureau, 1991), n.p.

177. In: Jessica Harrison-Hall, *Vietnam Behind the Lines: Images from the War, 1965–1975* (Chicago, IL: Art Media Resources, 2002).

178. In fact, the repeal of Don't Ask, Don't Tell in the U.S. military appears to be both accepted and embraced. See: Travis J. Tritten, "Gay, Lesbian Troops Perform in Drag at Kadena Air Base Fundraiser," *Stars and Stripes*, March 2, 2014, http://www.stripes.com/news/gay-lesbian-troops-perform-in-drag-at-kadena-air-base-fundraiser-1.270747 (accessed March 3, 2014).

179. Weida, "Wonder(ing) Women."

Chapter 7

1. Tarak Barkawi, "Culture and Combat in the Colonies: The Indian Army in the Second World War," *Journal of Contemporary History* 41, no. 2 (2006): 325–55; Josie McLellan, "'I Wanted to Be a Little Lenin': Ideology and the German International Brigade Volunteers," *Journal of Contemporary History* 41, no. 2 (2006): 287–304; Catherine Merridale, "Culture, Ideology and Combat in the Red Army, 1939–45," *Journal of Contemporary History* 41, no. 2 (2006): 305–24; Antonius C.G.M. Robben, "Combat Motivation, Fear and Terror in Twentieth-Century Argentinian Warfare," *Journal of Contemporary History* 41, no. 2 (2006): 357–77; Samuel A. Stouffer, Arthur A. Lumsdaine, Marion H. Lumsdaine, Robin M. Williams, Jr., M. Brewster Smith. Irving L. Janis, Shirley A. Star, and Leonard S. Cottrell, Jr., *The American Soldier: Combat and Its Aftermath* (New York: Science Editions, 1965); Samuel A. Stouffer, A.A. Lumsdaine, M.H. Lumsdaine, R.M. Williams, Jr., M.B. Smith, I.L. Janis, S.A. Star, and L.S. Cottrell, Jr., *The American Soldier: Combat and Its Aftermath*, Vol. 2 (New York: John Wiley and Sons, 1949).

2. Glen H. Elder, Jr., and Elizabeth Colerick Clipp, "Combat Experience and Emotional Health: Impairment and Resilience in Later Life," *Journal of Personality* 57, no. 2 (1989): 311–41.

3. Robert Fulton, "Death and the Funeral in Contemporary Society," in *Dying: Facing the Facts*, ed. Hannelore Wass (New York: McGraw-Hill, 1979), 236–55; David G. Mandelbaum, "Social Uses of Funeral Rites," in *The Meaning of Death*, ed. Herman Feifel. (New York: McGraw-Hill, 1959), 189–217.

4. Judith Butler, *Precarious Life: The Power of Mourning and Violence* (London, UK: Verso, 2004).

5. Marcia Lattanzi and Mary Ellis Hale, "Giving Grief Words: Writing During Bereavement," *Omega* 15, no. 1 (1984–1985): 45–52; Jan Plecash, "Speaking of Death: Remembrance and Lamentation," in *Spectacular Death: Interdisciplinary Perspectives on Mortality and (Un)Representation*, ed. T. Connolly (Bristol, UK: Intellect, 2011), 97–122. Also, for discussion of recognizing "life" and its susceptibility to violence, see: Judith Butler, *Frames of War: When Is Life Grievable?* (London, UK: Verso, 2009).

6. Eyal Ben-Ari, "Epilogue: A 'Good' Military Death," *Armed Forces and Society* 31, no. 4(2005): 655. Also see discussion of dying for one's country in: Elaine Scarry, *The Body in Pain* (New York: Oxford University Press, 1985).

7. Mike Featherstone, "The Heroic Life and Everyday Life," *Theory, Culture, and Society* 9, no. 1 (1992): 159–82.

8. Ira Byock, *Dying Well: Peace and Possibilities at the End of Life* (New York: Riverhead, 1998); Clive Seale, "Heroic Death," *Sociology* 29 (1995): 587–613; Jack B. Kamerman, *Death in the Midst of Life* (Englewood Cliffs, NJ: Prentice Hall, 1988).

9. Carolyn Marvin and David W. Ingle, *Blood Sacrifice and the Nation: Totem Rituals and the American Flag* (New York: Cambridge University Press, 1999); Ben-Ari, "Epilogue"; Butler, *Precarious Life*.

10. Jon Davies, "War Memorials," in *The Sociology of Death*, ed. David Clark (Oxford, UK: Blackwell, 1993), 113.

11. Ben-Ari, "Epilogue."

12. Ben-Ari, "Epilogue"; Davies, "War Memorials"; Kamerman, *Death in the Midst of Life*; Seale, "Heroic Death."

13. Brigadier J. Nazareth, *The Psychology of Military Humour* (Olympia Fields, IL: Lancer, 2008).

14. Tanya Biank, *Army Wives* (New York: St. Martin's Griffin, 2006).

15. Alex Watson, "Self-Deception and Survival: Mental Coping Strategies on the Western Front, 1914–18," *Journal of Popular History* 41, no. 2 (2006): 247–68.

16. Antonin J. Obrdlik, "'Gallows Humor': A Sociological Phenomenon," *American Journal of Sociology* 47, no. 5 (1942): 709–16.

17. C.J. Chivers, "In Wider War in Afghanistan, Survival Rate of Wounded Rises," *New York Times*, January 8, 2011: A1.

18. Robert S. Laufer, M.S. Gallops, and Ellen Frey-Wouters, "War Stress and Trauma: The Vietnam Veteran Experience," *Journal of Health and Social Behavior* 25, no. 1 (1984): 65–85; Simon Wessely, "Twentieth-century Theories on Combat Motivation and Breakdown," *Journal of Contemporary History* 41, no. 2 (2006): 269–86.

19. Hew Strachan, "Training, Morale and Modern War," *Journal of Contemporary History* 41, no. 2 (2006): 211–27.

20. Edgar Jones, "The Psychology of Killing: The Combat Experience of British Soldiers During the First World War," *Journal of Contemporary History* 41, no. 2 (2006): 229–46.

21. Paul Achter, "Unruly Bodies: The Rhetorical Domestication of Twenty-First-Century Veterans of War," *Quarterly Journal of Speech* 96, no. 1 (2010): 46–68.

22. Ana Carden-Coyne, "Ungrateful Bodies: Rehabilitation, Resistance and Disabled American Veterans of the First World War," *European Review of History* 14, no. 4 (2007): 543–65.

23. Crosby Hipes, "The Framing of PTSD: Narratives of Mental Health Workers and Veterans" (master's thesis, University of Arkansas, 2009).

24. Bill Briggs, "Vets, Docs Worry Fort Hood Shootings Will Deepen PTSD Stigma," NBCNews.com, April 3, 2014, http://www.nbcnews.com/storyline/fort-hood-shooting/vets-docs-worry-fort-hood-shootings-will-deepen-ptsd-stigma-n71046 (accessed April 15, 2014); Kate Hoit, "The 'Dangerous' Veteran: An Inaccurate Media Narrative Takes Hold," *Vantage Point: Dispatches from the U.S. Department of Veterans Affairs*, March 6, 2012, http://www.blogs.va.gov/VAntage/6026/the-"dangerous"-veteran-an-inaccurate-media-narrative-takes-hold/ (accessed June 28, 2014).

25. Geoffrey Gorer, *Death, Grief, and Mourning* (New York: Doubleday, 1965); Michael C. Kearl, "Death in Popular Culture," in *Death: Current Perspectives*, ed. John B. Williamson and Edwin S. Shneidman (Mountain View, CA: Mayfield, 1995), 23–30; Arthur Asa Berger, *The Comic-Stripped American: What Dick Tracy, Blondie, Daddy Warbucks, and Charlie Brown Tell Us About Ourselves* (New York: Walker, 1972); Gerhart Saenger, "Male and Female Relations in the American Comic Strip," in *The Funnies: An American Idiom*, ed. David M. White and Robert H. Abel (New York: Free Press, 1963), 219–31.

26. José Alaniz, "Death and the Superhero: The Silver Age and Beyond," *International Journal of Comic Art* 8, no. 1 (2006): 234–48.

27. Shawn Gillen, "Captain America, Post-Traumatic Stress Syndrome, and the Vietnam Era," in *Captain America and the Struggle of the Superhero: Critical Essays*, ed. Robert G. Weiner (Jefferson, NC: McFarland, 2009), 104–15.

28. Sarah Brabant, "Death and Grief in the Family Comics," *Omega* 36, no. 1 (1997–98): 33–44; Wilbur Farley, "'The Disease Resumes Its March to Darkness': The Death of Captain Marvel and the Metastasis of Empire," *International Journal of Comic Art* 8, no. 1 (2006): 249–57.

29. Jay Casey, "The Dynamics of Quiet Heroism and Invisible Death in American Soldier Cartoons of the World Wars," *International Journal of Comic Art* 9, no. 1 (2007): 281–95.

30. Casey, "The Dynamics of Quiet Heroism."

31. In: Frank Brandt, ed., *Cartoons for Fighters* (Washington, D.C.: Infantry Journal, 1945).

32. In: Harry L. Katz and Vincent Virga, *Civil War Sketch Book: Drawings from the Battlefront* (New York: W.W. Norton, 2012), 137, 140, and 170.

33. Charles Johnson Post, *The Little War of Private Post: The Spanish-American War Seen Up Close* (Lincoln, NE: University of Nebraska Press, 1999), 53, 148, and 212.

34. Douglas G. Ward, *Topical Sketches* (Irvin Department of Rare Books and Special Collections,

Digital Collections: http://library.sc.edu/digital/collections/rts.html 1915–1916), 66.

35. Dave Breger, *Private Breger in Britain* (London, UK: Pilot, 1944), 71.

36. Norval Eugene Packwood, *Leatherhead: The Story of Marine Corps Boot Camp* (Quantico, VA: Marine Corps Association, 1951), 77.

37. John Sheppard, *Incoming! Military Cartoons* (Hoschton, GA: ShepArt Studios, 2007–2011), 8.

38. Jeff Bacon, *The Best of Broadside: A Humorous Look at Life in the Navy* (Newport News, VA: Deep Water, 1992), n.p.

39. Alban B. Butler, Jr., *"Happy Days!" A Humorous Narrative in Drawings of the Progress of American Arms, 1917–1919* (Chicago, IL: First Division Museum at Cantigny, 2011), 37.

40. Ibid., 36.

41. Ibid., 39.

42. Ibid., 29.

43. In: Mark Bryant, *World War I in Cartoons* (London, UK: Grubb Street, 2009), 125.

44. Bruce Bairnsfather, *Carry On Sergeant* (Indianapolis, IN: Bobbs-Merrill, 1927), 122.

45. Bruce Bairnsfather, *The Best of Fragments from France*, ed. Tonie Holt and Valmai Holt (South Yorkshire, UK: Pen and Sword Military, 1998), 8–9.

46. Ibid., 11.

47. Ibid., 21.

48. Ibid., 73.

49. Ibid., 72.

50. Frank Dunne, *Digger Days*, Australian War Memorial, http://trove.nla.gov.au/version/44131579.

51. Bill Mauldin, *Willie and Joe the World War II Years*, ed. Todd DePastino (Seattle, WA: Fantagraphics, 2011), 525.

52. Ibid., 450.

53. John Holmes, *FM 3.0 Secret Squirrel Stuff, Power Point Ranger Comics 341–510* (N.p.: Amazon Digital Services, 2014; Kindle e-book), loc. 14.

54. John Holmes, *Power Point Ranger, Vol. 1* (New York: World Audience, 2012), 72.

55. Sheppard, *Incoming*, 9.

56. Mauldin, *Willie and Joe*, 203.

57. In: Robert E. Bronner, *The Soldier's Pen* (New York: Hill and Wang, 2006), 93.

58. Cecil L. Hartt, *Humorosities by an Australian Soldier* (London, EC: Australian Trading and Agencies, n.d.), n.p.

59. Tom Zibelli cartoon in *Yank* 2, no. 14 (September 24, 1943): 24 (reprinted in *The Best of YANK The Army Weekly*, ed. Ira Topping [New York: Arno, 1980]).

60. In: Mark Bryant, *World War II in Cartoons* (London, UK: W.H. Smith, 1989), 113.

61. Vernon Grant, "Grant's Grunts," *Pacific Stars and Stripes*, March 9, 1969: 16.

62. Sheppard, *Incoming*, 14.

63. Perce Pearce, *Seaman Si* (N.p.: Great Lakes Bulletin, 1918), 32.

64. Mark Baker, *Private Murphy's Law* (Baltimore, MD: United Books, 1999), 44, 45, 46, 47, 48, 49, and 56.

65. In: Jason Chudy, "Reservist's Cartoons Detail Burdens of Desert Deployment," *Stars and Stripes*, August 9, 2004, http://www.stripes.com/news/reservist-s-cartoons-detail-burdens-of-desert-deployment-1.22605.

66. Holmes, *Power Point Ranger*, 80.

67. In: Bronner, *The Soldier's Pen*, 94.

68. In: Katz and Virga, *Civil War Sketch Book*, 135.

69. Tad Foster, *The Vietnam Funny Book: An Antidote to Insanity* (Novato, CA: Presidio, 1980), "The 'Dear John' Saga."

70. For example: Walter Mansfield cartoon in cartoon in *Yank* 3, no. 42 (April 26, 1945): 24 (reprinted in *The Best of YANK The Army Weekly*, ed. Ira Topping [New York: Arno, 1980]).

71. Jack Coggins, "Death of an Army," *Yank Magaine British Edition* 3, no. 13 (September 10, 1944): 11.

72. Howard Brodie illustration in cartoon in *Yank* 1, no. 39 (March 19, 1943): 9 (reprinted in *The Best of YANK The Army Weekly*, ed. Ira Topping [New York: Arno, 1980]).

73. Bairnsfather, *Best of Fragments from France*, 46–47.

74. Post, *Little War*, 212–13.

75. Bairnsfather, *Best of Fragments from France*, 122.

76. Jack Coggins, "Twelve Months Under Fire," *Yank Magazine British Edition* 2, no. 1 (June 20, 1943): 9.

77. Jessica Harrison-Hall, *Vietnam Behind the Lines: Images from the War, 1965–1975* (Chicago, IL: Art Media Resources, 2002), 81.

78. In: Mark Bryant, *Napoleonic Wars in Cartoons* (London, UK: Grubb Street, 2009), 158.

79. In: Tran Da Tu, *Writers and Artists in Vietnamese Gulags with Choé's Cartoons from Vietnam* (Washington, D.C.: Century, 1990), 26.

80. Butler, *Happy Days*, 21.

81. In: Alexander Woolcott, *The Command Is Forward—Tales of the A.E.F. Battlefields as They Appeared in The Stars and Stripes* (New York: Century, 1919), 142.

82. Ibid., 170/171.

83. Brodie cartoon in *Yank* 1, no. 39 (March 19, 1943): 10 (reprinted in *The Best of YANK The Army Weekly*, ed. Ira Topping [New York: Arno, 1980]).

84. John Holmes, *Power Point Ranger* online, http://www.pptranger.net/comics/2012–10–29-old_guard.

85. Holmes, *Power Point Ranger* online, http://www.pptranger.net/comics/2012–05–25-what_price_pptx.

86. See: Roman Rosenbaum, "Mizuki Shigeru's Pacific War," *International Journal of Comic Art* 10, no. 2 (2008): 362.

87. Butler, *Happy Days*, 105.

88. Holmes, *Power Point Ranger* online, https://www.facebook.com/photo.php?fbid=756145481075124&set=a.113279995361679.11895.113256155364063&type=1&theater.

89. Ann Jones, *They Were Soldiers: How the Wounded Return from America's Wars—the Untold Story* (Chicago, IL: Haymarket, 2013; Kindle e-book), loc. 90.

90. Post, *Little War*, 244/245.

91. Mauldin, *Willie and Joe*, 432.

92. W.C. Pope, *Pope's Puns*, "Tell My Mother,"

http://www.military.com/cartooncontent/0,14
763,Pope_111705,00.html.

93. Norval Eugene Packwood, *Leatherhead in Korea* (Quantico, VA: Marine Corps Gazette, 1952), 76.

94. Foster, *Vietnam Funny Book*, "The Trigger Finger and the Freedom Bird."

95. Ibid., "Corpsman, Medic, Doc."

96. U.S. Department of Veterans Affairs, "Symptoms of PTSD," *PTSD: National Center for PTSD*, January 3, 2014, http://www.ptsd.va.gov/public/PTSD-overview/basics/symptoms_of_ptsd.asp.

97. Holmes, *Power Point Ranger* online, http://www.pptranger.net/comics/2011–10–10-empathy_rhymes_with_stupidity.

98. Bairnsfather, *Best of Fragments from France*, 12.

99. Ibid., 32.

100. Abian A. Wallgren *Wally: His Cartoons of the A.E.F.* (N.p.: Stars and Stripes, 1919), "Bomb, Shell, and Shrapnel."

101. Maximilian Uriarte, *Terminal Lance Head Call: The First 100 MarineTimes Strips* (N.p.: Amazon Digital Services, 2013; Kindle e-book), loc. 594.

102. Bob Stevens, *"There I Was..." Flat on my Back* (Fallbrook, CA: Aero, 1975), 145.

103. Jake Schuffert, *"No Sweat" ... More 'n More* (Washington, D.C.: Army Times, 1970), 117.

104. Vernon Grant, "Grant's Grunts," *Pacific Stars and Stripes*, March 9, 1969, 16.

105. Holmes, *Power Point Ranger*, 93.

106. Bairnsfather, *Best of Fragments from France*, 114.

107. Vernon Grant, "Grant's Grunts," *Pacific Stars and Stripes*, March 16, 1969, 16.

108. Anonymous, *The Further Adventures of Doctrine Man!! Vol. 1* (Lexington, KY: Doctrine Man, 2013), 103.

109. Wallgren, *Wally*, "Shelling is Shocking."

110. Kerry L. Knox and Robert M. Bossarte, "Suicide Prevention for Veterans and Active Duty Personnel," *American Journal of Public Health* 102, no. S1 (2012): S8-S9; B.M. Kuehn, "Military Probes Epidemic of Suicide: Mental Health Issues Remain Prevalent," *JAMA* 3014, no. 13 (2010): 1152–58.

111. Halimah Abdullah, "Despite Prevention Efforts, U.S. Military Suicides Rise," *McClatchy Newspapers*, January 15, 2010, http://www.mcclatchydc.com/2010/01/15/82471/despite-prevention-efforts-us.html (accessed July 14, 2010); Bill Briggs, "One Every 18 Hours: Military Suicide Rate Still High Despite Hard Fight to Stem Deaths," NBCNews.com, May 23, 2013, http://usnews.nbcnews.com/_news/2013/05/23/18447439-one-every-18-hours-military-suicide-rate-still-high-despite-hard-fight-to-stem-deaths (accessed November 27, 2013); Jeffrey Brown, "Condolence Letter Policy Shift Opens Conversation on Military Suicides," *PBS Newshour*, July 7, 2011, http://www.pbs.org/newshour/bb/military/july-dec11/suicides_07–07.html (accessed May 20, 2013); Mental Health America, "A Letter for EVERY Life Lost," n.d., http://www.change.org/petitions/view/a_letter_for_every_life_lost.

112. Dick Wingert, *Hubert* (London, UK: Love and Malcomson, 1944), 37.

113. Shel Silverstein, *Grab Your Socks* (New York: Ballantine, 1956), 69.

114. Shel Silverstein, *Take Ten.... A Collection of Cartoons* (Tokyo: Pacific Stars and Stripes, 1955), n.p.

115. Mauldin, *Willie and Joe*, 433.

116. Vernon Grant, *Stand-by One!* (Hong Kong: Dublin Associates, 1969), n.p.

117. See discussion in: Siri Thoresen and Lars Mehlum, "Risk Factors for Fatal Accidents and Suicides in Peacekeepers: Is There an Overlap?" *Military Medicine* 169, no. 12 (2004): 988–93.

118. In: NavStress, "Outdoor Fun Relieves Stress," August 17, 2010, http://navynavstress.com/2010/08/17/outdoor-fun-relieves-stress/.

Chapter 8

1. Daniel N. Nelson, "Definition, Diagnosis, Therapy: A Civil-Military Critique," *Defense and Security Analysis* 18, no. 2 (2002): 157–70.

2. Paul Richard Higate, "Theorizing Continuity: From Military to Civilian Life," *Armed Forces and Society* 27, no. 3 (2001): 445. Also see: Bernard Boëne, "How 'Unique' Should the Military Be? A Review of Representative Literature and Outline of a Synthetic Formulation," *European Journal of Sociology* 31, no. 1 (1990): 3–59; Peter D. Feaver, "The Civil-Military Problematique: Huntington, Janowitz, and the Question of Civilian Control," *Armed Forces and Society* 23, no. 2 (1996): 149–78.

3. Mackubin T. Owens, "U.S. Civil-Military Relations After 9/11: Renegotiating the Civil-Military Bargain," *Foreign Policy Research Institute E-Notes*, 2011: http://www.fpri.org/enotes/201101.owens.civilmilitaryrelations.html.

4. Samuel P. Huntington, *The Soldier and the State: The Theory and Politics of Civil-Military Relations* (Cambridge, MA: Belknap Press of Harvard University Press, 1957); Thomas-Durell Young, "Military Professionalism in a Democracy," in *Who Guards the Guardians and How: Democratic Civil-Military Relations*, ed. Thomas C. Bruneau and Scott D. Tollefson (Austin, TX: University of Texas Press, 2006), 17–33.

5. Ruth Jolly, *Changing Step from Military to Civilian Life: People in Transition* (London, UK: Brassey's, 1996); Justin, "'Exceptional Americans': Is the Military's Disdain for Civilians Sustainable?" *The Soldier Citizen Sapiens Project*, July 14, 2011, http://soldiercitizensapien.wordpress.com/2011/07/14/exceptional-americans-is-the-militarys-disdain-for-civilians-sustainable/ (accessed July 28, 2013); Thomas Ricks, *Making the Corps* (New York: Scribner, 1997); Thomas E. Ricks, "The Enduring Solitude of Combat Vets," *Foreign Policy*, September 3, 2010, http://ricks.foreignpolicy.com/posts/2010/09/03/the_enduring_solitude_of_combat_vets.

6. Charles Dunlap, Mackubin Owens and Richard Kohn, "The Gap," *PBS News Hour*, November 1999: http://www.pbs.org/newshour/forum/november99/civil_military.html.

7. Robert L. Goldich, "American Military Cul-

ture from Colony to Empire," *Daedalus, the Journal of the American Academy of Arts and Sciences* 140, no. 3 (2011): 58.

8. Robert M. Gates, "Lecture at Duke University (All-Volunteer Force)," *U.S. Department of Defense*, September 29, 2010, http://www.defense.gov/Spee ches/Speech.aspx?SpeechID=1508; Donna Miles, "Chairman Calls for Military Self-Examination," *Joint Chiefs of Staff Official Web Site*, January 10, 2011, http://www.jcs.mil/newsarticle.aspx?ID=499.

9. Huntington, *The Soldier and the State*.

10. John P. Hawkins, *Army of Hope, Army of Alienation* (Tuscaloosa, AL: University of Alabama Press, 2001).

11. Howard Harper, "The Military and Society: Reaching and Reflecting Audiences in Fiction and Film," *Armed Forces and Society* 27, no. 2 (2001): 231–48.

12. Krista E. Wiegand and David L. Paletz, "The Elite Media and the Military-Civilian Culture Gap," *Armed Forces and Society* 27, no. 2 (2001): 183–204.

13. Katherine Kinney, "The Good War and its Other: Beyond Private Ryan," in *War Narratives and American Culture*, ed. Giles Gunn and Carl Gutiér-rez-Jones (Santa Barbara, CA: American Cultures and Global Contexts Center, University of California, 2005), 121–38.

14. Kathy Roth-Douquet and Frank Schaeffer, *AWOL: The Unexcused Absence of America's Upper Classes from Military Service—and How it Hurts Our Country* (New York: Collins, 2007).

15. Edwin R. Micewski, "Conscription or the All-Volunteer Force: Recruitment in a Democratic Society," in *Who Guards the Guardians and How: Democratic Civil-Military Relations*, ed. Thomas C. Bruneau and Scott D. Tollefson (Austin, TX: University of Texas Press, 2006), 208–34.

16. See: Jocelyn Bartone, Jesse J. Harris, David R. Segal, and Mady Wechsler, "Lightfighters' Wives," in *Peacekeepers and Their Wives*, ed. David R. Segal and Mady Wechsler Segal (Westport, CT: Greenwood, 1993), 14–57; Chris Jessup, *Breaking Ranks: Social Change in Military Communities* (London, UK: Brassey's, 1996).

17. Mady W. Segal, "The Military and the Family as Greedy Institutions," in *The Military: More than Just a Job?*, ed. Charles C. Moskos and Frank R. Wood (Washington, D.C.: Pergamon-Brassey's, 1988), 93.

18. David E. Rohall, Mady Wechsler Segal, and David R. Segal, "Examining the Importance of Organizational Supports on Family Adjustment to Army Life in a Period of Increasing Separation," *Journal of Political and Military Sociology* 27, no. 1 (1999): 49–65.

19. Bartone, Harris, Segal and Segal, "Lightfighters' Wives."

20. Segal, "The Military and the Family." Also see: Lewis A. Coser, *Greedy Institutions: Patterns of Undivided Commitment* (New York: Free Press, 1974).

21. Lolita M. Burrell, Gary A. Adams, Doris Briley Durand, and Carl Andrew Castro, "The Impact of Military Lifestyle Demands on Well-Being, Army, and Family Outcomes," *Armed Forces and Society* 33, no. 1 (2006): 43–58; Jessup, *Braking Ranks*.

22. See, for example: Burrell, Adams, Durand and Castro, "The Impact of Military Lifestyle Demands"; Segal, "The Military and the Family."

23. Tanya Biank, *Army Wives* (New York: St. Martin's Griffin, 2006), front cover.

24. See discussion in: Janet A. Kohen, "The Military Career Is a Family Affair," *Journal of Family Issues* 5, no. 3 J. (1984): 401–18. Also see: Tanya Biank, *Army Wives* (New York: St. Martin's Griffin, 2006).

25. Erin Sahlstein, Katheryn C. Maguire, and Lindsay Timmerman, "Contradictions and Praxis Contextualized by Wartime Deployment: Wives' Perspectives Revealed Through Relational Dialectics," *Communication Monographs* 76, no. 4 (2009): 421–42; Suzanne Wood, Jacquelyn Scarville, and Katharine S. Gravino, "Waiting Wives: Separation and Reunion Among Army Wives," *Armed Forces and Society* 21, no. 2 (1995): 217–36; Defense Centers of Excellence, *A Handbook for Family and Friends of Service Members Before, During and After Deployment* (N.p.: Vulcan Productions, 2010); Bartone, Harris, Segal, and Segal, "Lightfighters' Wives."

26. Ryan Kelty, Meredith Kleykamp, and David R. Segal, "The Military and the Transition to Adulthood," *The Future of Children* 20, no. 1 (2010): 181–207.

27. Jessup, *Breaking Ranks*, 136.

28. Christina M. Knopf, "Relational Dialectics in the Civil-Military Relationship: Lessons from Veterans' Transition Narratives," *Political and Military Sociology: An Annual Review* 40 (2012): 171–92; Jolly, *Changing Step*.

29. See: Lawrence Baron, "X-Men as J-Men: The Jewish Subtext of a Comic Book Movie," *Shofar: An Interdisciplinary Journal of Jewish Studies* 22, no. 1 (2003): 44–52; Matthew Diebler, "'I'm Not One of Them' Anymore': Marvel's X-Men and the Loss of Minority (Racial) Identity," *International Journal of Comic Art* 8, no. 2 (2006): 406–13; Neil Shyminsky, "Mutant Readers, Reading Mutants: Appropriation, Assimilation, and the X-Men," *International Journal of Comic Art* 8, no. 2 (2006): 387–405.

30. See: David A. Gerber, "Heroes and Misfits: The Troubled Social Reintegration of Disabled Veterans in *The Best Years of Our Lives*," *American Quarterly* 46, no. 4 (1994): 545–74.

31. Todd DePastino, "Willie and Joe Come Home," in *Willie and Joe Back Home*, by Bill Mauldin (Seattle, WA: Fantagraphics, 2011), ix.

32. Bill Hume and John Annarino, *When We Get Back Home from Japan* (Tokyo: Kyoya, 1953), back cover.

33. Julie L. Negron, *PCSing.... It's a Spouse Thing!* (N.p.: Lulu.com/JulieNegron, 2010).

34. Tom Zibelli cartoon in *Yank* 3, no. 16 (October 6, 1944): 24 (reprinted in *The Best of YANK The Army Weekly*, ed. Ira Topping [New York: Arno, 1980]).

35. Cecil L. Hartt, *Humorosities by an Australian Soldier* (London, EC: Australian Trading and Agencies, n.d.), n.p.

36. Shel Silverstein, *Grab Your Socks* (New York: Ballantine, 1956), 96.

37. Bill Mauldin, *Willie and Joe Back Home*, ed.

Todd DePastino (Seattle, WA: Fantagraphics, 2011), 3.

38. John Sheppard, *Incoming! Military Cartoons* (Hoschton, GA: ShepArt Studios, 2007–2011), 61.

39. Daryl Talbot, *Laughing in Cadence: Dress Right Dress Military Cartoons* (Stillwater, OK: New Forums, 2009), 74.

40. Vic Herman, *Winnie the WAC* (Philadelphia, PA: David McKay, 1945), n.p.

41. Mark Baker, *Private Murphy's Law* (Baltimore, MD: United Books, 1999), 23.

42. W.C. Pope, *Pope's Puns*, "Advanced Party," http://www.military.com/cartooncontent/0,14763, Pope_121505,00.html.

43. Steve Opet, *Opet's Odyssey*, https://www.facebook.com/photo.php?fbid=154765594584313&set=a.154761024584770.32717.137174599676746&type=3&theater.

44. Dave Breger, *Private Breger in Britain* (London, UK: Pilot, 1944), 18.

45. Hugh F. Kennedy cartoon in *Yank* 2, no. 25 (December 10, 1943): 24 (reprinted in *The Best of YANK The Army Weekly*, ed. Ira Topping [New York: Arno, 1980]).

46. Joseph Kramer cartoon in *Yank* 2, no. 1 (June 25, 1943): 32 (reprinted in *The Best of YANK The Army Weekly*, ed. Ira Topping [New York: Arno, 1980]).

47. Bill Mauldin, *Willie and Joe the World War II Years*, ed. Todd DePastino (Seattle, WA: Fantagraphics, 2011), 146.

48. Jake Schuffert, *"No Sweat" ... More 'n More* (Washington, D.C.: Army Times, 1970), 5.

49 Opet, *Opet's Odyssey*, https://www.facebook.com/photo.php?fbid=154763421251197&set=a.154761024584770.32717.137174599676746&type=3&theater.

50. Silverstein, *Grab Your Socks*, 97.

51. Schuffert, *No Sweat*, 127.

52. Pope, *Pope's Puns*, "Lingo," http://www.military.com/cartooncontent/0,14763,Pope_060711,00.html.

53. Hank Ketcham, *Half Hitch* (Greenwich, CT: Fawcett, 1970), n.p.

54 Mike Jones, *Ricky's Tour*, "Gone Long," http://www.military.com/cartooncontent/0,14763,Jones_041505,00.html.

55. Silverstein, *Grab Your Socks*, 88.

56. Mark Baker, *Sgt. Murphy: A "Pvt. Murphy's Law" Collection* (Alexandria, VA: Byrrd, 2008), n.p.

57. Ibid., n.p.

58. Negron, *PCSing*.

59. Kirkland Day, *Camion Cartoons* (Boston, MA: Marshall Jones, 1919), "When I Get Home After the War Such Things as These Might Happen!"

60. Holcomb, *Ups and Downs ... of Camp Upton...* (New York: Bescardi, 1917), "Getting Back to Civilization" and "More of the Same."

61. Ted Stanley, *Perils of a Private: Sketches of Camp Life* (Boston, MA: Small, Maynard, 1918), n.p.

62. Mauldin, *Back Home*, 11.

63. Gerard Otto cartoon in *Yank* 2, no. 52 (June 16, 1944): 24 (reprinted in *The Best of YANK The Army Weekly*, ed. Ira Topping [New York: Arno, 1980]).

64. Hume, *When We Get Back Home from Japan* (Tokyo: Kyoya, 1953), 99.

65. Talbot, *Laughing in Cadence*, 26.

66. K.F., *On Cyber Patrol*, Army Office of Information Assurance and Compliance, http://ciog6.army.mil/OnCyberPatrol/OCPComics/tabid/129/Default.aspx, February 12, 2013.

67. Chris Grant, *Bohica Blues*, in: Jason Chudy, "Reservist's Cartoons Detail Burdens of Desert Deployment," *Stars and Stripes*, August 9, 2004, http://www.stripes.com/news/reservist-s-cartoons-detail-burdens-of-desert-deployment-1.22605.

68. Mauldin, *Willie and Joe*, 52, 67, 113; Maximilian Uriarte, *Terminal Lance: #1–100 Compilation* (Veterans Expeditionary Media, 2011), 62.

69. Douglas G. Ward, *Topical Sketches* (Irvin Department of Rare Books and Special Collections, Digital Collections: http://library.sc.edu/digital/collections/rts.html 1915–1916), 58.

70. Dick Wingert, "Hubert," in *I Ain't Laughing, Sir: 40 Years of GI Humor from Stars and Stripes and Yank Magazine*, ed. Sid Schapiro (Stars and Stripes, 1982), 46.

71. In: Frank Brandt, ed., *Cartoons for Fighters* (Washington, D.C.: Infantry Journal, 1945), n.p.

72. George Baker, *The New Sad Sack* (New York: Simon and Schuster, 1946), "Happy Day."

73. Fred Levi, "Sailor with Baby Diaper," National Museum of American Jewish Military History, http://nmajmh.pastperfect-online.com/34213cgi/mweb.exe?request=record;id=7A3D5B4C-D21C-4054-AF00-578601797908;type=101.

74. Maximilian Uriarte, *Terminal Lance Head Call: The First 100 MarineTimes Strips* (Amazon Digital Services, 2013; Kindle e-book), loc. 1020.

75. Defense Centers of Excellence, *A Handbook for Family and Friends*.

76. Jim Weeks cartoon in *Yank* 4, no. 6 (October 5, 1945): 16 (reprinted in *The Best of YANK The Army Weekly*, ed. Ira Topping [New York: Arno, 1980]).

77. Sheppard, *Incoming*, 118; Klotz, in: *Out of Line: A Collection of Cartoons from Pacific Stars and Stripes* (Tokyo: Toppon, 1952), n.p.

78. Uriarte, *Terminal Lance*, 68.

79. Anonymous, *The Further Adventures of Doctrine Man!! Vol. 1* (Lexington, KY: Doctrine Man, 2013), 101.

80. Anonymous, *Doctrine Man Vol. 1*, 101 and 102.

81. Daryl Talbot, *Laughing in Cadence: Dress Right Dress Military Cartoons* (Stillwater, OK: New Forums, 2009), 45.

82. In: Robert E. Bronner, *The Soldier's Pen* (New York: Hill and Wang, 2006), 54.

83. Day, *Camion Cartoons*, "Day Dreams Some Where in France"; Robert K. Bindig artworks, 26 March 1945, Veterans History Project, AFC/2001/001/32475, American Folklife Center, Library of Congress, http://lcweb2.loc.gov/diglib/vhp/story/loc.natlib.afc2001001.32475/artworks.

84. Charmian Cannon, "Peg's War: A Story Told Through Letters," *Women's History Review* 22, no. 4 (2013): 591–606; Martha Hanna, "A Republic of Letters: The Epistolary Tradition in France During

World War I," *American Historical Review* (2003): 1336–61; D.C. Gill, *How We Are Changed by War: A Study of Letters and Diaries from Colonial Conflicts to Operation Iraqi Freedom* (New York: Routledge, 2010); Judy Barrett Litoff and David C. Smith, "Since You Went Away: The World War II Letters of Barbara Wooddall Taylor," *Women's Studies* 17 (1990): 249–76; Deborah Montgomerie, *Love in Time of War: Letter Writing in the Second World War* (Auckland: Auckland University Press, 2005); Susan VanKoski, "Letters Home, 1915–16: Punjabi Soldiers Reflect on War and Life in Europe and their Meanings for Home and Self," *International Journal of Punjab Studies* 2, no. 1 (1995): 43–63; David Vincent, *Literacy and Popular Culture: England 1750–1914* (Cambridge: Cambridge University Press, 1989).

85. Wallgren, in: John T. Winterich, ed., *Squads Write! A Selection of the Best Things in Prose, Verse, and Cartoons from The Stars and Stripes* (New York: Harper and Brothers, 1931), 89.

86. Ibid., 156–7.

87. Robert K. Bindig Collection (AFC/2001/001/32475), Veterans History Project, American Folklife Center, Library of Congress, digital collection at http://lcweb2.loc.gov/diglib/vhp/story/loc.natlib.afc2001001.32475/artworks; Samuel Lionel Boylston Collection (AFC/2001/001/1848), Veterans History Project, American Folklife Center, Library of Congress, digital collection at http://lcweb2.loc.gov/diglib/vhp/story/loc.natlib.afc2001001.01848/; Joseph Farris, *A Soldier's Sketchbook from the Front Lines of World War II* (Washington, D.C.: National Geographic, 2011); Robert G. Geisler, Jr., Collection (AFC/2001/001/76576), Veterans History Project, American Folklife Center, Library of Congress; Sumner Grant Collection (AFC/2001/001/20970), Veterans History Project, American Folklife Center, Library of Congress, digital collection at http://lcweb2.loc.gov/diglib/vhp/story/loc.natlib.afc2001001,20970/; Henry Lamb, "Illustrated Letters," Imperial War Museum, http://www.iwm.org.uk/collections/item/object/1030005166; Frank L. Mack, "Fancy Mail from a South Pacific APO," *Yank* 2, no. 14 (September 24, 1943): 7 (reprinted in *The Best of YANK The Army Weekly*, ed. Ira Topping [New York: Arno, 1980]); William Schmitt, "Envelope Cartoons," http://www.488thportbattalion.org/Envelopes.html; and see: Sue L. Hamilton, *Jack Kirby: Creator and Artist* (Edina, MD: ABDO, 2007), 17.

88. See: Robert McClelland Martin, "Illustration on V-Mail of liberation," Veterans History Project, AFC/2001/001/479, American Folklife Center, Library of Congress, http://lcweb2.loc.gov/diglib/vhp/story/loc.natlib.afc2001001.00479/enlarge?ID=pm0005001&page=1.

89. "My Personal Touch," *Reader's Digest Special Edition World War II: An Illustrated Celebration of Love Letters, Homecomings, and the American Family*. July 22, 2014: 67.

90. Marion Reh Gurfein, "The Goofein Journal," Veterans History Project, AFC/2001/001/799, American Folklife Center, Library of Congress, http://lcweb2.loc.gov/diglib/vhp/stroy/loc.natlib.afc2001001.00799/artworks/.

91. Lieut. Edward Streeter and G. William

Breck, *Love Letters of Bill to Mable; Comprising "Dere Mable," "Thats Me All Over, Mable," "Same Old Bill, Eh Mable!"* by Lieut. Edward (New York: Frederick A. Stokes, 1918, 1919); Florence Elizabeth Summers and Natalie Stokes, *Dere Bill: Mable's Love Letters to Her Rookie* (New York: Frederick A. Stokes, 1918, 1919).

92. Joseph V. Parrino, "Reading Letters from Home," Veterans History Project, AFC/2001/001/626, American Folklife Center, Library of Congress, http://lcweb2.loc.gov/diglib/vhp/story/loc.natlib.afc2001001.00626/enlarge?ID=pm0010001&page=1.

93. *First World War Soldier's Hand-Drawn Cartoon*, http://www.swansongrp.com/picdocs/wwitoon.html.

94. Perce Pearce, *Seaman Si* (N.p.: Great Lakes Bulletin, 1918), 25.

95. Henry Lamb, "Letter to Michael," November 6, 1918, Imperial War Museum, http://www.iwm.org.uk/collections/item/object/1030005166.

96. For examples: Alexander Woolcott, *The Command Is Forward—Tales of the A.E.F. Battlefields as They Appeared in The Stars and Stripes*, ill. C. LeRoy Baldridge (New York: Century, 1919), 74/75; Mark Baker, *Pfc. Murphy: Private Murphy's Law Book* (Baltimore, MD: United Books, 2005), 73; Barbra E. Bristol, *Meet Molly Marine* (N.p.: Robert J. Weaver, 1945), n.p.; Bindig artworks, 10 October 1944, 5 March 1945 and 11 April 1945; Sumner Grant creative works, August 1944 and November 1944, Veterans History Project, AFC/2001/001/20970, American Folklife Center, Library of Congress, http://lcweb2.loc.gov/diglib/vhp/story/loc.natlib.afc2001001.20970/.

97. For examples: Bindig, "Artworks," no date, http://lcweb2.loc.gov/diglib/vhp/story/loc.natlib.afc2001001.32475/artworks; Grant, "Creative Works, August 1944 and September 1944, http://lcweb2.loc.gov/diglib/vhp/story/loc.natlib.afc2001001.20970/.

98. Mauldin, *Willie and Joe*, 304.

99. Ibid., 517.

100. Jones, *Ricky's Tour*, "Care Package," http://www.military.com/cartooncontent/0,14763,Jones_070502,00.html.

101. In: Park Kendall, *Gone with the Draft: Love Letters of a Trainee* (New York: Grosset and Dunlap, 1941), 13.

102. Laura M. Ahearn, "True Traces: Love Letters and Social Transformation in Nepal," in *Letter Writing as a Social Practice*, ed. David Barton and Nigel Hall (Philadelphia, PA: John Benjamins, 2000), 199–208.

103. Pearce, *Seaman Si*, 78; Ketcham, *Half Hitch*, n.p.; Alex Gard, *Sailors in Boots* (New York: Charles Scribner's Sons, 1943), n.p.; Percy L. Crosby, *That Rookie from the 13th Squad* (New York: Harper and Brothers, 1918), n.p.

104. Pope, *Pope's Puns*, http://www.citamn.afrc.mil/shared/media/ggallert/hires/2014\03\AFG-140320–002.jpg; John Holmes, *Power Point Ranger* online, https://www.facebook.com/photo.php?fbid=710111175678555&set=pb.113256155364063.-2207520000.1403633499.&type=3&theater and https://www.facebook.com/photo.php?fbid=708886175801

055&set=pb.113256155364063.-2207520000.14
03633499.&type=3&theater.

105. Breger, *Private Breger in Britain*, 21.

106. Mauldin, *Willie and Joe*, 313.

107. Jeffrey Hall, *Downrange*, "Lard Burger (part 2)," http://www.military.com/cartooncontent/0,14 763,Downrange_013106,00.htm; Robert Mullan, Tim Hortons cartoon, http://www.oocities.org/hollywo od/theater/7041/humour.html.

108. Alban B. Butler, Jr., *Happy Days!" A Humorous Narrative in Drawings of the Progress of American Arms, 1917–1919* (Chicago, IL: First Division Museum at Cantigny, 2011), 61.

109. For example, the National Museum of Jewish Military History has a display of knives, forks, vases, jewelry, and cigarette cases made from bullet and shell casings.

110. Dave Breger, *Private Breger: His Adventures in Army Camp* (New York: Rand McNally, 1942), "Morale."

111. Mauldin, *Willie and Joe*, 107.

112. Miller, in: *Out of Line: A Collection of Cartoons from Pacific Stars and Stripes* (Tokyo: Toppon, 1952), n.p.

113. Opet, *Opet's Odyssey*, https://www.facebook. com/photo.php?fbid=154762557917950&set=a. 154761024584770.32717.137174599676746&type= 3&theater; Mauldin, *Willie and Joe*, 49.

114. Talbot, *Laughing in Cadence*, 54.

115. Baker, *Pfc. Murphy*, 36.

116. Grant, "Creative Works," November 1944, http://lcweb2.loc.gov/diglib/vhp/story/loc.natlib. afc2001001.20970/; Jack Ruge cartoon Maxwell cartoon in *Yank* 4, no. 28 (December 28, 1945): 23 (reprinted in *The Best of YANK The Army Weekly*, ed. Ira Topping [New York: Arno, 1980]).

117. Opet, *Opet's Odyssey*, https://www.facebook. com/photo.php?fbid=154765657917640&set=a. 154761024584770.32717.137174599676746&type= 3&theater.

118. Mauldin, *Willie and Joe*, 307.

119. Norval Eugene Packwood, *Leatherhead in Korea* (Quantico, VA: Marine Corps Gazette, 1952), 60.

120. Packwood, *Leatherhead in Korea*, 61.

121. Mauldin, *Willie and Joe*, 246.

122. Eric Thibodeau, at http://ericthibodeau. com/uss_missouri.htm.

123. Abian A. Wallgren *Wally: His Cartoons of the A.E.F.* (N.p.: Stars and Stripes, 1919), "Christmas Packages from Over Here."

124. Anonymous, *Doctrine Man Vol. 1*, 141 and 154.

125. Breger, *Private Breger in Britain*, 139.

126. See: Norval Eugene Packwood, *Leatherhead: The Story of Marine Corps Boot Camp* (Quantico, VA: Marine Corps Association, 1951), 43; Baker, *Private Murphy*, 51.

127. Bruce Bairnsfather, *Carry On Sergeant* (Indianapolis, IN: Bobbs-Merrill, 1927), 22.

128. Hall, *Downrange*, "Jury Duty II," http://www. military.com/cartooncontent/0,14763,Downrange_ 022806,00.html.

129. Marvin Kalb, "Provocations: A View from the Press," in *Taken by Storm: The Media, Public*

Opinion, and Foreign Policy in the Gulf War, ed. W. Lance Bennet and David L. Paletz (Chicago: University of Chicago Press, 1994), 4.

130. Jeff Bacon, *The Best of Broadside: A Humorous Look at Life in the Navy* (Newport News, VA: Deep Water, 1992), n.p.

131. Patrick O'Heffernan, "A Mutual Exploitation Model of Media Influence in U.S. Foreign Policy," in *Taken by Storm: The Media, Public Opinion, and Foreign Policy in the Gulf War*, ed. W. Lance Bennet and David L. Paletz (Chicago: University of Chicago Press, 1994), 231–49.

132. Robert M. Entman, *Projections of Power: Framing News, Public Opinion and U.S. Foreign Policy* (Chicago: University of Chicago Press, 2004); Mike Gasher, "Might Makes Right: News Reportage as Discursive Weapon in the War in Iraq," in *Bring 'Em On: Media and Politics in the Iraq War*, ed. Lee Artz and Yahya R. Kamalipour (Lanham, MD: Rowman and Littlefield, 2005), 209–24.

133. Daniel C. Hallin and Todd Gitlin, "The Gulf War as Popular Culture and as Television Drama," in *Taken by Storm: The Media, Public Opinion and U.S. Foreign Policy in the Gulf War*, ed. W. Lance Bennett and David L. Paletz (Chicago, IL: University of Chicago Press, 1994), 152; O'Heffernan, "A Mutual Exploitation Model."

134. Heinz Brandenburg, "Journalists Embedded in Culture: War Stories as Political Strategy," in *Bring 'Em On: Media and Politics in the Iraq War*, ed. Lee Artz and Yahya R. Kamalipour (Lanham, MD: Rowman and Littlefield, 2005), 225–37; Tony Cucolo, "The Military and the Media: Shotgun Wedding, Rocky Marriage, Committed Relationship," *Media, War and Conflict* 1, no. 1 (2008): 84–9.

135. Baker, *Pfc. Murphy*, 90.

136. Ibid., 93.

137. Jeff Bacon, *20 Years of Broadside* (Garden City, ID: Deep Water, 2006), 67.

138. In: Bronner, *The Soldier's Pen*, 119.

139. Mauldin, *Willie and Joe*, 487.

140. Bruce Bairnsfather, *The Best of Fragments from France*, ed. Tonie Holt and Valmai Holt (South Yorkshire, UK: Pen and Sword Military, 1998), 83.

141. Charles Johnson Post, *The Little War of Private Post: The Spanish-American War Seen Up Close* (Lincoln, NE: University of Nebraska Press, 1999), 52.

142. Mauldin, *Willie and Joe*, 284.

143. Ibid., 319.

144. Ibid., 374.

145. Ibid., 625.

146. Kennedy in: *Out of Line: A Collection of Cartoons from Pacific Stars and Stripes* (Tokyo: Toppon, 1952), n.p.

147. Art Gates cartoon in *Yank* 3, no. 41 (March 30, 1945): 24 (reprinted in *The Best of YANK The Army Weekly*, ed. Ira Topping [New York: Arno, 1980]).

148. See: Robert J. Griffin and Shaikat Sen, "Causal Communication: Movie Portrayals and Audience Attributions for Vietnam Veterans' Problems," *Journalism and Mass Communication Quarterly* 72, no. 3 (1995): 511–24; Bruce A. Williams, "From Romance to Collateral Damage: Media Treat-

ment of Civilians in Wartime and What It Means for How America Wages War," *The Communication Review* 12, no. 3 (2009): 227–38.

149. Bairnsfather, *Carry On Sergeant*, 142.

150. Vernon Grant, "Grant's Grunts," *Pacific Stars and Stripes*, February 23, 1969: 16.

151. Vernon Grant, *Stand-by One!* (Hong Kong: Dublin Associates, 1969), n.p.

152. Baker, *Private Murphy*, 27.

153. Uriarte, *Terminal Lance Head Call*, loc. 635.

154. Pearce, *Seaman Si*, 64.

155. Baker, *Sgt. Murphy*, n.p.

156. John Holms, *FM 1.0: Counter Boredom Operations: Power Point Ranger Comics 1–170* (N.p.: Amazon Digital Services, 2014; Kindle e-book), loc. 35.

157. Mauldin, *Back Home*, 51.

158. Ibid., 1.

159. Ibid., 8.

160. Ibid., 49.

161. Mark Baker, *PV-2 Murphy the Adventure Continues: A "Pvt. Murphy's Law" Collection* (Baltimore, MD: United Books, 2001), 18.

162. Baker, *PV-2 Murphy*, 19.

163. See: Kent Mitchell, "Educating 'Sillyvillians': The God-A** P-3," *Mitchell's Ramblings*, July 21, 2009, http://kentmitchellsramblings.blogspot.com/2009/07/educating-sillyvillians-dog-p-3.html (accessed June 14, 2014).

164. Bairnsfather, *Best of Fragments from France*, 35.

Conclusion

1. Ernest G. Bormann, Roxann L. Knutson, and Karen Musolf, "Why Do People Share Fantasies? An Empirical Investigation of a Basic Tenet of the Symbolic Convergence Communication Theory," *Communication Studies* 48, no. 3 (1997): 254–76.

2. John F. Cragan and Donald C. Shields. *Symbolic Theories in Applied Communication Research: Bormann, Burke, and Fisher* (Cresskill, NJ: Hampton, 1995); Ernest G. Bormann, "Fantasy and Rhetorical Vision: The Rhetorical Criticism of Social Reality," *Quarterly Journal of Speech* 58 (1972): 396–407.

3. Geoffrey Ingersoll, "OpEd: Stop Saying Vets Sacrificed 'for Nothing' in Iraq," *Marine Corps Times*, June 20, 2014, http://www.marinecorpstimes.com/article/20140620/NEWS01/306200074/OpEd-Stop-saying-vets-sacrificed-nothing-Iraq (accessed June 23, 2014).

4. Gary Owen, "Mandatory Iraq Veteran Post: Looking Back a Decade On," *It's Always Sunny in Kabul*, July 12, 2014, https://medium.com/its-always-sunny-in-kabul/a69dba9e27b5; http://www.army.mil/values/soldiers.html (accessed July 12, 2014).

5. Army.mil, "Soldier's Creed," *Army Values*, http://www.army.mil/values/soldiers.html.

6. Gerhard Kümmel, "A Soldier Is a Soldier Is a Soldier!? The Military and Its Soldiers in an Era of Globalization," in *Handbook of the Sociology of the Military*, ed. Giuseppe Caforio (New York: Springer, 2006), 417–33.

7. Carol Burke, "Marching to Vietnam," *Journal of American Folklore* 102, no. 406 (1989): 424–41; Scott Simon, "World War II Cartoons Come to Soldiers' Aid," *Listen to the Story* (February 13, 2010), radio broadcast, transcript at http://www.npr.org/templates/story/story.php?storyId=123684046.

8. Thom Shanker, "Masked Military Man is Superhero for Troops"; *New York Times*, November 18, 2010, http://www.nytimes.com/2010/11/19/us/19pentagon.html (accessed November 9, 2012).

9. Hope Hodge Seck, "Tattoos and Terminal Lance: The 5 Most Surprising Things We Learned from the Commandant's Live Q&A," *Battle Rattle*, March 17, 2014: http://blogs.militarytimes.com/battle-rattle/2014/03/17/tattoos-and-terminal-lance-the-5-most-surprising-things-we-learned-from-the-commandants-live-qa/ (accessed March 20, 2014).

10. Saul Elbein, "The Marine Corps' Comic-Book Hero," *Men's Journal* 23, no. 11 (November 2014): 20–1.

11. Charlie Sherpa, "The Winners of the 2013 Mil-Humor Awards!" *Red Bull Rising*, September 5, 2013, http://www.redbullrising.com/2013/09/the-winners-of-2013-mil-humor-awards.html.

12. Joe Burlas, "Army Cartoonist Meets Inspiration," *ArmyLINK News*, May 26, 2000: http://www.geocities.ws/koratmahknut/armycartoons.htm.

13. Timothy L. Hale, "Opet's Odyssey," *Double Eagle*, July 2012, 10–11, 15.

14. "About the Comic," *Beetle Bailey*, http://beetlebailey.com/about/.

15. Tonie Holt and Valmai Holt, "Introduction to the 'BB4H4H' Edition of Best of Fragments from France," in *The Best of Fragments from France* by Bruce Bairnsfather, ed. Tonie Holt and Valmai Holt (South Yorkshire, UK: Pen and Sword Military, 2009), 4.

16. In: Dorothea J. Byerly, *Up Came a Ripple* (East Orange, NJ: Greenwood, 1945).

17. Virginia Herman, "Forward," in *Winning the WAC: The Return of a World War II Favorite* by Cpl. Vic Herman (Encinitas, CA: KNI, Inc./Virginia Herman, 2002), 1.

18. Simon, "World War II Cartoons Come to Soldiers' Aid."

19. Maximilian Uriarte, *Terminal Lance Head Call: The First 100 MarineTimes Strips* (Amazon Digital Services, 2013; Kindle e-book), loc. 998.

20. Hale, "Opet's Odyssey."

21. Burlas, "Army Cartoonist Meets Inspiration."

22. W.C. Pope, *Pope's Puns: Above and Beyond* (Herkimer, NY: W.C. Pope Studio, 2009).

23. Jay Casey, "'What's So Funny?' The Finding and Use of Soldier Cartoons from the World Wars as Historical Evidence," in *Drawing the Line: Using Cartoons as Historical Evidence*, ed. Richard Scully and Marian Quartly (Clayton, Australia: Monash University ePress, 2009), 07.3.

24. Lee Anderson, *Battle Notes.... Music of the Vietnam War* (Superior, WI: Savage, 2003).

25. Meredith H. Lair, *Armed with Abundance: Consumerism and Soldiering in the Vietnam War* (Chapel Hill, NC: University of North Carolina Press, 2011; Kindle e-book).

26. For discussion of branch personalities, see: Carl H. Builder, *The Masks of War: American Military Styles in Strategy and Analysis* (Baltimore, MD: Johns Hopkins University Press, 1989).

27. See: Julia Carpenter, "For One Veteran, Showing Photos of His Deployment in Afghanistan Is 'Easier,'" *Washington Post*, May 5, 2014: http://www.washingtonpost.com/news/post-nation/wp/2014/05/05/for-one-veteran-showing-photos-of-his-deployment-in-afghanistan-is-easier/ (accessed May 6, 2014); "About Warrior Writers," *Warrior Writers*, 2012, http://www.warriorwriters.org/about.html.

28. Paul Rosenfeld, "What Combat Feels Like, Presented in the Style of a Graphic Narrative," *The Atlantic*, September 2013, http://www.theatlantic.com/video/archive/2013/09/what-combat-feels-like-presented-in-the-stule-of-a-graphic-novel/280029.

29. William T. Livingston Collection (AFC/2001/001/12715), Veterans History Project, American Folklife Center, Library of Congress, letter dated February 7, 1946.

30. Joseph J. Brenner Collection (AFC/2001/001/1014), Veterans History Project, American Folklife Center, Library of Congress; from correspondence, December–February 1945.

31. Kate Hoit, "The 'Dangerous' Veteran: An Inaccurate Media Narrative Takes Hold," *Vantage Point: Dispatches from the U.S. Department of Veterans Affairs*, March 6, 2012, http://www.blogs.va.gov/VAntage/6026/the-%E2%80%9Cdangerous%E2%80%9D-veteran-an-inaccurate-media-narrative-takes-hold/ (accessed June 28, 2014).

32. Drew Ferrol, "Veterans with PTSD Linked to Everything That Could Kill Your Children," *The Duffel Blog*, April 13, 2014, http://www.duffelblog.com/2014/04/media-veteran-ptsd-link/#!5S2Zf (accessed April 14, 2014).

33. See: Tanja Thomas and Fabian Virchow, "Banal Militarism and the Culture of War," in *Bring 'Em On: Media and Politics in the Iraq War*, ed. Lee Artz and Yahya R. Kamilipour (Lanham, MD: Rowman and Littlefield, 2005), 23–36.

34. Stephen M. Walt, "Two Chief Petty Officers Walk into a Bar...," *Foreign Policy*, April 7, 2014, http://www.foreignpolicy.com/articles/2014/04/07/why_cant_we_make_fun_of_the_military_anymore, para. 15.

35. Jay Casey, "What's So Funny," 07.1.

36. Hale, "Opet's Odyssey," 10.

Bibliography

AAP-6. *The NATO Glossary of Terms and Definitions.* Brussels, Belgium: NATO, 1989.

"About the Comic." *Beetle Bailey.* http://beetle bailey.com/about/. Accessed October 3, 2014.

"About Warrior Writers." *Warrior Writers*, 2012. http://www.warriorwriters.org/about.html. Accessed June 26, 2014.

Abraham, Linus. "Effectiveness of Cartoons as a Uniquely Visual Medium for Orienting Social Issues." *Journalism and Communication Monographs* 11, no. 2 (2009): 117–65.

Achter, Paul. "Unruly Bodies: The Rhetorical Domestication of Twenty-First-Century Veterans of War." *Quarterly Journal of Speech* 96, no. 1 (2010): 46–68.

Acuff, Jonathan M. "Generational Analysis and the Evolution of Military Doctrine and Strategy." In *Theory and Application of the "Generation" in International Relations and Politics*, ed. Brent J. Steele and Jonathan M. Acuff, 177–202. New York: Palgrave Macmillan, 2012.

Adams, Kenneth Alan, and Lester Hill, Jr. "Protest and Rebellion: Fantasy Themes in Japanese Comics." *Journal of Popular Culture* 25, no. 1 (1991): 99–127.

Ahearn, Laura M. "True Traces: Love Letters and Social Transformation in Nepal." In *Letter Writing as a Social Practice*, ed. David Barton and Nigel Hall, 199–208. Philadelphia, PA: John Benjamins, 2000.

Aichinger, Peter. *The American Soldier in Fiction, 1880–1963: A History of Attitudes Toward Warfare and the Military Establishment.* Ames, IA: Iowa State University Press, 1975.

Alaniz, José. "Death and the Superhero: The Silver Age and Beyond." *International Journal of Comic Art* 8, no. 1 (2006): 234–48.

Alfonso, Kristal L.M. *Femme Fatale: An Examination of the Role of Women in Combat and the Policy Implications for Future American Military Operations.* Drew Papers, no. 5. Maxwell Air Force Base, AL: Air University Press, 2009.

Amana, Harry. "The Art of Propaganda: Charles Alston's World War II Editorial Cartoons for the Office of War Information and the Black Press." *American Journalism* 21, no. 2 (2004): 79–111.

Ames, Genevieve M., Carol B. Cunradi, Roland S. Moore, and Pamela Stern. "Military Culture and Drinking Behavior Among U.S. Navy Careerists." *Journal of Studies on Alcohol and Drugs* 68, no. 3 (2007): 336–44.

Anderson, Blane. "Humor and Leadership." *Journal of Organizational Culture, Communications and Conflict* 9, no. 1 (2005): 137–44.

Anderson, Lee. *Battle Notes: Music of the Vietnam War.* Superior, WI: Savage, 2003.

Anonymous. "America's Entrance into the War." *The Round Table: The Commonwealth Journal of International Affairs* 7, no. 27 (1917): 491–514.

Anonymous. "Informal Social Organization in the Army." *American Journal of Sociology* 51, no. 5 (1946): 365–70.

Ansorge, Josef Teboho. "Spirits of War: A Field Manual." *International Political Sociology* 4 (2010): 362–79.

Army.mil. "Soldier's Creed." *Army Values*, http://www.army.mil/values/soldiers.html. Accessed June 16, 2014.

Astor, Gerald. *Terrible Terry Allen: Combat General of World War II—The Life of an American Soldier.* New York: Presidio, 2003.

Avant, Deborah D. "The Institutional Sources of Military Doctrine: Hegemons in Peripheral Wars." *International Studies Quarterly* 37 (1993): 409–30.

Bailey, Theodore Layton. *Military Courtesy.* New York: Review, 1919.

Bairnsfather, Bruce. *Carry On Sergeant!* Indianapolis, IN: Bobbs-Merrill, 1927.

Baldwin, Fred D. "No Sex, Please, We're American." *HistoryClub*, April 29, 2014. http://history.scout.com/story/1387336-no-sex-please-we-re-american?s=155. Accessed May 2, 2014.

Ballenger-Browning, Kara, and Douglas C. Johnson. "Key Facts on Resilience." *Naval Center for Combat and Operational Stress Control*, n.d. http://www.med.navy.mil/sites/nmcsd/ ncc osc/healthProfessionalsV2/reports/Documents/resilienceTWPFormatted2.pdf.

Banks, Amanda Carson, and Elizabeth Wein. "Folklore and the Comic Book: The Traditional Meets the Popular." *New Directions in Folklore* 2 (1998). http://hdl.handle.net/2022/ 7218. Accessed July 9, 2013).

Barcus, Francis E. "A Content Analysis of Trends in Sunday Comics 1900–1959." *Journalism Quarterly* 38, no. 2 (1961): 171–80.

Barkawi, Tarak. "Culture and Combat in the Colonies: The Indian Army in the Second World War." *Journal of Contemporary History* 41, no. 2 (2006): 325–55.

Barker, Martin, and Roger Sabin. "'Doonesbury Does Iraq': Garry Trudeau and the Politics of an Anti-War Strip." *Journal of Graphic Novels and Comics* 3, no. 2 (2012): 127–42.

Baron, Lawrence. "X-Men as J-Men: The Jewish Subtext of a Comic Book Movie," *Shofar: An Interdisciplinary Journal of Jewish Studies* 22, no. 1 (2003): 44–52.

Barsis. *They're All Yours, Uncle Sam!* New York: Stephen Daye, 1943.

Bartone, Jocelyn, Jesse J. Harris, David R. Segal, and Mady Wechsler. "Lightfighters' Wives." In *Peacekeepers and Their Wives*, ed. David R. Segal and Mady Wechsler Segal, 14–57. Westport, CT: Greenwood, 1993.

Bates, Benjamin R. "Audiences, Metaphors, and the Persian Gulf War." *Communication Studies* 55, no. 3 (2004): 447–63.

Baudrillard, Jean. "War Porn." Trans. Paul A. Taylor. *International Journal of Baudrillard Studies* 2, no. 1 (2005). http://www.ubishops.ca/ba udrillardstudies/vol2_1/ Taylor.htm/. Accessed July 9, 2013.

Beamish, Thomas D., Harvey Molotch, and Richard Flacks. "Who Supports the Troops? Vietnam, the Gulf War, and the Making of Collective Memory." *Social Problems* 42, no. 3 (1995): 344–60.

Beck, Ulrich. "The Sociological Anatomy of Enemy Images: The Military and Democracy After the End of the Cold War." In *Enemy Images in American History*, ed. Ragnhild Fiebig-von Hase and Ursula Lehmkuhl, 65–87. Providence, RI: Berghahn, 1997.

Belk, Russell W. "Material Values in the Comics: A Content Analysis of Comic Books Featuring Themes of Wealth." *Journal of Consumer Research* 14 (1987): 26–42.

Ben-Ari, Eyal. "Epilogue: A 'Good' Military Death." *Armed Forces and Society* 31, no. 4 (2005): 651–64.

_____. *Mastering Soldiers: Conflict, Emotion, and the Enemy in an Israeli Military Unit*. New Directions in Anthropology, vol. 10. New York: Berghahn, 1998.

Benoit, William L., Andrew A. Klyukovski, John P. McHale, and David Airne. "A Fantasy Theme Analysis of Political Cartoons on the Clinton-Lewinsky-Starr Affair." *Critical Studies in Media Communication* 18, no. 4 (2001): 377–94.

Berger, Arthur Asa. "Comics and Culture." *Journal of Popular Culture* 5, no. 1 (1971): 164–77.

_____. *The Comic-Stripped American: What Dick Tracy, Blondie, Daddy Warbucks, and Charlie Brown Tell Us About Ourselves*. New York: Walker, 1972.

_____. *Li'l Abner: A Study in American Satire.* Studies in Popular Culture. New York: University Press of Mississippi, 2006.

Berk, Ronald A. "Student Ratings of 10 Strategies for Using Humor in College Teaching." *Journal on Excellence in College Teaching* 7, no. 3 (1996): 71–92.

Beronä, David A. "Worldless Comics: The Imaginative Appeal of Peter Kuper's *The System*." In *Critical Approaches to Comics: Theories and Methods*, ed. Matthew J. Smith and Randy Duncan, 17–26. New York: Routledge, 2012.

Bhabha, Homi K. *The Location of Culture*. London, UK: Routledge, 1994.

Biank, Tanya. *Army Wives*. New York: St. Martin's Griffin, 2006.

"Biography: Spirited Work," WillEisnerwww. N.d. http://www.willeisner.com/biography/3-spirited-work.html. Accessed July 6, 2013.

"Biography: The Army Years and PS Magazine." *WillEisner.com*. N.d. http://www.willeisner. com/biography/5-the-army-years.html. Accessed July 6, 2013.

Birdwell, Michael. "'Oh, You Thing from Another World, You': How Warner Bros. Animators Responded to the Cold War (1948–1980)." *Film and History* 31, no. 1 (2001): 34–9.

_____. "Technical Fairy First Class? Is This Any Way to Run an Army?: Private SNAFU and World War II." *Historical Journal of Film, Radio, and Television* 25, no. 2 (2005): 203–12.

Black, James Eric (Jay). "Amoozin' but Confoozin': Comic Strips as a Voice of Dissent in the 1950s." *ETC: A Review of General Semantics* 66, no. 4 (2010): 460–77.

Black, John. "War, Women and Accounting: Female Staff in the UK Army Pay Department Offices, 1914–1920." *Accounting, Business and Financial History* 16, no. 2 (2006): 195–218.

Blackmore, Tim. "*300* and Two: Frank Miller and Daniel Ford Interpret Herodotus's Thermopylae Myth." *International Journal of Comic Art* 6, no. 2 (2004): 325–49.

Boëne, Bernard. "How 'Unique' Should the Military Be? A Review of Representative Literature and Outline of a Synthetic Formulation." *Euro-*

pean Journal of Sociology 31, no. 1 (1990): 3–59.

Bogart, Leo. "Comic Strips and Their Adult Readers." In *Mass Culture: The Popular Arts in America*, ed. Bernard Rosenberg and David M. White, 189–98. Glencoe, IL: Free Press, 1957.

Bormann, Ernest G. "Fantasy and Rhetorical Vision: Ten Years Later." *Quarterly Journal of Speech* 68 (1982): 288–305.

_____. "Fantasy and Rhetorical Vision: The Rhetorical Criticism of Social Reality." *Quarterly Journal of Speech* 58 (1972): 396–407.

_____. "Symbolic Convergence Theory and Communication in Group Decision Making." In *Communication and Group Decision Making*, 2nd ed., ed. Randy Y. Hirokawa and Marshall Scott Poole, 81–113. Thousand Oaks, CA: Sage, 1996.

_____. "The Symbolic Convergence Theory of Communication: Applications and Implications for Teachers and Consultants." *Journal of Applied Communication Research* 10, no. 1 (1982): 50–61.

Bormann, Ernest G., John F. Cragan, and Donald C. Shields. "An Expansion of the Rhetorical Vision Component of the Symbolic Convergence Theory: The Cold War Paradigm Case." *Communication Monographs* 63, no. 1 (1996): 1–28.

_____. "In Defense of Symbolic Convergence Theory: A Look at the Theory and Its Criticisms After Two Decades." *Communication Theory* 4, no. 4 (1994): 259–94.

Bormann, Ernest G., Roxann L. Knutson, and Karen Musolf. "Why Do People Share Fantasies? An Empirical Investigation of a Basic Tenet of the Symbolic Convergence Communication Theory." *Communication Studies* 48, no. 3 (1997): 254–76.

Bormann, Ernest G., Jolene Koester, and Janet Bennett. "Political Cartoons and Salient Rhetorical Fantasies: An Empirical Analysis of the '76 Presidential Campaign." *Communication Monographs* 45, no. 4 (1978): 317–29.

Bostdorff, Denise M. "Making Light of James Watt: A Burkean Approach to the Form and Attitude of Political Cartoons." *Quarterly Journal of Speech* 73 (1987): 43–59.

Botzakis, Stergios. "'To Be Part of the Dialogue': American Adults Reading Comic Books." *Journal of Graphic Novels and Comics* 2, no. 2 (2011): 113–23.

Bouhammer. "And You Thought I Was Lying About Man-Love Thursdays." *Bouhammer's Blog.* January 28, 2010. http://www.bouhammer.com/2010/01/and-you-thought-i-was-lying-about-man-love-thursdays/. Accessed December 29, 2013.

_____. "Their Thursday Night Is Our Saturday Night. *Bouhammer's Afghan and Military Blog.* July 18, 2006. http://www.bouhammer.com/ 2006/07/their-thursday-night-is-our-saturday-night/. Accessed December 29, 2013.

Boyer, Cherrie B., Mary-Ann B. Shafer, Richard A. Shaffer, Stephanie K. Brodine, Stanley I. Ito, Debra L. Yniguez, Dana M. Benas, and Julius Schachter. "Prevention of Sexually Transmitted Diseases and HIV in Young Military Men: Evaluation of a Cognitive-Behavioral Skills-Building Intervention." *Sexually Transmitted Diseases* 28, no. 6 (2001): 349–55.

Brabant, Sarah. "Death and Grief in the Family Comics." *Omega* 36, no. 1 (1997–98): 33–44.

Braithchaite, Dawn O., Paul Schrodt, and Jody Koenig. "Symbolic Convergence Theory: Communication, Dramatizing Messages, and Rhetorical Visions in Families." In *Engaging Theories in Family Communication*, ed. Dawn O Braithwaite and Leslie A. Baxter, 146–61. Thousand Oaks, CA: Sage, 2006.

Brandenburg, Heinz. "Journalists Embedded in Culture: War Stories as Political Strategy." In *Bring 'Em On: Media and Politics in the Iraq War*, ed. Lee Artz and Yahya R. Kamalipour, 225–37. Lanham, MD: Rowman and Littlefield, 2005.

Brandt, Frank, ed. *Cartoons for Fighters.* Washington, D.C.: Infantry Journal, 1945.

Brienza, Casey. "Producing Comics Culture: A Sociological Approach to the Study of Comics." *Journal of Graphic Novels and Comics* 1, no. 2 (2010): 105–19.

Broom, Cheryl, and Susan Avanzino. "The Communication of Community Collaboration: When Rhetorical Visions Collide." *Communication Quarterly* 58, no. 4 (2010): 480–501.

Brooten, Lisa. "Political Cartoons and Burma's Transnational Public Sphere." In *Southeast Asian Cartoon Art: History, Trends and Problems*, ed. John A. Lent, chapter 7. Jefferson, NC: McFarland, 2014.

Brotz, Howard, and Everett Wilson. "Characteristics of Military Society." *American Journal of Sociology* 51 no. 5 (1946): 371–5.

Browder, Laura. *Her Best Shot: Women and Guns in America.* Chapel Hill, NC: University of North Carolina Press, 2006.

Brown, David W. "The Irresponsibility Stupid and Dangerous Camouflage Patterns of the U.S. Military." *The Week*, January 22, 2013. http://theweek.com/article/index/238909/the-irresponsibly-stupid-and-dangerous-camouflage-patterns-of-the-us-military. Accessed April 13, 2014.

Brown, Katherine E., and Elina Penttinen. "'A "Sucking Chest Wound" Is Nature's Way of Telling You to Slow Down...' Humour and Laughter in War Time." *Critical Studies on Security* 1, no, 1 (2013): 124–6.

Brown, William B. "It Means Something: The Ghosts of War." In *Storytelling Sociology: Narrative as Social Inquiry*, ed. Ronald J. Berger and Richard Quinney, 245–63. Boulder, CO: Lynne Rienner, 2005.

Brunn, Stanley D., Harri Andersson, and Carl T. Dahlma. "Landscaping for Power and Defence." In *Landscapes of Defence*, ed. John R. Gold and George Revill, 68–84. Harlow, UK: Prentice Hall, 2000.

Brunyé, T., G. Riccio, J. Sidman, A. Darowski, and F.J. Diedrich. "Enhancing Warrior Ethos in Initial Entry Training." *Proceedings of the Human Factors and Ergonomics Society Annual Meeting* 50, no. 25 (2006): 2634–37.

Bryant, Mark. *Napoleonic Wars in Cartoons*. London, UK: Grubb Street, 2009.

_____. *Wars of Empire in Cartoons*. London, UK: Grubb Street, 2009.

Builder, Carl H. *The Masks of War: American Military Styles in Strategy and Analysis*. Baltimore, MD: Johns Hopkins University Press, 1989.

Burke, Carol. "Marching to Vietnam." *Journal of American Folklore* 102, no. 406 (1989): 424–41.

_____. "Military Speech." *New Directions in Folklore* 7 (2003): http://hdl.handle.net/2022/6905. Accessed February 15, 2013.

Burns, Richard Allen. "'This Is My Rifle, This Is My Gun...': Gunlore in the Military." *New Directions in Folklore* 7 (2003): http://hdl.handle.net/2022/6906. Accessed February 15, 2013.

Burrell, Lolita M., Gary A. Adams, Doris Briley Durand, and Carl Andrew Castro. "The Impact of Military Lifestyle Demands on Well-Being, Army, and Family Outcomes." *Armed Forces and Society* 33, no. 1 (2006): 43–58.

Butler, Alban B., Jr. *Happy Days!* Oxford, UK: Osprey, 2011.

Butler, John Sibley. "Race Relations in the Military." In *The Military: More Than Just a Job?*, ed. Charles C. Moskos and Frank R. Wood, 15–26. Washington, D.C.: Pergamon-Brassey's, 1988.

Butler, Judith. *Frames of War: When Is Life Grievable?* London, UK: Verso, 2009.

_____. *Precarious Life: The Power of Mourning and Violence*. London, UK: Verso, 2004.

Byerly, Dorothea J. *Up Came a Ripple*. East Orange, NJ: Greenwood, 1945.

Byock, Ira. *Dying Well: Peace and Possibilities at the End of Life*. New York: Riverhead, 1998.

Calvin, Paula E., and Deborah A. Deacon. *American Women Artists in Wartime, 1776–2010*. Jefferson, NC: McFarland, 2011. Kindle e-book.

Campbell, Donald T., and Thelma H. McCormack. "Military Experience and Attitudes Toward Authority." *American Journal of Sociology* 62, no. 5 (1957): 482–90.

Cannon, Charmian. "Peg's War: A Story Told Through Letters." *Women's History Review* 22, no. 4 (2013): 591–606.

Captstick, M.D. "Defining the Culture: The Canadian Army in the 21st Century." *Canadian Military Journal*, Spring 2003, 47–53.

Carabas, Teodora. "Tales Calculated to Drive You MAD: The Debunking of Spies, Superheroes, and Cold War Rhetoric in Mad Magazine's 'SPY vs SPY.'" *Journal of Popular Culture* 40, no. 1 (2007): 4–24.

Carbaugh, Donal. *Situating Selves: The Communication of Social Identities in American Scenes*. Albany, NY: State University of New York Press, 1996.

Carden-Coyne, Ana. "Ungrateful Bodies: Rehabilitation, Resistance and Disabled American Veterans of the First World War." *European Review of History* 14, no. 4 (2007): 543–65.

Carrier, David. "Caricature." In *A Comic Studies Reader*, ed. Jeet Heer and Kent Worcester, 105–15. Jackson, MS: University Press of Mississippi, 2009.

Carruthers, Susan L. "No One's Looking: The Disappearing Audience for War." *Media, War and Conflict* 1, no. 1 (2008): 70–6.

Cartwright, William. "An Investigation of Maps and Cartographic Artefacts of the Gallipoli Campaign 1915: Military, Commercial and Personal." *Geospatial Visualisation* 14 (2013): 19–40.

Casey, Jay. "The Dynamics of Quiet Heroism and Invisible Death in American Soldier Cartoons of the World Wars." *International Journal of Comic Art* 9, no. 1 (2007): 281–95.

_____. "'What's So Funny?' The Finding and Use of Soldier Cartoons from the World Wars as Historical Evidence." In *Drawing the Line: Using Cartoons as Historical Evidence*, ed. Richard Scully and Marian Quartly, 07.1–07.23. Clayton, Australia: Monash University ePress, 2009.

Caswell, Lucy Shelton. "Comic Strips." In *History of Mass Media in the United States: An Encyclopedia*, ed. Margaret A. Blanchard, 150–2. London, UK: Routledge, 1998.

_____. "Drawing Swords: War in American Editorial Cartoons." *American Journalism* 21, no. 2 (2004): 13–45.

Cates, Isaac. "The Diary Comic." In *Graphic Subjects: Critical Essays on Autobiography and Graphic Novels*, ed. Michael A. Chaney. Madison, WI: University of Wisconsin Press, 2011. Kindle e-book.

Cathcart, Adam. "Atrocities, Insults, and 'Jeep Girls': Depictions of the U.S. Military in China, 1945–1949." *International Journal of Comic Art* 10, no. 1 (2008): 140–54.

Chaney, Michael A. "The Animal Witness of the Rwandan Genocide." In *Graphic Subjects: Critical Essays on Autobiography and Graphic Nov-

els, ed. Michael A. Chaney. Madison, WI: University of Wisconsin Press, 2011. Kindle e-book.

_____. "Introduction." In *Graphic Subjects: Critical Essays on Autobiography and Graphic Novels,* ed. Michael A. Chaney. Madison, WI: University of Wisconsin Press, 2011. Kindle e-book.

Chapman, Graham, John Cleese, Terry Gilliam, Eric Idle, Terry Jones and Michael Palin. *The Complete Monty Python's Flying Circus: All the Words, Vol. 1.* New York: Pantheon, 1989.

Cheesman, Kerry. "Using Comics in the Science Classroom." *Journal of College Science Teaching* 35, no. 4 (2006): 48–51.

Chittenden, Varick A. "'These Aren't Just My Scenes': Shared Memories in a Vietnam Veteran's Art." *Journal of American Folklore* 102, no. 406 (1989): 412–23.

Cioffi, Frank L. "Disturbing Comics: The Disjunction of Word and Image in the Comics of Andrzej Mleczko, Ben Katchor, R. Crumb, and Art Spiegelman." In *The Language of Comics Word and Image,* ed. Robin Varnum and Christina T. Gibbons, 97–122. Studies in Popular Culture. Jackson, MS: University Press of Mississippi, 2001.

Civikly, Jean M. "Humor and the Enjoyment of College Teaching." In *Communicating in College Classrooms.* New Directions for Teaching and Learning, vol. 26, ed. Jean M. Civikly, 61–70. San Francisco, CA: Jossey-Bass, 1986.

Clark, Robert A. "Aggressiveness and Military Training." *American Journal of Sociology* 51, no. 5 (1946): 423–32.

Clarkson, Alexander. "Virtual Heroes: Boys, Masculinity and Historical Memory in War Comics 1945–1995." *THYMOS: Journal of Boyhood Studies* 2, no. 2 (2008): 175–85.

Clausewitz, Carl Von. *On War.* 1832. Ed. Frederic Natusch Maude. Trans. James John Graham. N.p.: Amazon Digital Services, 2011. Kindle e-book.

Cleveland, Les. "Songs of the Vietnam War: An Occupational Folk Tradition." *New Directions in Folklore* 7 (2003). http://hdl.handle.net/2022/6908. Accessed July 9, 2013.

Cohen, Eliot. "The Military." In *Understanding America: The Anatomy of an Exceptional Nation,* ed. Peter H. Schuck and James Q. Wilson, 247–74. New York: Public Affairs, 2008.

Cohn, Neil. "Un-Defining 'Comics': Separating the Cultural from the Structural in Comics." *International Journal of Comic Art* 7, no. 2 (2005): 236–48.

Collins, John M. *Military Geography for Professionals and the Public.* Washington, D.C.: Brassey's, 1998. Kindle e-book.

Collins, Randall. "Three Faces of Cruelty: Towards a Comparative Sociology of Violence." *Theory and Society* 1, no. 4 (1974): 415–40.

_____. *Violence: A Micro-Sociological Theory.* Princeton, NJ: Princeton University Press, 2008.

Committee on Public Information, *Bureau of Cartoons, Bulletin No. 16,* September 28, 1919, 1–2.

Conners, Joan L. "Hussein as Enemy: The Persian Gulf War in Political Cartoons." *Harvard International Journal of Press/Politics* 3, no. 3 (1998): 96–114.

Corbett, Julian. *Naval and Military Essays.* Cambridge: Cambridge University Press, 1914.

Corson, Mark W. "Operation Iraqi Freedom: Geographic Considerations for Desert Warfare." In *Military Geography from Peace to War,* ed. Eugene J. Palka and Francis A. Galgano, 149–80. New York: McGraw-Hill, 2005.

Coser, Lewis A. *Greedy Institutions: Patterns of Undivided Commitment* (New York: Free Press, 1974).

Cotton, Charles A. "Commitment in Military Systems." In *Legitimacy and Commitment in the Military,* ed. Thomas C. Wyatt and Reuven Gal, 47–66. New York: Greenwood, 1990.

Cragan, John F., and Donald C. Shields. *Symbolic Theories in Applied Communication Research: Bormann, Burke, and Fisher.* Cresskill, NJ: Hampton, 1995.

Crilley, Mark. "Getting Students to Write Using Comics." *Teacher Librarian* 37, no. 1 (2009): 28–31.

Cucolo, Tony. "The Military and the Media: Shotgun Wedding, Rocky Marriage, Committed Relationship." *Media, War and Conflict* 1, no. 1 (2008): 84–9.

Culbert, David H. "Walt Disney's Private Snafu: The Use of Humor in World War II Army Films." *Prospects* 1, October (1976): 81–96.

Daley, James G. "Understanding the Military as an Ethnic Identity." In *Social Work Practice in the Military,* ed. James G. Daley, 291–306. Binghamton, NY: Hawthorn, 1999.

Davidson, Sol M. "The Funnies' Neglected Branch: Special Purpose Comics." *International Journal of Comic Art* 7, no. 2 (2005): 340–57.

Davies, Jon. "War Memorials." In *The Sociology of Death,* ed. David Clark, 112–128. Oxford, UK: Blackwell, 1993.

Davis, Julie. "Power to the Cubicle-Dwellers: An Ideological Reading of *Dilbert.*" In *Comics and Ideology* vol. 2, ed. Matthew P. McAllister, Edward H. Sewell, Jr., and Ian Gordon, 275–300. Popular Culture Everyday Life. New York: Peter Lang, 2009.

Davis, Karen D., and Brian McKee. "Women in the Military: Facing the Warrior Framework." In *Challenge and Change in the Military: Gender and Diversity Issues,* ed. Franklin C. Pinch, Allister T. MacIntyre, Phyllis Browne and Alan C. Okros, 52–75. Kingston, Canada: Canadian Defence Academy Press, 2006.

Davis, Peter, director. *Hearts and Minds.* You-Tube video. Posted by "Sao Vàng." August 22, 2012. http://youtu.be/1d2ml82lc7s. Accessed March 20, 2014.

Davis, W.N. "Foreward." In *Wits of War: Unofficial GI Humor History of World War II* by Edwin J. Swineford, v. Fresno, CA: Kilroy Was Here, 1989.

Deaton, John E., S. William Berg, Milton Richlin, and Alan J. Litrownik. "Coping Activities in Solitary Confinement of U.S. Navy POWs in Vietnam." *Journal of Applied Social Psychology* 7, no. 3 (1977): 239–57.

DeBruyn, Dieter. "Patriotism of Tomorrow? The Commemoration and Popularization of the Warsaw Rising through Comics." *Slovo* 22, no. 2 (2010): 46–65.

Defense Centers of Excellence. *A Handbook for Family and Friends of Service Members Before, During and After Deployment.* N.p.: Vulcan Productions, 2010.

D'Emilio, John, and Estelle Freedman. *Intimate Matters: A History of Sexuality in America,* 3rd ed. Chicago, IL: University of Chicago Press, 2012. Kindle e-book.

Dennis, Jeffrey P. "Gay Content in Newspaper Comics." *Journal of American Culture* 35, no. 4 (2012): 304–14.

Dept. of the Army. *Foundations of Leadership MSL II.* Rev. ed. New York: Pearson Custom, 2008.

DePastino, Todd. *Bill Mauldin: A Life Up Front.* New York: W.W. Norton, 2008.

_____. "Willie and Joe Come Home." In *Willie and Joe Back Home,* by Bill Mauldin, vii–xix. Seattle, WA: Fantagraphics, 2011.

Der Derian, James. *Virtuous War: Mapping the Military-Industrial-Media-Entertainment Network.* 2nd Ed. New York: Routledge, 2009.

DeSousa, Michael A. "Symbolic Action and Pretended Insight: The Ayatollah Khomeini in U.S. Editorial Cartoons." In *Rhetorical Dimensions in Media: A Critical Casebook,* ed. Martin J. Medhurst and Thomas W. Benson, 204–30. Dubuque, IA: Kendall/Hunt, 1984.

DeSousa, Michael A., and Martin J. Medhurst. "Political Cartoons and American Culture: Significant Symbols of Campaign 1980." *Studies in Visual Communication* 8 (1982): 84–97.

Devarenne, Nicole. "'A Language Heroically Commensurate with His Body': Nationalism, Fascism, and the Language of the Superhero." *International Journal of Comic Art* 10, no. 1 (2008): 48–54.

Diebler, Matthew. "'I'm Not One of *Them* Any more': Marvel's X-Men and the Loss of Minority (Racial) Identity." *International Journal of Comic Art* 8, no. 2 (2006): 406–13.

DiPaolo, Marc. *War, Politics and Superheroes: Ethics and Propaganda in Comics and Film.* Jefferson, NC: McFarland, 2011.

Dittmer, Jason. *Captain America and the Nationalist Superhero.* Philadelphia, PA: Temple University Press, 2013.

_____. "Fighting for Home: Masculinity and the Constitution of the Domestic in *Tales of Suspense* and *Captain America.*" In *Heroes of Film, Comics and American Culture: Essays on Real and Fictional Defenders of Home,* ed. Lisa M. Detora. Jefferson, NC: McFarland, 2009. Kindle e-book.

Dixon, Norman F. *On the Psychology of Military Incompetence.* New York: Random House eBooks, 2011. Kindle edition.

Dobrivojevic, Ivana. "Cartoons as a Powerful Propaganda Tool: Creating the Images of East and West in the Yugoslav Satirical Press." In *Drawing the Line: Using Cartoons as Historical Evidence,* ed. Richard Scully and Marian Quartly, 10.1–10.16. Clayton, Australia: Monash University ePress, 2009.

Dodge, Bernard J., and Allison Rossett. "Heuristic for Humor in Instruction." *Performance and Instruction* 21, no. 4 (1982): 11–32.

Douglas, Allen. *War, Memory, and the Politics of Humor: The Canard Enchaîné and World War I.* Berkeley, CA: University of California Press, 2002.

Douglas, Allen, and Fedwa Malti-Douglas. "From the Alergian War to the Armenian Massacres: Memory, Trauma, and Medicine in *Petit Polio* of Farid Boudjellal." *International Journal of Comic Art* 10, no. 2 (2008): 282–307.

Douglas, Mary. *Purity and Danger.* London, UK: Routledge, 1966.

Dower, John. *Yellow Promise/Yellow Peril: Foreign Postcards of the Russo-Japanese War.* Massachusetts Institute of Technology, 2008. Digital book at http://ocw.mit.edu/ans7870/21f/21f.027/yellow_promise_yellow_peril/yp_essay01.html. Accessed October 10, 2014.

Drew, Dennis, and Don Snow. *Making Strategy: An Introduction to National Security Processes and Problems.* Maxwell Air Force Base, AL: Air University Press, 1988.

Duffy, Margaret. "High Stakes: A Fantasy Theme Analysis of the Selling of Riverboat Gambling in Iowa." *Southern Communication Journal* 62 (1997): 117–32.

_____. "Web of Hate: A Fantasy Theme Analysis of the Rhetorical Vision of Hate Groups Online." *Journal of Communication Inquiry* 27, no. 3 (2003): 291–312.

Duffy, Michael. "Vintage Audio—How Ya Gonna Keep 'Em Down on the Farm." *FirstWorldWar.com,* August 22, 2009. http://www.firstworldwar.com/audio/howyagonna.htm. Accessed January 5, 2014.

Duncan, Randy, and Matthew J. Smith. *The Power of Comics: History, Form and Culture.* New York: Continuum, 2009.

Dunivin, Karen O. "Military Culture: Change and

Continuity." *Armed Forces and Society* 20, no. 4 (1994): 531–47.

Dunlap, Charles, Mackubin Owens and Richard Kohn. "The Gap." *PBS News Hour,* November 1999. http://www.pbs.org/newshour/forum/november99/civil_military.html. Accessed November 27, 2011.

Edelman, Murray. *Constructing the Political Spectacle.* Chicago, IL: University of Chicago Press, 1988.

Edwards, Janis L., and Huey-Rong Chen. "The First Lady/First Wife in Editorial Cartoons: Rhetorical Visions Through Gender Lenses." *Women's Studies in Communication* 23, no. 3 (2000): 367–91.

Edwards, Janis L., and Carol K. Winkler. "Representative Form and the Visual Ideograph: The Iwo Jima Image in Editorial Cartoons." *Quarterly Journal of Speech* 83 (1997): 289–310.

Edwards, Jason A. "Defining the Enemy for the Post-Cold War World: Bill Clinton's Foreign Policy Discourse in Somalia and Haiti." *International Journal of Communication* 2 (2008): 830–47.

Edwardson, Ryan. "The Many Lives of Captain Canuck: Nationalism, Culture, and the Creation of a Canadian Comic Book Superhero." *Journal of Popular Culture* 37, no. 2 (2003): 184–201.

Egolf, Jamie. "Political Commentary and Dissent in the Tapestry and Cartoon Strip." *International Journal of Comic Art* 11, no. 2 (2009): 432–46.

Eisenhower, Dwight D. "Military-Industrial Complex Speech, 1961." *The Avalon Project.* N.d. http://avalon.law.yale.edu/20th_century/eisenhower001.asp. Accessed June 27, 2013.

Eisner, Will. *Expressive Anatomy for Comics and Narrative: Principles and Practices from the Legendary Cartoonist.* New York: Norton, 2008.
_____. *Graphic Storytelling and Visual Narrative.* New York: Norton, 2008.

Elbein, Saul. "The Marine Corps' Comic-Book Hero." *Men's Journal* 23, no. 11 (November 2014): 20–1.

Elder, Glen H., Jr., and Elizabteh Colerick Clipp. "Combat Experience and Emotional Health: Impairment and Resilience in Later Life." *Journal of Personality* 57, no. 2 (1989): 311–41.

Elkin, Henry. "Aggressive and Erotic Tendencies in Army Life." *American Journal of Sociology* 51, no. 5 (1946): 408–13.

El Rafaie, Elisabeth. *Autobiographic Comics: Life Writing in Pictures.* Jackson, MS: University Press of Mississippi, 2012.

Emad, Mitra C. "Reading Wonder Woman's Body: Mythologies of Gender and Nation." *Journal of Popular Culture* 39, no. 6 (2006): 954–84.

Entman, Robert M. *Projections of Power: Framing News, Public Opinion and U.S. Foreign Policy.* Chicago, IL: University of Chicago Press, 2004.

"Episode 4: Demonising and Dehumanising the Enemy." *Deconstructing Propaganda: World War II Comic Book Covers.* YouTube video. Posted by "DWilt55," May 2, 2011. http://youtu.be/poPnVcgpaYk. Accessed March 13, 2013.

"Episode 9: Images of the Enemy, Japan." *Deconstructing Propaganda: World War II Comic Book Covers.* YouTube video, posted by "DWilt55," October 1, 2013. http://youtu.be/tId_EcrkDOQ. Accessed March 25, 2014.

ESRC. "Soldiers Who Desecrate the Dead See Themselves as Hunters." *Economic and Social Research Council,* 2012. http://www.esrc.ac.uk/news-and-events/press-releases/21182/Soldiers_who_desecrate_the_dead_see_themselves_as_hunters.aspx. Accessed July 21, 2013.

Farber, Manny. "Comic Strips." In *Arguing Comics: Literary Masters on a Popular Medium,* ed. Jeet Heer and Kent Worcester, 91–3. Jackson, MS: University Press of Mississippi, 2009.

Farley, Wilbur. "'The Disease Resumes Its March to Darkness': The Death of Captain Marvel and the Metastasis of Empire." *International Journal of Comic Art* 8, no. 1 (2006): 249–57.

Featherstone, Mike. "The Heroic Life and Everyday Life." *Theory, Culture, and Society* 9, no. 1 (1992): 159–82.

Feaver, Peter D. "The Civil-Military Problematique: Huntington, Janowitz, and the Question of Civilian Control. *Armed Forces and Society* 23, no. 2 (1996): 149–78.

Fehrenbach, T.R. *This Kind of War: The Classic Military History of the Korean War.* 50th Anniversary Edition. New York: Open Road Integrated Media, 2014. Kindle edition.

Fiebig-von Hase, Ragnhild. "Introduction." In *Enemy Images in American History,* ed. Ragnhild Fiebig-von Hase and Ursula Lehmkuhl, 1–40. Providence, RI: Berghahn, 1997.

Finlay, David J., Ole R. Holsti, and Richard R. Fagen. *Enemies in Politics.* Chicago, IL: Rand-McNally, 1967.

Fish, Lydia. "Informal Communication Systems in the Vietnam War: A Case Study in Folklore, Technology and Popular Culture." *New Directions in Folklore* 7 (2003): http://hdl.handle.net/2022/6907. Accessed February 13, 2013.

Fitzgerald, Paul E. *Will Eisner and PS Magazine: An Ongoing Legacy of Nitty Gritty Laughs and Deadly Serious How-To Comics for Generations of America's Warriors.* Fincastle, VA: Fitzworld.com, 2009.

Foss, Sonja K. "Fantasy-Theme Criticism." Chap. 5 in *Rhetorical Criticism: Exploration and Practice.* 2nd ed. Prospect Heights, IL: Waveland, 1996.

Foster, Hal. *The Return of the Real: The Avant-Garde at the End of the Century.* Cambridge, MA: MIT Press, 1996.

Frank, Nathaniel. *Gays in Foreign Militaries 2010: A Global Primer.* Santa Barbara, CA: University of California, 2010. http://www.palmcent er.org/files/FOREIGNMILITARIESPRIMER 2010FINAL.pdf/. Accessed January 26, 2014.

Franke, Volker. *Preparing for Peace: Military Identity, Value Orientations, and Professional Military Education.* Westport, CT: Praeger, 1999.

Freidman, Barabara. "'The Soldier Speaks': *Yank* Coverage of Women and Wartime Work." *American Journalism* 22, no. 2 (2005): 63–82.

Fulton, Robert. "Death and the Funeral in Contemporary Society." In *Dying: Facing the Facts,* ed. Hannelore Wass, 236–255. New York: McGraw-Hill, 1979.

Fussell, Paul. *The Great War and Modern Memory: The Illustrated Edition.* New York: Sterling, 2009.

Gasher, Mike. "Might Makes Right: News Reportage as Discursive Weapon in the War in Iraq." In *Bring 'Em On: Media and Politics in the Iraq War,* ed. Lee Artz and Yahya R. Kamalipour, 209–24. Lanham, MD: Rowman and Littlefield, 2005.

Gates, Robert M. "Lecture at Duke University (All-Volunteer Force)." U.S. Department of Defense. September 29, 2010. http://www.de fense.gov/Speeches/Speech.aspx? SpeechID= 1508. Accessed September 30, 2010.

Genter, Robert. "'With Great Power Comes Great Responsibility': Cold War Culture and the Birth of Marvel Comics." *Journal of Popular Culture* 40, no. 6 (2007): 953–78.

Gerber, David A. "Heroes and Misfits: The Troubled Social Reintegration of Disabled Veterans in *The Best Years of Our Lives.*" *American Quarterly* 46, no. 4 (1994): 545–74.

Gerde, Virginia, and R. Spencer Foster. "X-Men Ethics: Using Comic Books to Teach Business Ethics." *Journal of Business Ethics* 77, no. 3 (2008): 227–30.

Gieryn, Thomas F. "A Space for Place in Sociology." *Annual Review of Sociology* 26 (2000): 463–96.

Gill, D.C. *How We Are Changed by War: A Study of Letters and Diaries from Colonial Conflicts to Operation Iraqi Freedom.* New York: Routledge, 2010.

Gillen, Shawn. "Captain America, Post-Traumatic Stress Syndrome, and the Vietnam Era." In *Captain America and the Struggle of the Superhero: Critical Essays,* ed. Robert G. Weiner, 104–15. Jefferson, NC: McFarland, 2009.

Gillespie, Angus. "Sea Service Slang: Informal Language of the Navy and Coast Guard." In *Warrior Ways: Explorations in Modern Military Folklore,* ed. Eric A. Eliason and Tad Tuleja, 116–36. Logan, UT: Utah State University Press, 2012.

Glaser, Daniel. "The Sentiments of American Soldiers Abroad Toward Europeans." *American Journal of Sociology* 51, no. 5 (1946): 433–8.

Goldich, Robert L. "American Military Culture from Colony to Empire." *Daedalus, the Journal of the American Academy of Arts and Sciences* 140, no. 3 (2011): 58–74.

Goldstein, Joshua A. *War and Gender: How Gender Shapes the War System and Vice Versa.* Cambridge, UK: Cambridge University Press, 2001.

Gombrich, E.H. *The Image and the Eye: Further Studies in the Psychology of Pictorial Representation.* London, UK: Phaidon, 1982.

Goodwin, Jan. "The VA Health-Care System's Dishonorable Conduct." *Good Housekeeping* (March 2010): 160–6, 218–22.

Gordon, Ian. "Nostalgia, Myth, and Ideology: Visions of Superman at the End of the 'American Century.'" In *Comics and Ideology* vol. 2, ed. Matthew P. McAllister, Edward H. Sewell, Jr., and Ian Gordon, 177–94. Popular Culture Everyday Life. New York: Peter Lang, 2009.

Gorer, Geoffrey. *Death, Grief, and Mourning.* New York: Doubleday, 1965.

Graham, Richard L. *Government Issue: Comics for the People, 1940s–2000s.* New York: Abrams Comicarts, 2011.

Green, Ernest J. "The Social Functions of Utopian Architecture." *Utopian Studies* 4, no. 1 (1993): 1–13.

Gregory, W. Edgar. "The Idealization of the Absent." *American Journal of Sociology* 51, no. 1 (1944): 53–4.

Griffin, Robert J., and Shaikat Sen. "Causal Communication: Movie Portrayals and Audience Attributions for Vietnam Veterans' Problems." *Journalism and Mass Communication Quarterly* 72, no. 3 (1995): 511–24.

Grigorescu, Lt. Lucian. *Camouflaged Emotions: Stoicism in the Military.* Quantico, VA: United States Marine Corps, Command and Staff College, 2009.

Grimaldi. "Is There Humor in Afghanistan?" *The Public Manager* 30, no. 4 (2001): 55–6.

Grinspan, Jon. "'Sorrowfully Amusing': The Popular Comedy of the Civil War." *Journal of the Civil War* 1, no. 3 (2011). Kindle edition.

Groensteen, Thierry. *The System of Comics.* 1999. Trans. Bart Beaty and Nick Nguyen. Jackson, MS: University Press of Mississippi, 2007.

Hajdu, David. *The Ten-Cent Plague: The Great Comic-Book Scare and How It Changed America.* New York: Picador, 2009.

Hale, Timothy L. "Opet's Odyssey." *Double Eagle* July (2012): 10–11, 15.

Hall, Kelley J. and Betsy Lucal. "Tapping into Parallel Universes: Using Superhero Comic Books in Sociology Courses." *Teaching Sociology* 27 (January 1999): 60–6.

Hall, Stuart. "The Spectacle of the 'Other.'" In *Representation: Cultural Representation and Signifying Practices,* ed. Stuart Hall, 223–79. London, UK: Sage, 1997.

Hallin, Daniel C., and Todd Gitlin. "The Gulf War as Popular Culture and as Television Drama." In *Taken by Storm: The Media, Public Opinion and U.S. Foreign Policy in the Gulf War*, ed. W. Lance Bennett and David L. Paletz, 149–63. Chicago, IL: University of Chicago Press, 1994.

Hamilton, Sue L. *Jack Kirby: Creator and Artist*. Edina, MD: ABDO, 2007.

Hanna, Martha. "A Republic of Letters: The Epistolary Tradition in France During World War I." *American Historical Review* (2003): 1336–61.

Hanson, Thomas E. "Forward." In *The Roots of Military Doctrine*, by Aaron P. Jackson, iii–iv. N.p.: Combat Studies Institute Press, 2013.

Harper, Howard. "The Military and Society: Reaching and Reflecting Audiences in Fiction and Film." *Armed Forces and Society* 27, no. 2 (2001): 231–48.

Harries-Jenkins, Gwyn. "Institution to Occupation to Diversity: Gender in the Military Today." In *Challenge and Change in the Military: Gender and Diversity Issues*, ed. Franklin C. Pinch, Allister T. MacIntyre, Phyllis Browne and Alan C. Okros, 26–51. Kingston, Canada: Canadian Defence Academy Press, 2006.

Harrison-Hall, Jessica. *Vietnam Behind the Lines: Images from the War, 1965–1975*. Chicago, IL: Art Media Resources, 2002.

Hart, Roderick P. "Cultural Criticism." Chap. 11 in *Modern Rhetorical Criticism*, 2nd ed. Boston, MA: Allyn and Bacon, 1997.

Hart, William B., II, and Fran Hassenchal. "Culture as Persuasion: Metaphor as Weapon." In *Bring 'Em On: Media and Politics in the Iraq War*, ed. Lee Artz and Yahya R. Kamalipour, 85–100. Lanham, MD: Rowman and Littlefield, 2005.

———. "Dehumanizing the Enemy in Editorial Cartoons." In *Communication and Terrorism: Public and Media Responses to 9/11*, ed. Bradley S. Greenberg, 123–51. Cresskill, NJ: Hampton, 2002.

Harvey, R.C. *Milton Caniff's Male Call: The Complete Newspaper Strips: 1942–1946*. Neshannock, PA: Hermes, 2011.

Harvey, Robert C. *The Art of the Funnies: An Aesthetic History*. Studies in Popular Culture. Jackson, MS: University Press of Mississippi, 1994.

———. "Comedy at the Juncture of Word and Image: The Emergence of the Modern Magazine Gag Cartoon Reveals the Vital Blend." In *The Language of Comics Word and Image*, ed. Robin Varnum and Christina T. Gibbons, 75–106. Studies in Popular Culture. Jackson, MS: University Press of Mississippi, 2001.

———. "How Comics Came to Be: Through the Juncture of Word and Image from Magazine Gag Cartoons to Newspaper Strips: Tools for Critical Appreciation Plus Rare, Seldom Witnessed Historical Facts." In *A Comic Studies Reader*, ed. Jeet Heer and Kent Worcester, 25–45. Jackson, MS: University Press of Mississippi, 2009.

Harwell, Richard. *Margaret Mitchell's Gone with the Wind Letters 1936–1949*. New York: Macmillan, 1976.

Hawkins, John P. *Army of Hope, Army of Alienation*. Tuscaloosa, AL: University of Alabama Press, 2001.

Hearts and Minds. Directed by Peter Davis (1974; Criterion Collection). YouTube video, posted by "Sao Vàng." August 22, 2012. http://youtu.be/1d2ml82lc7s. Accessed March 20, 2014.

Heer, Jeet, and Kent Worcester. "Introduction." In *A Comic Studies Reader*, ed. Jeet Heer and Kent Worcester, xi–xv. Jackson, MS: University Press of Mississippi, 2009.

Henman, Linda D. "Humor as a Coping Mechanism: Lessons from POWs." *Humor* 14, no. 1 (2001): 83–94.

Herman, David. "Spatial Reference in Narrative Domains." *Text* 21, no. 4 (2001): 515–41.

Herman, Virginia. "Forward." In *Winnie the WAC: The Return of a World War II Favorite*, by Cpl. Vic Herman, 1. Encinitas, CA: KNI, Inc./Virginia Herman, 2002.

Heuer, Lt.C. Martin. "Personal Reflections on the Songs of Army Aviators in the Vietnam War." *New Directions in Folklore* 7 (2003): http://hdl.handle.net/2022/6909. Accessed July 9, 2013.

Higate, Paul Richard. "Theorizing Continuity: From Military to Civilian Life." *Armed Forces and Society* 27, no. 3 (2001): 443–60.

Hill, Deborah J. *Humor in the Classroom: A Handbook for Teachers*. Springfield, IL: Charles C. Thomas, 1988.

Hipes, Crosby. "The Framing of PTSD: Narratives of Mental Health Workers and Veterans." M.A. thesis, University of Arkansas, 2009.

Hockey, John. *Squaddies: Portrait of a Subculture*. Exeter, UK: Exeter University Press, 1986.

Hogan, Jon. "The Comic Book as Symbolic Environment: The Case of Iron Man." *ETC: A Review of General Semantics* 66, no. 2 (2009): 199–214.

Hollingshead, August B. "Adjustment to Military Life." *American Journal of Sociology* 51, no. 5 (1946): 439–47.

Holt, Tonie, and Valmai Holt. "Introduction to the 'BB4H4H' Edition of Best of Fragments from France." In *The Best of Fragments from France* by Capt. Bruce Bairnsfather (compiled and ed. Tonie and Valmai Holt), 4. South Yorkshire, UK: Pen and Sword Military, 2009.

Hönicke, Michaela. "'Know Your Enemy': American Wartime Images of Germany, 1942–1943." In *Enemy Images in American History*, edited Ragnhild Fiebig-von Hase and Ursula Lehmkuhl, 231–78. Providence, RI: Berghahn, 1997.

Horton, Mildred McAfee. "Women in the United

States Navy." *American Journal of Sociology* 51, no. 5 (1946): 448–50.

Howery, Carla B. "*Get Real Comics* Reveal a Sociological Touch." *Footnotes,* February 2007. http://www.asanet.org/footnotes/feb00/fn07.html. Accessed July 19, 2013.

Hudson-Rodd, Nancy, and Sundar Ramanathaiyer. "Cartooning the Iraq War: No Laughing Matter." *International Journal of Comic Art* 8, no. 1 (2006): 532–45.

Hume, Bill, and John Annarino. *Babysan: A Private Look at the Japanese Occupation.* Tokyo: Kasuga Boeki, 1953.

_____. *When We Get Back Home from Japan.* Tokyo: Kyoya, 1953.

Huntington, Samuel P. *The Soldier and the State: The Theory and Politics of Civil-Military Relations.* Cambridge, MA: Belknap Press of Harvard University Press, 1957.

Huntley, Mary I. "Take Time for Laughter." *Creative Nursing* 15, no. 1 (2009): 39–42.

Huntley, Mary, and Edna Thayer. *A Mirthful Spirit: Embracing Laughter for Wellness.* Edina, MN: Beaver's Pond, 2007.

Hutchinson, Katharine H. "An Experiment in the Use of Comics as Instructional Material." *Journal of Educational Sociology* 23, no. 4 (1949): 236–45.

Ingraham, Larry H. *The Boys in the Barracks: Observations on American Military Life.* Philadelphia, PA: Institute for the Study of Human Issues, 1984.

Ioniță, Denise Teodora, Andrade Victoria Suciu, Mihaela Suhalitca, and Oana Voitovici. "Political Cartoons." *Journal of Media Research* 3, no. 11 (2011): 28–44.

Irwin, Anne. "The Problem of Realism and Reality in Military Training Exercises." In *New Directions in Military Sociology,* ed. Eric Oullet, 93–133. Whitby, ON: de Sitter, 2005.

Isabella, Tony. *1,000 Comic Books You Must Read.* Iola, WI: Krause, 2009. Kindle e-book.

ITS Crew. "Military Acronyms, Terminology and Slang Reference." *Imminent Threat Solutions.* January 5, 2012. http://www.itstactical.com/intellicom/language/military-acronymstermin ology-and-slang-reference/. Accessed January 5, 2014.

Ivie, Robert L. *Democracy and America's War on Terror.* Rhetoric, Culture, and Social Critique. Tuscaloosa, AL: University of Alabama Press, 2005.

_____. "Democracy, War, and Decivilizing Metaphors of American Insecurity." In *Metaphorical World Politics,* ed. Francis A. Beer and Christ'l De Landtsheer, 75–90. East Lansing, MI: Michigan State University Press, 2004.

_____. *Dissent from War.* Bloomfield, CT: Kumarian, 2007.

_____. "Images of Savagery in American Justifi-

cations for War." *Communication Monographs* 47 (1980): 279–94.

_____. "Metaphor and the Rhetorical Invention of Cold War 'Idealists.'" *Communication Monographs* 54 (1987): 165–82.

Jackson, Aaron P. *The Roots of Military Doctrine.* N.p.: Combat Studies Institute Press, 2013.

Jackson, Bradley G. "A Fantasy Theme Analysis of Peter Senge's Learning Organization." *Journal of Applied Behavioral Science* 36, no. 2 (2000): 193–209.

Jacobs, Dale. "Beyond Visual Rhetoric: Multimodal Rhetoric and Newspaper Comic Strips." *International Journal of Comic Art* 9, no. 1 (2007): 502–14.

Jaffe, Alexandra. "Saluting in Social Context." *Journal of Applied Behavioral Science* 24, no. 3 (1988): 263–75.

Jahn, Hubertus F. "Kaiser, Cossacks, and Kolbasniks: Caricatures of the German in Russian Popular Culture." *Journal of Popular Culture* 31, no. 4 (1998): 109–22.

Janowitz, Morris. *The Professional Soldier: A Social and Political Portrait.* New York: Free Press, 1960.

_____. *Sociology and the Military Establishment.* New York: Russell Sage Foundation, 1959.

Jarman, Baird. "The Graphic Art of Thomas Nast: Politics and Propriety in Postbellum Publishing." *American Periodicals* 20, no. 2 (2010): 156–89.

Jenkinson, Jacqueline. "'All in the Same Uniform'? The Participation of Black Colonial Residents in the British Armed Forces in the First World War." *Journal of Imperial and Commonwealth History* 40, no. 2 (2012): 207–230.

Jessup, Chris. *Breaking Ranks: Social Change in Military Communities.* London, UK: Brassey's, 1996.

Jolly, Ruth. *Changing Step from Military to Civilian Life: People in Transition.* London, UK: Brassey's, 1996.

_____. *Military Man, Family Man.* London, UK: Brassey's Defence, 1987.

Jones, Ann. *They Were Soldiers: How the Wounded Return from America's Wars—the Untold Story.* Chicago, IL: Haymarket, 2013. Kindle edition.

Jones, Brian Adam. "The Sexist Facebook Movement the Marine Corps Can't Stop." *Task and Purpose.* August 20, 2014: http://taskandpur pose.com/sexist-facebook-movement-marine-corps-cant-stop/. Accessed August 20, 2014.

Jones, Edgar. "The Psychology of Killing: The Combat Experience of British Soldiers During the First World War." *Journal of Contemporary History* 41, no. 2 (2006): 229–46.

Jones, Jeffrey P. *Entertaining Politics.* 2nd ed. Lanham, MD: Rowman and Littlefield, 2010.

Joseph, Genie. "Laughter Is Best Medicine for Military Families." *U.S. Army,* April 15, 2011.

http://www.army.mil/article/55071/Laughter_is_best_medicine_for_military_families/. Accessed July 19, 2013.

Kalb, Marvin. "Provocations: A View from the Press." In *Taken by Storm: The Media, Public Opinion, and Foreign Policy in the Gulf War*, ed. W. Lance Bennet and David L. Paletz, 3–6. Chicago: University of Chicago Press, 1994.

Kamerman, Jack B. *Death in the Midst of Life.* Englewood Cliffs, NJ: Prentice Hall, 1988.

Kassarjian, Harold H. "Males and Females in the Funnies: A Content Analysis." In *Personal Values and Consumer Psychology*, ed. Robert E. Pitts, Jr., and Arch G. Woodside, 87–109. Lexington, MA: Lexington, 1984.

_____. "Social Values and the Sunday Comics: A Content Analysis." In *Advances in Consumer Research*, vol. 10, ed. Richard P. Bagozzi and Alice M. Tybout, 434–38. Ann Arbor, MI: Association for Consumer Research, 1983.

Katz, Harry L., and Vincent Virga. *Civil War Sketchbook: Drawings from the Battlefront.* New York: W.W. Norton, 2012.

Kaźmierczak, Janusz. "Raymond Williams and Cartoons: From Churchill's Cigar to Cultural History." *International Journal of Comic Art* 7, no. 2 (2005): 147–63.

Kearl, Michael C. "Death in Popular Culture." In *Death: Current Perspectives*, ed. John B. Williamson and Edwin S. Shneidman, 23–30. Mountain View, CA: Mayfield, 1995.

Keen, Sam. *Faces of the Enemy: Reflections of the Hostile Imagination.* San Francisco, CA: Harper and Row, 1986.

Kefford, Ali. "The Original GI Jane." Reprinted from "A Strip for Victory." *Skylighters.* N.d. http://www.skylighters.org/jane. Accessed July 19, 2013.

Kellen, Konrad. *Conversations with Enemy Soldiers in Late 1968/Early 1969: A Study of Motivation and Morale.* Prepared for the Office of the Assistant Secretary of Defense/International Security Affairs and the Advanced Research Projects Agency. Santa Monica, CA: Rand, 1970.

Kelty, Ryan. "Citizen Soldiers and Civilian Contractors: Soldiers' Unit Cohesion and Retention Attitudes in the 'Total Force.'" *Journal of Political and Military Sociology* 37, no. 2 (2009): 133–59.

Kelty, Ryan, Meredith Kleykamp, and David R. Segal. "The Military and the Transition to Adulthood." *The Future of Children* 20, no. 1 (2010): 181–207.

Kemnitz, Thomas Milton. "The Cartoon as a Historical Source." *Journal of Interdisciplinary History* 4, no. 1 (1973): 81–93.

Kent, Christopher. "War Cartooned/Cartoon War: Matt Morgan and the American Civil War in *Fun* and *Frank Leslie's Illustrated Newspaper*." *Victorian Periodicals Review* 36, no. 2 (2003): 153–81.

Kercher, Stephen E. "Cartoons as 'Weapons of Wit': Bill Mauldin and Herbert Block Take On America's Postwar Anti-Communist Crusade." *International Journal of Comic Art* 7, no. 2 (2005): 311–20.

King, Andrew. "The Word of Command: Communication and Cohesion in the Military." *Armed Forces and Society* 32, no. 4 (2006): 493–512.

Kinney, Katherine. "The Good War and Its Other: Beyond Private Ryan." In *War Narratives and American Culture*, ed. Giles Gunn and Carl Gutiérrez-Jones, 121–38. Santa Barbara, CA: American Cultures and Global Contexts Center, University of California, 2005.

Klish, Reneé. *Art of the American Soldier: Documenting Military History Through Artists' Eyes and in Their Own Words.* Washington, D.C.: Center of Military History, 2011.

Knapp, Robert H. "A Psychology of Rumor." *The Public Opinion Quarterly* 8, no. 1 (1944): 22–37.

Knopf, Christina M. "'Hey Soldier, Your Slip Is Showing!' Militarism vs. Femininity in World War II Comic Pages and Books." In *Ten Cent War*, ed. James Kimball and Trischa Goodnow. Jackson, MS: University Press of Mississippi, forthcoming.

_____. "Relational Dialectics in the Civil-Military Relationship: Lessons from Veterans' Transition Narratives." *Political and Military Sociology: An Annual Review* 40 (2012): 171–92.

_____. "Sense-Making and Map-Making: War Letters as Personal Geographies." *NANO* 6 (2014): http://www.nanocrit.com/issues/6-2014/sense-making-map-making-war-letters-personal-geographics.

Knopf, Christina M., and Eric J. Ziegelmayer. "Fourth Generation Warfare and the U.S. Military's Social Media Strategy: Promoting the Academic Conversation." *Air and Space Power Journal—Africa and Francophonie* 4 (2012): 3–22.

Knox, Kerry L., and Robert M. Bossarte. "Suicide Prevention for Veterans and Active Duty Personnel." *American Journal of Public Health* 102, no. S1 (2012): S8–S9.

Kohen, Janet A. "The Military Career Is a Family Affair." *Journal of Family Issues* 5, no. 3 (1984): 401–18.

Krensky, Stephen. *Comic Book Century: The History of American Comic Books.* Minneapolis, MN: Twenty-First Century, 2008.

Kuehn, B.M. "Military Probes Epidemic of Suicide: Mental Health Issues Remain Prevalent," *JAMA* 3014, no. 13 (2010): 1152–58.

Kuipers, Giselinde. "'Where Was King Kong When We Needed Him?' Public Discourse, Digital Disaster Jokes, and the Functions of Laughter after 9/11." *Journal of American Culture* 28, no. 1 (2005): 70–84.

Kukkonen, Karin. "Popular Cultural Memory: Comics, Communities and Context Knowledge." *Nordicom Review* 29, no. 2 (2008): 261–73.

Kümmel, Gerhard. "A Soldier Is a Soldier Is a Soldier!? The Military and Its Soldiers in an Era of Globalization." In *Handbook of the Sociology of the Military*, ed. Giuseppe Caforio, 417–33. New York: Springer, 2006.

Kunzle, David. *Father of the Comic Strip: Rodolphe Töpffer*. Jackson, MS: University Press of Mississippi, 2007.

Kuusisto, Riikka. "Heroic Tale, Game, and Business Deal? Western Metaphors in Action in Kosovo." *Quarterly Journal of Speech* 88, no. 2 (2002): 50–68.

Lair, Meredith H. *Armed with Abundance: Consumerism and Soldiering in the Vietnam War*. Chapel Hill, NC: University of North Carolina Press, 2011. Kindle edition.

Landis, Carole. "Forward," in *Winnie the WAC*, by Cpl. Vic Herman, 1–4. Philadelphia, PA: David McKay, 1945.

Lang, Kurt. "Military Organizations." In *Handbook of Organizations*, ed. John G. March, 838–78. Chicago, IL: Rand McNally, 1965.

Langley, Travis. "Freedom Versus Security: The Basic Human Dilemma from 9/11 to Marvel's *Civil War*." *International Journal of Communication* 11, no. 1 (2009): 426–35.

Laraudogoitia, Jon Pérez. "The Comic as Binary Language: An Hypothesis on Comic Structure," *Journal of Quantitative Linguistics* 15, no. 2 (2008): 111–35.

_____. "The Composition and Structure of the Comic," *Journal of Quantitative Linguistics* 16, no. 4 (2009): 327–53.

Lattanzi, Marcia, and Mary Ellis Hale. "Giving Grief Words: Writing During Bereavement." *Omega* 15, no. 1 (1984–1985): 45–52.

Laufer, Robert S., M.S. Gallops, and Ellen Frey-Wouters. "War Stress and Trauma: The Vietnam Veteran Experience." *Journal of Health and Social Behavior* 25, no. 1 (1984): 65–85.

"Laughter Yoga in the Canadian Military," *Laughter Yoga International*, May 23, 2013. http://www.laughteryoga.org/news/news_details/441. Accessed July 19, 2013.

Leab, Daniel J. "Cold War Comics." *Columbia Journalism Review*, Winter 1965, 42–7.

Lefèvre, Pascal. "The Unresolved Past: Repercussions of World War II in Belgian Comics." *International Journal of Comic Art* 9, no. 1 (2007): 296–310.

Lendrum, Rob. "Queering Super-Manhood: The Gay Superhero in Contemporary Mainstream Comic Books." *Journal for the Arts, Sciences, and Technology* 2, no. 2 (2004): 69–73.

Lent, John A. "Cartooning, Public Crises, and Conscientization: A Global Perspective." *International Journal of Comic Art* 10, no. 1 (2008): 352–86.

Lent, John A., and Xu Ying. "Cartooning and Wartime China: Part One—1931–1945." *International Journal of Comic Art* 10, no. 1 (2008): 76–139.

Lepre, George. *Fragging: Why U.S. Soldiers Assaulted Their Officers in Vietnam*. Lubbock, TX: Texas Tech University Press, 2011.

Leonhard, Robert R. *Fighting by Minutes: Time and the Art of War*. Westport, CT: Praeger, 1994.

Leuprecht, Christian. "Demographics and Diversity Issues in Canadian Military Participation." In *Challenge and Change in the Military: Gender and Diversity Issues*, ed. Franklin C. Pinch, Allister T. MacIntyre, Phyllis Browne and Alan C. Okros, 122–46. Kingston, Canada: Canadian Defence Academy Press, 2006.

Lewis, Ralph. "Officer-Enlisted Men's Relationships." *American Journal of Sociology* 52, no. 5 (1947): 410–19.

Ley, David. *A Social Geography of the City*. New York: HarperCollins, 1983.

Litoff, Judy Barrett, and David C. Smith. "Since You Went Away: The World War II Letters of Barbara Wooddall Taylor." *Women's Studies* 17 (1990): 249–76.

Litzenberg, Homer. "Preface." In *Leatherhead in Korea*, by SSGT Norval E. Packwood, Jr., 1–2. Quantico, VA: Marine Corps Gazette, 1952.

Lopes, Paul. *Demanding Respect: The Evolution of the American Comic Book*. Philadelphia, PA: Temple University Press, 2009.

MacCallum-Stewart, Esther. "The First World War and British Comics." *University of Sussex Journal of Contemporary History* 6 (2003): 1–18.

MacDougall, Robert. "Red, Brown and Yellow Perils: Images of the American Enemy in the 1940s and 1950s." *Journal of Popular Culture* 32, no. 4 (1999): 59–75.

Madison, Nathan Vernon. *Anti-Foreign Imagery in American Pulps and Comic Books, 1920–1960*. Jefferson, NC: McFarland, 2013.

Madrid, Mike. *Supergirls: Fashion, Feminism, and Fantasy, and the History of Comic Book Heroines*. Minneapolis, MN: Exterminating Angel, 2009.

Maggio, J. "Comics and Cartoons: A Democratic Art-Form." *PS: Political Science and Politics* 40, no. 2 (2007): 237–9.

Malinowski, Jon C. "Peleliu: Geographic Complications of Operation Stalemate." In *Military Geography from Peace to War*, ed. Eugene J. Palka and Francis A. Galgano, 91–112. New York: McGraw-Hill, 2005.

Malone, John D., Kenneth C. Hyams, Richard E. Hawkins, Trueman W. Sharp, and Fredric D. Daniell. "Risk Factors for Sexually-Transmitted Diseases Among Deployed U.S. Military Personnel," *Sexually Transmitted Diseases* 20, no. 5 (1993): 294–98.

Mandelbaum, David G. "Social Uses of Funeral Rites." In *The Meaning of Death*, ed. Herman Feifel, 189–217. New York: McGraw-Hill, 1959.

Maresca, Frank W. *A Soldier's Odyssey: To Remember Our Past as It Was*. N.p.: Trafford, 2012.

Marín-Arrese, Juana I. "Cognition and Culture in Political Cartoons." *Intercultural Pragmatics* 5, no. 1 (2008): 1–18.

Marshall, Bridget M. "Comics as Primary Sources: The Case of Journey into Mohawk Country." In *Comic Books and American Cultural History*, ed. Matthew Pustz, 26–39. New York: Continuum, 2012.

Marvin, Carolyn, and David W. Ingle. *Blood Sacrifice and the Nation: Totem Rituals and the American Flag*. Cambridge, UK: Cambridge University Press, 1999.

Massey, Doreen. *For Space*. Los Angeles, CA: Sage, 2005.

Matthews, Kristina L. "The ABCs of *Mad* Magazine: Reading, Citizenship, and Cold War America." *International Journal of Comic Art* 8, no. 2 (2006): 248–68.

_____. "A Mad Proposition in Postwar America." *Journal of American Culture* 30, no. 2 (2007): 212–21.

Matton, Annette. "From Realism to Superheroes in Marvel's *The 'Nam*." In *Comics and Ideology*, vol. 2, ed. Matthew P. McAllister, Edward H. Sewell, Jr., and Ian Gordon, 151–76. Popular Culture Everyday Life. New York: Peter Lang, 2009.

Mauldin, Bill. *Up Front*. 1945. New York: W.W. Norton, 2000.

Maw, Dolly. "Herman's Hacienda." *San Diego Magazine*, July 1971, 68–9, 91 and 94.

McAllister, Matthew P., Edward H. Sewell, Jr., and Ian Gordon, eds. *Comics and Ideology*, vol. 2. Popular Culture Everyday Life. New York: Peter Lang, 2009.

McCloud, Scott. *Understanding Comics: The Invisible Art*. New York: HarperPerennial, 1993.

McCloy, Thomas M., and William H. Clover. "Value Formation at the Air Force Academy." In *The Military: More Than Just a Job?*, ed. Charles C. Moskos and Frank R. Wood, 129–49. Washington, D.C.: Pergamon-Brassey's, 1988.

McClure, Peggy, and Walter Broughton. "Measuring the Cohesion of Military Communities." *Armed Forces and Society* 26, no. 3 (2000): 473–87.

McFate, Montgomery. "The Military Utility of Understanding Adversary Culture." *Joint Force Quarterly* 38 (2005): 42–8.

McGarty, Craig, Vincent Y. Yzerbyt, and Russel Spears. "Social, Cultural, and Cognitive Factors in Stereotype Formation." In *Stereotypes as Explanations: The Formation of Meaningful Beliefs About Social Groups*, ed. Craig

McGarty, Vincent Y. Yzerbyt, and Russel Spears, 1–15. Cambridge, UK: Cambridge University Press, 2002.

McGrath, Karen. "Gender, Race, and Latina Identity: An Examination of Marvel Comics' *Amazing Fantasy* and *Araña*." *Atlantic Journal of Communication* 15, no. 4 (2007): 268–83.

McKeever, Bruce. "Framing the Enemy: A Study of American Military Training in Modern War." Paper presented at the annual meeting of the Eastern Sociological Society, Baltimore, MD, February 2014.

McLaughlin, Jeff. "9–11–01: Truth, Justice and Comic Books." *International Journal of Comic Art* 8, no. 1 (2006): 412–25.

McLellan, Josie. "'I Wanted to Be a Little Lenin': Ideology and the German International Brigade Volunteers." *Journal of Contemporary History* 41, no. 2 (2006): 287–304.

McLelland, Mark J. "The Love Between 'Beautiful Boys' in Japanese Women's Comics." *Journal of Gender Studies* 9 (2000): 13–25.

Medhurst, Martin J., and Michael A. DeSousa. "Political Cartoons as Rhetorical Form: A Taxonomy of Graphic Discourse." *Communication Monographs* 48 (1981): 197–236.

Mental Health America. "A Letter for EVERY Life Lost." N.d. http://www.change.org/petitions/view/a_letter_for_every_life_lost. Accessed July 14, 2010.

Merridale, Catherine. "Culture, Ideology and Combat in the Red Army, 1939–45." *Journal of Contemporary History* 41, no. 2 (2006): 305–24.

Mershon, Sherie, and Steven Schlossman. *Foxholes and Color Lines: Desegregating the U.S. Armed Forces*. Baltimore, MD: Johns Hopkins Press, 1998.

Merskin, Debra. "The Construction of Arabs as Enemies: Post–9/11 Discourse of George W. Bush." In *Bring 'Em On: Media and Politics in the Iraq War*, ed. Lee Artz and Yahya R. Kamalipour, 121–38, Lanham, MD: Rowman and Littlefield, 2005.

Merton, Robert K. *Social Theory and Social Structure*, revised ed. Glencoe, IL: Free Press, 1957.

Metcalf, C.W., and Roma Felible. *Lighten Up: Survival Skills for People Under Pressure*. Menlo Park, CA: Addison-Wesley, 1992.

Meyer, Leisa D. *Creating GI Jane: Sexuality and Power in the Women's Army Corps During World War II*. New York: Columbia University Press, 1996.

Micewski, Edwin R. "Conscription or the All-Volunteer Force: Recruitment in a Democratic Society." In *Who Guards the Guardians and How: Democratic Civil-Military Relations*, ed. Thomas C. Bruneau and Scott D. Tollefson, 208–34. Austin, TX: University of Texas Press, 2006.

Miles, Donna. "Chairman Calls for Military Self-Examination." Joint Chiefs of Staff Official Web Site. January 10, 2011. http://www.jcs.mil/news article.aspx?ID=499. Accessed July 28, 2013.

_____. "Edwards Team Stars in 'Ironman' Superhero Movie." U.S. Department of Defense. May 2, 2007. http://www.defense.gov/news/news article.aspx?id=33023. Accessed June 17, 2013.

_____. "Military, Hollywood Team Up to Create Realism, Drama on Big Screen." U.S. Department of Defense, June 8, 2007. http://www.defense.gov/News/Newsarticle. aspx?ID= 463 52. Accessed June 17, 2013.

Monahan, Evelyn M., and Rosemary Neidel-Greenlee. *A Few Good Women: America's Military Women from World War I to the Wars in Iraq and Afghanistan*. New York: Anchor, 2011.

Montgomerie, Deborah. *Love in Time of War: Letter Writing in the Second World War*. Auckland, NZ: Auckland University Press, 2005.

Moran, Carmen. "Allies Cartoon Humor in World War II: A Comparison of 'Willie and Joe' and 'Bluey and Curley.'" *International Journal of Comic Art* 6, no. 2 (2004): 431–45.

Moser, John E. "Madmen, Morons, and Monocles: The Portrayal of the Nazis in *Captain America*." In *Captain America and the Struggle of the Superhero*, ed. Robert C. Weiner, 24–35. Jefferson, NC: McFarland, 2009.

Moskos, Charles C. "Institutional and Occupational Trends in Armed Forces." In *The Military: More Than Just a Job?*, ed. Charles C. Moskos and Frank R. Wood, 15–26. Washington, D.C.: Pergamon-Brassey's, 1988.

Moskos, Charles C., and John Sibley Butler. *All That We Can Be: Black Leadership and Racial Integration the Army Way*. New York: Basic, 1996.

Moss, Dori. "The Animated Persuader." *PS: Political Science and Politics* 40, no. 2 (2007): 241–44.

Mundey, Lisa M. *American Militarism and Anti-Militarism in Popular Media, 1945–1970*. Jefferson, NC: McFarland, 2012.

Murray, Williamson. "Does Military Culture Matter?" *Foreign Policy Research Institute* 43, no. 1 (1999): 134–51.

Nakar, Eldad. "Memories of Pilots and Planes: World War II in Japanese *Manga*, 1957–1967." *Social Science Japan Journal* 6, no. 1: 57–76.

Nardini, J.E. "Survival Factors in American Prisoners of War of the Japanese." *American Journal of Psychiatry* 109, 4 (1952): 241–8.

National Archives. "Propaganda: Home Front." *The Art of War*, http://www.nationalarchives.gov.uk/theartofwar/prop/home_front/INF3_0229.htm. Accessed February 1, 2014.

Nazareth, Brigadier J. *The Psychology of Military Humour*. Olympia Fields, IL: Lancer, 2008.

Negron, Julie L. *PCSing.... It's a Spouse Thing!* N.p.: Lulu.com/JulieNegron, 2010.

Neidel-Greenlee, Rosemary, and Evelyn Monahan. *And if I Perish: Frontline U.S. Army Nurses in World War II*. New York: Knopf, 2003.

Nelson, Daniel N. "Definition, Diagnosis, Therapy: A Civil-Military Critique." *Defense and Security Analysis* 18, no. 2 (2002): 157–70.

Neuhaus, Jessamyn. "How Wonder Woman Helped My Students 'Join the Conversation': Comic Books as Teaching Tools in a History Methodology Course." In *Comic Books and American Cultural History*, ed. Matthew Pustz, 11–25. New York: Continuum, 2012.

Newton, Julianne H. "Trudeau Draws Truth." *Critical Studies in Media Communication* 24, no. 1 (2007): 81–5.

Newton, Stephanie. "Bailey Strip Gets Attitude Adjustment." In *Mort Walker Conversations*, Conversations with Comic Artists, ed. Jason Whiton, 168–170. Jackson, MS: University Press of Mississippi, 2005.

Nickels, Cameron C. *Civil War Humor*. Jackson, MS: University Press of Mississippi, 2010.

Nijboer, Donald. *Graphic War: The Secret Aviation Drawings and Illustrations of World War II*. Ontario: Boston Mills, 2011.

Nöth, Winfried. "Narrative Self-Reference in a Literary Comic: M.-A. Mathieu's *L'Origine*." *Semiotica* 165–1/4 (2007): 173–90.

Nuciari, Marina. "Women in the Military: Sociological Arguments for Integration." In *Handbook of the Sociology of the Military*, ed. Giuseppe Caforio, 279–98. New York: Springer, 2006.

Nyberg, Amy Kiste. "Comic Books." In *History of Mass Media in the United States: An Encyclopedia*, ed. Margaret A. Blanchard, 149–50. London, UK: Routledge, 1998.

_____. "Comics Journalism: Drawing on Words to Picture the Past in *Safe Area Goražde*." In *Critical Approaches to Comics: Theories and Methods*, ed. Matthew J. Smith and Randy Duncan, 116–28. New York: Routledge, 2012.

_____. "Theorizing Comics Journalism." *International Journal of Comic Art* 8, no. 2 (2006): 98–112.

Obrdlik, Antonin J. "'Gallows Humor'—A Sociological Phenomenon." *American Journal of Sociology* 47, no. 5 (1942): 709–16.

O'Brien, Tim. *The Things They Carried*. 1990. Boston, MA: Mariner, 2009.

O'Heffernan, Patrick. "A Mutual Exploitation Model of Media Influence in U.S. Foreign Policy." In *Taken by Storm: The Media, Public Opinion, and Foreign Policy in the Gulf War*, ed. W. Lance Bennet and David L. Paletz, 231–49. Chicago: University of Chicago Press, 1994.

O'Neill, Patrick. "The Comedy of Entropy: The Contexts of Black Humour." *Canadian Review of Comparative Literature* 10, no. 2 (1983): 145–166.

Ormrod, Joan Stewart. "Graphic Novels." In *Ency-

clopedia of Contemporary British Culture, ed. Peter Childs and Mike Storry, 236–7. London, UK: Routledge, 1999.

Oswald, Justin M. "Know Thy Enemy: Camel Spider Stories Among U.S. Troops in the Middle East." In *Warrior Ways: Explorations in Modern Military Folklore*, ed. Eric A. Eliason and Tad Tuleja, 38–57. Boulder, CO: Utah State University Press, 2012.

Owens, Mackubin T. "U.S. Civil-Military Relations After 9/11: Renegotiating the Civil-Military Bargain." *Foreign Policy Research Institute E-Notes*, 2011: http://www.fpri.org /en otes/201101.owens.civilmilitaryrelations.html. Accessed June 20, 2012.

Pagliassotti, Dru, Kazumi Nagaike and Mark McHarry. "Editorial: Boys' Love Manga Special Section." *Journal of Graphic Novels and Comics* 4, no. 1 (2013): 1–8.

Palka, Eugene J. "Operation Enduring Freedom: The Military Geographic Challenges of Afghanistan." In *Military Geography from Peace to War*, ed. Eugene J. Palka and Francis A. Galgano, 321–42. New York: McGraw-Hill, 2005.

Parker, Cathy. *Freedom of Expression in the American Military: A Communication Modeling Analysis*. New York: Praeger, 1989.

Paul, J. Gavin. "Ashes in the Gutter: 9/11 and the Serialization of Memory in DC Comics' *Human Target*." *American Periodicals* 17, no. 2 (2007): 208–27.

Pelusi, Christian. "Cartoonist Bruce Higdon Draws Military Kids to his USO Fort Campbell Classes." *USO News*, August 27, 2012. http://www.uso.org/bruce-higdon-cartoon-class-fort-campbell/. Accessed July 19, 2013.

Plecash, Jan. "Speaking of Death: Remembrance and Lamentation." In *Spectacular Death: Interdisciplinary Perspectives on Mortality and (Un)Representation*, ed. T. Connolly, 97–122. Bristol, UK: Intellect, 2011.

Pope, W.C. "Introduction." In *Above and Beyond: Pope's Puns and Other Air Force Cartoons*, by W.C. Pope, 4–5. Herkimer, NY: WC Pope Studio, 2009.

Posen, Barry. *The Sources of Military Doctrine*. Ithaca, NY: Cornell University Press, 1984.

Press, Charles. *The Political Cartoon*. Toronto, ON: Associated University Presses, 1981.

Prividera, Laura C. and John W. Howard III. "Masculinity, Whiteness, and the Warrior Hero: Perpetuating the Strategic Rhetoric of U.S. Nationalism and the Marginalization of Women." *Women and Language* 29, no. 2 (2006): 29–37.

Purdue Libraries. *Military Doctrine: A Reference Handbook*. Brownbag Presentation, November 4, 2009.

Pustz, Matthew, ed. *Comic Books and American Cultural History*. New York: Continuum, 2012.

Putnam, Linda, Shirley A. Van Hoeven, and Connie A. Bullis. "The Role of Rituals and Fantasy Themes in Teachers' Bargaining." *Western Journal of Speech Communication* 55 (1991): 85–103.

Rarick, David. L., Mary B. Duncan, David G. Lee and Laurinda W. Porter. "The Carter Persona: An Empirical Analysis of the Rhetorical Visions of Campaign '76." *Quarterly Journal of Speech* 63, no. 3 (1977): 258–73.

Rawlings, Nate. "Tat-us Quo: Despite Strict New Army Rules Other Branches Keep Tattoo Policies Intact." *Time*, September 26, 2013. http://nation.time.com/2013/09/26/tat-us-quo-des pite-strict-new-army-rules-other-branches-keep-tattoo-policies-intact/. Accessed October 1, 2014.

Rawls, Walton. *Disney Dons Dogtags: The Best of Disney Military Insignia from World War II*. New York: Abbeville, 1992.

Reznick, Jeffrey S. *"Snoopy as the World War I Flying Ace.* Jane O'Cain. Produced by the Charles M. Schulz Museum and Research Center and toured by ExhibitsUSA. College Park, MD: College Park Aviation Museum, Aug. 30-Nov. 30, 2008." *International Journal of Comic Art* 11, no. 1 (2009): 554–56.

Ribbens, Kees. "World War II in European Comics: National Representations of Global Conflict in Popular Historical Culture." *International Journal of Comic Art* 12, no. 1 (2010): 1–33.

Riches, Adam. *When the Comics Went to War*. Edinburgh, UK: Mainstream, 2009.

Ricks, Thomas. *Making the Corps*. New York: Scribner, 1997.

Ricks, Thomas E. "The Enduring Solitude of Combat Vets." *Foreign Policy*, September 3, 2010. http://ricks.foreignpolicy.com/posts/2010/09/03/the_enduring_solitude_of_combat_vets. Accessed July 27, 2013.

Rico, John. "Why Soldiers Take Photos." *Salon*, April 22, 2012. http://www.salon.com/2012/04/23/why_soldiers_take_photos/. Accessed July 9, 2013.

Rifas, Leonard. "Cartooning and Nuclear Power: From Industry Advertising to Activist Uprising and Beyond." *PS: Political Science and Politics* 40, no. 2 (2007): 255–60.

Robben, Antonius C.G.M. "Combat Motivation, Fear and Terror in Twentieth-century Argentinian Warfare." *Journal of Contemporary History* 41, no. 2 (2006): 357–77.

Robbins, Trina. *A Century of Women Cartoonists*. Northampton, MA: Kitchen Sink, 1993.

Robinson, Jerry. *The Comics: An Illustrated History of Comic Strip Art 1895–2010*. 1974. Milwaukie, OR: Dark Horse, 2011.

Roger, Nathan. "Abu Ghraib Abuse Images: From Perverse War Trophies Through Internet Based War Porn to Artistic Representations and Beyond." *At the Interface/Probing the Boundaries* 75 (2011): 121–38.

Rohall, David E., Mady Wechsler Segal, and David R. Segal. "Examining the Importance of Organizational Supports on Family Adjustment to Army Life in a Period of Increasing Separation." *Journal of Political and Military Sociology* 27, no. 1 (1999): 49–65.

Romero, Eric J., and Kevin W. Cruthirds. "The Use of Humor in the Workplace." *Academy of Management Perspectives* 20, no. 2 (2006): 58–69.

Rose, Arnold. "The Social Structure of the Army." *American Journal of Sociology* 51, no. 5 (1946): 361–4.

Rosen, Stephen Peter. "Military Effectiveness: Why Society Matters." *International Security* 19, 4 (1995): 5–31.

Rosenbaum, Roman. "Mizuki Shigeru's Pacific War." *International Journal of Comic Art* 10, no. 2 (2008): 354–79.

_____. "Motomiya Hiroshi's *The Country Is Burning*." *International Journal of Comic Art* 9, no. 1 (2007): 591–601.

Rosenfeld, Paul. "What Combat Feels Like, Presented in the Style of a Graphic Narrative." *The Atlantic*, September 2013. http://www.theatlantic.com/video/archive/2013/09/what-combat-feels-like-presented-in-the-stule-of-a-graphic-novel/280029. Accessed September 20, 2013.

Rostker, Bernard D., Susan D. Hosek, and Mary E. Valana. "Gays in the Military." *RAND Review* Spring (2011): http://www.rand.org/pubs/periodicals/rand-review/issues/2011/spring/gays.html/. Accessed January 26, 2014.

Roth-Douquet, Kathy and Frank Schaeffer. *AWOL: The Unexcused Absence of America's Upper Classes from Military Service—and How It Hurts Our Country.* New York: Collins, 2007.

Rottman, Gordon L. *FUBAR: Soldier Slang of World War II.* New York: Metro, 2007.

Round, Julia. "London's Calling: Alternate Worlds and the City as Superhero in Contemporary British-American Comics." *International Journal of Comic Art* 10, no. 1 (2008): 24–31.

Russell, Edmund P., III. "'Speaking of Annihilation'" Mobilizing for War Against Human and Insect Enemies, 1914–45." *Journal of American History* 82 (1996): 1505–29.

Sabrosky, Alan Ned, James Clay Thompson, and Karen A. McPherson. "Organized Anarchies: Military Bureaucracy in the 1980s." *Journal of Applied Behavioral Science* 18, no. 2 (1982): 137–53.

Saenger, Gerhart. "Male and Female Relations in the American Comic Strip." In *The Funnies: An American Idiom*, ed. David M. White and Robert H. Abel, 219–31. New York: Free Press, 1963.

Sahlstein, Erin, Katheryn C. Maguire, and Lind-

say Timmerman. "Contradictions and Praxis Contextualized by Wartime Deployment: Wives' Perspectives Revealed Through Relational Dialectics." *Communication Monographs* 76, no. 4 (2009): 421–42.

Salisbury, Peter. "Giles's Cold War: How Fleet Street's Favourite Cartoonist Saw the Conflict." *Media History* 12, no. 2 (2006): 157–75.

Sansone, Leonard. *The Wolf.* New York: United, 1945.

Sasson-Levy, Orna. "Constructing Identities at the Margins: Masculinities and Citizenship in the Israeli Army." *The Sociological Quarterly* 43, no. 3 (2002): 357–83.

Savage, William W., Jr. *Comic Books and America, 1945–1954.* Norman, University of Oklahoma Press, 1990

Scarry, Elaine. *The Body in Pain.* New York: Oxford University Press, 1985.

Schneider, Matthias. "Der Fuehrer's Animation: Animation and Propaganda in the German Reich." Trans. Annette Gentz. *International Journal of Comic Art* 6, no. 2 (2004): 172–81.

Schoner, Scott R. "A Survey of Doughboy Humor in World War I." *International Journal of Comic Art* 9, no. 2 (2007): 288–315.

Scodari, Christine. "Operation Desert Storm as 'Wargames': Sport, War, and Media Intertextuality." *Journal of American Culture* 16, no. 1 (1993): 1–5.

Scott, Cord. "'Frankly, Mac, This "Police Action" Business Is Going Too Damn Far!'" Armed Forces Cartoons during the Korean Conflict." Paper presented at the Korean War Conference: Commemorating the 60th Anniversary, hosted by the Victoria College/University of Houston-Victoria Library, June 24–26, 2010.

_____. "The 'Good' Comics: Using Comic Books to Teach History." *International Journal of Comic Art* 8, no. 1 (2006): 546–61.

_____. "The Return of the War Comic: A Revival of Military Themes and Characters in Comic Books." *International Journal of Comic Art* 10, no. 2 (2008): 649–59.

_____. "Written in Red, White, and Blue: A Comparison of Comic Book Propaganda from World War II and September 11." *Journal of Popular Culture* 40, no. 2 (2007): 325–43.

Scully, Richard, and Marian Quartly. "Using Cartoons as Historical Evidence." In *Drawing the Line: Using Cartoons as Historical Evidence*, ed. Richard Scully and Marian Quartly, 01.1–01.13. Clayton, Australia: Monash University ePress, 2009.

Seale, Clive. "Heroic Death." *Sociology* 29 (1995): 587–613.

Segal, David R. *Recruiting for Uncle Sam: Citizenship and Military Manpower Policy.* Lawrence, KS: University Press of Kansas, 1989.

Segal, Mady W. "The Military and the Family as Greedy Institutions." In *The Military: More*

Than Just a Job?, ed. Charles C. Moskos and Frank R. Wood, 79–97. Washington, D.C.: Pergamon-Brassey's, 1988.

Shackelford, Damon Bryan. *Delta Bravo Sierra: Rally Point: Vol. 1, Year 1, 2008.* Lexington, KY: www.deltabravosierra.us, 2008.

Shalit, Ben. *The Psychology of Conflict and Combat.* New York: Praeger, 1988.

Shannon, Lyle W. "The Opinions of Little Orphan Annie and Her Friends." In *Mass Culture: The Popular Arts in America*, ed. Bernard Rosenberg and David M. White, 212–17. Glencoe, IL: Free Press, 1957.

Shaw, Matthew J. "Drawing on the Collections." *Journalism Studies* 8, no. 5 (2007): 742–54.

Sheppard, John. *Incoming! Military Cartoons.* Hoschton, GA: ShepArt Studios, 2011.

Sherpa, Charlie. "The Winners of the 2013 Mil-Humor Awards!" *Red Bull Rising.* September 5, 2013. http://www.redbullrising.com/2013/09/the-winners-of-2013-mil-humor-awards.html (access September 11, 2013).

Shibusawa, Naoka. *America's Geisha Ally: Reimagining the Japanese Enemy.* Cambridge, MA: Harvard University Press, 2006. Kindle e-book.

Shields, Donald C., and C. Thomas Preston, Jr. "Fantasy Theme Analysis in Competitive Rhetorical Criticism," *National Forensic Journal* 3 (1985): 102–15.

Shields, Patricia. "Sex Roles in the Military." In *The Military: More than Just a Job?*, ed. Charles C. Moskos and Frank R. Wood, 99–114. Washington, D.C.: Pergamon-Brassey's, 1988.

Shigematsu, Setsu. "Dimensions of Desire: Sex, Fantasy, and Fetish in Japanese Comics." In *Themes and Issues in Asian Cartooning: Cute, Cheap, Mad, and Sexy*, ed. John A. Lent, 127–64. Bowling Green, OH: Bowling Green State University Popular Press, 1999.

Shiokawa, Kanako. "Cute but Deadly: Women and Violence in Japanese Comics." In *Themes and Issues in Asian Cartooning: Cute, Cheap, Mad, and Sexy*, ed. John A. Lent, 93–126. Bowling Green, OH: Bowling Green State University Popular Press, 1999.

Shirlow, Peter. "Fundamentalist Loyalism: Discourse, Resistance and Identity Politics." In *Landscapes of Defence*, ed. John R. Gold and George Revill, 85–101. Harlow, UK: Prentice Hall, 2000.

Shirom, Arie. "On Some Correlates of Combat Performance." *Administrative Science Quarterly* 21 (1976): 419–32.

Shyminsky, Neil. "Mutant Readers, Reading Mutants: Appropriation, Assimilation, and the X-Men." *International Journal of Comic Art* 8, no. 2 (2006): 387–405.

Siebold, G.L. "The Essence of Military Group Cohesion." *Armed Forces and Society* 33, no. 2 (2007): 286–95.

Silk, Christina, Rachelle Boyle, Annie Bright, Merilyn Bassett, and Nicola Roach. *The Case for Cultural Diversity in Defence.* Report for the Defence Equity Organisation of the Australian Defence Organisation. 2000. http://www.defence.gov.au/fr/reports/ Cultural Diversity.pdf. Accessed July 27, 2013.

Simon, Scott. "World War II Cartoons Come to Soldiers' Aid." *Listen to the Story.* February 13, 2010. Radio broadcast. Transcript at http://www.npr.org/templates/story/story. php?storyId=123684046. Accessed July 17, 2013.

Sjoberg, Laura. "Agency, Militarized Femininity and Enemy Others." *International Feminist Journal of Politics* 9, no. 1 (2007): 82–101.

Skilling, Charles. "Kilroy Was Here." *Western Folklore* 22, no. 4 (1963): 276–77.

Sloan, Geoffrey. "Military Doctrine, Command Philosophy and the Generation of Fighting Power: Genesis and Theory." *International Affairs* 88, no. 2 (2012): 243–63.

Snider, Don M. "The U.S. Military in Transition to Jointness: Surmounting Old Notions of Interservice Rivalry." *Airpower Journal*, Fall 1996, 16–27.

Soeters, Joseph. "Value Orientations in Military Academies: A Thirteen Country Study." *Armed Forces and Society* 24, no. 1 (1997): 7–32.

Soeters, Joseph L., Donna J. Winslow, and Alise Weibull. "Military Culture." In *Handbook of the Sociology of the Military*, ed. Giuseppe Caforio, 237–54. New York: Springer, 2006.

"Speaking of Pictures.... GI's Blowzy Frauleins Hurt Germans' Feelings." *Life Magazine*, June 17, 1946, 12–13.

"Speaking of Pictures.... A Soldier Cartoonist Makes a WAC His Heroine." *Life Magazine*, March 19, 1945, 12–14.

Spears, Russell. "Four Degrees of Stereotype Formation: Differentiation by Any Means Necessary." In *Stereotypes as Explanations: The Formation of Meaningful Beliefs About Social Groups*, ed. Craig McGarty, Vincent Y. Yzerbyt, and Russel Spears, 127–56. Cambridge, UK: Cambridge University Press, 2002.

Spencer, David R. "The Press and the Spanish American War Political Cartoons of the Yellow Journalism Age." *International Journal of Comic Art* 9, no. 1 (2007): 262–80.

_____. "Visions of Violence: A Cartoon Study of America and War." *American Journalism* 21, no. 2 (2004): 47–78.

Spigel, Lynn. *Welcome to the Dreamhouse: Popular Media and Postwar Suburbs.* Durham, NC: Duke University Press, 2001.

Spiggle, Susan. "Measuring Social Values: A Content Analysis of Sunday Comics and Underground Comix." *Journal of Consumer Research* 13 (1986): 100–13.

Spillman, Kurt R., and Kati Spillman. "Some Sociobiological and Psychological Aspects of

'Images of the Enemy.'" In *Enemy Images in American History*, ed. Ragnhild Fiebig-von Hase and Ursula Lehmkuhl, 43–64. Providence, RI: Berghahn, 1997.

Stern, Edith M. "Nurses Wanted: A Career Boom." *Survey Graphic*, February 1942, 79 and 179.

Stouffer, Samuel A., Arthur A. Lumsdaine, Marion H. Lumsdaine, Robin M. Williams, Jr., M. Brewster Smith. Irving L. Janis, Shirley A. Star, and Leonard S. Cottrell, Jr. *The American Soldier: Combat and Its Aftermath.* New York: Science Editions, 1965.

Stouffer, Samuel A., A.A. Lumsdaine, M.H. Lumsdaine, R.M. Williams, Jr., M.B. Smith, I.L. Janis, S.A. Star, and L.S. Cottrell, Jr. *The American Soldier: Combat and Its Aftermath.* Vol. 2. New York: John Wiley and Sons, 1949.

Stouffer, Samuel A., E.A. Suchman, L.C. Devinney, S.A. Star, and R.M. Williams, Jr., *The American Soldier: Adjustment During Army Life.* Vol. 1. Princeton, NJ: Princeton University Press, 1949.

Strachan, Hew. "Training, Morale and Modern War." *Journal of Contemporary History* 41, no. 2 (2006): 211–27.

Strömberg, Fredrik. *Comic Art Propaganda.* New York: St. Martin's Griffin, 2010.

Sugawa-Shimada, Akiko. "Rebel with Causes and Laughter for Relief: 'Essay Manga' of Tenten Hosokawa and Rieko Saibara, and Japanese Female Readership." *Journal of Graphic Narratives and Comics* 2, no. 2 (2011): 169–85.

Suid, Lawrence. *Guts and Glory: The Making of the American Military Image.* Lexington, KY: University Press of Kentucky, 2002.

Swafford, Brian. "The Death of Captain America: An Open-ended Allegorical Reading of Marvel Comics' *Civil War* Storyline." *International Journal of Comic Art* 10, no. 2 (2008): 632–48.

Talbot, Daryl. *Laughing in Cadence: Dress Right Dress Military Cartoons.* Stillwater, OK: New Forums, 2009.

Terret, Thierry. "American Sammys and French *Poilus* in the Great War: Sport, Masculinities and Vulnerability." *The International Journal of the History of Sport* 28, nos. 3–4 (2011): 351–71.

Their, J. Alexander, and Azita Ranjbar. "Killing Friends, Making Enemies: The Impact and Avoidance of Civilian Casualties in Afghanistan." *United States Institute of Peace Briefing*, July 2008, http://www.usip.org/sites/default/files/resources/USIP_0708_2.PDF. Accessed March 25, 2014.

Thibodeau, Ruth. "From Racism to Tokenism: The Changing Face of Blacks in *New Yorker* Cartoons." *Public Opinion Quarterly* 53, no. 4 (1989): 483–94.

Thomas, Jr., Ronald C. "Hero of the Military-Industrial Complex: Reading Iron Man Through Burke's Dramatism." In *Heroes of Film, Comics and American Culture: Essays on Real and Fictional Defenders of Home*, ed. Lisa M. Detora. Kindle e-book. Jefferson, NC: McFarland, 2009.

Thomas, Tanja, and Fabian Virchow. "Banal Militarism and the Culture of War." In *Bring 'Em On: Media and Politics in the Iraq War*, ed. Lee Artz and Yahya R. Kamilipour, 23–36. Lanham, MD: Rowman and Littlefield, 2005.

Thompson, Jason. "PULPman Profiles: Vernon Grant." *PULP: The Manga Magazine* 5, no. 12 (May 12, 2001). Archived at http://web.archive.org/web/20041020025320/www.pulp-mag.com/archives/5.12/pulpman.shtml. Accessed July 8, 2013.

Thoresen, Siri, and Lars Mehlum. "Risk Factors for Fatal Accidents and Suicides in Peacekeepers: Is There an Overlap?" *Military Medicine* 169, no. 12 (2004): 988–93.

Thorkelson, Nick. "Cartoons Against the Axis: World War II Bonds Cartoons from the Terry-D'Alessio Collection. Sandy Schecter with Special Thanks to Hilda Terry and Art Spiegelman. New York City, NY: Museum of Comic and Cartooning Art, October 8, 2005-February 6, 2006." *International Journal of Comic Art* 8, no. 1 (2006): 591–94.

Thrift, Nigel J., and Dean K. Forbes. "A Landscape with Figures: Political Geography with Human Conflict." *Political Geography Quarterly* 2, no. 3 (1983): 247–64.

Topping, Ira, ed. *The Best of Yank the Army Weekly, 1942–1945.* New York: Arno, 1980.

Trnka, Susanna. "Living a Life of Sex and Danger: Women, Warfare, and Sex in Military Folk Rhymes." *Western Folklore* 54, no. 3 (1995): 232–41.

Turner, Roger. "Laughing at the Weather? The Serious World of Weather Cartoons." *History of Science Society Newsletter*, January 2009. http://www.hssonline.org/publications/Newsletter2009/January2009Turner.html. Accessed June 27, 2013.

Tyson, Jeni. "Compassion Fatigue in the Treatment of Combat-Related Trauma During Wartime." *Clinical Social Work* 35, no. 3 (2007): 183–92.

Urry, John. "The Sociology of Space and Place." In *The Blackwell Companion to Sociology*, ed. Judith R. Blau, 3–15. Malden, MA: Blackwell, 2004.

U.S. Department of Veterans Affairs. "Symptoms of PTSD." *PTSD: National Center for PTSD.* January 3, 2014. http://www.ptsd.va.gov/public/PTSD-overview/basics/symptoms_of_ptsd.asp. Accessed June 13, 2014.

VanKoski, Susan. "Letters Home, 1915–16: Punjabi Soldiers Reflect on War and Life in Europe and their Meanings for Home and Self." *International Journal of Punjab Studies* 2, no. 1 (1995): 43–63.

Van Laar, Collette. *Increasing a Sense of Community in the Military: The Role of Personnel Support Programs.* Santa Monica, CA: RAND, 1999.

Versluys, Kristiaan. "Art Spiegelman's *In the Shadow of No Towers*: 9–11 and the Representation of Trauma." *MFS Modern Fiction Studies* 52, no. 4 (2006): 980–1003.

Vessey Jr., John W. "Preface." In *Military Geography for Professionals and the Public*, ed. John M. Collins. Washington, D.C.: Brassey's, 1998. Kindle e-book.

The Vietnam Graffiti Project. "The Graffiti." *Vietnam Graffiti*, 2009–2010. http://www.vietnamgraffiti.com/the-graffiti. Accessed October 28, 2014.

Vincent, David. *Literacy and Popular Culture: England 1750–1914.* Cambridge, UK: Cambridge University Press, 1989.

Volkan, Vamik D. *The Need to Have Enemies and Allies: From Clinical Practice to International Relationships.* Northvale, NJ: Jason Aronson, 1988.

Vultee, Fred. "Dr. FDR and Baby War: The World Through Chicago Political Cartoons Before and After Pearl Harbor." *Visual Communication Quarterly* 14 (Summer 2007): 158–75.

Waldmeir, Joseph J. "What's Funny About That? Humor in the Literature of the Second World War." *Journal of American Culture* 12, no. 3 (1989): 11–8.

Walker, Mort. "Forward." In *Above and Beyond: Pope's Puns and Other Air Force Cartoons*, by W.C. Pope, 3. Herkimer, NY: WC Pope Studio, 2009.

_____. *The Lexicon of Comicana.* 1980. Lincoln, NE: iUniverse.com, 2000.

Walt, Stephen M. "Two Chief Petty Officers Walk Into a Bar..." *Foreign Policy*, April 7, 2014. http://www.foreignpolicy.com/articles/2014/04/07/why_cant_we_make_fun_of_the_military_anymore. Accessed April 9, 2014.

Wanzo, Rebecca. "The Superhero: Meditations on Surveillance, Salvation, and Desire." *Communication and Critical/Cultural Studies* 6, no. 1 (2009): 93–7.

Watson, Alex. "Self-Deception and Survival: Mental Coping Strategies on the Western Front, 1914–18." *Journal of Popular History* 41, no. 2 (2006): 247–68.

Watson, Bruce. *The Navajo Code Talkers.* Pune, India: New World City, 2011. Kindle e-book.

Weatherford, Doris. *American Women and World War II.* Edison, NJ: Castle, 2008.

Weems, Mickey. "Taser to the 'Nads: Brutal Embrace of Queerness in Military Practice." In *Warrior Ways: Explorations in Modern Military Folklore*, ed. Eric A. Eliason and Tad Tuleja, 139–60. Boulder, CO: Utah State University Press, 2012.

Weida, Courtney Lee. "Wonder(ing) Women: Investigating Gender Politics and Art Education Within Graphica." *Visual Culture and Gender* 6 (2011): 97–107.

Wessely, Simon. "Twentieth-century Theories on Combat Motivation and Breakdown." *Journal of Contemporary History* 41, no. 2 (2006): 269–86.

Westbrook, Robert B. "'I Want a Girl, Just Like the Girl That Married Harry James': American Women and the Problem of Political Obligation in World War II," *American Quarterly* 42, no. 4 (1990): 587–614.

Whiton, Jason, Ed. *Mort Walker Conversations.* Jackson, MS: University Press of Mississippi, 2005.

Wichhart, Stefanie. "Propaganda and Protest: Political Cartoons in Iraq During the Second World War." In *Drawing the Line: Using Cartoons as Historical Evidence*, ed. Richard Scully and Marian Quartly, 08.1–08.21. Clayton, Australia: Monash University ePress, 2009.

Wiegand, Krista E., and David L. Paletz. "The Elite Media and the Military-Civilian Culture Gap." *Armed Forces and Society* 27, no. 2 (2001): 183–204.

Williams, Andrew Paul, Justin D. Martin, Kaye D. Trammell, Kristen Landreville, and Chelsea Ellis. "Late-Night Talk Shows and War: Entertaining and Informing Through Humor." *Journal of Global Mass Communication* 3, no. 1–4 (2010): 131–38.

Williams, Bruce A. "From Romance to Collateral Damage: Media Treatment of Civilians in Wartime and What it Means for How America Wages War." *The Communication Review* 12, no. 3 (2009): 227–38.

Williams, Kristian. "The Case for Comics Journalism: Artist-Reporters Leap Tall Conventions in a Single Bound." *Columbia Journalism Review*, March/April (2005): 51–55.

Winslow, Donna J., Lindy Heinecken, and Joseph L. Soeters. "Diversity in the Armed Forces." In *Handbook of the Sociology of the Military*, ed. Giuseppe Caforio, 299–310. New York: Springer, 2006.

Winterich, John T., ed. *Squads Write! A Selection of the Best Things in Prose, Verse and Cartoons from the Stars and Stripes.* New York: Harper and Brothers, 1931.

Witek, Joseph. *Comic Books as History: The Narrative Art of Jack Jackson, Art Spiegelman, and Harvey Pekar.* Jackson, MS: University Press of Mississippi, 1989.

_____. "The Dream of Total War: The Limits of a Genre." *Journal of Popular Culture* 30, no. 2 (1996): 37–45.

Wolk, Douglas. *Reading Comics: How Graphic Novels Work and What They Mean.* Cambridge, MA: Da Capo, 2007. Kindle e-book.

Woo, Benjamin. "The Android's Dungeon: Comic-Bookstores, Cultural Spaces, and the

Social Practices of Audience." *Journal of Graphic Novels and Comics* 2, no. 2 (2011): 125–36.

Wood, Suzanne, Jacquelyn Scarville, and Katharine S. Gravino. "Waiting Wives: Separation and Reunion Among Army Wives." *Armed Forces and Society* 21, no. 2 (1995): 217–36.

Woodward, Rachel. *Military Geographies.* Malden, MA: Blackwell, 2004.

Worcester, Kent. "Symposium—The State of the Editorial Cartoon: Introduction." *PS: Political Science and Politics* 40, no. 2 (2007): 223–6.

Wright, Bradford W. *Comic Book Nation: The Transformation of Youth Culture in America.* Baltimore, MD: Johns Hopkins University Press, 2001.

Yang, Mei-ling. "Creating the Kitchen Patriot: Media Promotion of Food Rationing and Nutrition Campaigns on the American Home Front During World War II." *American Journalism,* 22, no. 3 (2005): 55–75.

Yellin, Emily. *Our Mothers' War: American Women at Home and at the Front During World War II.* New York: Free Press, 2004.

Yellin, Keith. *Battle Exhortation: The Rhetoric of Combat Leadership.* Columbia, SC: University of South Carolina Press, 2008.

Yoshimura, K., 2008. "Essei Manga no Tokucho [Characteristics of Essay Manga]." In *Manga no Kyokasho* [*A Textbook of Manga*], ed. I. Shimizu, T. Akita, T. Naiki, and K. Yoshimura, 196–8. Kyoto: Rinkawa Shoten, 2008.

Young, Thomas-Durell. "Military Professionalism in a Democracy." In *Who Guards the Guardians and How: Democratic Civil-Military Relations,* ed. Thomas C. Bruneau and Scott D. Tollefson, 17–33. Austin, TX: University of Texas Press, 2006.

Zelizer, Craig. "Laughing Our Way to Peace or War: Humour and Peacebuilding." *Journal of Conflictology* 1, no. 2 (2010): 1–9. E-journal.

Ziv, Avner. "The Influence of Humorous Atmosphere on Divergent Thinking." *Contemporary Educational Psychology* 8, no. 1 (1983): 68–75.

_____. "Teaching and Learning with Humor: Experiment and Replications." *Journal of Experimental Education* 57, no. 1 (1988): 5–15.

Zwagerman, Sean. "A Day That Will Live in Irony: September 11 and the War on Humor." In *The War on Terror and American Popular Culture: September 11 and Beyond,* ed. Andrew Schopp and Matthew B. Hill, 209–21. Cranbury, NJ: Rosemont Publishing and Printing, 2009.

Zweibelson, Ben. "Building Another Tower of Babel: Why Acronyms Are Ruining Shared Military Understanding." *Small Wars Journal,* May 7, 2013. http://smallwarsjournal. com/ jrnl/art/building-another-tower-of-babel. Accessed July 3, 2013.

Index

Numbers in *bold italics* indicate pages with illustrations.